AFTER WHITENESS
UNMAKING AN AMERICAN MAJORITY

MIKE HILL

NEW YORK UNIVERSITY PRESS
NEW YORK AND LONDON

NEW YORK UNIVERSITY PRESS
New York and London
www.nyupress.org

Copyright © 2004 by New York University

Library of Congress Cataloging-in-Publication Data
Hill, Mike, 1964–
After whiteness : unmaking an American majority / Mike Hill.
p. cm. — (Cultural front [series])
Includes bibliographical references and index.
ISBN 0–8147–3542–8 (cloth : alk. paper) —
ISBN 0–8147–3543–6 (pbk. : alk. paper)
1. Whites—Race identity—United States.   2. United States—Race relations.
3. White men—United States—Psychology.   4. Heterosexual men—United States—Psychology.
5. National characteristics, American.   6. United States—Census, 22nd 2000.
7. Multiculturalism—United States.   8. Group identity—Political aspects—United States.
9. Educational, Higher—Political aspects—United States.
10. Educational, Higher—Social aspects—United States.   I. Title.   II. Series.
E184.A1H527   2003
305.809'073—dc22   2003016635

New York University Press books are printed on acid-free paper
and their binding materials are chosen for strength and durability.

Manufactured in the United States of America
c 10 9 8 7 6 5 4 3 2 1
p 10 9 8 7 6 5 4 3 2 1

THIS BOOK IS DEDICATED TO THE MEMORY OF
MICHAEL SPRINKER, 1950–1999.

THOUGHT WAITS TO BE WOKEN ONE DAY BY THE MEMORY OF
WHAT IT WAS, AND TO BE TRANSFORMED INTO TEACHING.
—THEODORE ADORNO

CONTENTS

ACKNOWLEDGMENTS

My first debt of thanks is to friends and family who buoyed my commitment to the writing of this book while I struggled under the usual, and not so usual, kinds of pressures. With unending support David and Sandra Hill watched me tiptoe—sometimes stumble—through the academic minefield they saw smoking from afar. Many other intimates and comrades hovered close by and helped animate the spirit, if not the substance, of this long-in-coming work. Ann Fitzgerald and Paul Lauter, Robert Vorlicky, David Linton, John and Pricilla Costello, Kevin Frye, Donald Mendelson, Jon Robyn, Rosyln Berger, Melvin Jackson, Sema Ozogul, and Carina Yervasi are foremost among them.

Fellow graduate students at SUNY Stony Brook, where I never dreamed of whiteness while completing my English Ph.D., are now colleagues spread out across the country. Today they help narrow the cold divide between institutional and ordinary life, and it is my good fortune to be able to call them friends. These are Devoney Looser, Mona Narian, Barbara Smith, Jhan Hochman, Sheilja Sharma, David Sair, Jim Paxson, Jeffrey Williams, Anthony Jarrels, Jon Scott, David Macauley, Greg Laguero, Michael Bernard-Donals, and Pat Kahana. Clifford Siskin's now legendary graduate seminars at Stony Brook remain a productive source of edification. As any one of his former students who may read this book will know, Siskin's influence is detectable in its every twist and turn. Kevin Frye, whom I have already named, I also add to my list of important Stony Brook alums. He should receive yet a third nod of appreciation (and a wink) for taking the pictures in this book of the Promise Keepers' 1997 march on Washington, D.C., and for having dared to escort its author there.

Michael Sprinker, to whom the work here is dedicated, died while I was making an institutional move that he helped facilitate. Only in his absence do I realize the necessity of his life for my writing to continue. That I continue writing anyway, and in spite of his absence, is I hope a testimony to his lasting influence on my professional and political well being.

Beyond Stony Brook, the camaraderie of H. Aram Veeser and Paul Lyons has provided as much enlightening diversion as support. Ross Chambers has been a willing reader of my work since I became his student at the School of Criticism and Theory as far back as 1992. His encouragement and gentle criticism of the first draft of this book helped move it along to completion, whatever its lingering faults. Thank you, Ross, for reading and for getting me read. I also owe thanks for the occasional word of encouragement from esteemed scholars and fellow travelers such as Len Davis, Fred Pfeil, Eric Lott, Chris Newfield, Robyn Wiegman, Henry Giroux, Steve Martinot, Barbara Foley, Gale Wald, Crystal Bartolovich, Amitava Kumar, Jamie Owen Daniels, Jennifer Brody, Leslie Siskin, and countless anonymous voices at conferences and speaking events who engaged my work. Ted Allen has been an inexhaustible resource concerning the invention of the white race, and a powerful inspiration, in the several years I have been lucky enough to call on him. Warren Montag remains a key collaborator, teacher, and friend. I would also like to thank Michael Bérubé for the inclusion of *After Whiteness* in the Cultural Front series.

Of all the readers of this book in its nascent stages, none has been more formative than Sharon Holland. Whatever inadequacies still exist here, the book's successes are the index of a silent collaboration with her as she read along until its completion. Sharon's generosity as a reader nudged me to where I hoped I might be going in the writing I had yet to work through. She waved me forward with as much insistence as hospitality in the direction of what I only realized later was the substance of my thoughts. Every first-time author should get that kind of invitation and that kind of read.

This book was conceived during my time teaching at Marymount Manhattan College, in New York City. The University at Albany is the place where nearly all of it was later written. So let me thank those colleagues and students I have not already mentioned at both institutions. At Marymount, for taking an interest in my work, thank you Radhika Balakrishnan, Ann Jablon, Peter Baker, Paula Mayhew, Richard Niles, Eleanor Bazzini, Olive Crothers, Anwar Zadini, and Lucian Salidar. At Albany, first, thank you Tom Cohen for getting me work here and for keeping it going. Helen Elam's encouragement has been at times life sustaining. Randall Craig, Jeffrey Berman, Pierre Joris, Jennifer Fleischner, Donald Byrd, and Dick Goldman have been exceptionally generous in keeping me grounded during the years it took to complete this book. For their concern I am thankful. Rosemary Hennessy, Teresa Ebert, Charles Shepherdson, Mary Valentis, Cary Wolfe, and David Wills have supported my research agenda and continue to make Albany an appropriately challenging and engaging place to work. Gareth Griffiths, my current departmental chair, has provided a space of intellectual freedom such that books like this one may find a legitimate place among the ranks. Of the several faculty added to Albany's roster of late, Mark Anthony Neal, Edward Schwarzschild, and Lisa Thompson have expressed much-appreciated interest in future collaboration around themes commonly addressed in my work and theirs. I especially want to thank Bret Benjamin for his resolute friendship, rare institutional stamina, and genuine political commitment in difficult times. Thanks also to Laura Wilder, friend and colleague at large. Of the many students I have encountered at Albany, let me single out Todd Emerson Bowers for his contribution to this book.

Beyond U.S. affiliations, I want to express gratitude to Tatiana Venediktova, my host in Moscow, Russia, during a Fulbright Summer School where I offered several lectures on whiteness in 2002. Thank you also to John Ryder, Academic Director, Office of International Programs, SUNY–Moscow State University Center on Russia and the United States, for brokering my visit east. To Toby Clyman, and to fellow U.S. lecturer Sacvan Bercovitch, and the many students in American studies I encountered at Uskoye, thank you for making my Russian experience hospitable and unfamiliar in exactly the right combination.

Though he has since moved from New York University Press, I am indebted to Niko Pfund, who contracted this book and its precursor without much more to go on than our mutual conviction, barely speakable at the time, that somehow whiteness mattered. It is gratifying to have worked with Eric Zinner on the manuscript itself, and to have this book included among so many others I have long admired that Eric has ushered forth. For his labor on the manuscript, for the diligent work of Emily Park, and for the investment of others on the New York University Press editorial and marketing staff in the production of this

ACKNOWLEDGMENTS

book, I am thankful. A special note of thanks to Sarah Johnson, who read early versions of the manuscript, as she has other projects of mine. For copyediting and for correcting other infelicities in the prose, my thanks to Despina Gimbel at NYU Press.

Finally, I want to thank Laura Mendelson for reading the many drafts of the manuscript before and after it was circulated, rewritten, and circulated again. More than that heroic task, I am grateful for the other, better time we have shared together over the last six years. Thanks for going through all of this with me, and for a glimpse at life on the other side of work.

AFTER WHITENESS

INTRODUCTION
AFTER WHITENESS EVE

No whiteness is so white as the memory of whiteness.
—William Carlos Williams

The antiseptic setting of the Hyatt Dulles hotel must have reassured the suits and ties that, whatever else would be said, they were gathered in a gentlemanly way on behalf of "white genetic solidarity." That archaic-sounding phrase summed up the American Renaissance (hereafter AR) conference held in Herndon, Virginia, one oddly mild February weekend in 2002. With nearly three hundred participants, this was the largest assembly of the group since its founder and president, Jared Taylor, summoned the first meeting in 1994. The theme of the 2002 event struck a chord barely thinkable in the congregation's early days. This year the conference invited the men of AR to focus their attention, less on non-European immigrants and citizens of color, and more on the vicissitudes of white identity as it seemed to disappear before our eyes.

Remarkable to the 2002 event, AR gathered precisely to fantasize about, rather than eschew, life on the country's racial margins. (I say *fantasize* because as of 2000 citizens identifying as white in the United States accounted for 71 percent of the population, hardly conclusive of the national majority's unmaking.)[1] That recent historical achievement we call the white race, the group never tired of opining, is about to be historically discarded. In many ways, of course, the 2002 event was consistent with the previous four conferences. The affair was again pitched as "an opportunity to hear some of the most courageous academics, journalists, and scientists of our time discuss the forces that will determine our future."[2] But the newly loaded question of that future, not yet one year after the attacks of September 11, is what the AR conferees sought to whip into racially recognizable shape. Indeed, there was a sort of psycho-temporal fantasy being concocted here, part nostalgia and part prophecy, with a particularly American combination of desire and loathing stirred in. The men of AR were engaged in a weekend mourning ritual over what they kept referring to as the death of the white race—and this, while whiteness was everywhere still animated and brutally alive. Within the patriotic ether of post-9/11, the group's goal was to mingle the story of white identity's more glorious past with a prevailing despair over its widely storied passing. In doing so, the group pointed toward the dream of white racial purity (and permanence) that it could evidently no longer actually afford. The general claims of the conference were easy enough to predict. Foreign violence from within and foreign violence from without U.S. borders now constitute the twin beasts dogging authentic American identity. But in response to the combined aggression in New York and Washington, D.C., white folk must get clear about domestic racial issues just one or two steps removed. We need to join phenotypical ranks to secure our nation's future. We must make it a priority to confront such things as immigration, black-on-white crime, and the unhappiest form of bioterrorism yet known in the phantasmatic fatherland, rampant miscegenation. Laced within AR's patriotic fervor, then, was the evidently more urgent matter of the U.S. Population Reference Bureau prediction. You will know it, in one form or another: "Sometime during the second half of the twenty-first century, the arbiters of the core national culture for most of its existence, are likely to slip into minority status."[3] And so, sealed into the conventioneer's haze of an airport hotel, we white guys sought "the memory of whiteness."

My purpose at the AR conference was to get a story, to hold my nose and mix it up with people looking more or less like me. I would then report back on the experience as a sort of antiracist exposé for the *Journal of Blacks in Higher Education*.[4] Toward that end, I spent three agonizingly isolated days among my kind, mulling over a fantasy of whiteness now storied to be gone. More irritating than that, these days turned out to produce certain moments of intimacy that I would have liked to let go unnoticed. Hearing the ideas circulating around a coming white minority by the buttoned-down men of AR, I could not help making some unseemly comparisons closer to home. I could not help recollecting the remarkable excitement generated around the once unremarkable race not three years before, when the academic rush to whiteness I had helped encourage with an earlier edited volume reaped an eerily similar exuberance.[5] The story I was getting, but found myself wanting to resist, was a story I struggled to keep from recognizing as a version of my own.

Since the mid-1990s, whiteness has been a prominent topic at more mainstream and well-respected academic gatherings, such as the American Social Science Association, the Modern Language Association, the Institute for Culture and Society, the American Studies Association, and the like. Somehow the idea of particularizing whiteness as a normative historical fiction, combined with an under-interrogated desire to see that race on the margins, carried good professional and even political currency. Indeed, at some of those venues I have been able to present material that ended up in *After Whiteness,* in effect joining what has become a kind of academic rush to distinguish what was once assumed (by most white folk, anyway) to be an undistinguished, invisible, and undivided race.[6] What seems like a long time ago, and at once, a time too close at hand, humanities research in the 1990s saw a kind of academic great white hype about a topic AR members would have recognized with ease.[7] The ambivalent words "I write on whiteness" were the only credentials needed to get me an invitation to sit down at the 2001 assembly with Nick Griffin, the affable, sinister head of the racist British National Party, and a white guy, it turns out, remarkably well attuned to the plight of white working-class men. My point is simply to say that, while covering the AR story, I noticed how the same kinds of hopes and fears garnering whiteness its share (and then some) of academic attention were meshing too easily with the tortured hearts and twisted minds I mixed with at the AR conference. This was MLA through the ethnographic looking glass. As soon as I paid the cab, got a receipt for later reimbursement, and checked in to the conference hotel like all the other attendees, I knew this would be academic multiculturalism turned precisely on its head. Wrapped with more or less sociable manners, at the expected location, and in requisite business attire, white racial self-interest was never "so white," once again.

The presidential address in the Grand Ballroom midway through the conference only consolidated this nerve-wracking feeling of inversion. The AR founder and current chief, Jared Taylor, mingled a description of white marginality with a future for white folk that he wanted to take back from the nation's coming multicolored fate. The task, he insisted, was to hasten the inevitable mainstreaming of white racial self-interest and to celebrate the premonitions of nationalism that the current fantasy of a white-minority country should proceed to arouse and inflame. At a location in sight of the U.S. Capitol, Taylor wanted to see democratic jurisprudence repealed, *habeas corpus* surrendered, and the reach of an all-powerful domestic spy ring enlarged to maintain our white-national security. Beyond these evidently too moderate actions, Taylor wanted the forced segregation of communities and schools, mass deportation, forcible repatriation, and above all, racially based fertility control. This was the U.S.A. Patriot Act just a click beyond Senator Trent Lott's nostalgic endorsement of the segregationist politics behind Strom Thurmond's 1948 Dixiecrat presidential campaign. Taylor's presidential address was meant to spawn the rebirth of a nation. At the same time, his was a pitch for a form of racist nationalism meant to burst forth from within a respectable white-collar core. He wanted to arouse the bankers and real estate brokers, the lawyers and academics, the political advisors and the one school board member, who spoke in turn at AR about the coming white minority. It was this professional vanguard who could most capably articulate the challenges of white-racial marginalization, Taylor said. It was they who were in the most secure positions to criticize, if not abolish, the racial status quo.

With the *merely* conservative-sounding conference subtitle, "In Defense of Western Man," the eugenically based *cri de coeur* of past AR conferences attempted this time to reach out from above, like Nick Griffin's civic-minded handshake, to the excitable white guy next door. Fred Pfeil would have called this excitable white guy, tongue-in-academic-cheek, "the new subaltern subject of Post-Fordism."[8] And this description would be technically right, at least according to the numbers, since the real earnings of white men in the United States, having dipped during the 1970s and 1980s, declined faster than those of any other group during the recession of 1999–2001.[9] Diminished wages aside, during Taylor's presidential address I had to keep asking myself whether his excitable white guy was me. The domestic crisis of the state, declining wages, the manipulations of a flexible workforce, diversity management, and other such manifestations of post-Fordist political economy are the express concerns of a book like *After Whiteness*. And they are concerns, more disturbingly to its author, that AR's mixed-class rank and file would have been willing enough to consider—in a life-or-death kind of way.

Taylor's pitch got a good deal spicier than a civic-minded handshake accidentally aimed at me, as the presidential address concluded. "In the homespun wisdom of my grandmother," he said, "race was our most extended family." After CUNY philosophy professor Michael Levin's eugenicist screed that afternoon, of course, there was nothing surprising in Taylor's ancestral racist musings.[10] But in what followed, the call for "biological loyalty" was made more intense by the revelation of AR's more occulted preoccupation. Taylor proceeded to trace the graphically *sexualized* nature of white racial disintegration, episodes he assured us that were all but unmentionable in respectable circles like our own. Against his better judgment, then, Taylor claimed that he *had* to include this material. It provided mighty inspiration for addressing all the other outrages against the white American majority that were documented at the conference so far. No, this time he meant neither the hijacking of commercial airlines nor the bioterrorism of making mixed-race babies, but something still more lamentable than either of those offenses, something Taylor "[had] to talk about . . . no matter how horrible." The emblem and the outcome of a post-white America, he whispered in confidence, was "black-on-white male rape." Taylor's own reluctance to pronounce this suitably torrid hypothesis made for an odd anticipation in the room. Having accomplished such high dramatic tension, he then made what to some may have sounded like an odd request. He appealed to his audience to identify with—really, in some sense, to embody—the lost figure of white male "solidarity" that he found in the allegory of homosexual rape. This "solidarity" was best achieved, Taylor's heated logic seemed to run, as a direct consequence of the black/white homosexual violation, the very image he begged his audience to envision. "Group solidarity in prison," Taylor rallied, "means that rape of one is rape of all." "Whites [have] become blacks' personal property [in prison]." And in prison, as in the ballroom where we made our fantasies that night, we must "fully commit to each other." We must "commit to each other," Taylor charged, or risk a "long-term suicide" that kills heterosexual masculinity and the white race in one swipe.

Two more scenes in this story. During questions from the floor a middle-aged white man approached the microphone. Next to the speaker's athletic six-foot frame, the questioner looked risibly and self-consciously diminutive. He was sweating, I remember, and had an air of fealty toward the AR president that seemed to bring him to the brink of tears. "I commit to you, Jared Taylor," he said. "If somebody attacks you, or anybody in this room, I will come to your aid." Here again I had to ask myself, was I *already* in Jared Taylor's aid? Was I joined to him insofar as we two white male "radicals" in sports jackets and ties share an interest—if an inverted one—in telling stories about the passing of whiteness? More shameful than that, were we to be positioned the same way, as the country imagines whatever remains in the *racial* majority's wake? (There are, of course, always other ways than *race* to tally identity's numbers.)[11] The title of this book, *After Whiteness,* could as easily have been the title of Taylor's plenary address. And as reported to me by his U.S. presidential campaign advisor, Patrick Buchanan's new book, *The Death of the West,* was supposed to be *The Death of Whitey,* after all.[12]

That irritating thought was not altogether soothed when later, following dinner and drinks, matters turned from the violently intimate nature of Jared Taylor's presentation to a more public and political discussion (this progression, too, marking a certain inversion of the norm). After a short break Taylor resumed the dais, as was his way by now, and introduced "a man whose talk would go down best after a few beers." The reveler in question was Nick Griffin, my contact from the afternoon's earlier discussion about mobilizing excitable white working-class men. In the final presentation of the night, Griffin was to address the surprise electoral successes of his British National Party, which he touted alongside the rise of other such movements in Germany and France. In the King's own English, Griffin began his talk by speaking the usual racist missives. He reminded us "not [of our] conservative, but [of our] revolutionary movement." "We white racialists must put away our boots, and put on our suits," he said, affirming a dress code already enforced. "There is nothing left to preserve except the color of our children's skin." "I want white genocide trials for the likes of Blair and Clinton, [and would see them] hanging from the nearest lamp post." And so on, and so forth, to the roar of applause mixed with back slapping, foot stomping, and laughter. But another beer (or another Chardonnay) and two standing ovations later, it became clear that the two forms of nationalist "white racialism" at work in his and Taylor's speeches were not really the same. Somewhere, in the midst of what was supposed to be a lot of white racist good cheer, for one fleeting moment the BNP's nationalism and whatever it was that Taylor's organization imagined to the right of Buchanan and Thurmond were not in touch with the same species of hate. Griffin's distinctly U.S. white-collar audience, in spite of the strong desire to make merry, appeared to choke on the bitter pill he called, without flinching, "class struggle." Griffin did not articulate the fact that U.S. CEOs were taking home on average in 2000 about five hundred times the salary of the middle-income worker, compared with "only" twenty-five times that amount in the 1960s. Neither did he weave into his dissatisfaction with international corporatization the sad fact that real income has fallen since 1970 for U.S. workers, and continues to fall.[13] But rather remarkably and, it turns out, awkwardly for most of his audience that night, Griffin's racist invective ended with one or two quotations from Marx. In thinking about our earlier discussion, as well as any number of other less onerous fantasies about class consciousness when whiteness is gone, I found that Griffin's citation of Marx provided the oddest mix of hope and despair in my mind. It would have been tempting to go another round after hours with him in the lobby to see if Griffin could be nudged off his racist soapbox while keeping his working-class fidelities in place. But at this late point in the weekend of conference proceedings, who had that kind of resilience? What is more, who would really want to admit to the confusing prospect that opposing evaluations on the white majority's so-called death could mimic one another on class?

What was clear in Griffin's plenary address, beyond our inverted twin fantasies of a unified post-white labor force, was our mutual insistence that all current political options have "betrayed the working class." Griffin's economically based appeal to whiteness had preceded the avalanche of corporate scandals in 2002. He was, therefore, relieved from having to further antagonize his host and the AR membership with concrete examples of the big money rip-offs of workers. But his appeal to Marx would not have played any better to his fellow racists had the timing been different than it was. Griffin wanted to peddle a version of white genetic solidarity that strongly opposed the globalization of the free market and the further exploitation of labor. He meant to bemoan—as leftist scholars critical of whiteness (myself included) have done for some time—what he called "reductions in the wages of the ordinary worker." But in the minds of a relatively well-off group of men like those who made up his audience that night, it was decided to leave that behind. Any emerging anticapitalist *ressentiment* would fix itself in an all-white America. Griffin finally chose not to press the economic point too hard, and the emphasis on white solidarity soon won back its former pride of place.

I use the story of my experiences at the AR conference to introduce *After Whiteness* because the idea of a coming white minority has captured both popular and academic imaginations with effects that are ambivalent, at best. Indeed, that formulation, "white minority," might be put a little more precisely. The recent popularity of whiteness, at least within academe, has created the not unreasonable suspicion that so much white-on-white debate merely signals the opportunistic gaming of a multicultural administrative system. Even with an attempt like the one that follows to make sense out of *how we make sense* of what no longer worms away from critique, those welcomed charges are sure to advance. So I concede from the start that any work on whiteness will be full of holes and contradictions.

In the volume that began this project, *Whiteness: A Critical Reader,* I suggested that an initial wave of work on the topic attempted to break what Frantz Fanon referred to as the "ontogenetic" seal of white normativity.[14] That first wave of work challenged both the absence of whiteness from discussions of race, that is, its pretense to unmarkedness or purity, and the risible assumption that the white majority as such would continue beyond its specific historical moment. But even in 1997, when well-known scholars in what one still hesitates to call a field, agreed to contribute to that early volume, there was the sense that a critical rush to whiteness would be symptomatic of the very problem of hegemony *Whiteness* wrestled to demolish. My suggestion back then was that academic work on whiteness should not expect to rid itself of the contradictions it pins on mass culture. This point, borne as it was from materialist theoretical training, seemed to me to mark the threshold of a second wave of research on the topic. While nobody uses (or did use) the term "whiteness studies" unless in ironically damning ways, it is true that by twentieth century's end writing on whiteness was a part of academic culture in the awkwardly popular sense. This is why I ended my 1997 summation of the phenomenon (which admittedly brackets centuries of unrecognized critical encounters with whiteness) by referring to a transitional moment within feminism during the early 1980s.[15] My sense in reading that archive was, and still is, that the relations between identity and difference are historically (but not whimsically) portable. My other sense was that, over time, they are also prolific.

The phrase "over time" in that last sentence is critical and essential to the work that follows in the present book. The task at hand is to make sense of a set of unprecedented changes in the dynamics of racial identity in the United States. The task is no longer simply to mark the unmarked and unremarkable status of whiteness as such, the way it was less than a decade ago. That much has happened, with results that have ranged from the most naive forms of romancing the other to the insidious militancy of white genetic self-defense. The more difficult work I now have in mind still runs along the lines that Marilyn Frye, Toni Cade Bambara, and other feminists of color set out to draw in the later 1980s. It takes seriously what I alluded to above regarding the white racists of AR as "a psycho-temporal" problem where the stakes are life-and-death. I am interested, in other words, in a way of describing how the white majority's imagined move into the past is coordinated with its thoroughly agitated status in the present, and I want to do so for a future that I am sure is beyond the capacity of white guys like me to know. The core concern of *After Whiteness,* then, is to explore the remnants of white identity as a way of mobilizing one's democratic commitments within what might be called (a little awkwardly, I realize) an economy of absence. More to the point of the 1980s feminist work with which I introduced the earlier book, this one traces the demise of unmarked subjectivity as a way of placing white folk face to face with the kinds of political exigencies we are used to handling at some appropriately distant remove. From here we might ask some difficult questions: how, for example, does the imagined disappearance of the white majority—the nation's incipient temporal hallucination—work to produce the kinds of continuities with fascism that I have alluded to in reference to AR? By extension, how can the phantasm of a post-white America keep from ratcheting up the prevailing sense of nationalist fervor already in our midst?

Recent scholarship on race has increasingly turned to the historical pressures now besetting the fiction Americans still insist on calling the white race. In doing so, it has marked the same attention to whiteness that made it possible for AR's men to echo, if not exactly endorse, the reckless claim that whiteness in the United States is effectively leaving the country. The ambivalent prospect of an end to whiteness haunts progressive scholarship on race as much as it haunts the paranoid visions of white-collar racists on the other side of the ethnographic looking glass.[16] For both groups, ironically, whiteness is both gone and still very much here. And if such a body of discourse called whiteness studies actually exists, there is a sense that the blind proliferation of this work creeps toward an ugly metamorphosis that will keep it from progressive goals. Perhaps whiteness studies might better be dubbed *after*-whiteness studies, thus keeping the temporal irony of its absent presence at the forefront and in play. Scholarship on whiteness typically begins with the awkward premise that the very object it presumes to study is something less to be preserved than to be uprooted, if not abolished, one happy day. That work, wittingly or not, serves to nudge to the surface the troubling sense that the critical study of whiteness was destined to come up against the limits of modern epistemology. Thus the more general theoretical concern that runs through the course of this book is to advance the agenda of a post-white analytic, that is, to assess how we presume to know and value a thing by the fact of its not being there.

No figure of racial phantasmagoria has been more popular and, in her own way, less actually *there* than Eve, the computer-generated multiracial cover girl for *Time* magazine's 1993 special issue, "The New Face of America." Eve, you may recall, is a composite image of fourteen different racial and ethnic identities, digitally morphed into a muted picture of the nation's uncharted post-white future. The name Eve is, of course, biblically provocative. She clearly reestablishes a Genesis myth within the Puritan tradition of American exceptionalism. Eve avows a nationally reinvigorated origin of the species, an ironic "rebirth of the nation," in a prelapsarian, ultimately *species*-less pitch for heterosexual coupledom. In Lauren Berlant's astute evaluation, the image represents the latest ruse of "normative citizenship" as "hygienic governmentality" moves unimpeded into "the abstracted time and space of the private."[17] Eve generates "the embrace of heterosexuality for national culture" (*QW*, 208), she writes, "turn[ing] the loss of white cultural prestige into a gain for white cultural prestige" (*QW*, 200). Michael Warner casts the face of Eve as a "divine Frankenstein," a normative monster who ushers in the hegemonic optimism of "a happy monoracial culture" that is predicated on making mixed-race babies.[18] "It is not

SPECIAL ISSUE

TIME

Take a good look at this woman. She was created by a computer from a mix of several races. What you see is a remarkable preview of . . .

THE NEW FACE OF AMERICA

How Immigrants Are Shaping the World's
First Multicultural Society

symbolic femininity," he writes, "but practical heterosexuality that guarantees the monocultural nation" (*PCP,* 189). Even Susan Gubar's relative optimism about Eve, that "morphing postulates a visual elasticity beyond racial dualism," is tempered by Donna Haraway's wanting to shiver off the effects of "numbing" that Eve's muted visage delivers.[19] These critical responses to a face of mixed-race identity, and to its mixed messages, underscore a caveat that *After Whiteness* obeys at every turn. Beware the end of American whiteness, which might be nothing more than the fulfillment of its ends.

But the image has a certain popular allure that may, or may not, be so reductively admonished. In her appeal to the many scholars of culture and race (me included) who go on reproducing her face in our books, Eve's frustrating silence almost absorbs the criticism laid at her nonexistent feet. If she is Frankenstein, she is also part Bartleby. In the rush to get a properly critical hold on this phantasmatic icon of post-whiteness, Eve manages without even trying to underscore what I keep calling the mobilization of absence in time (or here, literally, in *Time*). Her own popularity exists on account of her omni-critical dumbness, I want to say. Her silent face inspires a certain nervousness all around as she both declares, and effectively hides, our national future. Indeed, her message, if there is one, might be that this future, like Eve herself, is for the first time not self-evidently present to the nation that struggles to claim it. Perhaps then e*ve* in lowercase is a better way to think of what I would claim is the more richly ambivalent historical terrain on which the white race may yet be unmade. In this sense, Eve's (or eve's) virtual visage might elicit that peculiar temporal mix I noted at the AR conference. That was a mix, recall, of our uncertainty about the passing of the white majority and the anticipation of a future that surely cannot be known in advance. In that sentence I am simply suggesting, again, that on the brink of what many are now imagining is a post-white American future (call that brink an "after-whiteness eve"), it remains a matter of both popular and academic uncertainty as to what will emerge in its place.

As a scholar who perhaps more than any other single figure might be called, no doubt reluctantly, a founding father of so-called American whiteness studies, David Roediger, too, is critically measured in his evaluation of Eve. He echoes the other scholars I have mentioned, in many ways. Roediger is clear about how this mixed-race assemblage of commercial media culture is "link[ed] to a multiracial denial of racial reality" insofar as the facts of exploitation and poverty remain out of view. But to complicate that denial, Roediger evokes Alexander Saxton, who writes that "white racism is essentially a theory of history."[20] With this I take Saxton to be saying, as I too want to say throughout *After Whiteness,* that we may well critique, even as we reanimate, the events we declare to be past. "We organize and write, like it or not," Roediger says, "in the face of Eve's appeal, and the appeal of Eve's face frankly causes serious problems for anti-racists" (*CW*, 15). The term "in the face of" may well be taken to mean *in spite of* Eve's nefarious "nativist folklore credibil[ity]" (*CW*, 10). But the words "like it or not" and "appeal" also bespeak Roediger's reluctant admission that U.S. academics may well have to begin where the rest of their countrymen do. We will have to begin, that is, with the contradictions at work in the mass culture about which we speak.

After Whiteness never leaves the contradictions that surround the virtual visage of Eve. This book is therefore part forensic report, part user's guide, and maybe part hallucination. Its core question asks how an emergent post-white national imaginary figures into public policy issues, into the habits of sexual intimacy, and into changes within public higher education, at a moment when white racial change has declared its ambivalent debut.

Part One of the book examines the congressional and popular debates over multiracial identity that surrounded the census leading up to the 2000 count. Here, I argue, a new form of identity politics leaves behind the civil rights legacy and signals the crisis of the liberal state. In my account of racial self-recognition, the constitutional mandate for enumerating citizenship reaches a revealing point of computational unease. Census counting is now beset with forms of ontological complexity that press upon identity itself as the formal basis of democratic governing. The first two sections of Part One trace the unlikely, but ultimately successful, addition of a check-all-that-applies option to racial self-enumeration for the 2000 census. Along the way, I offer a brief account of the crucial link between 1960s civil rights legislation and the forms of official race classification as constructed for the last two census counts. I do this in order, first, to interrogate the precarious idealism behind the notion of consistent racial self-recognition. Second, I am interested in the civil rights movement's influence on the census in order to link the various forms of *mis*recognition that now accompany the act of racial self-regard. The ontological permutations I want to trace in multiracialism signal a crisis within the liberal state where multitudes replace identity as such. The third section of Part One adjoins the U.S. census debates to developments regarding identity and the law that have occurred within Critical Race Theory. I am also interested in changes at work in what David Theo Goldberg calls the racial state. The goal here is to bring the contingencies of state-authorized racial self-categorization to bear on questions of juridical procedure. I maintain that the state's postmodern interest in race is doubly coercive *and* protective, inclusive *and* exclusive. As the claims upon civil rights justice proliferate and intensify, the state has developed an accompanying experimental interest in racial heterogeneity. But this interest, paradoxically, also enables the state's presumed domestic obligations to all but disappear.

The fourth section of Part One applies the lessons of the preceding sections to the question of civil society in more general terms. Here, too, I want to complicate the Enlightenment ideals of intersubjectivity that multiracialism might seem to uphold. Of particular interest in this fourth section is the influential work of Jürgen Habermas on communicative reason, as well as Charles Taylor's seminal endorsement of a politics of mutual, over purely self-, recognition. My claim is that the form of neo-Hegelianism espoused by these two distinguished social theorists never quite escapes Hegel's nationalist longings, and indeed, is inadvertently sympathetic to a multiracial rebirth of the nation. The overall goal of my discussion of Habermas and Taylor (and secondarily, Hegel) is to trace civil society's apparent disintegration, as much as to foster a more pronounced collision between individual and political life. I want to critique a liberal progressive-activist tendency that upholds a post-white national order by emphasizing racial oppositions and retaining civil rights solutions to them. The fifth and final section of Part One explores post-formalist conceptions of identity in the wake of civil rights, and offers a cursory rethinking of class as a way of coming to better terms with the immanent force of racial multitudes. In general, the goal of Part One of *After Whiteness* is to situate the state's official turn to racial subjectivity as a way of governing via dissensus. The racial divisions that formally hindered civil society from ever becoming fully established are being removed, or so congressmen and multiracial activists would have us believe. And with that removal, or that alleged removal, identity politics are altered so that having a race matters less, and matters more, to the vanishing liberal state.

Part Two of the book traces the way whiteness is both surrendered and defended given the affective twists and turns expressed by two groups that are organized around white masculinity. In this account of the Christian men's group the Promise Keepers (PK) and the neofascist organization the National Alliance (NA), I am interested in sussing out the volatile psychic investments that white heterosexual men have in men of color. The psychic intensity exhibited by each of these two groups, at their opposite extremes, advances a "radical" reclamation of traditional family structures. My analysis of PK and NA thus reveals how love and hate, arousal and repression, authority and submission, humility and pride cooperate in contemporary white masculinity. The anxieties produced by growing inequities of wealth are lived differently by today's white men than simply by cordoning off color from whiteness, as in former times. Class angst is lived, not simply through modern forms of white racial separatism, but via a postmodern, erotically charged softening of mutable racial distinctions.

The initial sections in Part Two trace the accelerated rise of the Christian men's group the Promise Keepers in the early and mid-1990s. Touted as the largest evangelical movement in U.S. history, this group exhibits the pursuit of white racial reconciliation, and binds it to the dictates of masculine heterosexuality, specifically, to fatherhood and marriage. PK is only one of a number of formal organizations promoting what has been called the U.S. marriage movement. But given the group's fundamental multicultural interests, it is curious that PK is bound (even if covertly) to the right-wing public policy groups that support it. In line with these groups, the ideological lineaments PK attaches to the heterosexual family become supercharged. But oddly, PK does this by appealing to hypermasculinized forms of self-sacrifice that are hinged to white racial transgression. The second section in Part Two develops this hypothesis with further examples from PK literature (and, less explicitly, from my own participation at PK events). Here I detail how PK's interest in pursuing cross-racial forms of heteromasculine intimacy becomes the platform on which the achingly uncertain future of whiteness depends. The work of masculine recovery resides in the cultivation of a post-white sensibility within what PK terms "a father-shaped void." At stake in this deliciously loaded phrase is the very heart of what I am calling "a fascism of benevolence." By this phrase, I mean to highlight a process of white racial self-negation that returns in the inverted form of sexual self-reassertion. My general point regarding heterosexual masculinity is that the love and hate of color operate in common, and at the same time.

Subsequent to initial work on PK, the argument takes a more theoretical turn to discuss the role self-negation plays in forming what Theodor Adorno calls the authoritarian personality. The goal of this intermediary section will be to construct the conceptual bridges that join PK's gentler approach to race (the love of color) to the explicitly neofascist aims of the National Alliance (the hate of color). Here I follow the lead of Paul Apostolidis's impressive book on Adorno and the Christian right, which despite its subtle analysis of conservative religious radio culture leaves the issue of sexuality more or less to the side. I use Apostolidis's work on Christian family policy groups to set up the psychic hinge revealed by the PK/neofascism connection with which I will eventually conclude. I also turn in this intermediary section to the work of Judith Butler and David Eng on the racial moorings of masculine heterosexuality. Eng's pathbreaking book on the relation between heterosexual masculinity and race is especially important for contextualizing my analysis of PK. However, my analysis differs from his on what seems to me an overly schematic account of the psychic life of heterosexual white men. Eng and Butler commonly suggest that racial repudiation satisfies the mandates of white racial purity—an important formulation for anatomizing the neofascist imaginary in, for example, the infamous National Alliance novel I examine later, *The Turner Diaries*. But even when I apply the Butler-Eng hypothesis to this best-selling racist book, their theses do not explain the partnering of race and sexuality as it occurs within PK. In this group, white masculine sexuality plays out in terms that are exactly opposite to those that presume to maintain white racial purity through color's strict repudiation. A carefully cultivated, if also extremely volatile, form of post-white sensibility is the unlikely basis by which heterosexuality is secured in PK. Indeed, PK and U.S. neofascism share the same heterosexual logic, I will finally suggest. But they do so via a kind of mirrored libidinal inversion. Both groups seek to preserve masculinity, but the more curious point is that they do so by mobilizing exactly the opposite extremes regarding race and whiteness. According to an unlikely composite of racial benevolence and U.S. neofascism, white men's relation to alterity is writ *doubly* as an attraction *and* an aversion to the future forms of racial multiplicity they cannot quite embody.

Part Three of *After Whiteness* is a critical account of identity studies and diversity within the contemporary public research university. Of concern here, to begin with, is the replacement of public support for the university with market-oriented forms of corporate funding that are indicative of the vanishing liberal state. The initial two sections trace the vexed effects of academic corporatization, among other places, within English studies. I also produce here a critical reassessment of Clark Kerr's administrative classic, *The Uses of the University* (and related subsequent books), and evoke Bill Readings's influential hypotheses in *The University in Ruins*. My general purpose, following that watershed book, is to connect the alleged collapse of traditional English studies to the public university's withering claim on democratic purpose. From different quarters and with diverging agendas, both Kerr and Readings surmise the same problem. For Readings, it is the rise of social dissensus and cultural "de-referentialization." Kerr signals the postmodern university's rise by a far simpler name, the advance of what he calls the "mob" beyond the multiversity's gates. Both Readings and Kerr allege that an earlier social contract between knowledge and the public has effectively come apart. And while they may use different language to say so, both authors allude to how such a moment of coming apart is the result of a kind of forcing together, indeed, a collision between the once assumedly separate realms of work and knowledge production. This coming apart of the modern university's former public purpose and the current collision between thought and material life are best understood, I will argue, as symptoms of academic labor struggle. Related to this struggle, and in many ways central to it, is the issue of diversity or multiculturalism. Within the corporate university scheme, I contend, the current flirtation with post-whiteness remains, at least partly, a highly managed affair. Cultural brokering within administrative circles organizes new and more fluid orders of work. Whether or not (more optimistically) that fluidity may give way to forms of democratic collaboration with labor as its most critical component remains very much to be seen.

Having measured the university's stake in multiculturalism by contextualizing it within academic labor politics, the third section of Part Three fine-tunes the discussion by turning to the curious rise of so-called whiteness studies. Here I want to explore the ambivalent institutional locale of this relatively new-sprung branch of critical ethnography, which is, in effect, an accidental field, if a field at all. The argument here is that the recent attention paid to whiteness, as well-intended as its practitioners plead it was and it is, is best considered within the conditions of institutional ruin that whiteness studies cannot help but reveal. It has become a common enough charge that the spate of work that amassed on whiteness throughout the 1990s has served to exacerbate the problem of white hegemony that it only pretended to unmask. Critical responses to whiteness studies are of great importance, since they are attuned to the ways this work plays out materially, that is, how it tends to run contrary to an author's best intentions. But there is a creeping redundancy in the soon-to-be hoary debate about the political efficacy of academic work on whiteness. My argument is that the contradictions surrounding whiteness studies remain one of its most salient and worthwhile features. In this sense, the study of whiteness was never—and with hard enough work will never be—an unproblematically unified institutional force. And this is so, not because whiteness studies scholars have resolved the contradictions upon which their writing secretly rests. Rather, a lack of institutional force is the *only force* the ruined university allows. The turn to whiteness in academe is symptomatic, in other words, of an increasingly exploitative labor environment that is itself predicated on cultural absence.

The fourth section of Part Three connects the infelicitous rise of whiteness studies to one of the most definitive, if also highly contested, developments within humanities scholarship in recent decades. In this section of the argument, I want to widen my concern over multicultural knowledge production and whiteness to include the boom in Cultural Studies (hereafter CS) as it entered the United States from the United Kingdom during the early 1990s. Bill Readings's ideas about de-referential knowledge and the forms of social dissensus pursuant to it—what is in fact a critical reinscription of Clark Kerr's fear of the mob—are points here brought to bear on the legacy of the British New Left. The specific problem of interest here is a historical one concerning how writing and work are related. That an overdue encounter with labor in the ruined university occurs simultaneous to the collapse of writing's representational function is the point Readings makes about the rise of CS. This point recalls the collision between writing and work, and with that, what I have been calling the economy of absence that is endemic to academic life. In my account of CS's investment in popular culture, the renowned Marxist cultural historian E.P. Thompson will be an essential figure. Here I will turn to his work on the eighteenth-century British working class, in particular, his writing on the crowd as a way to link back to Kerr's fear of the mob. Thompson, as is well known, was one of the key New Left originators of British CS in the 1960s. Moreover, he is celebrated in North America as one of CS's founding fathers and sometimes its guiding conscience. I will argue that Thompson's work on the eighteenth-century laboring masses is seminal to the way U.S. CS wrongly uses popular culture to fortify its own troubled representational status. Thompson's difficulties with Louis Althusser (as a stand-in for theory, in general) betray an under-historicized notion of political economy as it relates both to identity and knowledge production. Thompson glosses the historicity of this tripartite arrangement and allows, apropos the unlikely figure of Adam Smith, a false moral continuity between identity and object, and again, between writing and work.

Finally, section five of Part Three turns to the question of representational misfires within writing from the angle of contemporary literary studies. Such authoritative figures as Alvin Kernan and Harold Bloom bemoan the Western literary canon as something irretrievably lost. Literary studies, the charge proceeds, has been invaded by new knowledge, namely, the cobelligerent upstarts of multiculturalism and CS. But the storied demise of Western literature, like whiteness, remains attractive in the ruined university precisely because so many people gain authority by evoking its loss. In that sense, the whiteness studies trend and the dead-end turn to pop culture that plagues English are not antagonists to the traditional literary work once found there. Indeed, according to the institutional logic I will try to describe, race studies and CS are literature's unlikely bedfellows and partners in crime. All three function according to an economy of absence that organizes the humanities in ruined academe. In the wake of identity studies and so much interdisciplinary work, the current afterlife of traditional literary studies—a field that insists on being addressed precisely as "dead"—is once again symptomatic of a larger set of problems that adjoin writing to mass politics and race.

One figure who is sufficiently popular, multicultural, *and* literary—and who I want to suggest is up to something like finding labor conflict within an economy of absence—is Toni Morrison. The text I have in mind is her award-winning work of nonfiction, *Playing in the Dark: Whiteness and the Literary Imagination*. In this text, Morrison provides an account of Africa as a figure of absence that, while historically excluded, is indeed generative of canonical

American literature. This hypothesis provides effective grounds for thinking critically through the normativizing effects of whiteness. But her deft attention to causality as that which is generatively gone (I will have been calling this labor power) has even further-reaching implications than this. *Playing in the Dark* makes use of writing's necessarily dissensual ends. It shows how historically unclaimed affective arrangements can become the basis for more democratic reconfigurations of how we work and live in the future. In such a way, Morrison's own work gestures beyond the ruined university, finding in its irrefutable disasters the necessary hope for a democracy whose time is not yet known. A more modest contribution to the achievement of that goal is the best I might hope for in writing *After Whiteness.*

INCALCULABLE COMMUNITY

MULTIRACIALISM, U.S. CENSUS 2000, AND THE CRISIS OF THE LIBERAL STATE

LABOR FORMALISM

The problem of the twentieth century is . . .

—W. E. B. Du Bois

The epigraph above from Du Bois, which I leave deliberately incomplete, is perhaps one of the most oft repeated aphorisms ever cited in contemporary scholarship on race. In that sense, to those familiar with such work, the phrase may sound a little worn. But then again, how else to begin to think about color and categorization, which of course includes thinking about whiteness, than through the extraordinary figure of Du Bois? Even in the simple reluctance to repeat his celebrated phrase yet once more, the epigraph evokes a problem about citation (and re-citation) and therefore gets one thinking from the start about repetition and time as well as category. The epigraph presents what I want to argue is an appropriately nonsynchronistic form of racial reckoning between Du Bois's historical moment and ours, a rift that indeed nags the whole field of identity studies. It forces us to come to terms with that other problem, *the* problem of the argument that follows, which is how the infamous "color line" (the part of the phrase I left out above) proceeds to change. In a roundabout way, I am simply suggesting that scholars of race have to ask a new question. That question is not what *is* "the problem of the twentieth century," but what *was* it? How in not being here, or not here exactly, is the "color line" different in the twenty-first century than before? And a question going differently to the linked issues of category and repetition, is the "problem of the twentieth century" our problem, in whatever guise the "our" of a new century may chance to recognize itself?

Du Bois's declaration was made originally at his address to the American Negro Academy in 1900, and of course he harkend back to the phrase himself throughout his long and ideologically varied career.[1] But a century and counting later, the phrase intimates a certain paradox it may not have signaled in its day. To cite Du Bois at present should mark the limits that distinguish his time and ours, and reveal a rather more elaborate and unwieldy intra-linear racial order than 1900 allowed him to surmise. At the same time, my wanting to repeat him a century later should mark the centrality of race to social justice in the United States, even when that center refuses to hold. The issue at present, I want to suggest, is not merely a hesitation to say again about "the color line" what by political necessity one has to go on saying. The new century reveals citational problems that are different from before. As part of this difference, racial identities exceed their former boundaries. And within our most plastic and accelerated historical moment, race works against the very name(s) of "color" that it continues to promote. At the dawn of the twenty-first century, one witnesses a numbers and identity problem that disrupts whatever connection one might fathom between history, its catastrophic relation to the present, and the better future hoped for by evoking "color" like Du Bois. The problem of the twenty-*first* century is the problem of color *lines,* as the aphorism must now be emended, with a new and indomitable emphasis on the plural. In repeating Du Bois's maxim at a time when the original seems almost to go without saying, remarking on a plurality of "color lines" calls to mind another set of divisions. In the materialist spirit proper to his cause, this means the struggle to elucidate a unity that is as elusive and dynamic as any other. By this I mean what some scholars call the *collar* line, that is, the divisions and redivisions of labor.

To underscore the historical incompatibility of racial self-belonging and labor struggle, and to foreshadow my own analysis of the 2000 census debates, recall the conclusion of Du Bois's epic historical work, *Black Reconstruction.* Here the longing for a cross-racial working-class political synthesis is presented as both a missed opportunity and a tragically absent ideal. Indeed, the Du

Boisian desire to seek a racially transcendent form of labor solidarity retains titanic influence on the writings of historians of the white working class, such as Theodore Allen, David Roediger, Noel Ignatiev, and others.[2] The Cincinnati mobs of 1828, the Congress of Trade Unions in 1850, the presidential election of 1868, the exclusion of black workers from the American Federation of Labor in 1935 all mark events that worked in Du Bois's appraisal to "frustrate any mass movement towards the union of white and black labor."[3] Here, around the key phrase "mass movement," Du Bois puzzles over the historical incapacity of what he calls "the shibboleth of race" to make progressive sense of class divisions. In this account, white and black workers fail to suss out the tangled contradictions of racialized self-interest and miss the chance to identify across racial lines. The more damnable point, made with regularity in radical white labor history at the twentieth century's end, is that nominally ethno-European workers chose instead to cash in on the "public and psychological wages of whiteness" (*BR*, 700). White racial identity preempted labor struggle according to this schema, instead of softening the color boundary on political grounds and making common cause with the greater "mass" interest implicit in the unity of labor. But the convening of the "masses" as a "unity" becomes a problem as soon as one leans a little on the idea of collective action as simply the erection of one diametric opposition (working/ruling class) on the grave of a preceding diametric opposition (black/white racial). American labor historians in the wake of Du Bois tend to treat class in terms of the categorical reformulation of oppositional self-consciousness, and achieving a greater transparency of self-interest. They are, in this sense, labor formalists. And as such, they are inevitably limited by categorical difference having become so prolific and by trusted oppositions now breaking down.

The conceptual precursor of labor formalism is found in a certain version of Marx, which (though I will not do so here) is in need of revision. In his October 1864 "Inaugural Address to the First International," Marx comments on the exemplary "fraternal concurrence" exhibited by the workers of Manchester who willingly suffered the shortage of cotton from the blockaded U.S. South out of support for the war against slavery.[4] This account of international unity, writ in Enlightenment terms as sympathetic ("fraternal") identification, was the premise for working-class organization as mapped in *The Critique of the Gotha Programme*. Class unity is written here as a matter, "not [of] content, but . . . [of] form." Referring to the *Communist Manifesto*, Marx goes on to elaborate this notion of labor unity as a series of concentric "frames": "the framework of the present-day national state, . . . itself in its turn [framed] economically 'within the framework' of the world market, [framed] politically 'within the framework' of the systems of states."[5] Ungenerous readers will detect in this scheme the tendency toward viewing the social order as comprising too neatly a series of concentric categorical rings. The idea that politically effective self-reflection brings differently exploited individuals into a unified oppositional "mass" runs through Marx. It extends to more recent Marxist-humanist cultural theorists such as E. P. Thompson (whom I will discuss at length in Part Three), perhaps one of the most respected British theorists of "mass" agency there is.

By a more recent name, what I am calling labor formalism is premised upon what William Julius Wilson dubs the split-labor theory of class difference.[6] According to this idea, which Wilson wants rightly to complicate, racially based forms of uneven compensation divide workers against their better interests; and these better interests they can only understand if they define themselves in class, rather than in racial, terms. Cross-racial labor alliances—Du Bois's "masses" writ as such—are identifiable only to the extent that they are also presumed to be grounded by oppositions that are stable long enough to be self-consciously overcome. Black/white racial decomposition writ in this way ought to intimate positive political change over time, at least insofar as this division remains dialectically sutured to class as definitive of racial belonging.[7] In this scheme, it becomes the business of class struggle to transcend racial difference, so that labor may emerge in the future with full historical membership. But what about when racial decomposition is the order of the day, officially, and at a moment when capitalism has never been more secure, nor increasingly more brutal? The complication I want to introduce by this question signals the displacement of racial opposition with racial multiplicity. And this complication is implicit in the account of multiracialism and its relation to an emergent post-liberal state that will follow. What if the historically specific black/white racial opposition begins to unfold, as I will argue is beginning to happen, while this unfolding sacrifices its Du Boisian promise to class struggle? If the polarity implicit in *the* "color line" ought to be trumped by the primary division of labor, then one might also say that this trumping has occurred in scholarly circles without elaborating on a certain ambivalence evidently also implicit in collective agency as such. What I called before the tragically absent opportunities of "mass" agency gain their force here. Between accelerated forms of color consciousness in the United States and an understanding of class interest that has never been more missed, identity finds itself at a terminal crossroads. At this crossroads, the *disunity* of "masses" never looked more inviting, nor more politically charged. As I want to explore more fully below, this charge involves bringing self-recognition and economic redistribution closer together than even Du Bois might have thought.

To think along the *lines* of contemporary racial self-belonging (again, along lines that are plural), and to do so in a way that retains the spirit, if not the letter, of Du Bois's materialist charge, the next section will focus on the discussions about multiracial identity that surrounded the historically unprecedented complexities of the 2000 U.S. census. This section of the argument traces a series of congressional debates whereby the unlikely, but ultimately successful, addition of a check-all-that-applies racial option was added to the census. Along the way, I offer a brief account of the crucial link between 1960s civil rights legislation and the forms of official race classification as constructed for the last two census counts. I do so, as stated more generally above, to complicate the idea of racial self-recognition and to link the various forms of *mis*recognition that accompany that act to the terminal permutations of a waning liberal state. From here, a subsequent section brings the discussion of the census to bear on certain issues regarding identity and the law that are relevant to Critical Race Theory. At stake in my account of this work is to adjoin the issue of state-sanctioned racial self-categorization to what I argue are the doubly coercive *and* protective dynamics that constitute juridical procedure.

A fourth section directs the computational unease that surrounded the 2000 census debates to more general concerns having to do with the perceived disintegration of civil society. Here, too, I want to complicate the Enlightenment ideals of democratic intersubjectivity that multiracialism seems, at least superficially, to uphold. Of particular interest is the influential work of Jürgen Habermas on communicative reason. I am also concerned with Charles Taylor's seminal defense of a multicultural politics of mutual, over purely self-, recognition. The charge here is that a form of neo-Hegelianism evident in the work of these two social theorists never quite escapes Hegel's nationalist longings. Indeed, the call for multiracial self-description potentially helps to set the stage for a kind of post-racial rebirth of the nation. The overall goal of my discussion of Habermas and Taylor (and secondarily, Hegel) is to trace civil society's evident disintegration. More than that, I want to collapse what Nancy Fraser usefully describes as the falsely dichotomous division between (cultural) recognition and (material) redistribution.[8] The fifth section returns to Du Bois's evocation of "the masses" to advance a cursory exploration of collective agency in the wake of one set of formal strictures implicit in the discourse of rights. This section intimates certain potentialities around affect and intimacy outside common racial self-recognition. In that sense, it makes an effective transition to Part Two of the book on the love and hate of color in the two men's movements I describe there.

My general purpose below is to examine the relation between official forms of racial self-disclosure and a shift in the rules of civil rights–based governmentality. I want to critique a liberal progressive-activist tendency that upholds a post-white national order by proliferating racial oppositions and retaining civil rights solutions to them. Ultimately, my charge is that the liberal state is disintegrating through the intensification of the very premises that founded it. The point of detailing this process is meant to limn a new and unholy consolidation between a neoliberal left discourse of rights and a contemporary right-wing assault on the political significance of individual difference. If, in tracing how the "color line" is pluralized, I move race in a less customary post-formalist direction, it should also be said that I intend to remain faithful to Du Bois's core concerns and objectives: the "masses," categorical necessity, unnamed relational rights, and the "psychological" stipends of whiteness in the domain of "the public" are all essential elements of the argument that follows. Michael Warner has it right. "The political meaning of the public's self-alienation," he writes, "is one of the most important sites of struggle in contemporary culture."[9] What follows seeks to unpack the "political meaning" distilled in Warner's term "public self-alienation." I want to determine how public forms of self-recognition are silently partnered with a politics of misrecognition in official conversations about race. In a time of radical demographic change, a time of fundamental shifts in an all but disintegrated civil society, and not least, a time when the lingering, by now phantasmatic question of class unity is emerging differently, and again, the problem(s) of "color line(s)" could not be greater.

So we return to the oft-repeated epigraph provided by Du Bois: "The problem of the twentieth century is the problem . . ." etc. The hesitation one feels in repeating this phrase (the missing supplement implied by my "etc.") marks a unique place in the history of U.S. racial discontent. The 2000 census has occurred with unprecedented computational unease and contradiction this—its twenty-second—time around. Is "the problem of the twentieth century" conceivable in twenty-first-century terms? Or does the combination of urgency and sheer repetition one hears in Du Bois's famous phrase intimate new difficulties holding forth around an old desire? At stake in the hesitation to echo Du Bois is the attempt to forgo an assumption that too readily adjoins the old and the new. That assumption underwrites the false idea that racial (re)iteration and difference are more or less symmetrical in the peaceable communicative domain of a renewable Enlightenment *socius*. In reaching for the Du Boisian maxim I wanted to begin with but cannot, I find instead a more difficult combination of phrases. Something like Jean Francois Lyotard's remark that "Majority does not mean large number, it means great fear," combined with the insistence of Hegel, who says, "the state is . . . self-conscious ethical substance," seems rather more to the point.[10] "Majorities," "numbers," "self-consciousness," "the state"—these terms mark a new and troubled arrangement within the identity/politics matrix. Between the emptying out of identity's emancipatory presumptions and the incalculable proliferation of our publicly discernible forms, democracy's future will rest in the balance.

DISSENSUS 2000

> It were not until I come to Harlem that one day a Census taker dropped around my house and asked me where were I born and why, also my age, and if I was still living. I said, "Yes, I am here, in spite of all."
>
> —Jesse B. Semple

In Langston Hughes's short story "Census," taken from the collection *Simple's Uncle Sam,* Jesse B. Semple describes his encounter with a Harlem census taker a decade before the civil rights movement. Semple's response to the enumerator is as minimal, at least at first, as it is uncooperative. "I am here," he says, "in spite of all." "All of what?" the census taker then responds. "Give me the Data."[1] But that misfire in communication is precisely the point. The story is about identifying what fails to count. Published in 1965, "Census" is inarguably invested in the civil rights movement that reached its apex in that watershed year. Semple's declaration seems to contradict the desire for racial self-disclosure, or at least seems to reveal a certain contradiction Hughes insists on pointing out, *avant la lettre,* that is immanent to the legacy of civil rights.

"Census" does not signal the task of the movement "simply" as a struggle to be recognized and counted by the state. The individual remains inassimilable in this short story. Indeed, the undeclared "I" resists the "all" that Semple mentions, insofar as that "all" is presumed to already be known. Semple is "here," but "in spite" of "all," that is, whether or not that "all" allows Semple to count. The force of Semple's declaration is about recognizing "still" present and "still" silent collectivities. And it exists at the moment self-description performs an act of social protest by being here, and not here, all at once.

As the story continues, the census enumerator's insistence upon counting Semple (on his terms) runs up against the evidently nonquantifiable markers of identity that are tied, in this instance, to work. This mention of labor is what creates the greatest conflict in "Census," throwing the question of color into an incalculable kind of relief. "Include my feet on that Census you are taking," Semple demands. "My feet have helped make America rich, and I am still standing on them" (2). The visceral signs of class exploitation on Semple's aching body create an incidental and allusive presence in the enumerator's mind, and one that "still" does not adhere correctly to the "Data." The blisters Semple goes on to describe are too ordinary, too ordinary to count. (Perhaps the census taker has them as well?) And the alternative forms of counting that Semple demands by "still" (the word is oft-repeated in the story) standing there remain unspecified within his persistence. Blisters are a skin problem, of course, but one that, unlike race, exceeds the census taker's skin intelligence according to the 1950 count. That much the story makes clear. But it also makes clear that the relations of work and the production of "riches," while going unnamed by the census taker, retain some allusive presence in the story itself ("still here," and still unaddressed in "American" society). Semple's many years of work are essential to the creation of the nation's "riches," as he well knows, yet they remain beyond their due political tally. There is no "all" except work in "Census," and that alternative totality the census taker discards at the command of other "Data." The enumerator must calculate that peculiar form of "American" racial inclusivity wherein Semple "run[s] errands for white folks" (1) while being "Jim Crowed." But signaling the paradox of counting as it does, the story makes clear that Semple's work is persistent even, indeed especially, as it escapes the interest of the state.

The critique implicit in the story "Census," then, is not one of failing to conform to "the Data." It is not one that encourages officially sanctioned forms of self-recognition. Indeed, it seems almost to portend the contradictions implicit in the state's regard for race, and to speak beyond them to another moment in that uneasy relationship. While "Census" is situated within the civil rights victories that marked the year of its publication, the story time travels, I would suggest. "Census" seems to situate civil rights at a certain historical limit, one that could only be recognizable from the point of view of a future Hughes may not have known. In this sense, too, the story is about recognizing "still" present and "still" silent forms of racial significance. There are identity claims the state may not see, and that remain to be announced. I use the word *remain* here in both senses, that is, as a way of thinking about race as something that is clearly still among us, but because changeable, something also that portends a future not yet here. Ever more flexible forms of "rich American" inclusivity foster a version of national "all"-ness that ensures that more people, and more different kinds of people, are counted. But the relations of work "still" do not count. In "Census," computing identity aright dictates a need for racial self- and state recognition, while it caps any interest whatever in who works and who profits. Race becomes extraordinarily noticeable in the story, since enumeration demands it. But at the same time, the census taker makes racial identity look politically banal: the association between being "Jim-Crowed" and Semple's labor is jettisoned, paradoxically speaking, exactly insofar as he *counts*. Here work is moved beneath the skin, graphically, in the form of the blisters on which Semple "still" somehow manages to stand.

The Langston Hughes short story bears directly on recent debates about the 2000 census. Like Semple, these debates bring renewed pressure to the vexed question of what counts, and what fails to count, as official forms of racial self-disclosure. In this sense, Ian Hacking's cautionary stipulations regarding governmental biopower may serve as an appropriate Foucauldian reminder. The enumeration of individuals within the public sphere, Hacking remarks, has always "aimed at the preservation of the state."[2] "The first Enlightenment 'state,'" he elaborates, "is . . . the United States of America, whose very name was invented by Richard Price, publisher of the work of Thomas Bayes that we now call Bayesian statistics. . . . The very name of the first Enlightenment state was invented by a 'statistician'" (289). And yet, to regard the connection between racial self-recognition and the preservation of the state as an example of purely instrumental power, as Hacking (in fact, *contra* Foucault) seems to do, glosses over the ways civil rights is historically enmeshed, even determined by, class struggle.[3] Thus it must be noted, early and expressly, that the way of problematizing racial self-recognition as I shall proceed to do is not meant to reduce the civil rights movement root-and-branch to a blithely culturalist escape of class (more on class and culturalism in Part Three of this book). Diane McWhorter's comprehensive account of the civil rights struggles of Birmingham—industrial home of "the world's largest corporation"—is clear on this score: race-minded activists and the representatives of organized labor were regarded by the coal and steel industry's entrepreneurial elite as the twin antagonists of free enterprise in the South.[4] "The bombing of the Sixteenth Street Baptist church," as she chronicles that brutal event, "was the endgame in the city fathers' long and profitable tradition of maintaining industrial supremacy through vigilantism" (25). Still, despite the understandable attraction of the Birmingham civil rights movement to the U.S. Communist Party, as the movement matured it did not escape the tragedy of internal division and the forms of barefaced appropriation that I am about to describe as a new tactic of post-liberal governmentality.[5] Indeed, census historians, who chronicle the trajectory of racial counting from the constitutionally mandated first U.S. census count of 1790 to more recent examples of multiracial self-disclosure, make a set of unimpeachable points: the habits of affiliation the public may assign to race are changeable; and they are mandated as much by desire as law.

Civil rights are inseparably tied to statistical enumeration. The ambivalence of this attachment will be described more clearly in a moment, as the legacy of civil rights is seen to mutate into a set of policies and initiatives that Freedom Riders and lunch counter sitters would clearly decry. For now it is important simply to establish the civil rights association between race and the law. The myriad forms of antidiscrimination legislation that occurred between 1964 and 1968 continue to set the legal context for discussing the state's interest in racial self-disclosure.[6] From the race-conscious 1960s forward, the constitutional duties of the U.S. Census Bureau have become increasingly intertwined with the equal protection clause of the Fourteenth Amendment. The Voting Rights Act of 1965, perhaps the most important example of this interrelation, continues to bind the census to constitutional mandates for reapportioning minority voting districts.[7] Encouraged by the Voting Rights Act, as well as expanded federal legislation barring discrimination in employment (1964) and housing (1968), public scrutiny on the undercounting of minority populations would become an important means of legal redress against public disenfranchisement from the 1970 census forward. The politics of counting, newly rendered by the movement precisely *as* politics, is the invaluable legacy of these earlier civil rights achievements.

In tracing the legacy of this "second Reconstruction" to debates concerning the 2000 census, we need to recall two related changes in the gathering of racial data: first, progressively minded race-conscious legislation, combined with experiments in statistical sampling that began in the 1940s, produced a new emphasis on self- over observer-enumeration. In attempting to reduce the kind of enumerator error produced by "eyeballing," statisticians hoped to close the distance between individually chosen and state-decreed forms of race recognition. Racial categories on the census tended from this moment forward to place a new emphasis on self-description and assumed that it would be unproblematically sutured to the law. A kind of fragile circularity between racial self-disclo-sure and categorical impermanence was here introduced. In order to ensure that race, jurisprudence, and public access to classificatory procedures would be made to more or less happily meet, the Census Bureau needed once again to update its ever changing system of race categories. At the behest of the civil rights movement, this system would have to be, on the one hand, distinct enough to differentiate the races but, on the other hand, inclusive enough to make individuals classifiable by choice, as much as state selection. At this moment, racial self-knowledge in the United States became a legal requirement imposed from within, as much as without. However, as shall become clearer below, race categories can double back over time, less happily, to re-enforce (or fail to re-enforce) the sacred state-identity relation. Indeed, when race is presumed to be a common matter of state and individual interest, racial distinction is subject to occasional and, it turns out, increasingly fractious outbreaks of classificatory complexity and computational unease.

But before I limn an episode of just such an outbreak, the close connection between the civil rights legacy and the U.S. census should be emphasized one final time. From the mid-1960s onward, civil rights burdened the Census Bureau with a three-part task: to calculate historically relevant and publicly decidable forms of racial self-recognition; to provide the most accurate and inclusive race counts; and, most problematically, to surrender an activity of racial naming that was once performed by bureaucrats and statisticians to the more volatile dictates of political group interest. In her comprehensive study of the history and development of the U.S. census since its republican inception, Margo Anderson describes the new pressures brought to the census by civil rights with appropriate conclusiveness: by the close of the 1960s, racial counting "ceased to be simply a technical problem of Census field procedures: it became an explosive political issue."[8]

If this explosion was at all diffused in the decade that followed the 1960s, it was done so hastily, momentarily, and with what history would reveal to be the seeds of a potentially fatal set of contradictions. Anderson traces how the Office of Management and Budget (OMB), as mandated by civil rights legislation enacted the previous decade, was beset with the task of organizing what remained the official racial categories until the watershed moment of the 2000 census. In 1977 the OMB issued its Statistical Policy Directive 15, which named the longest-standing set of state-recognized race categories in more than two hundred years. These five categories are American Indian or Alaska Native, Asian and Pacific Islander, Black, White, and a Hispanic/non-Hispanic ethnic category.[9] In the years leading up to the 2000 census, any number of glossy magazines, newspaper editorials, and other journalistic ventures proceeded to jump-start the minimal analytical pressures necessary to worry the OMB official five.[10] American Indian, for example, designates "persons having origins in any of the original peoples of North America," but excludes native Hawaiians, effectively rendering them "Asian" immigrants. For reasons that can hardly be accounted for by increasing birthrates, according to the 1990 census the American Indian population was up 255 percent since 1960. The "Asian" category overturns the former Japanese/Chinese distinction, which was operative during the internment of the former during World War II and which, up until 1943, served to underwrite anti-immigration statutes excluding the latter.[11] Today the "Asian" category contains such ostensibly different peoples as Samoans, Guamians, Cambodians, Filipinos, and Laotians. Until 2000, Black mandated the one-drop rule of hypo-decent, otherwise associated with the 1896 "separate but equal" doctrine known as Jim Crow. But since "black" technically contains all people of African heritage, it covers the entire color spectrum. So in fact does "white," which includes among its official members North Africans, Arabs and Jews, and all peoples from India and the Middle East. Hispanic, which would have been counted as part of a "Mexican" race in 1930, but not so in 1940, was until 1960 subsumed under "white."

Indeed, the problem of officially categorizing a pan-ethnic Latino plurality, which exceeds the once presumed reliable marker of national origin (find here: not only Mexicans and Puerto Ricans, but Salvadorians, Guatemalans, Ecuadorians, indigenous South and Central American immigrants, such as Zapotecs, Yaquis, et al.), remains the surest sign of the inadequacies of bureaucratic expedience.[12] Given the relative stability or decline in the growth of populations within *race* classifications, the category of Hispanic as an *ethnicity* functions as a kind of interdivisional racial buffer between black and white. While the fastest-growing minority group in the country (in California, which had seventy-two Latino-majority cities in 1990, the population has surpassed the nominally minoritized white citizenry), Hispanic continues to hold the status of *ethnicity*, mediating the evidently purer, late-nineteenth-century black/white *racial* opposition. Hispanic therefore can legally include blacks from the Dominican Republic, blond, fair-skinned, blue-eyed Argentineans, and Mexicans who would otherwise be Native Americans if they happened to be born on the north side of the Rio Grande after 1857. (To fine-tune the Hispanic category, the 1970 census attempted to introduce what it called a Central or South American distinction. More than 1 million people made that choice; but after following up the experiment with census observer-enumerators, researchers found that the majority of these "Central" or "South Americans" were identified as ethno-Europeans from such places as Kansas, Alabama, and Mississippi.)[13]

Roman de la Campa's foreword to *Magical Urbanism,* Mike Davis's book on the new Latino majority in Los Angeles, is worth recalling as one thinks through the political promises and pitfalls revolving around the Hispanic ethnic category.[14] De la Campa is aware of the shortcomings surrounding the term, its capacity as presently deployed by the census to function as what I called above a black/white racial buffer. But he is also keen to salvage the radical democratic potential occasioned by a renewed Latino presence in the United States precisely because this black/white division may be redivided, if not overcome. Both de la Campa and Davis draw upon the "browning" of the western states in order to more fully imagine a politically reinspired white-minority nation. In so imagining, both want to move the discussion of race beyond the black/white binary toward a rejuvenated and updated sense of collective political agency. The "crossover insights" provided by the contemporary Latino-American encounter, de la Campa suggests, run "the languages of social science into uncharted territory when attempting to account for the post–melting-pot period of American history" (*MU,* xiii). The statement evokes a form of ethnically inspired statistical indeterminacy that is aimed at the heart of the fiction called whiteness. Its hope is that a more nuanced consideration of racial division and interdivision will therefore emerge. "Latino demographic growth . . . [may realize] its potential for social and political change [in] its new claim on the American imaginary," he writes (*MU,* xi). And as Mike Davis similarly expounds, Latino ethnic identity sought beyond race to highlight a form of "cultural syncretism that may become a transformative template for the whole society" (*MU,* 15). These statements are important to the discussion of multiracialism in the 2000 census. They are important because, while they mirror those debates in terms of the penchant for cultural syncretism, they reveal a symptomatic indecidability over whether or not the political outcome of post-binaristic forms of racial redivision will look anything like the progressive goals to which de la Campa and Davis aspire. The worthwhile pitch in *Magical Urbanism* is for what might be called a new Latino multiculturalism. This would bracket the more restrictive issue of racial identity and replace it (though how is not exactly said) with a reinvigorated emphasis on material redistribution.

Davis and de la Campa are, of course, technically correct to remark upon a new extremity of multiples as racial theorists and demographers in the United States imagine its post-white national future. Latinos, specifically Mexican immigrants and their U.S.-born children, became California's new majority in the 1990s. This event marked the first time since the 1858 Treaty of Guadalupe Hidalgo that whites did not constitute the state's racial majority. And indeed, compelling examples of the "Californization of America" are abundant and easy to recite.[15] During the civil rights period of the 1960s in which the OMB "official five" were devised, less than one-eighth of the population was classifiable as racial minorities. This is contrasted to 1990 statistics, in which more than one-fourth of the population classified themselves as such. Widely circulated information like this, combined with a marked turn toward non-European immigration after the lift of the National Origins Act of 1956 (between 1961 and 1965, 42 percent of legal immigrants came from Europe; between 1978 and 1981, 12 percent did), has created a deluge of proclamations from all walks of political life, nervously or excitedly anticipating what Dale Maharidge calls "the coming white minority."[16] And it is common knowledge, too, that the new "majority-minority" will present a more racially complex picture than in the days of civil rights. In the 1960s, for example, when the United States first legislated race-conscious social remedies, blacks made up 96 percent of the minority population, Hispanics 3.9 percent.[17] In the 1990s, Hispanics surpassed blacks as the largest minority population, and will account for two-thirds of total U.S. population growth by midcentury.[18] If arriving on the scene with certain studied fever and fret, the "*cafe au lait* society" is already in our midst.[19] But does greater racial complexity increase or effectively diminish the democratic potential of a post-binaristic, indeed a post-racial political imaginary, especially as regards the civil rights obligations of the state?

While it is true that current race and ethnic classifications would put so-called whites at a mere one-third (33.7 percent) of California's total population nationwide by 2025 and make whites a national minority population by 2052, one has to attend carefully to Davis's hope that Latinos will "tropicalize the national vision of the 'city on a hill'" (57) and give renewed vigor to the nation's withered democratic aspirations. While it may be politically advantageous (and empirically accurate) to reject the racially binaristic thinking of the 1960s civil rights era, it is nevertheless the case that blacks remain the poorest racial minority in the United States per capita, with annual incomes 20 percent below that of Latinos, and 45 percent below that of whites.[20] In flat economic terms, Davis's post-white American political errand seems to fall more likely where Andrew Hacker placed it some time ago in his renowned book, *Two Nations: Black and White, Separate, Hostile, Unequal.*[21] But as previously mentioned regarding *Magical Urbanism,* Davis and de la Campa want to foreclose the stalemate of an identity-based labor vanguardism in which static black/white color oppositions trump the more elusive matter of wages and work. Given that the coming majority will supersede the historical fiction of whiteness, they require a more fluid identity in order to renew labor's mission of hope. Toward this end, they want to suggest, Latino multiculturalism might be called upon to provide a category of belonging that is both sufficiently massive and mixed.

34

Does this speculation on post-binaristic Latino agency escape the problems of identity politics that it seeks to dismiss? The form by which one may recognize the majority presence of an otherwise incalculable "race," "ethnic," or "cultural" collective called "Latino" is a difficult matter to surmise. On the one hand, Davis accurately outlines California's new demography and its subsequent redivisions of ethnicity and race. On the other hand, the optimism that this new arrangement might prove politically redemptive betrays a certain tension, if not a contradiction, over the question of mixedness and the renewal of collective political agency as itself an oppositional force. The identity of Latino is assumed to be sufficiently anchored in its own categorical moorings so that it may bring forth the dissolution of a sclerotic black/white racial binary. But beyond the "one drop definition of racial Otherness" (*MU*, xvii), itself relegated to "an old-fashioned black-and-white screen" (*MU*, 8), lie two problems. The first is how to characterize the force of a new Latino political agency outside the schema of oppositional difference. Second, there is the nagging effect of mobilizing ethnicity such that the claims of racial justice on the state are dissolved altogether. What happens to civil rights–inspired forms of racial identity in the post-binaristic future intimated here? The question is crucial, since the distribution of wealth is still stubbornly sutured to a recognizably race-divided social order. The vision portrayed by Davis's twenty-first-century political landscape, at least on this reading of it, becomes vulnerable to certain forms of neoconservative smoke screening that dismiss race from class-based discourse root-and-branch.

Consider, for example, the way Walter Benn Michaels empties race politics in his influential book *Our America*.[22] Here, Michaels uses the term "native modernism" to reveal the regrettable "identitarian ambitions" that lurk in even the most pluralistic diagnoses of race. "Cultural identity," a term Michaels critiques elsewhere to grant the scientific fallibility of race, "must resort to some version of the essentialism it begins by repudiating. . . . This accounts for how people can 'claim' or not a culture merely by behaving in a certain way."[23] The claiming of a specific culture, he suggests, presents an impossible contradiction, a need both for category and its repudiation, which is implicit in any act of racial self-disclosure. In the place of this contradiction, Michaels offers a neoconservative desire to give up on race altogether. While Davis, too, wants to dispel previous forms of black/white racial division in his ideas about Latinos, he would clearly find Michaels's dismissal of cultural belonging a politically unsatisfying move.

To give Davis's argument a second, more generous look, it is important to recall one of his key words, mentioned already, "cultural syncretism." Joined with Davis's corresponding pitch for a "renaissance of American labor" (142), this term takes on a sense that exceeds, even while it includes, the term "culture," which worries Michaels on the grounds that it also includes contradiction. We know that *Magical Urbanism* seeks to move race politics beyond the binary, away from the "frozen geometries" of black/white racial opposition, and in the direction of pan-Latino cultural belonging. And we know that belonging to Latino multiculturalism borders on contradiction, since its own oppositional exigencies are designed, among other things, to displace the strictures of racial opposition in the name of labor and class. But in Davis's argument, closely read, this contradiction can appear more productive than it does at first sight. The kind of agency Davis appears to have in mind has political potential, as the book is careful to say, insofar as the Latino displacement of whiteness *has not yet had its time.* In other words, the combined form of agency Davis refers to as Latino is itself only namable in relation to the categorical necessities it must also resist. This would seem, *pace* Michaels's dismissal of this contradiction as politically anesthetizing, precisely the place to recall Du Bois's "masses" as the *absent* unity of labor. In this sense, Semple, too, resembles something of Latino plurality. Davis forgoes developed theorization in this area. And fuller consideration of how the "masses" might release the ambivalent forms of agency locked into the nation's racial past will have to wait until the later parts of my own argument in this book.

For now, however, this much can be said about the discarding of racial binaries as they were advanced in the formative moments of the civil rights movement. In that earlier era, the attempt was to secure a progressive link between identity, categorical belonging, and state responsibility, and to do so well in advance of whatever politics might emerge from the law later on. Put simply, race in the civil rights era was evidently more countable, but less multiple; more easily reducible to racial opposition, but less able to account for racial mutability, than is the case at the dawn of the twenty-first century. In Davis's argument, the contradictions implicit in a post-white national imaginary bespeak an absent or, at least, a less determinably calculable coherence of economically disenfranchised bodies for which there is yet no name. This, again, was Semple's story. Ironically, the lesson of the last two decades of state-sanctioned racial attention is beginning to signal the undoing of statistical sensibility at its very core. Combined with a popular obsession with the coming white minority, the problem of mixed identity suggests that the struggle for statistical selfhood is moving toward what are at best ambivalent forms of post-white racial redivision. Henry Louis Gates offers a cautionary point that bears directly on the nation's new exigency of racial numbers. "The simple affirmation of indeterminacy," he writes, "cannot staunch the very human pain of racial stigmata. Statistical they may be: they bleed just the same."[24] The apparent undoing of racial identity after civil rights begs a good deal more scrutiny than has generally occurred. This process turns more broadly, I want now to suggest, not just on a new indeterminacy regarding racial belonging, but indeed, on more radical degrees of political self-readjustment. By this I mean a degree of self-readjustment that is, nonetheless, superficially inspired by the lexicon of civil rights. I say "superficially" because the self-readjustment civil rights now inspire may well serve to end the state's relation to identity precisely in the name of civil rights. To begin to develop this charge, let me now turn to one of the most pressing issues raised in the debates over the 2000 census, the rise of state-authorized multiracial self-recognition. These debates are in step with popular pronouncements of the coming white minority, and they mesh in complicated ways with the heady impulse to move beyond a black/white racial binary.

Since the Warren court overturned the sixteen final state laws banning miscegenation (*Loving v. Virginia,* 1967),[25] the rising numbers of mixed marriages have been declared far and wide, and with at least quasi-democratic fanfare. In 1960, for example, there were 149,000 mixed marriages nationwide; by 1990, 1.5 million. The "multiracial baby boom" is apparently upon us. In 1992, as has been widely reported, so-called monoracial black births increased by 27 percent; white births, by 15 percent. For the first time in U.S. history the number of bi- and/or multiracial babies appears to be increasing faster (260 percent) than the rate of monoracial births (15 percent).[26] The number of biracial black/white babies grew by almost 500 percent, with a total of some 2 million multiracial children in 1990.[27] With an apparent increase in the multiracial population of 547 percent over the last thirty years, this kind of number crunching is designed to project revolutionary shifts with regard to race mixing. Indeed, without an official mandate to count multiracial peoples until 2000, the 1990 census reported that the category "other" grew more than any of the OMB official five—by 45 percent, to 9.8 million people. That number was larger than the entire Asian American population at that time (Root, xvii). No wonder that the figure of Eve, the computer-generated multiracial portrait on the cover of *Time* magazine's 1993 special issue, "The New Face of America," has become a figure of such legendary (if still imaginary) status.[28] It is an increasingly well-marketed twenty-first-century assumption that "the world's first multicultural society" will see the standard forms of racial self-categorization collapse by reproductive default.

Since the early 1990s, when the data on multiracial populations began to circulate ever more widely, some sixty multiracial organizations have appeared.[29] Organizations such as Charles Byrd's Multiracial Voice and Susan Graham's Project RACE ("Reclassify All Children Equally") have become influential in the attempt to recalibrate race categories at both the state and federal level. Graham's organization, which began in 1991 in Georgia as a 501c(3) nonprofit corporation, has prompted multiracial legislation in Ohio, Illinois, Georgia, Indiana, and Michigan. A federal law requiring a multiracial option in the classification of race (H.R. 830) was introduced in the United States House of Representatives in 1997 by Representative Thomas E. Petri (R-Wisconsin).[30] A march on Washington in 1996 and a march in Los Angeles in 1997 also provide evidence of the movement's increasing grassroots momentum. While Representative Petri's bill ultimately failed, the struggle for what multiracial activists claim is the latest extension of the civil rights movement continues unabated. Just as it is illegal to die in the United States unless by a disease prescribed by the World Health Organization, activists claimed that the race categories of the 1990 census "rob[bed] people of their identity." It effectively amounted, they charged, to the federal obstruction of the hard-fought civil rights victory of self- over observer-enumeration.[31]

Consider the case for having the state recognize multiracial identity, to begin with, on the activists' terms: in 1990 the five largest school districts in the United States counted more than a hundred races and ethnicities. Forty-one percent of schools report that they have students for whom the OMB official five are totally inaccurate. And about 27 percent of schools have chosen to defy those categories, letting the federal government re-aggregate the numbers as they will.[32] This story is made more complex by the fact that school districts, unlike the U.S. census after civil rights, are allowed to observer-enumerate— meaning that students, their parents, and enrollment officers often disagree about how this or that identity might be described. As of the late 1990s, nine states have enacted multiracial legislation or mandates and many others are attempting to do so. Thus until the 2000 census, a person could travel between Indiana and California and change races—moving, for example, from the black or white option in one state to the multiracial option of both and neither, in another.

In November 1998, after four years of intensive study by thirty-plus federal agencies, after thousands of pages of congressional testimony and demographic analysis at a cost of more than $100 million, the OMB decided not to include a multiracial category for the 2000 census. However, on March 10, 2000, the OMB issued its new guidelines on racial tabulations and entered uncharted demographic territory. With other minor changes in the civil rights–inspired official five, the OMB released its new "Standards for Maintaining, Collecting, and Presenting Federal Data on Race and Ethnicity." This mandate allows an option to "mark one or more races" for the first time since the initial U.S. census in 1790.[33] Even limiting one's choice to just two combinations, this new law stands to increase the tabulation from five to 128 possibilities.[34] Currently there is no final proposal to suggest how data from the 2000 census will be made compatible with the last two census reports.[35] Early reports from the tallies of 2000 carried a new caveat, that "exact figures are uncertain because Americans, for the first time, were allowed to check off more than one race on the 2000 Census form."[36] With this complication in mind, the OMB has recommended that "disruption could be minimized if information from persons who have marked multiple boxes could be used to tabulate responses in the race categories currently specified in Directive 15."[37]

For the multiracial movement, which continues to press for an autonomous multiracial category, the outcome of the 2000 census debates was a qualified victory. In the discourse of Project RACE and its constituency, the right to be counted as one would choose simply means the full extension of a civil rights–inspired emphasis on self-enumeration. Race is addressed as the matter of getting identity correct in one's own eyes and in the eyes of the state. But in pursuing the multiracialism debate a bit further, one begins to see how an individual's right to self-recognition, paradoxically, releases the state from previous civil rights obligations. In this sense, the nationalist end of liberalism is found dormant in the logic of its originally benevolent *ends*. In effect, all and no race relations now seem to exist in the eyes of a racially emancipated state. Multiplicity is unleashed upon identity, and the organizational capacity of the state is both maximized and evaporated within the very act of saying, "I am . . ."

Consider here the appeal of multiracialism described by G. Reginald Daniel as a "strategy of resistance."[38] Like so many others, Daniel is eager to "challenge the dichotomization of blackness and whiteness that originates in Eurocentric thinking" (13). And in step with the rampant theorization of a post-white national imaginary, the "egalitarian order" (189) that Daniel has in mind comes specifically on the heels of "deconstruct[ing] the Eurocentric dichotomy as well as the hierarchical valuation of blackness and whiteness as mutually exclusive and unequal" (3). Moreover, the necessary dissolution of the black/white binary and the concurrent proliferation of racial identity across and between that old single color line are "the fruits of the civil rights movement of the 1950s and 1960s, [and] thus [build] on the egalitarian, pluralist tenets of the racial movements of the 1960s, which sought to achieve the equality of difference" (6, 11, 121, 190). The problem with this formulation is that the civil rights legacy is extended to a point that each and all differences count equally, while none do. A schema such as this wields pluralism in such a way that consolidates neoliberal left attention to race with its conservative dismissal, in one fell swoop. The de-racialization of state policy has come of age in the unlikely form of a post-white national imaginary. More curiously still, this process sees the civil rights legacy diminished in the movement's very name. Compare Daniel's hasty pitch for black/white racial deconstruction to the congressional hearings in 1993 on the addition of a multiracial census category. There it was a welcome proposal across party lines that racial coherence is in general misguided, and that no one race is categorically pure.[39] As if congressional leaders had lapped up the last decade of anti-essentialist identity theory, race is referred to in these debates always in the terms of a "categorical convenience," one that is necessarily "misleading over time" (1). "Terms such as 'majority,' 'principal minority,' and 'minority' may be outdated," we are reminded (39). The "illusion of racial purity . . . may no longer have the same basis in reality [as it] may once have had" (68). Anti-essentialism is now a matter of state record. And it effectively functions to release the state of its former civil rights obligations. The more curious point, once again, is the way this process is occurring. The emancipation of the state from race-based civil rights claims takes place, not through the repression of race, but through the accommodation and enforcement of the proliferation of racial difference such that racial justice disappears. It cannot be said, in other words, that racial identity is denied by the state. Rather, the state both widens and makes more precise the self-descriptive possibilities accessible to its citizens. Racial *intra*relationality proliferates to a fatal point where, one might say, race signifies itself all the way to nonexistence. The pitch now is that citizens belong to no category save what they would choose. The new juridical attention to race gains such a level of intensity, I am suggesting, that the state/subject relation is both unraveled and made absolute.

In his book *Racial Subjects,* David Theo Goldberg draws on Foucauldian notions of governmentality and discipline in order to offer a historical critique of the U.S. census. Like Hacking, mentioned above, Goldberg calls census self-enumeration the quintessential example of the state's "ideological mandate."[40] "Identity is conceived, manufactured, and fabricated in and through forms," he writes. And this "provides governmentality with everything that amounts to knowledge in the scientific-technical mode necessary to administration" (*RS,* 31). Goldberg provides similar insights in his more recent book, *The Racial State.* Here the state itself is metonymic for modernity, which is based on "the power to exclude . . . to dominate through the power to categorize differentially and hierarchically, to set aside by setting apart."[41] Insofar as the modern state is bent on the "reproduction of homogeneity" (*TRS,* 241), it is a veritable machine of "exclusion," according to Goldberg, who repeats the term "exclusion" for emphasis some eighteen times in the book's introduction. Racial self-disclosure is for Goldberg a matter of "discipline." And he uses this watchword to critique the ways identity is putatively sealed off by its own delusion of autonomous self-reflection (*qua* Foucault's infamous panopticon).[42] Either identity is made docile via its own presumed governability, or it becomes suitably resistant and is reoriented toward greater "openness" and heterogeneity. Toward that latter alternative, Goldberg argues for "renewably open-ended self-identification [that] would quite literally undermine . . . the identity of information via categorization" (*RS*, 32). Instead of legislated self-disclosure apropos the census and civil rights, he insists upon the "right to refuse" race classification altogether (*RS*, 45). Goldberg argues for "open-ended . . . self-identification [in order to] undermine the social control of racial naturalism" (57).

In his more recent book, Goldberg advances more complex alternatives to static racial categorization than he does in the earlier text. Here he presents an interest in the critical capacity of what he calls "noisy and bothersome gaps" (*TRS*, 2). These moments of ontological absence are implicit, he suggests, in any act of racial representation, especially those that draw state interest. I will eventually return to Goldberg's qualified exploration of "multi-identification" and "flexible citizenship" (*RS*, 276) in the concluding part of my own argument some distance ahead. My present point with regard to the multiracial movement is sympathetic with Goldberg's notion of the exclusionist racial state; but I want to make a slightly finer point about the state's emergent interest in race that seems to exceed the disciplinary governmental tactics he critiques. Indeed, the term "exclusion" could not be *less* appropriate for launching a critique of contemporary governmentality. The combination of opposing alternatives between "exclusion" and "openness" that Goldberg offers in his work on the census, I would suggest, is no longer tenable for describing what is evidently a transition from the modern *disciplinary* state to what might be called its postmodern *de-disciplinary* epoch. I use that latter term to highlight the official dissolution of racial categories precisely through close attention to them. The cellularizing (to use an apt Foucauldian term), or formal partitioning, of racial identities may have been the condemnable secret of modern sovereignty. But ontological obsession according to kind is what the postmodern state disregards by granting a check-all-that-applies option for the census. Goldberg draws attention to the more common Enlightenment strategy of the state as a disciplinary or ideological apparatus, hailing identities on the order of social individuation and control.[43] According to this model, individuals are effectively homogenized, fixed into recursive but still distinguishable social norms, which the state serves to enforce and reproduce. My suggestion, to the contrary, is that the state is at work differently (or at work, according to difference). Its conservative nature has advanced, indeed has calcified, in a counterintuitive way, via the hyper-liberalization of racial self-regard. Identity's options in relation to the state do not reduce to being either fixed or open, repressed or free to resist, as modernity might have put the matter. At work in the debates over the 2000 census is a curious de-ontological admixture of both free and repressed modes

41

of being. Identities are still hailed by the state, to be sure, but in the interest of ontological *attrition*. This, to say again, is what might be called a *de*-disciplinary governmental tactic. The state's concern for identifying peoples according to an increased racial "openness" and fluidity means that its reliance on self-description for administering social order tends to both increase and retreat. That this retreat may occur as the state furthers its imposition into private life and as public debate degenerates into extreme forms of patriotic correctness is only further evidence that civil rights discourse has been evacuated by a totalitarian drift.[44] The postmodern practice of governing I am trying to describe is thus not the same as Goldberg's apt anatomy of modern racial governmentality. The state power I have in mind operates, not via categorical fixity or racial "exclusion," but precisely through the "open-endedness" he wants to retain as a form of supposed political resistance.

One more example from the 1993 congressional debates is worth noting on this score. In the testimony from the multiracial activists mentioned above, the claim that the nation is becoming less white (77 percent in 2000, down from 80 percent in 1990)[45] is adjoined to the more nettlesome charge that 70 to 90 percent of the current black population is racially mixed.[46] "Almost everybody," Republican committee chairman Thomas Sawyer (R-Ohio) is happy to remark, "is fifth generation somewhere" (*Hearings,* 102). Categorical speculation on this order was something the NAACP and other leading civil rights groups find understandably disquieting.[47] Given the demographic shifts multiracial activists are fond of alleging, it is feared that the number of blacks identified in future census counts would be made not only unreliable compared with earlier data, but indeed, might look to be on the decline.[48] Multiracial activists seek the right to self-enumerate outside the OMB official five. However, as the NAACP insists with some cause, racial self-recognition on this order threatens to nudge previous claims of black racial coherence to the edges of multicultural anarchy. How can de facto civil rights infringements be the objects of legal redress if racial distinctions proliferate to the point of their de jure disappearance? As the state's relation to identity is both loosened and tightened at once, time-honored theories about the relation between identity and democracy may have slipped into some other dimension altogether.

THE WILL TO CATEGORY

You don't have a right not to be identified.

—Rudolph Giuliani

No, the quote from Mayor Giuliani cited above was not given in response to the terrorist attacks on New York City on September 11. More than a year before that, the mayor addressed a relatively minor health-related issue, something more akin to human services than the Patriot Act. But what about the obligation to belong? In the Giuliani quote, identity and rights take on an odd association, reversing an earlier appeal to be identified by the state as a matter of gaining equal protection under civil rights. Here the refusal to be identified is the act the state cannot allow. And, as this double negative implies, *not* allowing *no* identity is enforced as a legal mandate premised on the appeal of positive self-expression. One is not exactly forced to belong, so much as one finds oneself belonging by ontological default. And yet what I have been discussing with regard to multiracial self-recognition seems to complicate this logic further still. Racial difference has never been more highly encouraged nor more actively recognized as a premise of governing than it was for the 2000 census. But the more curious point is that two forms of seemingly antagonistic intensity—the state's will that we be identified and the kinds of intragroup dissolution of former race categories—find a strange partnership. Identity emerges as *both* self-expression and negation as the liberal state reinvents itself at the opposite political extreme. The state's concern with identity, I have been suggesting, is slowly dissolving its previous civil rights obligations. It has done so, as the examples I have cited duly show, by moving beyond racial formalism, selecting instead a certain deployment of post-formalist racial multiplicity that promotes the kind of categorical misfire rejected by the NAACP. Given the more fluid and, it must be said, equally strict examples of governmental interest in racial identity that we have witnessed so far, what can be said about race in the post–civil rights era? Before answering that question, let me further sum up the stakes of the multiracial debates already examined.

The politics of self-recognition that I have traced in my account of the 2000 census debates could be reduced to three general conclusions. The first conclusion is simply to concede what has become a commonplace thesis in scholarly as well as governmental circles. As everyone everywhere now seems to agree, race is a historically changeable social construction.[1] Republican congressmen and post-Enlightenment race theorists join each other in touting this boilerplate theme. But the fact that anti-essentialism is approaching postmodern common sense should not make it a trivial matter. To the contrary, that a constructionist theory of race has become ordinary news ought to provoke a look at how post-formalist assumptions about identity alter the jurisprudence of rights. Racial abundance threatens to terminate the legal specificity of race. The intent today is to embrace increasingly specific forms of racialized self-disclosure. A new and accelerated civil rights lexicon increases the number of race categories that individuals may legally claim. On this order, race is everywhere significant and nowhere identifiable in the old formalist sense. The NAACP's awkward defense of the one-drop rule of hypo-descent (formerly associated with Jim Crow) is good evidence of the current difficulties implicit in a post–civil rights approach to racial self- and state recognition. The changeable and constructed nature of race means, in effect, that in order to maintain its own waning categorical integrity racial identity must stave off intraracial permutation. This is so because permutation is what identity cannot have if it is to remain categorically defensible. The changes we have witnessed regarding standard racial divisions means the negotiation of a certain dangerous crossroads, which is where the NAACP now lives: either (a) new racial identities would be added onto the current system in a way that keeps new identities apart from previous racial distinctions (system theorists on the order of Niklas Luhmann would call this an example of operational closure);[2] or, more likely (b) the mixing of racial categories would eventually reach a level of complexity such that those categories threaten to collapse. Global anthropologists insist that the world's 184 independent nations contain more than 5,000 race or ethnic groups, more than 12,000 diverse cultures.[3] How to imagine governing according to those numbers? As is evident in the case of U.S. multiracialism, certain vacillations in self-recognition come forward when the state moves to incorporate more and more racial difference. I referred to this process before as a sign of *de*-disciplinary governmental power, developing Goldberg's application of Foucault to show postmodern tactics of sovereignty. This latest process of governing is distinct from previous civil rights struggles to liberalize the state and to get government officially interested in the racial identities it once denied. Under this new set of protocols, the state has admitted racial interest with ever greater nuance, but it has done so such that race itself is evacuated of former political significance.

My second conclusion comes out of the first, which declared the end of the liberal state and the appropriation of racial fluidity as a new governmental concern: if race categories are sociopolitical creations that tend to redivide over time, self-recognition within a *single* race becomes an increasingly impracticable pursuit. There is little serious argument today that identities cannot be reduced to the headings under which they are prone—indeed, legislated—to belong. Thus (conclusion number two) race categories presume a temporal index that to stay secure they also must deny. Once time is admitted to the understanding of identity, we see that race tends toward a point of categorical interrelation that empties it of previous political content. The case in point, of course, was the multiracial argument for officially recognized forms of racial recombination. The dangerous crossroads toward which plurality seems liable to march thus repeats what I called before a Du Boisian problem of racial citation and re-citation. As stated before regarding his reference to the color line, the divisions of race have extended, multiplied, and redoubled on the contemporary political scene. And thus the state's obligation to recognize race on the order of civil rights is thwarted, paradoxically, by its heightened racial expertise.

The social constructionist theory of race and what I just insisted is the (largely denied) temporal index within which race categories signify and do not are two points worth developing in relation to Critical Legal Studies (CLS) and Critical Race Theory (CRT).[4] Before adding my third and final conclusion to these two already listed, let me pause for a moment and discuss this work at greater length. The debates in CLS and CRT hinge on the same question of anti-essentialism that we have already addressed. And depending where scholars in each group stand on the racial construction/mutability issue, they will have either more or less interest in preserving civil rights–based jurisprudence. Both groups are to some extent dissatisfied with the ruse of legal formalism, which posits the assumption of a color-blind rule of law.[5] To various degrees, scholars in both movements embrace a constructionist theory of race. They differ greatly, however, over how to assess the full consequences of anti-essentialism, insofar as that position renders all formal racial distinction vulnerable to intradivision. Some working in CLS reveal a Foucauldian slant that is similar to David Theo Goldberg's understanding of disciplinary governmentality. They are therefore highly skeptical, as are some in CRT, about the ideological implication of rights-based discourse. These legal scholars hold that "the idea of legal rights is one of the ways that the law helps legitimate the social world by representing it as rationally mediated by rules of law."[6] The juridical subject is thus regarded less as the *beneficiary* of legal protection and redress than as an *effect* of a coercive state order already in process when identity speaks for the law. Highlighting the limits of the civil rights movement in particular, Peter Gabel emphasizes the connection between a belief in rights and the ideological effects of state power. "A belief in the state," he writes, "is a flight from the immediate alienation of concrete existence into a split-off sphere in people's minds in which they imagine themselves to be a part of an imaginary political community." "Hegemony," Gabel continues, "is reinforced through 'state abstraction' because people believe in and react passively to the mere illusion of political consensus."[7] On the inadequacies of "Enlightenment rationalism" as such, Richard Delgado sums up Derek Bell's founding thesis of "interest convergence."[8] Bell argues with regard to the watershed event of school integration, the "crown jewel of U.S. Supreme court [civil rights] jurisprudence (*Brown v. Board of Education* [1954])," that "civil rights advances for blacks have always coincided with changing economic conditions and the self-interests of whites" (*CRT,* 19). This is not (yet) to introduce a theory of class to the divisions of races, since CRT "has yet to develop a . . . theory of class" (*CRT,* 107). But I do want to emphasize with this string of quotes the severely anti-essentialist wing of the CLS and CRT movements. The very idea of state-sanctioned racial redress is complicated by this work. Here the state can only respond to race in a compromised, politically loaded, if not downright anti-progressive manner.

Other CRT scholars such as Kimberlé Crenshaw, however, want to take issue with the "vulgar anti-essentialist" attack on the legacy of civil rights as "mere illusion." "The oppositional dynamic" of black oppression, Crenshaw writes, and the "exclusion, and subordination as Other, initially created an ideological and political structure of formal inequality against which rights rhetoric proved to be the most effective weapon" (*CRT,* 116). Crenshaw suggests, in step with a re-newed understanding of the importance of civil rights, that "the deconstruction of white race consciousness might lead to a liberated future for both blacks and whites" (*CRT,* 118). And yet the term "deconstruction," within her own desire to qualify "vulgar anti-essentialism" on behalf of "oppositional dynamics," points to a certain impasse within CLS and CRT circles. On the one hand, Juan F. Perea, for example, rejects Andrew Hacker's "two nations" theory and makes the familiar, if still underqualified, claim that the black/white "binary paradigm interferes with liberation and equality."[9] On the other hand, Angela Harris cites Toni Morrison on behalf of "black exceptionalism."[10] One branch of the CRT movement gives ample credence to racial fluidity. The other branch plots differ-ence within a more or less stable oppositional dynamic, in order to secure civil rights claims to individual as well as group justice. Richard Delgado is satisfied to draw attention to the stalemate as such, for the moment, setting the vexed question of "intra-minority relations" aside (*CRTI,* 57).

The impasse with CLS and CRT is important because it bears directly on what I have been arguing is the termination of a civil rights interest in race via the very extension of that interest. In cutting-edge legal theory there is rampant skepticism about the legislation of justice based on state-determined forms of racial identity. Others qualify this anti-essentialist slant, claiming that to dis-miss the transformative legacy of civil rights would be historically irresponsible. In the case of multiracialism and the 2000 census debates as I have described them, both impulses are at work: *both* a radical anti-essentialist theoretical mindset *and* a grassroots commitment to civil rights are claimed in what comes to mark a transmutation of modern governmental technique. The social con-structionist notion of race and the endorsement of a post-white national imagi-nary are encouraged by the state in the simultaneous appropriation and demoli-tion of rights. Like Goldberg, Gabel implies that the way toward political emancipation lies in tossing off formal subjectivity as misguided. Disciplined identity as such is predicated on officially mandated choices that privilege the state's interest in social unity above all others. But as we have seen, race has be-come an anti-essentialist affair by official decree, as much as by civil rights ac-tivism. It is not simply that the state's and its citizens' interests have become in-separable within the iron fist of Foucauldian biopower, as Goldberg might put the matter. Rather, there is a kind of mutuality between race and government that is both maximized and degenerated at once. Racial difference is developed to a point where racism no longer matters to the law. Indeed, as we have seen, the multiracial demand for state recognition portends the end of civil rights for those staking a claim on the movement's hard-fought political legacy; yet this occurs, paradoxically, by the extension of that legacy itself.

My third conclusion can now be introduced, since it is an attempt to better limn this crucial paradox and to give it theoretical clarity. Recall that the first conclusion I offered was nothing more than to echo a commonplace charge. The consequences of that charge are not less significant for being common, or indeed, as in the case of the 2000 census, for being signed onto by the post-liberal state. Thus I noted, second, a *de*-disciplinary governmental strategy that was hitched to what I called the temporal index of race. Racial identities tend to multiply and redivide over time, and few groups have made better political use of this than Republican congressional leaders. As witnessed by the NAACP's awkward defense of the one-drop rule, identity is sooner or later nudged outside the former paradigms that coordinate racial self-recognition. My third and final point is also borne out by the debates over multiracialism and the 2000 U.S. census. If race categories are relational and are mediated by additional categories that emerge over time, then much more needs to be said about the nature of this peculiar form of mediation. This, then, is conclusion number three: the claim to self-recognition within multiracialism also initiates certain forms of *mis*recognition that occur within previous racial categories. The principle of ontological laissez-faire that is touted by the multiracial movement is founded on the ability to ignore this conflict. Self-recognition is writ here as a constitutionally mandated act of social belonging. But the right to self-identify always also prohibits alternative collective realities. Indeed, in the instance I have been describing, mixed identity outright dissolves the limits that codify previously established racial groups. This should help further develop the picture of postmodern governmentality that exists on the other side of Goldberg's disciplinary state. Once bound to procedures of self-recognition that excluded difference and isolated individuals through rigid classificatory rules, the state mobilizes race differently now. Rather than identifying individuals as categorically fixed, attentive civil government relies on the promotion of fluid racial multitudes. Beyond repression or disciplinary fixity, then, the practice of governing in its neoliberal guise maximizes a form of violence implicit in self-description as such.

In closing this section on the 2000 U.S. census debates, and before moving on to various critical responses bemoaning the end of the liberal state, let me clarify in more fully conceptual terms some of the specifics offered so far. Two items, while not unpacked in precisely these terms, have been central to our previous considerations. These are, first, the issue of ideology or governmental power; and second, the changing relation between identity and otherness as recognized by individuals and by the state. Recall that for many of the scholars discussed, rights-based discourse is part of the ideological state apparatus. It is an example of state hegemony, which effectively works to keeps identities divided and at odds. This hypothesis can be traced to Louis Althusser, whose work on ideology is well-known, but bears abbreviated repetition here, as we set up one final look at the 2000 census. For Althusser, in short, ideology is defined as a set of imaginary relations that *interpellate* individuals, giving identity a false sense of unity as belonging to whatever apparatus (nation, school, religion, family) of the modern state. Ideology thus functions, in Althusserian terms, to keep the masses from confronting the material conditions that rob them of their labor and turn it into capital. By extension, a properly materialist critique of subjectivity means the collectivization of individual will. The nature of this new form of collectivity is specified by Althusser as class struggle, which is active—though opaquely—in our daily toils.

On the question of identity and class struggle writ this way as collective unconscious, consider along with Althusser a cursory allusion to Marx. In an early commentary on Hegel's *Philosophy of Right,* Marx writes that "the state issues from the multitude in their existence as members of families," and moreover, that "family and civil society constitute themselves as the state."[11] Implicit in this evocation of "the multitude" is Marx's renowned inversion of Hegel, which was in turn central to his earliest formulations of historical materialism. For Hegel, the private sphere of individuality is socially produced such that identities become the "natural basis" for a state, which in turn "consists of them." "The state is," he writes, "self-conscious ethical substance, the unification of the family principle with that of civil society."[12] For Marx, *contra* Hegel, identity is at once a "premise of the state" and, as the state's "genuinely active element," one of its primary "modes of existence" ("CCH," 16–17). Subjectivity thus designates less the ethical basis for governmental consensus than a practice of governing already at work in the socially grounded act of self-recognition. What Foucault would much later call the "'governmentalization' of the state" becomes in this light the sorting of "multitudes" on behalf of an agreeable civic totality. That totality is agreeable because the "multitude" is at once voluntarily adherent to the normative principles of social categorization and restrained by other individuals who are similarly inclined.[13] Althusser's concern with ideology was to focus on this process of governmentalizing identity on the way toward critiquing Hegel's ideal citizen-subject.[14] Here he is concerned to point out the constitutive function of identity's opposite, that is, to point out what I called above the performance of misrecognition implicit in any act of self-description over time. It is important to point out that, *contra* Hegel, Althusser maintains that identity's occulted relation to its others does not arrive at a point of intersubjective consensus that, as he would say, Hegel wants finally to secure.[15] For Althusser, borrowing selectively from Lacanian theories of object relations, the subject's being predicated

THE WILL TO CATEGORY

on forces and identities that it cannot admit is understood as a matter of (class) conflict.

The implications of Althusser's critique of the ethical (read modern, or liberal) state are apparent in the way census enumerators are trained to coax information from the occasional reluctant respondent. The *Non-Response Follow-Up Enumerator Manual* for the 2000 count spends a good deal of effort on "how to handle refusals."[16] The enumerator is reminded not to "threaten or antagonize the person" by drawing undo attention to the illegal nature of a "confirmed response refusal." Rather, the advice is to "remain calm . . . and try to persuade him or her to cooperate" (*NF,* 11–10). Further, the enumerator is given a copy of "Privacy Notice D-31." This notice, which the census taker is instructed to read to the refusing recipient, highlights what Althusserians might refer to as the rotten twin pillars propping up every state apparatus. These are, of course, the appeals to "privacy" and "community." "*Your* privacy is protected," the notice reads. "We appreciate *your* participation and the participation of *others* in *your* community" (emphasis mine). The insertion of that second "your" before "community" is what binds the first and second "your" to the "others" whom the enumerator wants you to know are *your* own. And this faux pitch for community happens, not just locally, but in the farther-reaching eyes of the real "we" in play here, the prying representatives of the state who will remind you, if need be, that you have no right not to be identified. ("Scan the [enumerating] group with your eyes," another training manual reads.)[17] There could be no clearer example of the *interpellative* powers of the state to align subjects and objects and isolate them from intrasubjective social conflict. And there could be no more decisive indication that this power is based on enforcing the presumption, however "calmly," that one can distinguish between who one is and is not.

Like Goldberg and some CLS theorists who would describe the census as an ideological state apparatus, I want to uncover the covert *exclusionist* objectives of "Privacy Notice D-31." The state enforces racial homogeneity, those race critics might be inclined to say. But that reading of the census as it is currently deployed is also partly mistaken, as I have been suggesting, since the state now encourages—indeed, demands—racial heterogeneity, as it has in no previous time. The pitch for "your community" means in practice that you could self-enumerate multiracially and effectively undo your community by "your" very act of "participation" in it. The contest for multiracial state recognition thus complicates Althusser's theory of ideology, at least the cursory version of it I have rendered above. As we have seen, multiracialism maintains that the excluded object on the other side of subjective differentiation is neither fully adequated nor passive, but is a mixed value and one that is subject without warning to change. The absent other is mixed, not fixed, it might be said. And this is what makes identity itself (think here of the NAACP's adherence to the one-drop rule) such a newly problematic governmental problem. Fluidity, not discipline, is the governmental order of the day, and this is so in spite of the enumerator's false appeal to "community." Racialized identity under conditions such as these takes on the status of a "multitude," indeed. But this "multitude" stumbles without much attention, save from clever Republican congressmen, toward a post-white national future that both extends and diminishes rights.

It should be a matter of regret on the left that the agency I am calling here, after Marx (and Du Bois), a "multitude" (or masses) has been hinged so completely to the advance of right-wing public policy. To the extent that multiracial self-recognition threatens to disorient the state's civil rights interests, multiplicity remains circumscribed within the retrograde politics it may also be poised to challenge. Singularities, not categories, occupy a location within the remnants of civil society that were formerly quantifiable in black/white oppositional terms. Consider, in closing, an example from one of the studies done by the state as part of its decision to recognize multiracial identity. As part of the advice necessary to render the OMB's acceptance of a "check all that applies" option for the 2000 census, the Office of Survey Methods and Research Bureau performed a series of surveys called the "Race and Ethnic Target Test."[18] What the demographers wanted to discover in these target tests, put simply, was whether or not people know themselves as government would know them. Would identity be adequately *adequated*, to invoke Althusserian language, or would statisticians be forced to come to terms with unforeseen fractures in the apparatuses of social discipline? Left to their own devices, the population sampled by the RETT demographers reported an unprecedented number of a-categorical distinctions. These included, for example, "mason," "Muslim," "American," "Christian," and "rebellious teenager," distinctions that are illegal for the purposes of the census.

And yet the more substantive catastrophes of developing specifically "racial" forms of multiplicity are more eagerly admitted by the state. They are admitted especially—indeed, almost exclusively—by conservative politicians and pundits. The U.S. Libertarian Party and right-wing potentates such as Newt Gingrich, Dinesh D'Souza, and George Will are all on public record in support of the multiracial movement. That they express their support by laying claim to the legacy of civil rights makes their interest in the intradivisions of race that much more pernicious.[19] "Consistent with Martin Luther King's vision," writes D'Souza, "the government should stop color coding its citizens."[20] George W. Bush's nomination of Gerald Reynolds as assistant secretary for civil rights confirms the trend of dismantling racial discrimination laws from within the juridical system. Reynolds, a well-known opponent of affirmative action, would be

51

responsible for overseeing Title IX, which prohibits sex discrimination in education and sports programs. That such a nominee is courted by an administration that touts the most diverse presidential cabinet in U.S. history underscores a unique trend of multicultural conservatism.[21]

Ward Connerly, architect of the anti-immigration initiative Proposition 187, University of California Regent, and author of the anti–affirmative action "California Civil Rights Initiative" (CCRI), writes in a similar vein.[22] Connerly's risible claim is to "restore the original meaning and purpose of the U.S. Civil Rights Act," as the California Initiative is subtitled. Proposing to amend the California Constitution, CCRI proclaims a reemphasis on a "fundamental civil rights principle" that presumes to disregard race altogether in public employment, education, and state contracting. In an article reprinted in Susan Graham's Project RACE newsletter, Connerly embraces the multiracial movement as what he calls "the California trend." Like Congressman Petri, who led the congressional support for a multiracial census category, he claims to do so on behalf of the "abandonment of terms such as 'minority' [which will] reflect the reality that Americans are not part of any socially defined 'racial' group." Connerly concludes that "there is no 'majority' or 'minority.'"[23] His more recent efforts include the "Racial Privacy Initiative," which he proclaims would free Californians from being "straight-jacketed into choosing from racial and ethnic classifications that fit an ever-shrinking pool of people."[24] Intending to get the initiative on the California state ballot in 2004, Connerly evokes the same language as the federal "Privacy Notice," which census enumerators are supposed to use in order to counter the odd racial refusenik. "Privacy" in his case would make the gathering of racial data of any kind illegal in the state of California. Once again, we see here that the connection between race and jurisprudence develops paradoxically. Racial justice is abolished in the name of a post-white— but decidedly right-wing—extension of the civil rights agenda. Liberal notions of transparent self-description mingle comfortably with the conservative desire to end race-based legal redress. In the post-white national imaginary, civil rights are expunged on the very authority civil rights once commanded. And for the first time in U.S. history the nation invents racism without the need for race.

My suggestion, then, returns us to the Du Boisian problem of racial citation and re-citation. The problem of the twenty-first century that I have been exploring regarding the 2000 census sees a unique fusing of racial heterogeneity and national homogeneity, each at its increasingly apparent extremes. Grassroots agitation for liberalizing the descriptive possibilities of U.S. citizens has won an undeniable victory in the latest adjustments to the census. In 2000 the state has maximized its interest in racial difference, while its former obligations to civil rights are seen to wither away. This double move for and against race is the proper context for assessing renewed academic interest in the promises of cultural miscegenation. As we transition to the next section of my argument, which develops the relation between civil society and an emergent neonationalism in more conceptual terms, renewed devotion to so-called post-ethnic America deserves a bit more scrutiny.

The term "post-ethnic" is David Hollinger's. But such scholars as Ross Posnock, Naomi Zak, and Werner Sollors offer positions that run parallel to his use of the term and to the multiracial debates I have been describing so far.[25] Beginning with the boilerplate "race-as-social-formation" thesis, each of these scholars offers what I have cautioned above is an insufficiently developed understanding of the effects of racial choice. The civil rights–inspired insistence on self-enumeration is directly evoked in this work, even while that insistence turns paradoxically back against the movement's original historical objectives. Whether through "voluntary affiliation" (Hollinger),[26] "volitional allegiances" (Sollors),[27] or unchecked "individual freedom" (Zak),[28] maximizing the opportunities for racial self-recognition is presumed to enrich both personal and political life. And in keeping with the postmodern state's promotion of subjective nonfixity, the alternative pitch by these critics is for "dual public recognition" and "postmodern fluidity" (Posnock, 104, 105); the pursuit of "ethnic options" that eventuate in "multiple . . . [and] new cultural combinations" (Hollinger, 41, 116); "inventiveness of syncretism" (Sollors, 15); and the dismissal of "coherent personal identities" (Zak, 7)—a list of this kind could continue.

For all these scholars, multiracialism is singled out by name as the best hope for a stronger and more internally diverse "American" identity that is finally purged of the intranational divisions of race. Again, the new divisions within races (no longer simply between them) function to shore up a greater opposition that effectively divides "America" from the world. For Sollors, a newly miscegenated "America" emerges through the encouragement of black/white marriage and reproduction, a heterosexual reparation for racial difference that I will explore at greater length in Part Two of this book. For "cultural miscegenationists" (Posnock's term, 98) at large, "the universalist tenor of civil rights" (102) is embraced insofar as it dismantles race altogether. In challenging the "American adherence to the one-drop rule" of hypo-descent, the "recognition of racial mixture," it is hoped, "re-invigorates the constitutional tradition of the United States" (Hollinger, 29, 118). As a matter of voluntary allegiance, multiracialism is presumed to work as follows: it brings racial identification to a state of "tragic contradiction" (Hollinger, 9), one that empties the formality of race—as we have already seen—in the name of race itself. In this peculiar combination of

THE WILL TO CATEGORY

rights-based discourse and anti-essentialist rhetoric, "cultural miscegenation" reveals a stealthy endorsement of what I called, vis-à-vis Goldberg, a de-disciplinary conception of the post-racial nation-state. This endorsement severs a previous obligation between civil rights and the practice of governing, and it does so with the special insult of deploying freedoms once located there. *Beyond Ethnicity* (Sollors), "Before and After Identity Politics" (Posnock), *Post-Ethnic America* (Hollinger) are all titles of important works on the multiracial nation to come. They are also, I am suggesting, temporal provocations that bespeak a curious disjunction between the past and future significance of racial self-description.[29] Categories are time bombs, as we have witnessed in the 2000 census debates. That they are mutable and relationally inflected needs no further emphasis. The more important point is that, as those relations change over time, racial categories tend to turn against themselves and redivide, leaving only traces of whatever previous political significance they may formerly have had. This, once again, is the alienating historical dynamic that places the NAACP on such soft ground, defending the one-drop rule of hypo-descent as a matter of political expediency.

The fact that the multiracial movement has tended to be pitched against racial formalism presents a difficult challenge to an entire legacy of civil rights appeals to government. Having shifted without the slightest procedural inconsistency from liberal enactments of self-recognition to the fatal evocation of mass incomparability, race consciousness no longer leads to the jurisprudence of racial equality. Instead, in the cultural miscegenationist redivisions of race, racial difference is nudged toward the accidental renewal of what Eric Lott aptly dubs consensus nationalism.[30] Only here, the more precise way to put the point might be *dissensus* nationalism. What we have in the United States at present is identity politics turned oddly rightward by those evidently more capable than the left in mobilizing incalculable masses. The barefaced appropriation of civil rights on this new national order can be used, I want now to suggest, to enter the general debate over the twisted fate of the nation-state and of civil society as such. My goal in what follows is to connect the perfidious rightward trajectory of a new politics of racial multitudes to an insistence on the left, no less objectionable, that the defense of civil society is our last best hope for imagining more democratic futures.

REBIRTH OF A NATION?

Policy is about "right" names, names that pin people down to their place and work. Politics is about "wrong" names—misnomers that articulate a gap and connect with a wrong.

—Jacques Rancier

The various endorsements of cultural miscegenation outlined above proclaim a new and more fully democratic moment in the history of U.S. race relations. That work, I have suggested, is a thinly veiled extension of the multiracial movement's argument for public policy changes on how races should be counted, and how race should count.[1] My point in connecting the two was to trace the emergence of an ideal American collectivity, one that is in the process of displacing racial politics, paradoxically, in the guise of racial proliferation, if not dissensus. As I have been arguing in the two previous sections, the organizational objectives that race categories achieved in the civil rights epoch have been inverted in the very name of civil rights. The struggle for self-recognition has succeeded only too completely in the eyes of the state. And racial identity is evidently on the verge of degenerating into an erstwhile long-ing for the kind of color-blind unity the state once demanded by force. My ac-count of the debates over multiracial self-enumeration and the 2000 census was meant to trace a form of volunteerism that unleashes the emergence of a multi-tude of a-categorical identities and racially expressive political misfires. The fed-eral government's interest in anti-essentialist approaches to identity, to evoke the epigraph from Rancier, operates to forgo a "politics" of computational un-ease for a "policy" that exploits the ways "naming" also designates "a wrong." The "gap" between "politics" and "policy" that Rancier insists upon keeping *critically* open is foreclosed by the facile assumption that democratic practice means getting names aright. More troubling still, I have tried to suggest, is that a "politics" of multiracial self-recognition has been seamlessly conjoined to the rightward "policy" initiatives advanced by multicultural conservatives, such as those pursued by Ward Connerly. In effect, if not in deliberate strategy, multira-cialism and cultural miscegenation reveal a formerly unspeakable convergence of interests. U.S. neoliberalism and rank conservatism are interchangeable in the new social order. The identity "politics" of a post-ethnic academic left and the "policies" of the multicultural right work in their unique capacities to reju-venate the idea of "America" as the exceptional and universal nation. They do so, moreover, under the pretense of benevolent globalization.

As we move in this section of the argument from the census debates to a more direct encounter with what I intimated before is the new *dissensual* na-tionalism, that last sentence above needs some clarification. The advance of ne-oliberal market relations along the NAFTA axis, the regulation of third world debt, the international enforcement of market fundamentalism by the Interna-tional Monetary Fund and the World Bank, the superexploitation of interna-tional labor, and so on, are well-documented signs of the times.[2] U.S. assets abroad have increased in staggering proportions, from $519 billion in 1977 to $1,960 billion in 1991 at the end of the definitive Reagan-Bush years. Foreign assets in the United States reached $2,321 billion (almost half the GNP) during that same period.[3] Up until the terrorist attacks of September 11, 2001, politi-cians and the popular press rhapsodized that the idea of national boundaries was becoming increasingly outmoded. And concurrent to the new planetary forces of capitalism, the superficial extension of democratic rights to the former Eastern bloc and Central and South America is celebrated with knee-jerk ebul-lience in the face of abject poverty.[4] Whatever disorienting fate may befall U.S. civil society, it would seem to be occurring at a moment that mixes the unprece-dented reach of U.S. foreign policy with the domestic transfer of wealth toward a very few at the top.

So I do not mean to suggest by signaling the crisis of the liberal state a dwindling of U.S. international influence.[5] On the contrary, indications seem more likely to validate Alfredo G. A. Valladão, who in his book by the same provocative title proclaims that "the twenty-first century will be American."[6] "America today," he writes, is the focal point "of the first revolution in history to have reached the entire planet, casting doubt on established certainties and undermining ancient institutions, even the sovereignty of nation states; including the United States of America" (*TC*, xv). Nicos Poulantzas's much earlier 1975 thesis regarding the "internationalization of the nation state" provides equally important context for assessing the domestically troubled future of U.S. civil society, even at the nation's moment of international ascent.[7] According to this thesis, suitably paraphrased by Leo Panitch, the transformative force of multinational capitalism "leads to the dissolution of the national bourgeoisie as a coherent concentration of class interests; but far from losing importance, the host state actually becomes responsible for taking charge of the complex relations of international capital for the domestic bourgeoisie."[8] The corporate consultant Kenichi Ohmae uncritically celebrates the fact that "investment . . . is no longer geographically constrained."[9] Ohmae jettisons the notion of a domestic state altogether, preferring instead international corporate geographical boundaries, which he calls "region states" (*EN*, 5). These new boundaries replace "artificial political borders" and "lie entirely within or across the borders of a nation state. Traditional nation states have become unnatural," Ohmae continues, "even impossible. Business unites in the global economy" (*EN*, 4). His conclusion is that "changing the battle ground from nation to cross-border region will be at the core of 21st-century corporate strategy" (*EN*, 21). Insofar as the domestic crisis of the United States, which I am suggesting ironically includes a strategy of accelerated U.S. racial inclusivity, also includes the internationalization of U.S. market values, by all accounts, the trend seems to be in the direction of a new form of "World-American" economic rule (South Korea, it has been said, "is now owned and operated by our Treasury.")[10] The U.S. nation is clearly accelerating its role in the accumulation of international capital. And the idea of the welfare state, which Masao Miyoshi rightly comments was always "more chimerical than real," disintegrates beneath our feet.[11] The reason the picture of American globalization is worth introducing here is that it brings politics back into the domestic policy initiatives on race that signal the dawn of a post–civil rights epoch. In the clash between the internationalization of corporate America and the model of the liberal state, the nation finds itself free from the former citizenship responsibilities it may once have pretended to have. America may now participate in a world market system without the weight of internal dissent. Multiracial dissensus, I am suggesting then, is the domestic metonym for U.S.-inspired forms of postmodern empire.[12] The "U.S. Defense Planning" documents having been leaked to the press in 2002, David Armstrong flatly declares in *Harper's Magazine* that "the Plan is for the United States to rule the world."[13] This pursuit of renewed imperial ambition occurs while the internal coherence of the bourgeois nation-state creeps toward peaceable collapse. Nothing could be more appropriately—nor more tragically—timed than the kind of seal-the-borders patriotism and us-*versus*-them international aggression that are a matter of course in the Bush Doctrine.[14] And nothing could be more apropos to what I have been calling a post–civil rights epoch than Supreme Court Justice Sandra Day O'Connor's remark that "we are likely to experience more restrictions on our personal freedom than has ever been the case in our country."[15]

Accordingly, Poulantzas and Valladão offer an argument regarding globalization wherein the U.S. nation-state is internally weakened while it externally expands. The disintegration of civil rights in the United States occurs under the global conditions of neoliberalism that are completely appropriate to it. I have tried to tease out this process of disintegration in the admittedly limited instance of the 2000 census. Here, the rise of what I called the de-disciplinary state presents a disastrously cooperative relation between legislated racial adjudication and the collapse of former race categories. This relationship, I have been trying to show, originates paradoxically out of the discourse of rights. My point was that the proliferation of race categories the withering of a previous obligation to belong, and with that, portends the silent dissolution of the benevolent liberal state. Concurrent to multiracialism, a new tactic in the procedures of governing seems to offer citizens the kind of freedom that terminates belonging while enforcing it as never before. Identity claims proliferate beyond the formal capacities of race to contain them. The racial subject is officially encouraged to diversify in such a way that self-recognition loses its former political success. Thus it might be said that to imagine an "America" without whiteness at this historical moment presumes an imperialism of freedom.[16] Multiracialism brings on an apparent weakening of civil society, though it does so via civil society's own means. My further-reaching point is that the evacuation of the previous identity/state relation co-conspires with an internationalization of "American" morality that is appropriate to claiming the world's wealth.

With the thesis of de-disciplinary internationalism in mind, I want now to shift gears and examine the stark resurgence of interest in defending neo-Hegelian conceptions of identity and civil society. The longed-for better days of the Enlightenment *socius* belie our having to contend with the politics of an epoch that is increasingly alien to civil rights goals. Preferring neither the dismissal of civil society nor, exactly, its preservation, I want to argue that planetary capitalism adjoins these two seemingly antagonistic impulses on its own behalf. Holding steadfast to the devil it knows, the renewed demand for a multicultural politics of recognition and, commensurately, the desire to preserve and expand the public sphere reveal the persistence of dissensual multitudes that Part One of this book has been charting all along. In the following discussion of such influential social theorists as Charles Taylor and Jürgen Habermas, the effect of multiplicity on naming and recognition tends toward the ironic hollowing out of U.S. civil society that we have already witnessed. That this occurs while Western forms of social morality are introduced elsewhere at gunpoint gives us another glimpse of "World-America."

The predominant tenor of current scholarship on democratic social orders shows optimistic high regard for rejuvenating the promises of civil society, or put more familiarly, the public sphere. From the time of its publication in 1989, the English translation of Jürgen Habermas's book *The Structural Transformation of the Public Sphere* (originally published in German in 1961) has had an especially far-reaching impact on the understanding of the Enlightenment and its continued relationship to contemporary political life.[17] What sustains the public sphere today as the object of a certain historical longing is the apparent emergence in the eighteenth century of a civil society independent of the state in which autonomous individuals exchanged arguments in a manner analogous to the way they exchanged commodities in the market (*STPS*, 46–47). For Habermas, the market, liberated from the artificial interference of the mercantile system but not yet compromised by the formation of monopolies, would necessarily give rise to an abundance that would neutralize class antagonisms, as well as to an economic rationality whose primary characteristic would be the optimization of products and services. In the same way, a public sphere, liberated from the state and from any threat of coercion but not yet the site of class conflict, permitted the emergence of a world of rational critical exchange in which the merely ornamental discourses of aristocratic affect gave way to genuine arguments that were adjudicated solely according to "audience oriented subjectivity" and the criterion of reason (*STPS*, 49). Here Habermas has provided governmental modernity with its most theoretically sophisticated defense. An account of early-eighteenth-century Britain as one "blissful" (and all too fleeting) moment in the history of capitalist societies, which by virtue of the fact that unlike anticapitalist utopias, it actually existed, seemed to Habermas originally, and to leading U.S. intellectuals at present, to offer a set of realistic objectives for liberal social reform (*STPS*, 59).

Indeed, according to John Keane in *Civil Society: Old Images, New Visions*, the velvet revolutions of central-Eastern Europe have formed a unique partnership with the predominate turn in U.S. social theory toward what he calls "the renaissance of civil society."[18] Habermas's notion of the public sphere is characteristically solicited as the touchstone for this rebirth of modernity. Keane seeks to fortify a world "of mutual solidarity and free and open communication" (17), a model of civil society based on the interactions of civic morality, "such norms as trust, reliability, punctuality, honesty, friendship, the capacity of group commitment, and non-violent mutual recognition" (18). Similarly, in *Civil Society, Democracy, and Renewal,* Robert K. Fullinwider calls for reinvigorated attention to "the networks of interaction [that] broaden our sense of self, developing the 'I' in the 'we' . . . enhancing the participants' 'taste' for collective benefits."[19] It is this "politics of recognition" that, according to Benjamin Barber in the same volume, underwrites our "civic discipline." True to the dictates of social modernity outlined by Habermas's influential account of the public sphere, the renewal of "discipline" in this context is alleged to "sustain both increased social cohesion and greater liberty for individuals." "By establishing among citizens themselves a high degree of normative agreement about rights and responsibilities," Barber continues, "civic communities can remain resilient and cohesive with far less direct control of individuals than in less internally disciplined societies."[20] Citations of this sort are unvaried and abundant.[21]

Habermas's notion of an "inter-subjective politics of recognition," which almost singularly underwrites predominate endorsements of civil society, has been vulnerable to critique if only in that, as he has come to admit, liberal democracy in its blissful mercantile-capitalist, British eighteenth-century phase is historically founded on the carefully guarded principle of exclusivity.[22] We have already seen a capable critique of modernity's reliance on *both* exclusionist habits *and* democratic promise in David Theo Goldberg's book *The Racist State* (more on this text in the final section below). Attendant to the acquisition of property and capital by a new middle class (which Habermas brackets from the rise of "communicative reason") is the matter of alterity in its distinctly modern form. For every private, rights-bearing (white and male) citizen, there are the nagging problems of the "patriarchal conjugal family," British imperialism, the first standing army, and the state and local police (*STPS,* 18–19). The establishment of a universally accessible public sphere wherein the free and open exchange of ideas creates the ideal conditions for "mutual recognition" is precisely *that,* an "ideal," and as such, something that tends to belie somewhat more nefarious realities. But this objection to civil society on the grounds of its exclusionist historical nature has not hindered the lasting popularity of *The Structural Transformation,* which by Habermas's own admission has had a distinctly American afterlife. Habermas has responded to the multicultural and feminist objections that his early work has privileged the bourgeois public sphere (which in reality was or is only one among others) by pluralizing the concept.[23] The public sphere is thus discussed in terms more appropriate to cultural difference as no longer "bourgeois," either in its origins or in its actual functioning at present. Instead, Habermas has come to recognize that if there is indeed a plurality of spheres, there is also a sphere of all spheres. The public sphere thus conceived is the totality formed by the communicative interaction of all groups, even nominally dominant and subaltern.

For the early Habermas, the constant concourse of these groups in the communicative realm (where rational-critical debate stands above relations of power and an intellectual contest of ideas is fundamentally independent of and even opposed to the materiality of forces) has worn away their antagonisms to produce something like a genuine "general interest." Here, beneath a consensual umbrella within which differences are communicatively resolved, all individuals who seek mutual recognition have a stake in the preservation of society at large. In Habermas's later writings, the realm of communicative action similarly takes place in a public sphere that is protected by the state, but distinct from it. Here such differentials as property and power also disappear from view.[24] No longer does class demarcate the negative boundaries of civil society, as in the eighteenth century. The distinct groups that emerge in the zone of material conflict are neither rooted in irreconcilable difference nor forged in a struggle against illegitimate power. As Habermas insists, once liberated from the Marxist tradition, we are free to dissociate the diverse communities that make up civil society from the processes of capital accumulation and class struggle. We must seek to understand them as purely "voluntary associations" (read here: self-recognizable subjects) that have emerged "spontaneously," that is, in no way determined by relations of subordination (*BFN,* 366–67). The recognition that a plurality of spheres have always made up the public sphere compels us to admit that irrespective of rank, status, or property, and independent of material differences, there has existed at least from the dawn of capitalism in Europe a universalism of the human "as human," even if it was never fully realized as such (*STPS,* 36).

Habermas's response to the problem of alterity, as intersubjectively recoupable, rests on an updating of Hegel. The argument for preserving the public sphere against those differences merges the pitch for a miscegenated neonationalism with the pseudo-ethical charges of the racially fine-tuned, if also racially *dissensual,* state. "We are still," Habermas opines in *The Philosophical Discourse of Modernity,* "contemporaries of the young Hegelians."[25] Followed by Axel Honneth and, to a more qualified extent, Charles Taylor, Habermas seeks within Hegel an intersubjective "politics of recognition" that lays explicit claims to the universalist legacy of civil rights.[26] Hegel's early Jena manuscripts (unavailable for more than a century after their original composition in 1801) offer in Habermas's and Honneth's account a rejuvenated Hegel, purged of the nationalist forms of German idealism apparent in his later years. By the time of *Phenomenology of Spirit* (1807), Honneth writes, "the conceptual model of a 'struggle for recognition' had lost its central position within Hegel's theory."[27] Similarly for Habermas, "the critique of subjectivity," that is, "ethical life" described in the Jena period as "the reciprocal dependencies of inter-subjectivity," is "puffed up into an absolute power" (*PDM,* 29). As the state is elevated in Hegel's *Philosophy of Right* to "the reality of the substantive will," rationality tends toward "self-glorification" over "self-critical self-renewal" (*PDM,* 55). This, Habermas contends, is what a rejuvenated Jena-inspired undertaking of modern intersubjectivity would be able to avoid.

Charles Taylor offers a decidedly less critical version of an intersubjective politics of recognition than Habermas and Honneth in that his endorsement of the state and of national "spirit" is less qualified. The "basic need" of "modern [*sic*] man [is] the recognition of their fellows. The recognition of oneself in others . . . the recognition of the universal . . . brings us to the reality of the *Geist.*"[28] Unable or unwilling to jettison the Hegelian sublimation of identity to governmental order, Taylor sees "the state" as "a community in which universal subjectivities can be bound together while being recognized as such" (*Hegel,* 431), "the highest embodiment of *Sittlichkeit* ['ethical life'] which is implicit in the notion that man is the vehicle of rational will" (*Hegel,* 428). Habermas and Honneth want to provide an alternative account of identity that brings rational order to intersubjective fluidity, while attempting to avoid the imposition of the state. "The politics of recognition" as described by Habermas as an "agreement on self-understanding" would seem to "guarantee different ethnic groups, and their cultural forms of life, equal rights of co-existence" without reducing identity to nation.[29]

But taken together the two different neo-Hegelian endorsements of a "politics of recognition" offered by Taylor on the one hand and Habermas and Honneth on the other lead by separate approaches to the rebirth of the nation that I noted above as a miscegenated new "World-American" order. Whether fixed within a national template, as in the case of Taylor, or located outside the needs of nationality, as in Habermas's account, self-recognition is presumed to contain a multiplicity of cultures that reduce to nationality, if only by default. And as we have seen in the 2000 census debates, the state's recognition of the differences pushed forward from within the public has meant the end of governmental modernity as such.[30] Moreover, the intersubjectivity that is recognized by multiracialism undermines the very foundations of civil society upon which intersubjectivity supposedly rests. Categorical self-recognition, as we have established repeatedly, is always predicated on misrecognition. This is what enables the indefensible advance of conservative public policy on the matter of race, Rancier's "naming" as a political "wrong." Through "a politics of equal respect," Taylor suggests that "the rigidities of procedural liberalism" are given a more "hospitable variant" of total inclusivity.[31] Following George Herbert Mead, he maintains that we merely need to "recognize the equal value of different cultures" and "acknowledge their worth" in order to become our better selves ("PR," 64). "Mis-recognition" under "the presumption of equal worth," he continues, "has now graduated to the rank of a harm that can be heartedly enumerated" ("PR," 64). For Taylor, recognition equals mutuality, which in turn equals a consensual cultural basis for the ethical substance of the state. But again, as we have seen, the distance between mutual recognition and the "harm" (or "wrong") of misrecognition that Taylor wants to hold onto no longer exists as a liberal governmental practice. They occur simultaneously, as the NAACP now realizes, such that the state is released from previous civil rights claims precisely by the more careful "enumeration" of Taylor's "harm."

In his anticipated book, *The Inclusion of the Other,* Habermas similarly reconceives modern natural law as "citizens coming together voluntarily to form a legal community of free and equal associates."[32] Here "intersubjectivity" is understood as "a theory of rights that requires"—in common with Taylor—"a *politics of recognition* that protects the integrity of the individual in the life contexts in which his or her identity is formed" (*IO,* 113; emphasis mine). "The juridified ethos of the nation-state," he continues, "*cannot come into conflict with civil rights* as long as the political legislation is oriented to constitutional principles, and this [orientation is linked] to the idea of actualizing basic rights" (*IO,* 137; emphasis mine). What else do the debates over multiracialism and the U.S. census reveal, if not this tragic conflict between the juridical subject *and* civil rights? For Habermas, as distinct from Taylor at least on this count, the emphasis on "mutual recognition" becomes the basis for "post-national self-understanding" (*IO,* 119). The insistence on the "juridified ethos of the nation-state" realizes its full potential in Habermas's call for an "actually institutionalized cosmopolitan legal order."[33] The "inclusion of the other" thus eventuates in a supranational collective identity that is premised on the U.S. nation-state and its coveted forms of mutual recognition. "The political culture of the United States," Habermas continues, "enables everyone to maintain two identities simultaneously, to be both a member and a stranger in his or her own land" (*IO,* 118). The international public sphere presumes a "World-America."

Thus the difference between Taylor's and Habermas's ethics of mutual recognition constitutes less a point of contrast than twin paths leading to the same American-planetary destination. Taylor is content to proceed according to the "state as ethical substance" thesis, criticized by reformed neo-Hegelians whose primary focus is Hegel's early Jena period. For Honneth and Habermas, however, emphasis on the early Hegel overlooks his infamous contention in *Lectures on the Philosophy of World History* (1822–28) that the point of contrast for modernity itself was "the undifferentiated and concentrated unity" of "the African."[34] Note here that the designation of "African" is *not* reducible to a simple black/white binary, or if it is, that binary is predicated less on racial *difference* than on an "undifferentiated" *multiplicity.* That multiplicity is then *racially* objectified against the white West as an incalculable (or "undifferentiated") "African" mass. In the moment of the de-disciplinary state, almost two centuries after Hegel, racial differentiation begins to unravel, and that formerly "African" multitude somehow finds its way back through one of modernity's temporal portals to the postmodern U.S. census debates. Thus multitudes persist from within dissensual nationalism, and the agency of masses, as in Du Bois, retains its unrepresentable status. Habermas seeks to extend the project of civic morality as international consensus to the world, envisioning a cosmopolitan rebirth of modernity, in spite of its rank historical exclusions and in the face of its Western domestic collapse. The internationalization of the public sphere, it appears, can only happen with the enhancement of a politics of recognition that Taylor insists on at home. My charge is that both Taylor's and Habermas's positions uniquely endorse "World-American" rule. They do so by promoting while effectively evacuating the democratic promises of civil society at the same time. Taylor's tacit nationalism and Habermas's cosmopolitan public sphere tend, paradoxically, to endorse the same "global-American" prospects. Together they imply what is both a new-nationalist and a post-racial world order. Recalling Poulantzas, the (international) restoration of the U.S. nation-state is accompanied in the current epoch by its internal collapse. In their common insistence on the politics of recognition, Taylor (nationally) and Habermas (globally) tacitly encourage this event.

Insofar as multiracialism and the census are concerned, the ruse of intersubjectivity contains a fatal contradiction that inspires the advent of multitudes against which Taylor and Habermas pitch the unitary philosopheme of consensus. As we have seen in multiracial claims on federal jurisprudence, the "juridical ethos of the [U.S.] nation state," *contra* Habermas, not only "comes into conflict with civil rights," but indeed terminates the state's interest in protecting civil rights on civil society's own terms. This termination, to repeat, occurs through the very politics of recognition that both Taylor and Habermas prescribe. In the example of the 2000 census debates, the legal right of public self-disclosure is predicated by a surreptitious violence upon previous categories of belonging. This hazard, I have suggested throughout, releases a domestic crisis of subjective incalculability, a fatal computational unease, wherein the agency of multitudes displaces identity as such. On one hand, this impasse signals a terminal contradiction within civil society. On the other hand, however, the emergence of racial incalculability on the scene of U.S. public policy retains something of Hegel's fear of "undifferentiated" masses, something that is well worth our continuing to pursue. There is a complex trade-off at work here as the potential of not yet calculable forms of community struggles to invent itself, and we will return to it in the fourth section below. For now let it stand that, while the state gestures toward a juridical ethos that seeks the recognition of all races and all race combinations, it leans toward the possibility of recognizing none in particular. "American" identity, perhaps uniquely at this moment, is at the point of realizing a certain release from governmental jurisdiction out of the sheer multiplicity of its forms. Perhaps the real potential of this detachment helps explain the anxious swing toward patriotic fervor in the opposite extreme. The disciplinary state historicized by Goldberg and others emerges on the international scene at the moment it presents its domestic collapse, I am suggesting. This is not the same as claiming that the state as such no longer exists. More modestly, I suggest that the *liberal* state no longer does, and that this disintegration occurs, paradoxically, through the intensification of the state's own logic. Habermas exhorts the global transference of intersubjective self-understanding, while self-recognition advances toward a point of fatal multiplicity at home. My point is that the cosmopolitan public sphere is foreshadowed by an internal disintegration of modern liberalism that takes place in equality's name. To evoke Antonio Negri and Michael Hardt on this count, the move from "capital's instrumentalization of the state"—as in a modern disciplinary society—"to the capitalist state's . . . integration of civil society" evidently means that civil society as such disappears.[35]

The odd aspect of this disappearance is that the end of the liberal nation-state does not reduce to the matter, as Habermas would have it, of a historically decisive face-off between the global completion of liberalism on the one hand and the canny escapism of domestic postmodern singularity on the other. As Taylor would have it, the politics of recognition is markedly on the increase in the United States as the twenty-first century begins. The debates over the 2000 census, and the post-white hype around an American minority-majority are ample evidence of this. Curiously, the proliferation of racial identity itself and the imagined demise of whiteness have occasioned the return of an incalculable multitude that Hegel too simply called "Africa." And it is this multitude that the state is now forced to admit to in its march toward globalization. The very ubiquity of liberalism brings it to the verge of internal collapse. Within the public sphere, mutual recognition reaches a point of multiplicity that exceeds the intersubjective capacity to know it. This very moment of the weakening of civil society in the United States shadows the arrogant punctuality of American liberalism on the global scene. The public sphere is sought to be intensified (by Taylor) and exported (by Habermas) so that modernity achieves its rightful, world-dominant place. Thus the internationalization of Western civic morality is paired today, uniquely and disturbingly, with a politics of civil rights ill-equipped to mobilize the grumbling exigencies of its own numbers.

AMERICA, NOT COUNTING CLASS

The planetary petty bourgeoisie has . . . taken over the aptitude of the proletariat to refuse any recognizable social identity.

—Giorgio Agamben

Part One of this book began with a certain reluctance to repeat Du Bois's
famous maxim that "the problem of the twentieth century is . . ." *et
cetera*. By way of introduction, my intention in leaving out the key term "color
line" was to signal my sense of the overuse of this phrase. There has been no
more repeated *line* in race scholarship over the last twenty years than that one,
I remarked. The idea in not repeating it once again, or in *almost* not repeating
it, was not just an academic language game. I wanted to signal a more substantive political problem having to do with subjective citationality at the beginning of the twenty-first century. This had to do with the way races repeat, or
indeed, how races may fail to repeat, while they are encouraged by the state to
proliferate. Perhaps the form of agency I was trying to pin down in the wake of

multiracialism resides in the elliptical part of the famous quote from Du Bois—the "*et cetera*" I used to replace his key phrase (which should have been an "*et alia*," or rather, an "inter *alia*"). My abbreviation of the epigraph was meant to highlight a point about how time interrupts (and determines) what counts in America: the problem of the twenty-*first* century is and will be color *lines*, I said, with an indomitable emphasis on the plural. Racial self-recognition in one census category, I later said, always eventually means *mis*recognition in another. This is because race, as both activists and the federal government have hurried it along, changes, sometimes radically, over time. The subsequent account of the 2000 U.S. census and multiracialism was thus meant to keep what I have called the temporal index of race in play. With this term it was noted how racial identities historically multiply and eventually exceed the formal categories once presumed to contain them. Racial multiplicity thus tends to poise identity on the threshold of incalculable futures. Conservative policy makers have found clever ways of bringing this into line with a racially attentive disregard for race, as we have seen. The idea of a post-white America in the abstract looks equally good for the conservative right as for the liberal left.

I then moved to argue that the liberal-Enlightenment (or simply modernist) racial state was in the process of being displaced by *de*-disciplinary modes of governance. But as I was careful to point out, this occurs from within a civil rights–based logic, which contains both the promise of individual freedom and identity's eventual undoing. Race has officially become fluid, and perhaps too conveniently ineluctable, as the identity/state relation is torn apart at its historical seams. The state's attention to race (and not incidentally, to whiteness) apparently intensifies to the point of its own ironic dissolution. Thus in response to David Theo Goldberg, I added that the state is no longer racial on the simple grounds of race-based exclusivity. Rather, oddly enough, contemporary governmentality is predicated on racial inclusiveness, if also, finally, the political dissolution of race-based claims to justice. Governmentality no longer operates merely by repressing color on behalf of white preservation. Its more effective tactic is to encourage racial diversity and redivision at every turn, so that the phantom of a post-white America is imagined as going beyond real political consequence. The so-called coming white minority is thus tragically shadowed by reversals of civil rights legislation. My account of a multiracial politics of self-recognition, a liberal ideal that has been perfidiously hinged to the ideological program of the right, has provided ample evidence of this.

A strange multiplicity now burdens the legacy of civil rights. At the moment civil society and U.S. consumer culture reach their international zenith, Agamben's "planetary bourgeoisie" forecloses its attachment to modernity. That is to say, at the moment market capitalism has moved into its most expansive global phase, any former pretense toward domestic responsibility of the kind put in place from the New Deal through the civil rights movement is all but eviscerated. While Du Bois's (tragically absent) "mass" unity of labor still goes unnamed, postmodern racism enables the accumulation of international capital through carefully guarded forms of flexibility, jettisoning its former reliance on the fixed unity of race. The problem, then, is no longer that Du Bois's missing masses have been improperly individuated, racially divided, or excluded by a white-majority state, as in former times of struggle. The problem today is that identity has become unwittingly massified, and with still no way for labor to count. There has been too little initiative on the left to engage the late arrival of multitudes to public discourse outside the worn-out domestic register of individual rights. This was my point, recall, in putting Habermas and Taylor into contact with Valladão's provocative "World-America" thesis. In contrast to their neoliberal pitches, respectively, for an international *and* nationalist politics of recognition, my argument was that intersubjective consensus has reached a point of political termination. With the formal and official recognition of multiracialism as it is playing out in the United States, racial belonging exceeds its own numbers, revealing the state's interest in the violence implicit in self-description.

In sum, in Part One of this book I have tried to establish an association between the aleatory processions of time, the unplanned obsolescence of the bourgeois subject, and something only alluded to before, evoking Hegel's "Africa" as the persistence of mass agency in the wake of civil rights. In the absence of domestic racial unity, and given the rank appropriations by the right of race-conscious legislative equality, my final question seeks an unlikely partnership between Du Bois and Agamben: what "aptitude" remains for laboring multitudes to steal back from their masters? In the "age of democracy," the word "proletariat" as I read it retains an archaic quality that is crucial to its appropriateness for my purposes. Indeed, this appropriateness has everything to do with Agamben's wanting to retain the political good use of the "refus[al of] any recognizable social identity." The word "proletariat" is critically anachronistic, one might say, pointing as much to the well-documented failures of past worker utopias as to the urgency of claiming unrecognizable democratic futures. The epigraph does not suggest that one should or can refuse identification. Rather, it insists that self-recognition is itself the politically offending logic. That this offense may or may not be solicited on behalf of democratic agency means that collectivity should be reformulated in the gaps in representation that are always also found there. If the term "proletariat" is nostalgic, then all the better for it. The term should highlight an interruption in time; or rather, it should take advantage of the evacuation of official forms of racial self-categorization as they are hurried toward the temporal absenteeism of democratic identity as such.

Indeed, the "aptitude of the proletariat" should evoke the "*et cetera*," or the unnamed "*inter alia*," that is crisscrossed by twenty-first-century color lines. Mixed and moving "masses" replace fixed "minorities" beyond the discourse of rights, Agamben elsewhere remarks.[1] "Terms such as *sovereignty, right, nation, people, democracy,* and *general will,*" he continues, "by now refer to a reality that no longer has anything to do with what these concepts used to designate" (*MWE,* 110). Setting the terms "consensus" and "public opinion" similarly aside, Agamben deploys the term "proletariat" in a way that is closer to Jacques Derrida's insistence that there is "no justice without . . . an aporia" than it is the charge of totalitarian rule.[2] The agency Agamben (like Du Bois) has in mind is located precisely in the *absent* presence of democracy, its incalculable futures and pasts. Wedged into the temporal index of race, the term "proletariat" dictates the reluctant admission of an enduring problem of "too many." And the "proletariat," as Agamben recalls it, issues forth in its progressive antagonism in both citational registers that I have been exploring: the rhetorical and the juridical. Du Bois's "masses" exist as a "proletariat" in the technical sense of that term. It marks the struggle, recalling Jesse B. Semple, to hear silent numbers that, like him, are "still here."

Consider one final point dealing with the state and race, or with what Goldberg insists is its racially exclusionist historical nature. It is tempting to read Goldberg's formidable argument in *The Racial State* as simply an endorsement of assumedly radical heterogeneity, over the kind of homogeneity enforced as a modern governmental tactic. But while that book traces the state's enforcement of "the color line," its farther-reaching argument is more nuanced than a straight-ahead pitch to make that line more flexible and so more forgiving. Early in his historicization of modern governmentality, Goldberg offers a key qualification regarding domestic calls for and against racial pluralism: "it is not just that heterogeneity is or has been a challenge or a threat, opportunity or potential problem . . . it has always been both" (*RS,* 32). I read this qualification to be allowing room for the possibility, the one limned throughout my own argument here, that heterogeneity *and* homogeneity are at work in the state at historically varying degrees and with different effects over time. The multiracial debates should have made that more than clear. Indeed, on the very second page of *The Racial State,* the potentially more positive political consequences implicit in the state/identity decoupling I have traced are stated clearly. "To move on," that is, beyond the disciplinary grip of modern government, Goldberg suggests, we must "not . . . turn back but . . . begin to address the lacuna, the noisy and bothersome gaps" (*RS*, 2) that racial representation also always produces. These "gaps" are linked to "unspeakable" (*RS*, 251) "multiplicities" (*RS*, 276) that we must nonetheless also "address," and that are at work within the dubious (if also necessary) act of self-recognition in the register of race. I would suggest that in attempting to think beyond the racial state, Goldberg is unwittingly gesturing toward Agamben's "proletariat," which is equally Du Bois's "masses." Both, I am arguing, are found in Goldberg's favored postmodern racial "gaps." And, in that sense, both forms of collective agency allude to an incalculable community of subjects in the wake of the liberal state.

To suggest that a "proletarian" struggle exists within the changing techniques of government, as archaic as I mean that formulation to sound, is nothing more than to emphasize a point made throughout the first part of this book. The alternative to racial subjectivity is not otherness, but like Hegel's "Africa," is multiplicity. And the "aptitude" of this absent agent is borne out in the very substance of the de-disciplinary state. Whereas the state once functioned in its prophylactic ban on racial mixing so as to maintain classificatory certainty and white-majority rule, today, after whiteness, some other relation of power is at work. The imaginary unities of race are no longer depended upon by the state to reduce, and thereby manage, its occasional political openings. Rather, complexity is itself intensified on the order of the state's capacity to manage multitudes of difference. The "proletariat" is numbers, in this sense, but those numbers do not count in America. In Latin they are *proletarii*, or "prolific people," as Jacques Rancier reminds us. They are those who "merely live and reproduce without a name, without being counted as part of the symbolic order of the city . . . the class that dissolves classes, as Marx said."[3] The *proletarii* are Jesse B. Semple—"still here, in spite of all" and, one might say, because of "all" as well.

Under conditions that mark both the end of the liberal state and a post-white national imaginary, then, there is as much renewed interest as confusion about racial self-recognition. As race categories proliferate and the state/identity relation both loosens and becomes absolute, we may well expect what J. K. Gibson-Graham, Stephen Resnick, and Richard Wolff refer to as "the amplified affective charge of the laboring body."[4] Our discussion of the U.S. census has revealed certain inassimilable intensities on the question of political belonging.[5] Arguably, these intensities have begun to turn the liberal state upside down, producing examples of dissensual sociability that would be unimaginable in former times. Should there not also be some trace of this public intensity in the private domain, insofar as these two spheres are mutating and merging together? As different ways of construing racialized self-interest jockey for place in the post-white American imaginary, might we not expect intimacy to exhibit its share of new tensions and revealing contradictions as well? Part Two of this book goes on to address exactly that. Of concern here will be to think about post-whiteness as a psycho-social matter involving masculinity and family. As the rhetorical flip side to what has been offered regarding public policy in Part One of *After Whiteness*, it is to the equally curious affective charges surrounding race that we turn in Part Two.

A FASCISM OF BENEVOLENCE

GOD AND FAMILY IN THE
FATHER-SHAPED VOID

OF COMMUNISM AND CASTRATION

Where there is love, there is also communism and castration.
                                                    —Klaus Theweleit

Like any good epigraph, the one cited above is meant to invite further reading. Its job is to reach out to readers by signaling some ostensibly common interest, while perhaps defamiliarizing that something at the same time. Indeed, as these things go, sometimes the better the outreach, the more intense the estrangement. Epigraphs draw attention to a topic about which some general knowledge is presumed, but they also create curiosity by implying that there is something unknown near enough by. The epigraph is a fragment in search of wholeness that never quite comes, you could say. It produces a set of boundaries around this or that expected topic and anticipates a conclusive readjustment of those boundaries at some deferred later moment in the text. In the case of my epigraph, and pursuant to the ideas I want to tease out from its distilled provocation, the general topics are sexuality and power. Of particular interest to me is how these two items relate to one another within the anguished psychic performances of white heterosexual men.

While masculinity studies has more recently come to the fore, sexuality and power have, of course, been a longer-standing focus of scholarly inquiry.[1] And if one thing in general might be concluded about the academic fixation on subjectivity, it is that identity studies works best when it resists facile or reductive conclusions about the matter of desire (e.g., as manifestations of illusion, false consciousness, determined by economy, as an index of psychological repression, etc.). The vast attention to intimacy has produced some of the best of this nonreductive kind of work in cultural studies and, better still, in its more sophisticated cousin, queer studies. Both modes of inquiry have tried to lead a way through the gleaming shears of so much 1990s theory. They have tried to negotiate a way through, on one side, the presence of domination within every thought and gesture; and on the other side, an individual's capacity for resistance and agency, the sticky tenacity of democratic hope and potential. With that double bind front and center, then, the "love" mentioned in my epigraph might indeed best be approached in epigrammatic terms. Like epigraphs more generally, the term here should allude to ways the expected and the unfamiliar switch places and combine. I want, in other words, to take the question of desire outside the formulaic rules that treat it within the context of this or that mode of repression. Instead, what follows tries to increase and diversify those rules, precisely as a way to critique them. My objective is to specify the changing habits of affection between men, overturning, not creating, the expectations for what I called above the wholeness that never quite arrives. So before the scholarly fascination with gender, sexuality, and desire scurries back into the shadows of more sober times, let me introduce the following set of questions: given the imagined coming of a U.S. white minority, what about love, the myriad prohibitions and phantasmagoria wrapped up in racialized libidinal attraction? In Part One of this book, the general question ran as follows: in the wake of multiracial state recognition, and beyond the formal opposition of a black/white racial binary, whither the public sphere? In Part Two, I want to invert that initial line of thought and ask this: beyond the previous civil rights–based racial geometries already examined, what similarly inassimilable pressures may be weighing in on the psyche of (white) American men?

Using the case of the 2000 U.S. census, I have argued that the presumption to speak from a place of identity in general, that is, in a public or consensual-normative way, has paradoxically tended to displace the Enlightenment subject in the very name of civil society. The effect of this displacement, I further suggested, was a collective social arrangement whose principle of unity now strains the legal notions of individual rights. In short, the liberal left and conservative right have exchanged discourse and reversed. Radical-progressive thinkers wanting to move beyond that partnership are beset with what I called a politics of misrecognition, the struggle en masse for a body politic not yet named. Such a thesis was not proposed to reinvent the common *doxa* of postmodern excess. It was not my intention to celebrate fragmented subjectivity for the sake of an anything-goes form of pluralism (though one could say that the multitude is, indeed, ontologically empty). Rather, my interest in identity's apparent social dissolution was offered to signal the welcome disjointing of an ill-begotten partnership between the triumphs of neoliberalism (its victories—recall debates over multiracial civil rights—hiding precisely in its losses) and a renewed understanding of race. This interest in what I just called identity's social dissolution is where the second central question of this book becomes important. Beyond the critique of racial self-recognition already offered, what might be said about related political dramas that are attached to affection and intimacy? What might be said when new-sprung libidinal economies and heretofore implausible object choices begin to emerge in predictable ways? What happens when these object choices manifest themselves not (or not only) in specific boundary transgressions, but become evident, too, in how we mourn unclaimable social generalities and invent a new host of post-white psychological rules?

These questions hasten us from the function of epigraphs to the issue of ethics. Here again we have the problem of mingling the common with the unfamiliar, and of doing so in such a way that the common—in this case the normative white masculine subject—struggles to either be re-enforced by or reject his newly race-sensitive persona. Within this double bind, where whiteness is caught in the no-man's-land between the racially familiar and estranged, fascism comes to bear on the triumph of liberalism already born dead. The love that Theweleit has in mind in the epigraph I cut from *Male Fantasies* above is (on the order of epigraphs) a mechanism of both defense and attraction. Love in the sense Theweleit goes on to describe it maintains the enforced generality of race—the white race—even while it encounters what are decidedly masculinized forms of imagined self-dissolution. My argument, simply put, is that in the post-white national imaginary of U.S. men, color is processed in a sexual way. Moreover, color and sex are linked to a kind of erotic canalization of class conflict. This is what enables the devil's bargain between the forms of liberal self-expression and fascistic self-defense that I will begin to trace shortly. Fascism operates in the name of an exalted race that also posits certain hyperbolic forms of heterosexual masculine virility, as Theweleit maintains. I want to suggest that this, too, is the way contemporary white men operate in the United States. But more curious than that, white masculinity responds to the dreaded colorization of America by mirroring the logic of fascism and inverting racial loathing. Indeed, a heterosexually anxious mix of racial love *and* hate designates a common masculine response to the unmaking of the white majority. The fantasy of a white minority (that is, mourning whiteness before its actual death) is lived today through a racialized libidinal phalanx whereby new forms of self-division seek old forms of heterosexual repair.

By way of further introduction to my argument, a word or two more about Theweleit's stunning book, *Male Fantasies*. His analysis of fascism historicizes the psychodynamics of a historically specific group of men known as the Freikorps. These men constituted the "volunteer armies that fought and triumphed over the revolutionary German working class in the years immediately after World War I," and later became Hitler's core executives of terror.[2] The fear of communism mentioned in my epigraph from Theweleit, as Barbara Ehrenreich puts it in her foreword to his book, is the fear of "the communism of Rosa Luxemburg, promiscuous mingling, breaking down old barriers . . . a dread of engulfment by 'the other'" (*MF,* xv). The Freikorps "see the world divided into 'them' and 'us,' male and female, hard and soft, solid and liquid," she writes. They therefore "fight and flee the threat of their own desire" (*MF,* xvi). My hypothesis about the love and hate of color draws from this, but is divergent. I, too, want to show how the fascistic fear of racial liquidity is equally the desire for it. Otherness has never been more sought out nor more divisively manipulated than it is in U.S. culture and politics today. But my difference with Ehrenreich has to do with the stacking-up of crumbling opposites that she names as so many parallel sets. One cannot reduce the other in the contemporary scene, I shall argue, by setting up the divisions between "'us' and 'them,'" "male and female," "hard and soft," white and not, and so on, as if they were paired off in harmonious ideological alignment. The differences and oppositions that constitute sexuality and race are not correspondingly divided along a fixed organizational line (for example, as some Marxists used to say, "scientifically," of class). The (racial) double that constitutes, for example, the white/black opposition is within itself already also (sexually) divided. Within an emergent post-white imaginary, masculine subjectivity functions according to a historically specific ensemble of *differently* motivated differences than the parallel race and sex opposites held in place by early-twentieth-century German military men. Herein lies my general thesis, and the postulate that governs how I regard the twenty-first-century American men examined below. Contemporary white masculinity sustains itself, I want to suggest, less according to the old rules of *sexual* repression, and more by inventing new rules for *racial* promiscuity, on the sly, as a task that binds men together. As race is more welcomingly perceived as fluid, sex is more desperately conceived of as fixed. Indeed, the very idea of heterosexuality as the touchstone of normal masculine affection is dependent on the way race is infused with desire in our post-white national dream.

In this dream, I want further to argue, the psychic relation white heterosexual men have to men of color is comprised equally of two opposite affective modes, comprised, that is to say, of love and hate. This ambivalence, as we shall see, is what motors a rejuvenated popular movement toward traditional family structures and the sanctity of marriage. We may go on associating racial divisions with ruling-class interest, and indeed, I would argue, we should; but this association is less than instrumental in that those divisions are maintained via an affective balancing act that preserves and transgresses racial domination in the same heady moment: love and hate, arousal and repression, authority and submission, humility and pride all operate at the same time and at their mutual extremes in contemporary white masculinity. Call this the heterosexual high-wire act white men perform over racial terrain that is no longer solid ground. The anxieties produced by growing inequities of wealth are lived uniquely by white men in the twenty-first century. They are lived, not by the sexual cordoning-off of color from whiteness as in former times, but via an erotically charged softening of mutable racial distinctions. This is what I call in the title of Part Two a fascism of benevolence. By this I mean, in short, that both the love and hate of color are attendant to a perceived material crisis in the fading privileges of whiteness for a good many American men.

I want to limn what I referred to as a sexual high-wire act over race in the next four sections below. My first goal is to examine the rise of the Christian men's group the Promise Keepers in the mid-1990s. Touted as the largest evangelical movement in U.S. history, this group is useful for examining ways in which race-*bending* is enlisted on behalf of gender-*binding*. Race is attached here inseparably to the dictates of masculine heterosexuality, specifically, to fatherhood and marriage. Indeed, the Promise Keepers (hereafter PK) is only one of a number of formal organizations promoting what has been called the U.S. marriage movement. Given the group's fundamental multicultural interests, it is curious that PK is bound (even if covertly) to the right-wing public policy groups that support it. In line with these groups, the ideological lineaments PK attaches to the heterosexual family become supercharged. But oddly, it does this by appealing to hypermasculinized forms of self-sacrifice that are hinged to white-racial transgression. A second section develops this hypothesis with further examples from PK literature, promotional material, and, less explicitly, my own participation at PK events. Here I detail how PK's interest in pursuing cross-racial forms of heteromasculine intimacy becomes the platform upon which the achingly uncertain future of whiteness depends. The work of masculine recovery resides in the cultivation of a post-white sensibility that PK speakers refer to as "a father-shaped void." At stake in this deliciously loaded phrase is the very heart of what I am calling a fascism of benevolence. I want to unpack this term, once again, as a process of white racial self-negation that returns with renewed masculine vigor in the form of sexual self-reassertion.

The next section takes a more theoretical turn to discuss the role negation plays in forming what Adorno calls the authoritarian personality. The goal here will be to construct the conceptual bridges that join PK to the U.S. neofascist group the National Alliance. For this I follow the lead of Paul Apostolidis's fine book on Adorno and Christian right radio, which despite its subtle analysis of conservative religious popular culture leaves the issue of sexuality to the side. I use Apostolidis's work on Christian family policy groups to set up the PK/neofascism connection with which I will eventually conclude. With the same purpose in mind, I turn in this section to the work of Judith Butler and David Eng. Eng's groundbreaking work on the relation between heterosexual masculinity and race is especially important for contextualizing my analysis of PK, which ultimately differs from his own take on white men. Eng and Butler both suggest that racial repudiation satisfies the mandates of white racial purity—an important beginning point for anatomizing the neofascist imaginary in, for example, the widely selling National Alliance novel *The Turner Diaries*. But in applying the Butler-Eng hypothesis to this infamously racist book, as I will go on to do, I find that the appropriateness of their thesis does not explain the dynamics of PK. In this group, white masculine sexuality plays out in terms that are exactly the opposite of racial purity and repudiation. A carefully cultivated, if also extremely precarious, form of post-white sensibility is the unlikely basis on which PK seeks to secure heterosexual manhood. PK and U.S. neofascism share the same heterosexual logic, I want to suggest. But they do so via a kind of delicate inversion of their respective affective claim. Both groups seek to preserve masculinity by targeting race. The more curious point is that they do so by mobilizing precisely the opposite psychological extremes. They do so by claiming to love color, and by hating it, so as to placate the same class-conflicted, heteromasculine ends. As I detail in this section, together PK and the National Alliance present a complex picture of rejuvenated masculinity that is both post-white *and* violently pure. This bizarre psychic composite is worth unpacking, because (white) men's relation to alterity is writ *doubly* as the fascination with and aversion to a moment of racial multiplicity about which no one can be sure.

In *The Origins of Totalitarianism*, Hannah Arendt suggests that "organized loneliness is considerably more dangerous [than] unorganized impotence."[3] This phrase is significant to the account of evangelical Christian family men and neofascist fathers offered below. But Arendt's denunciation of "the Nazi or the Bolshevik" (*OT*, 5)—for her, cobelligerent historical beasts—hinges on an opposition that defines her own overly modest political investments. Worse than that, this opposition enables the rejuvenation of the masculine myth of fatherhood in an imagined post-white twenty-first century. For Arendt, and characteristic of the civil-society tradition that motivates her cause, the structuring principle of fascism is writ as uncorrected intimacy. On the one—"more dangerous"—side of her formulation, the male *isolato* is "organized" outside the modern strictures of "integration" and "common interest" (*OT,* 12). In this way he becomes what Arendt returns to time and again as the forbidden adversary of liberal consensus: "mass man." The chief characteristic of "mass man," she writes, "is not brutality and backwardness, but his isolation and lack of normal social relationships" (*OT,* 15). The word "impotency" in the first quote speaks precisely to the word "normal" in the second. Thus on the other—if unequally dangerous—side of "mass man," an additional normative hazard appears, here evoking the urgency of heterosexual reproduction. Like "loneliness," "unorganized impotence" is located in the intimate sphere, and is as likely as inassimilable masses to "pervert the standards and attitudes towards the public affairs of all classes" (*OT,* 9). Thus lurking within the figurative language of *The Origins of Totalitarianism* is a long-standing premise that the conjugal patriarchal family is the founding principle of the modern state and of liberal civil society. That same *socius* is what Arendt wishes to uphold against masses.[4] While receiving due interrogation from within feminism and queer studies, the family/state equation runs in materialist theory, from Hegel to Marx and Engels, through the Frankfurt School (namely, Max Horkheimer and Theodor Adorno), and most recently to Habermas. The "authority of the nation has seemed to depend on the authority of the family," Horkheimer writes in 1949.[5] Liberalism's empty triumph over masses, it would seem, depends on historically specific Oedipal ensembles that allude to (but, *pace* Freud, do not dictate) wider forms of collective belonging than the liberal state can allow.

In *Did Someone Say Totalitarianism?* Slavoj Zizek offers an alternative to Arendt's dismissal of "mass man." Here, Zizek comments on the habit of "dismiss[ing] the Leftist critique of liberal democracy as the obverse, the 'twin,' of the Rightist Fascist dictatorship."[6] He continues, "the elevation of Hannah Arendt into an untouchable authority [is] perhaps the clearest sign of the theoretical defeat of the Left—of how the Left has accepted the basic co-ordinates of liberal democracy ('democracy' versus 'totalitarianism'), and is now trying to redefine its (op)position *within* this space" (*DS,* 3; emphasis in the original). My intention is not to rehash the stalemate Zizek rightly wants to challenge. I want to avoid applying formulaic principles to fascistic psychological ensembles. Too often such treatments serve to sound a tired warning against radically massive forms of collective belonging on behalf of liberalism's renewal. I am looking for

81

a more specific intervention, one that offers a gender studies critique of masculinity with a distinctly materialist slant. From that mixed vantage point I want to delineate the sexual logic by which whiteness is made *and* unmade in America. Whiteness, as we have already established, is both absent and present, authorized and repressed, feared and desired, celebrated and denounced, disintegrated and strengthened, post-ed and recovered, everywhere and all at once. The general point of what follows is to detail a certain libidinization of race and a racialization of libido, both of which underwrite the fantastically paradoxical status of whiteness. The particular sexual link to race I have in mind is unique to our contemporary scene. It mobilizes the love and hate of color equally and without distinction, so as to placate a distinctly white and male form of class anxiety. In focusing on a fascism of benevolence, I want to show how desire still matters to politics, and matters gravely. I want to show how the forms of desire that animate liberal appeals to racial inclusivity in fact mimic the fascistically excited preconceptions of a post-white nation to come.

MUSCULAR MULTICULTURALISM

It is no accident that the modern manager, whose enterprises are to dominate the planet, is simultaneously sportsman and womanizer.

—Etienne Balibar

Of the most visible features of the Promise Keepers' dubious rise to glory, surely the desire to garner public visibility has *itself* been one of the more remarkable. Founded in 1990 by former University of Colorado football coach Bill McCartney, PK claims to have "reached nearly 5,000,000 men in 10 years of conference outreach."[1] These numbers beckon attention, as do other aspects of the group. Its meteoric financial rise; its claims to racial reconciliation; its volatile or—as PK put the matter for the 2001 convention theme—"extreme" message of faith; and its unofficial right-wing political affiliations are all significant elements of the PK pop cultural phenomenon. In the wake of September 11, 2001, the group adopted an explicitly militarized version of its message, hailing its membership to join in "storming [evil's] gates." Indeed, the group explicitly links "America's . . . war against terrorism" to a "return to the Church [in] its stance of spiritual warfare."[2] And for messages like this, PK has been as often celebrated as it has more justly been rebuffed within the narrow political spectrum of U.S. popular media. The specific import of PK commentary aside for a moment, that its largely white and male membership has garnered so much press is, to say again, worth pausing over. Indeed, PK has been the focus of numerous progressive magazines (giving rise to a special investigative unit with its own regular newsletter, *PK Watch*), mainstream television, magazines, and newspapers (e.g., C-SPAN, *Time*, the *New York Times,* etc.), and, of course, Christian media outlets (e.g., Pat Robertson's 700 Club and other like-minded venues).[3]

For standard left journalism, PK contains all the juicy cringe-worthy ingredients for a satisfying media exposé. Even if, as I shall argue more closely below, PK literature bespeaks a rather less secure self-understanding than sheer masculine-"managerial" world domination, its stadium rallies display the fiercely homosocial pathos of Balibar's ultraistic "sportsman." Indeed, this pathos operates to the point of unintended self-parody. The men of PK, for example, are as fond of engaging in mass forms of prayer as raucous team cheer as they are high-fiving for Jesus or barking hokey call-and-response refrains like "Every man needs a huddle!" Indeed, with a purported 64 percent of its membership declaring sexual temptation—"womanizing"—the most pressing moral problem they face, PK addresses masculine libido almost to the point of obsession. This is better put as married masculine libido, since a definitive 90 percent of PK's membership is purported to be married.[4] And yet part of the group's appeal is that the alleged indiscriminate sexual tendencies of PK married men are, with the right fraternal support, all the more satisfyingly tethered to the conjugal necessities of heterosexual fatherhood. (Family commitment is emphasized in PK literature, notwithstanding McCartney's admittedly self-obsessed career goals as a college football coach, his unhappy children, and his suicidal wife.)[5] Retrograde masculine posturing and glaring sexual hypocrisies fully in view, as the largest and, historically, the fastest-growing religious organization in U.S. history, PK has been as disturbing a mass movement to witness as it has been impossible to ignore.[6]

After an original gathering of seventy men in 1990, with little or no budget or staff, PK reached its popular apogee in 1997. Overshadowing the mythopoetic men's movement, it held sixty-two sold-out stadium rallies that year. Those rallies reached untold masculine millions via nationwide Christian radio simulcasts. At its height, PK claimed an annual budget of $117 million and a paid staff of 500 in 136 offices nationwide. To put those numbers in perspective, PK's budget was higher than the NAACP's in 1997; its staff larger than that of the AFL-CIO. The culminating event of PK's rise to popularity, "Stand in the Gap," won national and international news coverage by more than a thousand media outlets and brought a reported 700,000 to 1 million men to the Washington, D.C., Mall in October 1997. That number far surpassed the high estimate of 250,000 civil rights activists who assembled for the historic March on Washington in 1963 to hear Martin Luther King. "Stand in the Gap" was called by one nonpartisan reviewer "the largest gathering of people ever assembled at that location."[7] In recent years, the size and visibility of the PK organization have waned. Rather like the *pre*–Promise Keeping posture of socially diminished manhood itself, the PK organization has waned in notoriety and influence.[8] (Still, eighteen stadium rallies were scheduled across the nation for 2003.) Coach McCartney claims that the relative drop-off in PK participation has occurred because he has steered the group toward the issue of "racial reconciliation," just as he has steered it toward PK's (and much of the country's) touchstone reference: the assumed arrival of a white American minority sometime after 2050.[9] Promise six of the "Seven Promises of a Promise Keeper" is to "reach beyond . . . racial and denominational barriers." And indeed, Coach Mac makes good use of the fact that he has two grandchildren born of different men of color (though these were former college football players, who had unmarried conjugal relations with his daughter while he was coaching them).

The exposure of right-wing ties to the group's leadership has revealed inconsistencies in PK's repeated public assurances that it is a "politically neutral" organization, is "not politically motivated," and has "no political agenda."[10] Certain evidence speaks otherwise. The Christian activist James Dobson, for example, a conservative media mogul and CEO of the million-dollar-a-year-plus Focus on the Family coalition, publishes a large portion of PK authors. In 1992, when PK was low on start-up money and without the all-important direct mailing list, Dobson provided both. The right-leaning Campus Crusade for Christ provided Coach McCartney the platform for his initial moment of salvation.[11] And that group's leader, Bill Bright, well-known for his cries against the separation of church and state, provided 85 of PK's 452 full-time Colorado staffers in 1996. More notably still, onetime presidential candidate Pat Robertson came out in strong support of 1997's "Stand in the Gap," sponsoring guest appearances of PK leaders on his *700 Club* television program. Despite the fact that Robertson has over the years supported conservative candidates whose platforms included a range of anti–New Deal policies (for example, defunding state programs benefiting communities of color and cutting Head Start), Robertson has come out loud and long on PK's minimal charity work among vandalized black churches. And PK board member E. V. Hill has been active in Falwell's Moral Majority.

MUSCULAR MULTICULTURALISM

To complete the tally of transparent political offenses like these, the premier PK speaker, Tony Evans (more on Evans below), was heard at a past stadium event to link homosexuality to hell. Indeed, the homophobic elements within PK's leadership are especially noteworthy, even if they are rather less emphasized in PK's stadium events than one would think. For some in PK, homosexuality is the devilish flip side to fatherhood and marriage. PK cofounder David Wardell remarks, for example, "We're drawing a line in the sand here. . . . There has already been controversy about abortion and homosexuality. I hope there won't be physical confrontation; but look at Amendment 2 [an anti–gay civil rights initiative in Colorado] and the Act-Up people . . . coming in here."[12] In an "ex-gay" advertisement in the *New York Times,* an Amendment 2 advocacy group, Colorado for Family Values, evoked Coach McCartney by name as it proposed to close its Christian ranks and "face a very intense campaign to force homosexuality on to our cities, states, and nation."[13] A PK director, Reverend James Ryle, states, "The crisis of homosexuality . . . is a cultural revolution, which has poised our nation precariously on the brink of moral chaos."[14] Again, this language is not predominate in PK literature, nor is it explicit at its rallies, where multicultural speakers are careful to keep the message more positive. But occasional flat-footed gay bashing is consistent with the more vapid proclamations of homophobia that hover just outside PK's broader-pitched ideological tent. James Dobson provides the closest example of this. Indeed, a Dobson-financed group, the Family Research Council, describes the so-called ex-gay movement as "the Normandy landing in the larger cultural wars."[15]

It is obvious even in the most superficial examination of PK that those "larger cultural wars" are waged squarely in the intimate sphere. As Linda Kintz comments of Christian right culture more generally, PK promotes a politics of affect that moves "directly and intensively into the sacred site of the family."[16] Although Ann Burlien does not mention PK in her book, *Lift High the Cross,* right-wing evangelists perform what she calls a kind of affective "double-cross."[17] Especially in the way the church turns to the family, she notes, religious ideology too often "stigmatizes [the] abject" (*LH,* 196), "insisting on the 'same-as-me-ness' as a precondition for intimacy" (*LH,* 11). Why Burlien's observation is inapplicable to PK will become clear in a moment. For now, before I describe the rather more complex sex-race dynamic underpinning PK, it is essential to acknowledge how family politics have gained conservative momentum in the United States concurrent with the group's inception in 1990.[18] The family, which has somehow come to mean heterosexual married couples with children, provides an aggressive public policy platform at twentieth century's end. Lauren Berlant sees this as a symptom of the explicit politicization of intimacy on the right, what she calls the dubious rise of "infantile citizenship."[19]

(Consider, for example, the outcry against same-sex civil union legislation in Virginia, Vermont, Hawaii, Nevada, and Nebraska, on the grounds that gay partnerships are "anti-family.") While membership in the traditional religious conservative groups of the 1970s dropped precipitously during the 1990s (the Christian Coalition's annual budget is half of its $25 million high), conservative family policy councils have been as markedly on the rise.[20] Variously networked by GOP lobbyists, a total of thirty-five such groups existed at the state level in 2001. Many are affiliated with Dobson's Focus on the Family, which regulates and helps distribute "pro-family" voting guides beyond offering deep-pocket financial support and sponsoring PK radio broadcasts. Such alarmist diatribes as Maggie Gallagher's *Enemy of Eros: How the Sexual Revolution Is Killing the Family*, and *The Abolition of Marriage*, or James Q. Wilson's *The Marriage Problem: How Our Culture Has Weakened Families* are characteristic of the so-called U.S. marriage movement.[21]

Indeed, the rise of family policy groups is connected in important ways to a change in national policy on religion's role in public assistance. President George W. Bush's creation of an Office of Faith-Based Programs promises new and deeper connections between religion and government. Here the destitute and working poor are offered the hope of spiritual "redemption" over social "reform," as Bush proclaimed the year the federal court appointed him to office.[22] The president's faith-based initiative functions, characteristically, to transfer the lion's share of public funds into private hands (as if we needed another example of the devolution of the liberal state). Beyond that, so-called charitable choice solidifies the religious right's annexation of the family as a hard-won battle prize in the larger cultural wars. Bush's landmark bill—inspired from within the most "diverse" presidential cabinet in U.S. history—gives federal funds to religious charities, allowing them to ignore state and local civil rights laws exactly as the authors of the Colorado Amendment 2 intended.[23] Corresponding movements, like the Virginia-based Alliance for Marriage, propose a Federal Marriage Amendment that would change the U.S. Constitution to read: "Marriage in the United States shall consist only of the union of a man and a woman."[24] The legislation of intimacy on this order saw first light on the national stage in 1996, when Republican politicians introduced the Defense of Marriage Act. Here marriage is to be legislated, similarly, as "a legal union between one man and one woman."[25] Characteristic of the "marriage movement" on the whole, a group called Marriage Savers networks clergy in 146 cities in order to promote Christian-based Community Marriage Covenants.[26] These arrangements function as voluntary trials for the establishment of state laws allowing "covenant marriages," which enable couples to elect more juridically restrictive marital contracts (Louisiana enacted such a law in 1997).

Exactly what should we make of the newly torqued-up "defense" of the family—as if, like whiteness, what was once presumed unremarkable and omnipresent is now assumed to be just about gone? No doubt, to begin with, one part of the defense-of-family mantra is connected to the changing requirements of labor in America. It has been a long-standing and indispensable premise of feminist-materialist thought on the family that patriarchy and modern political economy constitute two historically inseparable systems. As an extension of Engels's still relevant thesis in *The Origin of the Family,* Juliet Mitchell famously wrote in 1973 of the transition from feudal to modern capitalist economic relations. "The family changed," she notes, "from being the economic axis of individual private property under feudalism, to being a focal point of the idea of individual private property under a [new] system of production—capitalism. The working class work socially in production for the private property of a few capitalists in the hope of individual property for themselves and their families."[27] Eve Sedgwick, in her ground-breaking book *Between Men,* extends this formulation to examine the specific issue of heterosexual male relations. Sedgwick rightly regards the patriarchal conjugal family as a mechanism that historically "propel[s] the worker *forward* to further feats of alienated labor, in the service of a now atomized and embattled, but all the more idealized home" (emphasis in the original).[28] Michèle Barrett and Mary McIntosh anatomize the "ideology of familialism," similarly, as "the eleva[tion] of the morality of the market into an entire social ethic [that] ignores all those members [i.e., children and women] who do not themselves enter the market. This is done," they continue, "by the sleight of hand of subsuming them as members of families into the individuality of their head of household."[29]

More recent work on "the postmodern family," a term introduced by Edward Shorter in 1975,[30] links unprecedented changes in traditional domestic patterns to post-Fordist economic demands. While "family values" rhetoric has reached a pitch of public fervor matching no other time in history, it is also the case that, since the 1970s, divorce has supplanted death as the primary cause of marital dissolution. Since 1996, which saw the Promise Keepers at its most popular stage, "no single family pattern [has been] statistically dominant." And more tellingly than that, "only a *minority* of U.S. households still contain married couples with children; and many of these include divorced and remarried adults" (emphasis mine).[31] At the same time as the literal *minoritization* of the nuclear family, the twenty-first century witnesses the proletarianization of women, once supposed to be shielded from capitalist labor relations in their subservience to the male-headed intimate sphere. (This is more accurately put as the "re-proletarianization" of women, since not until the 1920s did the majority of children in the United States live in male-head-of-household families where the wife remained at home.)[32] In 1950, for example, 33.9 percent of U.S. women were in the workforce. By the mid-1990s, that number grew to 57.9 percent, a clear majority of women. According to the 2000 census, nuclear households are down 23.5 percent, to an all-time historical low. The number of single mothers increased 25 percent since 1990, to more than 7.5 million households. And married households with children are now at a paltry 24 percent.[33] On top of the dismantling of the domestic sphere as a result of women leaving home for work, according to the *National Study of the Changing Workforce,* paid and unpaid work hours have been steadily increasing for both men and women workers since 1977. More than one in three workers brings work home more than once a week.[34]

That new and increasingly exploitative work conditions have wrought new demands on the nuclear family seems clear enough on the surface. As post-Fordism requires more fluid (and relative to men's real wages before 1977, decreasingly compensated) orders of labor, the notion of a separate, standard zone of private, male-headed domestic life seems less and less necessary for the accumulation of capital.[35] It would be temptingly easy (and not altogether wrong) to conclude that the reactionary posturing attendant to the marriage movement simply reflects the inexorable intrusions of wage labor upon a domestic sphere that capitalists no longer need. But the fragmenting effects of labor on normative private life should not be reduced to an anticapitalist defense of house and hearth. Statistics, like the ones I just cited, regarding the minoritization of the nuclear family should not, in other words, double back and inspire nostalgia for modes of patriarchal intimacy that still cling to golden-age memories of America's lost middle class. Materialist theories of how to evaluate the apparent post-Fordist dissolution of the traditional family differ along these lines. On one hand, the (public) demands of labor may be reflected in a (private) zone of intimacy, where that zone of intimacy is regarded as sheer ideological coercion. But on the other hand, if one does not cordon off the (public) relations of work from the (private) relations of desire in such overly functionalist terms, then the affective realm may retain some form of relative autonomy within capitalist labor relations.

Examples of the first approach, which should be called the "false consciousness" tendency, emanate from Engels's "origins of private property" thesis.[36] The second approach takes its charge from feminist complications of the modern public/private split. It makes the personal thoroughly political (and vice versa), as the well-known slogan goes. And in that, feminism presents a critique of the deterministic way of pairing economy and identity, a critique from which Marxism has not recovered. For example, Judith Stacy brackets post-Fordist demands for more flexible labor relations in order to celebrate the "postmodern family condition." She sees the new family, "like postmodern culture . . . as diverse, fluid, and unresolved . . . admix[ing] unlikely elements in an improvisational pastiche of old and new."[37] The suggestion here, breaking from Engels's deterministic approach, is that desire is no longer a seamless instrumental extension of the demands of wage labor. Rather, for Stacy, the world of public life and work and the intimate sphere of the postmodern family are no longer functionally separate from one another. Neither, within their newly synthesized domains, are the zones of publicity and privacy pure in and of themselves. Family life in late capitalism becomes a diffuse and more fluid arrangement, which subverts any previously necessitated public/private split. According to Stacy's postmodern collapse of this earlier historical division, affect is allowed to signify "more cosmopolitan, world beat, feminist, and democratic family rhythms" (13).

The optimism here is admirable, and it is characteristic of predominate trends in U.S. Cultural Studies (about which more in Part Three). But it could also be said, less admiringly, that Stacy makes too little of the question of labor. As I hoped to show with the previous discussion of multiracialism and the 2000 census, pitches for fluidity, multiplicity, and cosmopolitan combination may (and often do) contradict the politically progressive intentions they may start out pretending to have. Diversity in the post-white national imaginary takes on a standard, indeed, a generic appeal. And this paradox runs unabated through the crisis of the liberal state, to conservative policy agendas that enforce heterosexual marriage by law. That said, my discussion of the 2000 census was not offered so as to simply subvert the expected racial geometries of civil rights. I did not want merely to place cosmopolitan combination on the conservative side of the political line and racial separation on the other, more progressive side. I granted what is increasingly pointed out by scholars interested in class, that the postmodern condition tends to escape formal political reckoning. However, the only effective critique of this tendency possible, I would continue to argue, is to go on making that same concession: the political obfuscations attendant to subjective fluidity are implicit in the democratic possibilities that one might also find there. The position I am trying to stake out, in other words, is not one that rests on blithely celebrating postmodern fluidity over the oppressive forms of domestic isolation felt in former times. That, it might be argued, is where Stacy is finally headed. I would suggest that a rather more difficult task is also the politically better one. This would be to articulate which version of identity's multitudes, its various "admixtures" or "combinations," might be cited on behalf of a materially more equitable future. The conservative right has been remarkably more capable than the progressive left in mobilizing subjective fluidity for the sake of its nefarious goals. This point I now want to develop more fully.

90

On the issue of conservative postmodernism, consider, for example, Tony Evans. I mentioned Evans above as one of PK's most transparently offensive leaders. Indeed, common left-leaning media accounts charge Evans, correctly, with flat-footed sexism and rampant homophobia. The *Humanist* comments, for example, that Tony Evans "abhors the 'feminization of the church': . . . tell[ing] men to reclaim their role—without compromise—as head of house, and tell[ing] women that they should submit 'for the survival of our culture.'"[38] This message, the report continues, is characteristic of PK's "rigid fundamentalist family structure," which encourages "a strong 'we versus them' mentality."[39] The otherwise more radical journal *In These Times* focuses on Evans in exactly the same way. Frederick Clarkson cites Evans's now infamous lecture, "Reclaiming Your Manhood," as the group's most despicable moment. And it is certainly that. But the case against Evans, and more broadly PK, misses the subtler violations of the "we versus them mentality" that are more characteristic of the group's mass appeal. In a lecture that claimed so much media attention, which PK stopped showcasing almost immediately after it happened, Evans proclaims:

> I can hear you saying, "I want to be a spiritually pure man. Where do I start?" The first thing you do is sit down with your wife and say something like this: "Honey, I've made a terrible mistake. I've given you my role. I gave up leading this family, and I forced you to take my place. Now I must reclaim that role." Don't misunderstand what I'm saying here. I'm not suggesting that you *ask* for your role back, I'm urging you to *take* it back. (Emphasis in the original.)[40]

Again I would point out that this passage is reprinted or referred to by every anti-PK media exposé in print as characteristic of PK's sexist and homophobic foundation. *Front Lines Research* cites Evans's sermon as evidence of PK's "capitaliz[ation] of male backlash."[41] The *Progressive,* too, recalls his remarks to paint the usual picture of PK's "'we' as opposed to 'them' mentality." In this manner Evans's characteristic homophobia and his patriarchal call to family values "threaten a democratic pluralistic society,"[42] we read time and time again. But is PK really anti-pluralist in pursuit of its feverishly masculine "we"-mindedness?

I recite the common indictments against Evans, not wanting to diminish the reality of homophobia and patriarchy in PK, or in the United States at large. But the standard accounts of Evans as both anti-pluralist and misogynist miss the point of his far more complicated role in directing PK's vexed performances of masculine self-recovery. Popular treatment of the group too easily passes over the changing relationship between PK's transparent race and gender offenses and its more pronounced focus on *other* than feminine others.[43] In the voluminous writing by Evans pitched at PK stadium events, the dismantling of white identity is what PK's membership really pays (and prays) to see. By this account, the case against Evans misses a more vexing problem regarding the ethical substance of pluralism than the simplistic one available when race, gender, and class differences are sutured too neatly together. Judith Stacy's evocation of the postmodern family and Ann Burlien's hasty interest in ontological abjection are inapplicable with regard to PK. With Evans, white racial self-criticism reinforces the threatened psychic life of masculine heterosexuality.

Evans's book, *Let's Get to Know Each Other,* for example, is affectionately introduced by "Coach Mac" himself along racially transgressive lines. Elsewhere McCartney will publicize his most important religious epiphany as kneeling in the course of worship to wash the feet of a fellow Christian black man. This man was picked for the honor because he chastised PK's predominately white congregation as being effectively racist.[44] In Evans's argument in his book, the performance of white masculine submission is described with the kind of twisted cosmopolitan intimacy pitched as the linchpin of PK masculine redemption. Evans, too, chastises his readers for the "great hesitancy on the part of whites to sit at the feet of blacks with the expectation of learning."[45] But PK's arch-patriarch and dastard homophobe offers hope, after whiteness. "It is evident to any serious social observer," Evans writes, "that 'black is in'" (*LG,* 21). "The roots of human civilization," he continues, "are in Africa with black people" (*LG,* 22). The significance of these assertions lies in how PK's emergent post-white sensibility is situated so as to reclaim heterosexual manhood. Indeed, the rise of the multiracial U.S. citizen-subject we have already traced is essential to Evans's cosmopolitan resanctification of the traditional family. "Moses was married to an African woman . . . and it has been proven that other Israelites were also dark skinned" (*LG,* 25), he suggests. "Jesus" himself "was mestizo—a person of mixed ancestry" from which we all sprang (*LG,* 36). The term "mestizo" at once echoes and reverses such influential work in 1980s feminism as Gloria Anzaldúa's *Borderlands/La Frontera,* which proposes to reach beyond essentialist identity politics toward embracing "the dilemma of the mixed breed."[46] Evans draws selectively upon his own work in the civil rights movement of the 1960s. He calls upon his white brethren to begin a "new era" of "white self-assessment," asking with a form of provocation that must be, in proper measure, both welcomed and resisted: "does it rub you the wrong way to have an African-American man or woman in final authority over you?" (138).

Much more needs to be said, and will be soon, about the intricate multiracial, heterosexual logic outlined in PK books like Evans's. But to sum up what has been offered so far, the decline of the traditional family has occurred in two ways. The first is easy enough—indeed, too easy—to discern. In a literal sense, the conditions of labor now impinge on the traditional domestic arrangements that it once required, with the consequence of diminishing the real numbers of traditional male-headed heterosexual families. (For women this can be a positive event, but one that takes place nonetheless in the context of increased labor exploitation and the disintegration of a middle class.) Yet the numbers that document the minoritization of the nuclear family are meaningless, just as appeals to cosmopolitan fluidity are vacant, outside an account of how the figure of "minority" appears in a second, less calculable sense: family ideology in PK is supercharged by mass appeals to dissolve whiteness into color. The otherwise welcomed new era of white self-interrogation functions, like the census debates, in a counterintuitive way. The imagined place of whiteness on the demographic and psychological margins holds safe the coherence of heterosexual manhood. In this sense, the encroachments of capital upon the patriarchal family unsettle masculinity, and do so while race is called upon to make men whole again.

WHEN COLOR IS THE FATHER

The white family is the agenda of a certain system.

—Frantz Fanon

In this introductory phrase borrowed from Fanon, the word "system" is crucial. It designates the family's role in producing and regulating what he calls the "psycho-existential complex" of colonial black/white race relations. And this complex, not incidentally, is something Fanon wishes rightly to "destroy."[1] Without launching into a full-scale analysis of Fanon's apt critique of colonialism, I would like to note for my more limited purposes that his white family is the "agenda of a *certain* system" (emphasis mine). I take the word "certain" to be a second crucial term. It suggests that the family system is at work in a specific time and place, its "agenda" determined in part by a relation to other systems (of colonial dominance, labor, presumed heterosexual good health, as well as color). Fanon's family, therefore, is situated in a way that is historically particular to one imperial order.² In the context of French Martinique, *Black Skin, White Masks* sets out to interrogate and transform an inequitable "ontogenetic" black/white color opposition that is held in place by sexuality, fear, and desire. For Fanon, the reality of this situatedness is what remains opaque within the racial unconscious on both sides of a black/white color line.

Fanon is naming a dynamic we have already introduced in an initial look at PK. Whiteness is a sexually dependent category of belonging, a point that post-colonial theorists have been arguing after Fanon for some time. For Fanon the "ontogenetic" capacity of race produces false political asylum for "the white man," who is, he writes, "sealed in his whiteness" (*BS*, 9). White subjugation of this order enacts a backpedaling transference of difference, more accurately, a transference of hyperbolic sexual difference. This is projected upon the colonized black subject, who in turn adopts such sexual difference as part of his dissonant psychic composure. Through the sexual arrangement of racially ontogenetic (or sealed) opposition, whiteness reproduces itself in Fanon's psychological schema as the master signifier of a normative (though fictional) psychosexual unity. Moreover, white colonialist subjugation produces a "reactive" blackness for black masculinity as hermetically defined by white "negation" (*BS*, 36, 17). This results in a debilitating "self division" or "third person consciousness," "the Other . . . perceived on the level of the body image, absolutely the not-self—that is, the unidentifiable, the inassimilable" (*BS*, 110–11, 161). In Fanon's analysis, then, blackness is made "the scapegoat for white society . . . [which] opposes the expansion and triumphs of these myths" (i.e., "myths" of "liberalism," "civilization," "Enlightenment," etc.) (*BS*, 194).

I limn the concept of "ontogenesis" from Fanon by way of introducing further analysis of PK. But this introduction must also point out a contrast between PK's apparent psychic composure (and decomposure) and the kind of libidinized sealing-off of whiteness from blackness as it takes place in Fanon's colonialist imaginary. The question of white masculinity, given the psychological geographies evident in emergent fantasies of a post-white America, is ultimately not the same question that Fanon asks of colonial whiteness. Even if the agenda of the (white) family system is still a matter of agitated self-defense, white men are increasingly unlikely to be enmeshed in the same ensemble of differences, the same system of attractions and repulsions, that are anatomized in Fanon's work. The alternative system I want to limn below should reveal something different about the (white) family system given the way certain (white) men imagine the new politics of race. By this, I simply mean to foreshadow the next round of discussion on PK. Here I want to focus on the ways heterosexuality retains a self-defining interest in, not just blackness, but racial difference within a far more promiscuous scene than Fanon's. We must reexamine the psychodynamics of heterosexuality in white men within a period of historical self-adjustment, that is, now that the "ontogenetic" division (in the singular) that constituted the black/white axis of difference is slipping toward a rather more complicated future. This future, as I have been arguing from the onset of the book, is comprised in the post-white imaginary of exceeding numbers of racial divisions and intra-divisions (in the less calculable sense of the plural). Something peculiar is happening to the already peculiar invention of the white race: its ideal other, blackness, has begun to drift on a sea of racial difference that whiteness, too, is pretending to ride. Fanon describes the white repulsion of blackness, which, in that it is also a kind of colonial need for that difference, provides a glimpse of the white psyche as secretly dependent on its opposite. With PK, as we shall now see, there is a proliferation of racial difference beyond strict opposition, and with that, a certain psychic reversal. The secret of that colonial racial dependency could not be more actively (nor more agonizingly) publicized than it is by PK. White racial humility is pursued by the men of PK. Fanon's "ontogenesis" is willingly breached. And in this sense, racial difference functions for the group as a form of heterosexual masculine repair. That heterosexual masculinity is itself never far from the brink of disaster in PK is what gives its post-white racial posturing the quality of desperation they need to make their recovery.

Consider an additional set of examples from PK. "It was very easy for me to submit to Phil," writes Coach McCartney of Bishop Phillip Porter, another one of the coach's many "angry . . . [black] leader[s] in the African-American community."[3] As mentioned regarding Tony Evans above, the construal of whiteness as so much unbearable spiritual baggage is an important counterpart to the group's correspondent agenda of heteromasculine repair. Note, too, the reference to black anger and community leadership in the McCartney quote. The residual political forces of the turbulent 1960s are evacuated in this move, as Coach Mac proceeds to submit to Phil in an act of indefensible white-racial humility. Indeed, the oppositional relation of blackness to whiteness is emptied by PK in subsequent evocations of racial pluralism along similar lines. In *Let the Walls Fall Down,* Bishop Porter reflects warmly on PK's 1996 conference theme, "Break Down the Walls." The governing image of that season's gathering, as described by Porter, is McCartney "on his knees" (a sexual position, for some).[4] The point here is that *all* walls are broken down, and race politics lies equally in ruin. The binaristic racial opposition in, for example, civil rights is replaced by an appeal to white racial visibility and black *di*-visibility in one devastating shot. The preferred stance of PK in this sufficiently fluid environment shows "the ability to be weak," and as such, "pushes Coach to the forefront of the movement of breaking down walls for reconciliation" (96).

Glossy magazine pictures of multicolored groups of men tearfully embracing, "prayer tepees" on the Washington, D.C., Mall, clusters of private prayer "huddles" have become PK's unofficial emblems (see figs. 2–8). The D.C. rally, while deliberately evocative of Martin Luther King's presence in 1963, gave no priority to black men. But alongside its black preachers on the dais, PK included a Native American performing in traditional dress, Mexican folk singers, a rabbi on a shofar, Asian evangelists, and so on. This image is consistent, though differently charged, with PK's official publicity graphic for the event: bodiless male arms of cartoonishly varying hues all joined to carry the crown-embossed PK banner. That image itself is emblematic of PK's purposeful disembodying of color, which reduces race to masculine spiritual renewal in the name of a post-white imaginary. Echoing similar calls for "racial reconciliation," Bishop Porter asks white men to pursue a "critical moment" of self-reflection in a "world [that] is increasingly becoming an institution of non-Caucasian peoples" (98). Porter extends the evocation of a white-minority world in two directions, both forward toward an unnamed masculine future, and back toward a past that highlights his own involvement in "the first sit-ins" that started the civil rights movement in 1954. In Porter's appeal to civil rights, the legacy of black political leadership is emptied out, and whiteness is minoritized in the name of liberal inclusivity. Indeed, the struggles for black civil rights become, in Porter's account, the true origins of PK and its final goal. From "Colorado Civil Rights Commissioner" (*LW,* 118) in the 1960s, to "Chairman of the Board of Directors of Promise Keepers" today, he writes, "my life is a wonderful saga"

WHEN COLOR IS THE FATHER

(*LW,* 77). Wellington Boone's *Breaking Through* celebrates the (white) Nashville country singer Ricky Skaggs in a vein similar to Porter's. Like Porter's description of Coach McCartney, Skaggs is portrayed mimicking PK's white masculine performance of ritualized submission, "washing another [black] man's feet."[5] Joining the charge of Martin Luther King to PK's firebrand graphic of muscular multiracial banner waving (5), Boone sees this act as nothing short of racial "revolution" (*BT,* 50).[6] In *Right or Reconciled,* Joseph L. Garlington pits "God vs. Jim Crow." "It was Christian men and women," he writes, "who dared to face public anger and hatred in the initial battle for civil rights."[7]

To situate once again the arrangements of difference specific to this brand of muscular multiculturalism, a unique post-white sensibility is written into the conflicted psyche of PK's passively aggressive men. Race is solicited in PK rituals and readings in order to fill what another of its authors, Patrick Means, calls in *Men's Secret Wars* "a *father-shaped void* inside a man . . . [which] no woman will be able to fill" (emphasis mine).[8] In this phrase the opposition designated by "no woman" is not simply or unequivocally "man"; and neither, as it might be tempting to say, is it blackness. The opposite of femininity in PK, despite the group's hyperbolic masculine performances, is kept absent so that the group may coordinate a multitude of racial difference on the missing father's behalf. The opposition designated by "no woman" is color; but the meaning of that second term is heterosexually libidinized such that masculinity itself is mourned for no longer being able to exist (i.e., it is "voided"). For PK, racialized self-con-

sciousness prefigures the recovery of an anguished father whose shortcomings are experienced as the absence of his *own* dad. "Fail[ing] to affirm his masculinity" for wife and family (*MS*, 54), PK atones for the failures of masculinity not (or not primarily) by getting the patriarchal contract aright, but by dumping whiteness in the name of a recuperated sense of manhood in a vacuous multicultural zone. The "wound of masculinity" is perceptible by a self-conscious turn to whiteness as something, rather like the father, that was never really there. The ritual of white-racial submission is emblematized by Coach Mac, who is portrayed either "on his knees" to blackness (his "illegitimate" white-Samoan grandchildren being equally key here), or suffering badly from the costs of career. In McCartney's autobiography, *Sold Out* (revealingly subtitled *Being Man Enough to Make a Difference*), white masculine *difference* turns racial contrition into the melancholic task of patriarchal recovery. The book's centerpiece is McCartney's racial awakening, mixed seamlessly with his renewed promise to family commitment. And as its preface reminds us, "Coach is both our guiding mentor and loving dad. Think [of McCartney] as the finest father figure you ever had."[9]

PK's recharged hetero-*sexual* father figure is structured in a psychically unique manner in that it depends on the submissive posture of white-*racial* recombination. In *We Stand Together: Reconciling Men of Different Color*, PK author Dr. Rod Cooper pitches renewed masculinity in a way familiar to the group's appeal to a manly "mestizo condition." Here, what might have been offered up in racially binaristic black/white terms is replaced by a sexualized

WHEN COLOR IS THE FATHER

plurality. Cooper calls for a thoroughly pluralized form of white self-consciousness that is predicated on ("voided") masculine heterosexuality. Cooper continues, "We, as men, are living in a time when we are fighting for our lives as a gender. . . . As a gender, we are being devastated."[10] We need to "deal with the concepts of whiteness and white development," Cooper continues, and deal with it as men who are "incomplete without knowing and accepting other men—Asian, Black, Indian, Hispanic" (*WS,* 22). At an appropriately fevered pitch, racial division has, alas, "left its mark on a white man's identity" (*WS,* 137). And white men must, alas, and once and for all, "recognize . . . whiteness" (*WS,* 140) as such. As Coach Mac models this process and as PK performs it more generally, white masculine difference is achieved, it could be said, when color is the father. By this phrase, I simply mean that the marking of whiteness with color by PK (its belated "recognition") seeks a masculine familial outcome that, itself, never quite arrives. The group's right-wing political affiliations have been exposed with the appropriate effect of clarifying the stakes of PK membership. But a more complicated interrelation of systems is at work here than the glaringly offensive strain to hold on to the divisions that constitute the patriarchal family in the terms of gender alone. PK solicits white self-abnegation and posits within it the careful balance of a form of masculinity that is diminished and reclaimed in equal measure.

Scholarly writing on PK commonly fails to grasp the functionally nonreciprocal relationship between sexuality and race, reducing the group's popular appeal to either one of two arguments. On one hand, there are qualified endorsements of PK, which construe the group as a class-anxious gathering of mostly white men who gesture toward a racially more progressive future. On the other hand, more numerous examples of unqualified opprobrium focus on PK's sexist, antifeminist, and/or homophobic defense of heterosexual fatherhood. Though published by a popular commercial press, Ken Abraham's *Who Are the Promise Keepers?* is a stealthy promotional fluff-piece for PK that stands at one end of the endorsement/dismissal continuum.[11] (Indeed, the author con-

WHEN COLOR IS THE FATHER

tributed three articles to McCartney's edited volume, *What Makes a Man?*[12] Abraham is guardedly critical of PK's associations with right-wing groups like Dobson's Focus on the Family and the Family Research Council. However, he is also armed with an impressive set of statistics about the racial composition of PK's staff and speaking team (e.g., 30 percent of the leadership is of color, as are more than half of PK's speaking roster). Abraham thus stands firm with his book's primary conviction: "PK may be building stronger and more lasting bridges of racial reconciliation than any other movement in America—religious or otherwise" (*WA*, 73). Most of the authors in a volume edited by Dane Claussen are similarly inclined. Contributors make assurances that "PKer's are low in the area of authoritarian aggression" and "are not a group that threatens the rights of others."[13] PK is upheld in Abraham's book as "a supportive community in which [marginalized men of color] can resist harmful stereotypes . . . and both subtle and overt forms of discrimination" (*WA*, 77, 88). "I was approached several times by white men with tears in their eyes who apologized for previous racial attitudes and behaviors," one of the book's black contributors remarks.

Rounding off these endorsements and lending them rare eudemonic legitimacy from the left, Cornel West and Sylvia Ann Hewlett defend PK's multiracial family concerns in their unself-consciously titled book, *The War against Parents*.[14] Echoing certain features of the defense-of-family rhetoric seen in Dobson and elsewhere on the right, West and Hewlett cite three aspects of the

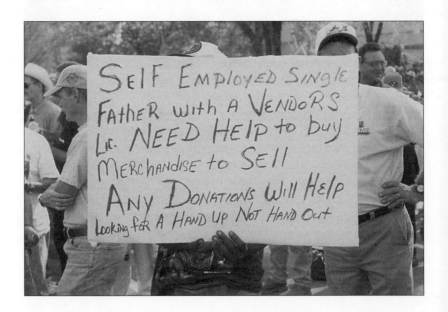

Promise Keepers that they argue require progressive groups to take heed. First, as they point out, the Promise Keepers are worried about wages. Though her evaluations of PK's "stealth campaign of misogyny and dominance" contrast markedly with West and Hewlett's, on this important point Susan Faludi makes the same connection between PK masculinity and economic angst: "Many of those in local PK groups [whom she interviewed] were . . . suffering from the post–Cold War restructuring of the economy, and struggling with domestic burdens in isolated bedroom communities."[15] PK men are half-consciously "shipwrecked in the service economy" (*SB,* 263), and they speak at length in interviews conducted by both West and Faludi of being "downsized in the workplace."[16] These concerns with the increasingly brutal impositions of work and downward class mobility bear out entirely in PK literature. In *The Power of a Promise Kept,* a collection of twelve "life stories" drawn from over eight thousand submissions vetted by PK's (black-led) executive board, the reader is identified across race in expressly class terms: "You'll find no *Fortune 500* CEOs revealing their secrets of success, . . . [but those of] men just like you."[17] These men "maybe . . . got fired from a job" (*PP,* 3), are "treated unfairly by a boss" (*PP,* 13), or, as a second PK volume puts the matter, are "hurt in the workplace [by] broken promises, [and] exploitation."[18]

For West and Hewlett, PK's broadly expressed class anxiety emanates from having to provide for a wife and children as the fulcrum of masculine achievement. "In the 1990s," they write, "white men are beginning to understand what it means to be irrelevant and redundant, what it feels like to experience invisible pain. As employers, government, and the culture increasingly moves against husbands and Dads, men everywhere are being crippled" (*WP,* 182). Coach Mc-Cartney identifies the same problem of class conflict: "for the first time in their lives, millions of Americans [and here he means white men and fathers] are losing confidence in their ability to achieve a more prosperous future or even to maintain their present economic condition" (*WP,* 95). West and Hewlett (and, no less, McCartney) want to adjoin the heterosexual-familial dimensions of the PK program to work-related issues. They want to do so in order to avoid "losing out on a rare opportunity to take the agony of crippled men and turn it into something good: a new commitment to husbandhood and fatherhood" (*WP,* 211). In a call reminiscent of PK's most ardent family-minded literature, West and Hewlett continue, "Our nation urgently needs many more men who are willing and able to come through for their family" (*WP,* 211). Thus, as the second reason for affirming PK from the left, West and Hewlett attempt to stave off the intensifying encroachments of neoliberal labor patterns by falsely separating traditional family relations from capitalism as such.

The word "traditional" is made less suspect in West and Hewlett's endorsement of PK in a way precisely consistent with how PK attempts to address its all-important father-shaped "void." They, too, reach for racial border crossing, and with two PK-like conditions: that class-inflected racial promiscuity is circumscribed by the patriarchal intimate sphere; and that it addresses the needs of "our nation."[19] In such a way, they update retrograde family relations by the "something good" of color so as to grasp at another absence signaled by the father-shaped void: the notoriously elusive historical advance of multiracial working-class resistance. For West and Hewlett, a post-white, racially unbounded coalition of class-minded individuals, working en masse for a more equitable future, is a promise worth keeping, even at the price of "patriarchy . . . or gay-bashing" (*WP,* 211). This unfortunate conclusion has proven ruinous for a U.S. left whose class, race, and sexual politics are well-known for never squaring up.[20]

The pitfalls of bracketing sexuality from analyses of race and class are no less evident in the more common inversions of West and Hewlett's sex-blind dismissals of PK. With greater sophistication—but with the same metronomic regularity as the left-liberal press—anti-PK scholarship brackets the group's "mestizo" sensibility so as to check off a common list of patriarchal violations. Marjorie Garber writes that PK's "anti-gay . . . fellowship of men" scapegoats "minor differences" so that "intolerance vanishes within the group."[21] The exact difference between the "differences" of race and sexuality (she is unconcerned to comment on class) is undeveloped in her essay. However, McCartney is taken to task because he "doesn't report that his unmarried daughter gave birth to two children, both fathered by players on [his] team" (*ON*, 301). PK literature and McCartney's own biography not only contradict this assertion, but indeed emphasize this racial transgression in ways consistent with PK's general pitch for "new mestizo" forms of masculine redemption. While McCartney laments his daughter's unmarried status, he blames himself for having failed as a father (i.e., for being "voided" by new conditions of work). That his grandchildren are born from Samoan and black fathers is well known by PK membership, and is featured unabashedly in all McCartney's speeches and books. Indeed, McCartney rarely misses the chance to comment lovingly on his emergent mestizo genealogy, which fits nicely with PK's notion of *racial* promiscuity as a *sexually* binding task. Jean Hardistry transforms the expected logic of sexual victimization into class terms, and deals PK's complex figuration of race out of the group's "anti–working class" politics. PK "manipulates working-class people," she suggests, "by providing [racial?] scapegoats for their frustrations and appealing to their fears."[22] Michael Kimmel and Michael Messner produce capable observations on PK's "essentialist retreat" to heterosexual manhood.[23] Messner contends that PK's biblically inspired commitment to masculine "categorical essentialism underlies Promise Keepers' rejection of feminist critiques of men's institutional power" (*PM*, 27). But the follow-up to this statement, that PK's "Biblical essentialism . . . encourages a blurring or ignoring of the differences among men" (*PM*, 27), is puzzling. In PK literature as a general rule, it is precisely an anti-essentialist notion of race that is employed to address the agonizing persistence of the father-shaped "void." That this absence is also always linked to class anxiety makes PK's anti-essentialist treatment of whiteness all the more pernicious, and the more difficult for cultural-leftists to assess. Kimmel is more accurate in his recognition that PK is "one of the few [and, one might add, largest] virtually all-white groups in the nation willing to confront white racism" ("PS," 116). Compared straight across with PK's more condemnable pitch for "masculine renewal" ("PS," 116), the group's treatment of gender falls short of the liberal forms of diversity Kimmel typically prefers.

Judith Newton supplies rare consideration of the race and sexuality matrix exhibited by PK. Moreover, she associates this set of relations with "transnational capitalist development and economic restructuring [as evident] in the increasing gap between rich and poor."[24] In one of the more astute lines written about PK, she suspects that "color functions largely as a form of justification for the continuation of white-male headship in a reinvented national community and home" ("RD," 40). Newton finds it "difficult to question the passion and sincerity of the racially mixed speakers, when they talk of seeing racism as a sin and of wanting to end racism in the church by the year 2000" ("RD," 41). But she offers, as an undeveloped sidebar, an account of PK's homophobia that serves only to deflate its pretensions toward a more racially equitable (if also newly nationalized) future. "Any organization," she writes, "that condemns homosexuality as a sin inevitably contributes to a climate in which discrimination and violence against gays can and do easily flourish" ("RD," 43).

Casting the question of homosexual "discrimination" in the too simple terms of categorical equality, Newton, like Kimmel, invokes the unhelpful assumption that bad sexual politics are just the veiled barbs of the insufficiently developed identity politics that puncture PK's otherwise inspiring post-white national bubble. The implication in even the best work on PK, like Newton's and Kimmel's, is that sexuality and color function according to a mirror logic of desire and mere inclusivity. On the contrary, PK's multiracial appeals to the "voided" heterosexual father present a set of motivations and alignments that underwrite the group's attraction to color and remain to be sufficiently limned. If nothing else, the limits of existing discourse on PK are indicative of how the studies of race, sex and gender, and class still tend to be cordoned off from one another in scholarly discourse. Either these are seen as completely separate ontological modalities or, conversely, they are cast as formally consistent systems that call for the same kind of attention and redress. Understanding how the slippery matter of "white confrontations of white racism" (Kimmel) is uniquely dependent on "*violent*" or "discriminatory" (Newton) sexual relations that also happen to be "*loving*" (emphasis mine), is too often reduced to the matter of spoiling what would otherwise be a fully realized world of democratic tolerance. Other lines of thought, traceable to fitful earlier attempts to join psychosexual analysis to race and class, are only beginning to emerge. In line with that kind of work, I offer below a suitable theoretical turn. This, I hope, will make for a more precise and useful analysis of the kinds of post-white ambivalence at work in the "father-shaped void."

A CERTAIN GESTURE OF VIRILITY

> There is a certain gesture of virility, be it one's own or someone else's, that calls for suspicion.
>
> —Theodor Adorno

Of the ample scholarship on evangelical Christianity's rise to prominence in the 1990s, Paul Apostolidis's *Stations of the Cross: Adorno and Christian Right Radio* is without doubt one of the most analytically nimble.[1] Apostolidis is duly "suspicious" of retrograde mobilizations of masculine affect, such as those Adorno censures in the epigraph cited above. However, in contrast to most scholars of the religious right, Apostolidis refuses to dismiss the popular appeal of right-wing evangelical Christianity root-and-branch. This movement, he suggests, does not merely represent a safe collating bin for the detritus of so much white and patriarchal backlash; and neither do conservative religious values contain the prized dormant kernel of liberal pluralism and racial equality. Instead of an argument wholly for or against neo-right Christian culture,

Stations of the Cross focuses on the telling contradictions that remain obscured in less nuanced studies of the country's most popular form of religious reawakening. The provocative thesis of this book, as the subtitle indicates, is indebted almost exclusively to Adorno. It is therefore best approached by a closer examination of the deceptively simple epigraph on "virility" that I use above.

In this epigraph, Adorno offers a predictable set of gender oppositions implied by his key masculine term. But before the "suspicion" about "a certain gesture of virility" finds its proper target, a second, intermediary clause keeps the issue alive and in play. Adorno's crucial phrase is "be it *one's own* or someone else's" (emphasis mine). It is crucial because this phrase iterates a certain critical self-reflexivity that is essential to Adorno's general theoretical objectives. Specifically, the part of the phrase—"be it one's own"—crosscuts the enterprise of objecting to masculine impudence as a matter of surefooted critical detachment. The phrase "be it one's own or someone else's" serves to burden the speaker with the same offending condition he would otherwise like to indict. In a characteristically ironic way, the speaker's final judgment on "virility" disintegrates the moment it becomes concrete enough to cause worry. Here, subjectivity becomes an effect of the antagonisms that might be easier to keep at some objectively descriptive remove. A conception of identity stemming from anything less reflexive would run afoul of Adorno's anti-Enlightenment thesis about what he calls the "insufficiency of the subject." In this Adorno maintains what is now a boilerplate postmodern position: the idea that identity is autonomous from relations of power that are, in fact, immanent to it is full of contradiction. Identity, it follows, is dependent on denying what Adorno calls "the guilt of life." This guilt, of course, is also always connected to life's pleasures, and in this, it is something all of us "unconsciously" share.[2]

Apostolidis constructs his plastic analytical claims upon this richly ambivalent theoretical ground. *Stations of the Cross* is an examination of James Dobson's Focus on the Family (hereafter FF), a group that, as indicated above, provided indispensable start-up financial and labor resources for PK, not to mention its all-important direct mailing list. More particularly, the book is a series of theoretically motivated analyses of FF's Colorado-based radio broadcasts (Colorado hosts the largest concentration of Christian right organizations in the country and is also home to PK). With between 1,200 and 1,600 stations providing Christian listening formats (and over two-thirds for profit), FF's radio shows and like-minded programs are, as Apostolidis shows, a formidable presence in U.S. culture today (*SC,* 22). FF's forty-seven-acre corporate headquarters, where its own prolific contributions to this media originate, is comprised of 1,300 employees and has an operating budget of over $100 million, more than five times that of the Christian Coalition (24). With fifty-two ministries beyond its radio offerings, FF is the largest and most influential of the emergent "family policy groups" yet seen.[3]

FF's decidedly right-wing evocations of the family, consistent at least at that level with PK, are comprised of the expected patriarchal offenses we have already listed. And while Apostolidis is forthright about the group's more explicit political messages regarding the family's heterosexual sanctity, the more provocative feature of his argument is its generous account of FF's capacity to exhibit certain veiled and contradictory forms of working-class agency. FF, he writes, "at once expresses, reproduces, and protests against post-Fordist experiences [of "declining wages," intensified production methods, and more intrusive work demands], according to its very constitution" (SC, 11). More characteristic of the book's theoretical underpinnings, Apostolidis continues, FF "can be seen as retaining a weak but abiding negative utopian ferment. . . . [With its] necessarily unsuccessful attempt to re-articulate a coherent narrative of religious salvation in a society rent by antagonisms, but still supporting the pretense of harmony, [FF] negatively illuminates those antagonisms and thereby preserves the hope of their radical, historical transcendence" (SC, 19).

The terms "negative utopian ferment," and "negative illumin[ation] of . . . antagonism," which motivate the thesis that FF "preserves . . . [a] radical transcendence" of (class) "antagonism," signal Apostolidis's heavy debt to Adorno. It is a debt, more particularly, to the Adorno of Negative Dialectics, the last major work completed by this Frankfurt School philosopher and arch anti-Hegelian. Left deliberately to the side in Apostolidis's book, though, is the earlier and better-known work of Adorno on "the culture industry," which took place under the pressures and stark revelations of World War II.[4] Adorno's pat dismissal of popular culture (most notoriously, of jazz) as the instrumental manipulation of the masses "leads us," according to Apostolidis, "to miss crucial, potentially radical aspects of mass cultural phenomena" (SC, 46). In addition, Adorno's seldom-read post–World War II work on the "authoritarian personality" is dismissed by Apostolidis for the same reason. It fails to allow for the "negative utopian capabilities" that he wants to recover in FF, which is a characteristic feature of U.S. Cultural Studies at large. As I will discuss further in a moment, the turn away from Adorno's psychoanalytic work on fascism is an infelicitous elision. I will detail below exactly why this work is important for coming to terms with the religious right. For now it is important to unpack the tenets of Adorno's interest in the negation of identity as transgressive political work, since this is what motivates Apostolidis's main thesis. From there we can reintroduce Adorno's work on fascism and show how this compensates for Apostolidis's inattention to sexuality as the crucial missing link between color and class.

A fitting approach to Adorno's theory of negative ontology is to recall a certain version of Hegel, particularly the version that attends to the matter of subject = object "adequation" that I outlined vis-à-vis Althusser in Part One of this book. To review, recall that Hegel describes the emergence of modern bourgeois society as a particular (and more or less peaceable) arrangement between identity and difference. This arrangement sought to achieve an intersubjective transcendence of individual particularity, which was, in turn, collectively lived out as "the ethical substance of the state."[5] To reduce this formulation still further, one could simply say that the positive value of subjectivity according to Hegel is incomplete without an encounter with its opposite, a negation. We should of course also recall the productive role of intimacy in Hegel. It was the modern family that made the individual ready for inclusion within the state's general will. While the emergence of the modern bourgeois family allows for Hegel the hypothetical transcendence of negation, the family's dynamic inner workings are left oddly underdeveloped in Apostolidis's account of FF. Had Adorno's cursory psychoanalytic work on the authoritarian personality been given more serious attention, I am suggesting, this might not have been the case. That omission aside for just a moment, it is essential to again restate Hegel's formative claim: in the presence of others—call this the potential for subjective negation—identity is provided with an intersubjective point of transcendent self-reflection. Charles Taylor, recall again, called this a politics of recognition. And he meant it in the Hegelian sense of moving the subject beyond a state of abhorrent or asocial particularity, and into a properly individuated realm commensurate with the state's general will.

Hegel's dream of full subjective integration is renounced by Adorno in characteristically Marxian terms as an "apology for the *status quo*."[6] For Adorno, the ideals of intersubjectivity under the conditions of wage labor portend a slick denial of the class conflict at work in the political unconscious. Accordingly, individuals remain strikingly particular, indeed radically singular, and do not, in fact, cohere in some macro-subjective ethical realm of civil society. Regarding the 2000 census, I called this failure to cohere the advent of a dissensual *socius*. And it is important to Adorno in a similar way, because the pretenses to coherence and wholeness as they exist under capitalism only too obviously fail to produce real (i.e., material) forms of equality and universality. In his book of aphorisms, *Minima Moralia,* Adorno contends that the ironic and disconnected quality of his chosen rhetorical form was itself a way to insist "in opposition to Hegel, on negativity."[7] Indeed, the best-known of the aphorisms in that book is the assertion—inverting Hegel's famous dictum from *The Philosophy of Right*— that "the whole is false" (*MM,* 50). (For Hegel, of course, conversely, "The whole is true.") The connection in Adorno between negation and particularity is vitally important, as much for understanding his profound renunciation of Enlightenment intersubjectivity as for grasping the successes and shortcomings of Apostolidis's assessment of FF. It might be said, according to Adorno, that particularity is the critical effect of motivated subjective negation. And it might be offered, by extension, that negation is itself never wholly describable by critics, because they are negated by the *socius* they seek to contest. Here Adorno's phrase "be it one's own" in the epigraph with which we began gains full reflexivity. The cultural critic who is situated within culture repeats the dynamic of negated subjectivity, and cannot presume anything that transcends self-alienation as the effect of his or her work. Identity is for Adorno predicated on the management of political misfires, which occur between individuals as they go through life denying their own collective better interests. This I called before a politics of *mis*recognition. And it finds a cultural analogue in the critic's necessary failure at making objects of study universally known. The term "failure" (as in negation) is thus not only a key word for understanding Apostolidis's account of FF, it is also related to his savvy reluctance to dismiss the group as only so much right-wing noise beneath him. The citizen-subject is produced for Adorno through a hypocritical denial of the (class) conflicts cordoned off from its specious sense of oneness with the world. So, too, the cultural critic must fail at producing the general truths about power relations that criticism cannot fully get beyond.

By drawing on Adorno's theory of critical failure, then, Apostolidis seeks "negative utopian ferment" within mass culture. Moreover, he does not presume that his own book stands outside that ambivalent mass cultural mix. This, too, is utterly in line with Adorno. For him the production of culture under capitalism cannot presume to harmoniously "transcend reality." Rather, culture exists "in the necessary failure of the passionate striving toward the identity" (quoted in *SC,* 36). The work of the theorist of mass culture, then, is equal to that of the alienated cultural object. Criticism "deciphers the gaps in the general idea of society as [falsely] reconciled community" (*SC,* 36). Apostolidis puts his own task another way. He intends "to analyze the object's structural form in terms of the relationship between the *general idea,* which the object is meant to express, and the *particular elements* (or 'moments' or materials), which have been combined so as to give that idea concrete expression" (*SC,* 36; emphasis in the original). That the particular cannot be reconciled to the general is here a condition described in post-formalist cultural terms; but this is also part and parcel of Adorno's insistence, *contra* Hegel, on subjective negation in the sociopolitical realm. For Adorno the general interest (an ideal of wholeness) exists in the contradictory pronunciation of its absence. And this absence is outlined by the "irreconcilability of the object's moments, . . . in the logic of the object's aporias, the insolubility located in the task [of cultural analysis] itself" (quoted in Apostolidis, 36). Materialist cultural critics thus make aporias politically discernable under conditions where the culture/politics distinction no longer exists. To cite Apostolidis once more, then: "The politics of FF are . . . very much a matter of silences, of aporias, of spaces between contradictory narrative strands that gesture mutely toward the chasms that mark the growing divisions between the secure and the exploited in America today" (SC, 30).

Is there anything significant that is missing here? Or to keep Adorno's abstract critical idiom in play a moment longer, is there something missing in the insistence that the cultural critic should seek to bring significance precisely to "what is missing" as the absent basis for political utopia? In my overly schematic review of Hegel, I remarked above and then set aside the notion that the conjugal patriarchal family was the historical precursor to the transcendence of negation that Adorno refuses to grant. I remarked that Apostolidis ought to have attended better to Adorno's oft-dismissed work on the authoritarian personality. Had he considered that work, he would likely have been more precise about the utopian "aporatic function" as he casts it regarding FF. On one hand, this notion initiates a provocative reevaluation of mass culture and the critic within it. (How the relation between mass culture and generative absence plays out in U.S. Cultural Studies is a topic I develop in Part Three of this book.) On the other hand, Apostolidis might have been more specific about the function of aporias as pop cultural transgression, as such transgression may exist case by case. The significant element that goes missing in Apostolidis's appeal to negation is sexuality, PK's father-shaped "void." For PK, the class- and race-inflected status of absence always contains a highly libidinized charge. The so-called "gap," as in the theme of the 1997 Washington, D.C., march—"Stand in the Gap"—happens to signal a specifically masculinized way of abridging absence by post-white (and, for that matter, post-black) appeals to racial pluralism. Thus, we need to fine-tune Apostolidis's formidable assessment of FF by considering sexuality more fully. This is by no means to diminish the group's performance of "negative utopian ferment." But by comparing how negation works in PK, I do want to insist on the primary relevance of desire to class and race matters as they play out on the religious right. In his account of FF as sublimated class struggle, I would argue that Apostolidis too hastily dismisses the sexual avenue of analysis. "Evangelical conservative narrativizations of post-Fordist experiences . . . [reveal] the disjunctures between communitarian ideology and exclusionary practices . . . between the new 'antiracist and feminist' ideologies and the deepening disempowerment of minorities and women," he concludes (SC, 213). The tendency here is symptomatic of a more general division between materialist and psychoanalytical approaches to subjectivity. One elides

A CERTAIN GESTURE OF VIRILITY

sexuality, while the other, too often, misses race or class. In the worthy name of class struggle, Apostolidis appears to collapse the offenses of racism into the *differently* tangled problem of heterosexuality, a problem identified most consistently by the "feminist ideologies" he leaves to others to explore. To apply Apostolidis's account of FF to its ideological cousin, PK, would mean having to come up with a theoretical schema that accounts for a different set of negative relations than the two-dimensional account he presents. This theoretical schema would have to account for a class-based "negative utopian" allusion to the form of "communitarian ideology" Apostolidis points out in FF. But the next level of analysis, at least regarding PK, would be to show how a specifically racialized form of self-negation produces the false positive heterosexual reveries that Apostolidis overlooks. Better attention to Adorno's encounter with Freud would have prevented this oversight. And it is to that work that, however briefly, we now turn.

Adorno's psychoanalytic work on the authoritarian personality can be introduced at this point in the interest of providing a more precise analysis of PK's configuration of post-white, heterosexual masculinity. "Authoritarianism and the Family Today," written with his lifelong friend and collaborator Max Horkheimer, is characteristic of Adorno's interest from the late 1930s through the 1950s in the psychodynamics of fascism.[8] Adorno begins his analysis, once again, with Hegel's premise that the bourgeois family prefigures the subject and the modern state. But Adorno, borrowing from psychoanalysis *contra* German idealism, sees in the family "a profound antagonism from the very beginning" ("AF," 359). This antagonism exists in the child's fragile relation to authority, that is, "the power of the father" ("AF," 361). Drawing from Freud's castration complex, Adorno maintains, in classical Freudian terms, that a healthy negotiation with the power of the father means that "a considerable amount of aggressiveness must be developed in the child against the authority which prevents him from having his first, but nonetheless his most important satisfactions. . . . By means of identification he takes the unattackable authority into himself. The authority now turns into his super-ego."[9]

Thus, masculine heterosexual satisfaction is properly developed, or not, under the threat of castration. And this threat was evidently muddled under the historical conditions that led to German fascism. From there, the correct objectification of the father, first as rival, then as heterosexual comrade, fails to occur. The caution in this Freudian scheme is that improperly canalized forms of masculine aggression and submission will find their way to the surface in the form of overt racist violence. Anthony Easthope provides a tidy summation of the "castration complex" as that which "occupies the gap *between* the two sexes, as the negative in which masculine is not feminine and feminine is not masculine."[10]

A CERTAIN GESTURE OF VIRILITY

In a way directly pertinent to Adorno's typology of fascism as "sadomasochistically" structured, Easthope continues, "the masculine myth aims to reconstruct castration on its own ground; it tries to read sexual difference as the difference from him" (*WM,* 195). The failure to read sexual difference in this way is for Adorno the psychological crux of the authoritarian personality: early rebellion against the father is repressed and retained in an unconscious level, coming to the fore only in a displaced form as "authoritarian aggressiveness" ("AF," 369). For Adorno, "the socially conditioned weakness of the father . . . prevents the child's real identification with him. . . . The growing child looks for a stronger, more powerful father . . . as it is furnished by fascist imagery" ("AF," 365). In this failure to identify with—*and* find the right distance from—the father, the child develops an inverted masculine libido, which he lives out in its likely political form: a masochistic craving for self-effacement that actually conceals racist aggression. This masochistic craving is thus transferred outward, and is turned into the opposite extreme as a sadistic passion for the persecution of (racialized) others. In Adorno's case, this meant the persecution of non-Aryans, Jews.[11]

Adorno's work on the psychodynamics of fascism reveals an unlikely heteronormative bias, however, as contemporary psychoanalytic theorists well know. There is, he writes, "a deep rooted affinity between homosexuality, authoritarianism, and the present decay of the family" ("AF," 370). And it is this homosexually inspired "decay" that locates the origins of the totalitarian mind. To be obeyed and give pleasure to the boss, in extreme and at once, is part and parcel of the authoritarian desire to commingle dependence and submission.[12] But for Adorno, this condition also "impli[ies] . . . anality, such as sadism, stinginess, . . . [and] compulsiveness."[13] Such biological reductions are unacceptable in a materialist theorist who otherwise works at every turn against static Freudian concepts of the Oedipal unconscious. Adorno's rendition of the father claims to present "a dynamic configuration" of "the rise of an anthropological species" (*AP,* 158). He thus describes his work as the "critical typology" of a "characteristically middle-class phenomenon" (*AP,* 158). In fact, however, Adorno's own apparent homophobia prevents adequate attention to historical detail.

At the prospect of a socially and economically diminished father figure—in PK's parlance, the "father-shaped void"—Adorno finds a homosexual violation of the family that looks a lot like PK's deepest fears. He, too, regards a breach in the heterosexual contract as a social aberration. That Adorno fails to treat heterosexuality in a materialist way should not be left without critique, nor has it been.[14] But what can be retained from Adorno should also be noted. His analysis of the psychodynamics of fascism gives us an account of how the *love and hate* of the ("voided") father are combined in the male psyche, and can be manifest under certain historical conditions at various extremes. The essential

Freudian insight here is this: an attraction to and a repulsion of other races are co-present and historically unstable within white masculinity. For Adorno, submission and aggression are just a click away, and moreover, race is what spins that dial. In Adorno's failure to answer his own materialist obligations to bring the weight of history more fully to bear on male sexuality, he missed the chance to loosen white racism from its heterosexual moorings.[15] That said, it is vital to retain his idea of the psychosexual proximity between love and hate in the fascist personality. Submission and aggression, attraction and repulsion, self-effacement and personal authority commingle within whiteness differently at various moments of its history. It is also important to retain from Adorno the task of explaining how familial feeling is mediated by extreme forms of racial preoccupation. As we shall see, PK's class-anxious white men live out a relation to race that mirrors Adorno's fascistic rejection of difference, but they do so in a wholly inverted form. If the authoritarian personality ineffectively repels castration and falls negatively in love with the objects it repudiates, then the new manifestations of white masculinity exemplified by PK proceed to turn that negation on its head. Remarkably, PK embraces Oedipal failure as race in the father-shaped "void." The group's interest in public outbursts of weeping are symptomatic of that. The still more remarkable aspect of this psychosexual surrender is that PK turns heterosexual loss into a post-white racial win by its appeal to color. The negation of race is not only inverted in PK, but is moved sideways into a sexual register so that color gives white men a second chance at getting castration aright.

My ultimate goal in what remains of the argument presented here in Part Two of the book is that PK's ritual of white-racial submission is, in fact, mirrored by its inversion, the neofascist repulsion of color exhibited by such U.S. hate groups as the National Alliance. On the way toward making that case, let me introduce three additional texts. I want now to consider two of Judith Butler's texts and David Eng's groundbreaking book on Asian masculinity, *Racial Castration*. Of particular value is Butler's treatment of subject differentiation as linked to melancholic self-beratement.[16] Here, she recasts the identity problem along the lines I have described referring to Adorno's theory of ontological negation. Like Adorno, in at least this sense, Butler seeks to retain political value in resolute particularity, reworking Hegel's interest in tidy social syntheses in such a way as to give the canceling out of identity its due democratic potential.[17] She is critical, above all, of subjective experience writ as self-sufficiency, that is, the known side of a properly adequated object choice. Rather, Butler is interested in the way repudiated desires negatively enable certain positive identity achievements, of which heterosexuality is one. "Becoming a man" requires in Butler's terms a double repudiation: a repudiation, in the first instance, of the feminine, which a man cannot be, but which nonetheless defines him in the desire for his opposite; and a repudiation, in the second instance, as the refusal by extension to desire other men (*SD*, 137–39). Thus, homosexuality is objectified by negative ontology, a social order predicated on multivalent forms of psychological repression. By renouncing homosexual attachment, heterosexuality is unconsciously indebted to the object choices it refuses to make—refuses to make, that is, so as to avoid the risk of immanent de-subjectivization. "If a man becomes heterosexual by repudiating the feminine," she asks, "where could that repudiation live except in an identification which his heterosexual career seeks to deny?" (*SD*, 137). By locating repudiation at the core of identity, then, Butler develops the negative ontology thesis several steps beyond Adorno's work on fascism. Indeed, she puts Adorno's understanding of the father in reverse. And by doing so, she links the various historical slippages between aggression and submission to the unattainable desire for maintaining strict heterosexual manhood. For Butler, masculine identity is problematized by that which it denies. More to the point, the persistence of the excluded object reemerges in one of two forms of manly self-beratement: either as gender melancholia, what she calls the "traces of an ungrieved and ungrievable love," or conversely, as rage (*SD*, 132–66).

I want now to think about how Butler's formulation of gender melancholia pertains to PK's white-masculine "love" of color, and eventually beyond that, to show how it applies to neofascism's "rage" against it. However, Butler's analysis of becoming and remaining "a man" must be qualified before we get to that point. Recall, in her notion of double repudiation, the first denial manhood needs (i.e., of the feminine) resides in the melancholic world of the second denial (i.e., for the men that heterosexuals cannot want to have). While this formulation is surely complicated enough, I want to suggest that PK's various combinations of disavowal and attraction are wired slightly differently through the added complication of race. For example, heterosexual identity may indeed live an ambivalent psychic life within the denial of same-sex desire. And this ambivalence is clearly manifest in melancholic same-sex disavowal. But what is sidelined in this formulation is PK's repeal of whiteness as essential to its heterosexual charge. Here I would also differ with David Savran, who argues in *Taking It Like a Man* that, through "masochistic fantasy," the white male subject can "feminize and/or blacken himself fantasmatically."[18] In the case of PK, race and gender do not flatten out neatly as the running together of the "feminized/and or black" would seem to suggest. Rather, this group presents heterosexually libidinized forms of "positive" subjectivization and white-racialized forms of "negative" de-subjectivization unevenly, and at the same time. PK embraces a certain negation of the white race and moves it sideways, toward a sexual realm where color affords white men the opportunity to readdress an ambivalent heterosexual bond. This, recall, is the ever important "gap" PK refers to by appealing to the "voided" father. PK mobilizes race, in other words, so as to keep Adorno's sliding scale of aggression and submission titled in the latter extreme (i.e., toward post-white racial humility). The group's hyperbolically benevolent interest in men of color barely hides the sexual cruelties that are never far behind.

It is useful to think about the Oedipalization of race as exhibited by PK in relation to David Eng's provocative book, *Racial Castration.* Building from the critical traditions that Apostolidis eschews, this book brings together "analyses of masculinity in Asian American literary and cultural productions with psychoanalytic, feminist, queer, postcolonial, and critical race studies."[19] Eng reveals how "racial difference repeatedly operates as a proxy for normative and aberrant sexualities and sexual practices" (*RC,* 6). Drawing in particular from *Totem and Taboo,* he offers an account of "the ways in which Freud's psychoanalytic project manages racial difference" (*RC,* 6). This takes place, he continues, "through a discursive strategy configured as the teleological evolution of normative [hetero]sexual practices and 'pathological' sexual perversions" (6). Eng takes Freud's "proscription on homosexuality in 'On Narcissism' . . . as also coming to signify [the] expunging of racial difference" (12). Here Eng's mobilization of Butler is consistent with what we referred to above as the double repudiation that necessitates becoming and remaining "a man." Both critics outline a properly Oedipalized repudiation of same-sex desire, which secures the boundaries of compulsory heterosexuality while the masculine subject "melancholically" grieves its ambivalent homosexual losses. Moreover, Eng joins Butler in a conflation of whiteness and heterosexuality that is more debatable or, at least, more selectively applicable to PK than it would seem at first glance. Drawing from *Bodies That Matter,* Eng appreciates Butler for "not only emphasiz[ing] the fact that a theory of heterosexual development cannot easily be dissociated from racial regulation, but also [for] suggest[ing] that heterosexuality gains its discursive power through its tacit coupling with hegemonic, unmarked whiteness" (*RC,* 13). The contention that heterosexuality and "unmarked whiteness" cannot be "dissociated" is a welcome and enabling premise. It provides compelling insights into "the costs of heterosexuality and whiteness not just from the Asian American male's point of view, but from that of the putatively normative, straight white male" (*RC,* 138). Indeed, the argument Eng provides regarding Asian American masculinity is unimpeachable based on the premises he provides and the texts he examines. But it is important to point out that white unmarkability is writ here as a heterosexually complicitous mechanism for maintaining its own fictive ontogenetic coherence.[20]

A CERTAIN GESTURE OF VIRILITY

That heterosexuality is always powered by "unmarked whiteness" (or vice versa) is a thoroughly refutable point in the psychic life of PK's white men. The "smooth alignment between heterosexuality and whiteness"—the attempts, in other words, "to secure heterosexuality and whiteness as universal norms in a colonial world order" (*RC,* 152)—simply does not apply to PK's interest in race. One final example of how color fills the group's "father-shaped void" will suffice to make PK's distinctly post-white defenses of racialized heterosexual fatherhood conclusive. The popular PK book *Breaking Down Walls* presents an "intertwined story of pain."[21] This book is coauthored by "two wounded men, one white, one black, unknown to each other [who] lived only a few miles apart in Chicago" (*BD,* 85). In telling the story of how they came to meet and care for one another, both men attempt to come to terms with "the loss of jobs and the breakdown of the family" (*BD,* 23). One author reaches a state of white racial self-consciousness that he insists will indeed mark him, and in a class-related way, as becoming different from white. This coveted "post-white" (his term) racial condition is born from what PK's mixed-race director of education, Rod Cooper, describes as the regenerative powers of having a white man "love" (Cooper's term) his own multiracial difference. Such "racial reconciliation," as we have seen, is a standard feature of PK. But it is made possible directly proportionate to a shared adherence to the rituals of "ordinary" (meaning heterosexual) manhood. This more completely reveals the group's unique figuration of the colorized Oedipal father, and foreshadows PK's proximity to the organized forms of aggression it would otherwise flatly deny.

In *Breaking Down Walls* it is important to emphasize that the multiracial, vaguely class-conscious, masculine "love" held out by PK mentor Rod Cooper in his book, *We Stand Together,* is linked in the end to winning a formerly gay man of color back to heterosexual norms.[22] This linkage is forged by a narrative that chronicles the association between Washington's white coauthor, Glen Kehrin, and "Clyde," an older (and sexually repugnant) black man whom Kehrin eventually takes into his home to become "Grandpa Clyde" to his children. The trouble with Clyde is that he "was active in the homosexual life style for nearly fifty years" (*BD,* 45). The racial boundary crossing that is fundamental to PK is here produced from within an antagonized (but also always essentially empty or "voided") zone of heteromasculine "pain." The platonic interracial "love" celebrated in *Breaking Down Walls,* which is supposed by Kehrin and Washington to be self-evident, is in fact, once again, predicated on fatherhood writ as an absence. "Grandpa Clyde" is no more able to fulfill the sexual preconditions of normative fatherhood demanded from him (he is both "homeless" and "gay") than the white coauthor is able to fulfill the traditional roles of fatherhood given his own pressing economic difficulties. But in this peculiar relation of "voids," Clyde's color is always "lovingly" addressed. The white coauthor's melancholic appeal to colorized fatherhood presents itself as a doubly unutterable bond. This unutterable bond exists, first, in a prefigured form by the "wounded" sense of fatherhood that Kehrin hopes Washington will share; but its unutterableness reaches full intensity in the form of a second, now *racialized* heterosexual investment in "gaps." Thus the appeal of one already missing father (Kehrin) is compounded by his reverse adoption of a second absent dad, the literally "homeless" (propertyless and gay) black "Grandpa Clyde." Thus three different conditions, schematically, of race, sex, and class, are brought into a systematic arrangement in the delicate man-to-man relations described here. But it is important to point out, *contra* Butler and Eng, that each condition is not of equal psychological value. Indeed, the multivalent term "homelessness" in *Breaking Down Walls* functions to pawn off Kehrin's white anxieties regarding property disenfranchisement as a problem of the gay and poor. However—and this point is crucial—this pawning off of a property issue is mediated not by leaving whiteness "unmarked," as in Eng's account, but by having a white man "love" another man's different race (e.g., Washington's blackness). Whiteness is discarded in this story so as to shore up a heterosexual crisis of fatherhood that originates equally out of the relations of class. This arrangement signals PK's unique willingness precisely to mark whiteness as racially divided. By adopting a "voided" (because "homeless") black father, Kehrin finds a way to have heterosexual security and surrender his whiteness at once. Thus, in the opposite way suggested by Eng, class-related forms of masculine crisis are redressed by PK's appeal to a universal "mestizo" condition that appeals to a heterosexual norm. Indeed, Kehrin assures us at strategic points in the narrative that "Satan's primary tool is to make us . . . comfortable with homogeneity." What we need to do instead, he suggests, with PK's typical interest in redemptive white-racial self-dissolution, is "be willing to open [our] closet[s] to reveal the hardships and failures of our lives" (*BD,* 186). Kehrin has done so through the reverse biracial adoption of an impoverished, black, gay man. And "Grandpa Clyde" must now fulfill the patriarchal duties his new title indicates, though without any guarantee. What is more tragic, he must do so twice over: once for Kehrin, his post-white reverse-adopted child; and a second time, for the grandchildren, who have been betrayed by their own absent father, as Kehrin laments.

According to the logic outlined in *Breaking Down Walls,* it would be wholly inaccurate to say, as one might in drawing from Butler's reworking of subjective negation, that "unmarked whiteness" keeps heterosexuality safe as the psychic racial twin of masculine desire. The negative ontology at work in PK is more precisely a multidimensional set of negative/positive combinations that organize race and sexual difference unequally, if at the same time. These nonmutual differences are sequenced and rearranged uniquely by the men of PK. The group addresses masculinity according to an Oedipal logic that complicates the binaristic quality that the word "negative" implies. Here "closets" (Kehrin's word) are numerous, and have only partially overlapping doors. Where economics is linked to anguish, in Clyde's case literally evacuating him from his "home," color reenters the psychological scene of diminished white patriarchy and occupies what is now a racialized (grand)father-shaped "void." The pain PK is so renowned for expressing is experienced by wounded middle-class white fathers who imagine themselves on the brink of social extinction. But this wound is lived, as *Breaking Down Walls* suggests, through the unlikely solicitation of poor and gay "Grand Fathers" of color, unlikely men who represent an even more desperate history of unavailable anguish, a "grander" "void," than white, heterosexual fatherhood can allow. In PK, the love for racial boundary crossing provides a ruse for more effectively upholding the strained task of heterosexual self-preservation. Male sexuality is patrolled and made normative by PK through an Oedipally motivated homosexual repudiation, to be sure. This occurs, though, in a different fashion than is delineated in Butler's hypothesis concerning sexual melancholy. And it is different from the Asian/white American crossroads mapped by Eng. For PK, homosexual repudiation is made possible through certain forms of white-racial promiscuity. This, I would gather, is why certain men in PK are able to declare themselves "post-white" while, in a disarmingly unironic manner, likening themselves to "the brides of Jesus" and to "cosmic Cinderellas . . . rescued by our Prince."[23]

The traces of heteromasculine ambivalence are felt in the case of PK through the denial of homosexual love, as contemporary queer theory would have it. Yet this ambivalence is differently troubling when white masculinity supercharges its sexual repudiations through the ideological template of white-racial submission. The second part of Butler's general hypothesis, recall, is that the jumbled circuitry of heterosexual self-beratement can produce as much repudiation as love. If this is so, then we ought to be able to find an example of PK's already twisted race/sex logic at the opposite extreme of so much white affection for racial difference. Such an example of "wounded" heterosexual manhood would not be easily repaired by benevolent "post-white" forays into racial promiscuity. Rather, it would manifest itself as suicidal glory, the proposed annihilation, once again through an essentially empty identification with the father, of all races other than white. Such a phenomenon, close enough at hand, brings us to a confrontation with the more violent end of Adorno's typology of Oedipal aggression and submission. Here we turn to U.S. neofascism, the ontogenetic flip side of PK's loving encounters with race.

THE EROS OF WARFARE

The monumentalism of fascism would seem to be a safety mechanism against the multiplicity of the living.

—Klaus Theweleit

Particularity above the general. Partial truths and half-lies over universal understanding. Objects proximate to identity. Subjects negated by their never fully adequated opposites. The strained desire for, and repudiation of, difference in the "father-shaped void." And now, "fascism . . . against the multiplicity of living." These concepts may read like a grocery list of postmodern theoretical standards. But perhaps we might attach to such a response that, like whiteness, the problem of ordinariness itself has taken on a new and puzzling significance. For it is an acknowledged effect of the postmodern condition, as worn-out as that phrase has become, to signify something different in the ordinary, while the ordinary is imagined to be gone. How else to explain today's interest in the critical study of whiteness, heterosexual masculinity, and the family—historical phenomena that were once presumed (by so many) as too banal to command much attention? Among other, more important things, a question like this ought to give the dry bones of postmodern theoretical discourse some much-needed sinews and flesh. What kind of beast this body might become, let alone where it might turn out to take us, is a matter one cannot pretend to know in advance. And yet certain patterns, certain possibilities and potentials emerge (while others continue to hide) around the presumed disintegration of whiteness.

We began Part Two of this book with an examination of the so-called decline of the nuclear family. The turn from there was to PK, its class-related love of color, and its disarming intent to break the seal of Fanon's black/white colonial difference. At issue in the analysis of PK so described was a reevaluation of the family as the mediator of white universality, designed, as Fanon would have had it, to enforce the agenda of a certain binaristic system. However, PK's evocation of the father operates in a different way, I have suggested, by deliberately crossing racial boundaries and making color occupy the patriarchal "void." David Eng's notion of racial castration helped, as did Butler's reworking of subjective negation, to expel Adorno's latent homophobia and develop his materialist and psychoanalytically inflected account of the white-racial unconscious. From there, I argued that the sexual logic behind race as it operates in PK is distinct from Eng's and Butler's theses. Whiteness and heterosexuality do not constitute the twin pillars of psychic universalism. In a way that contrasted with Eng's description of whiteness as related to Asian American masculinity, white-racial dissolution placates class anxieties in heterosexually determinate ways. Color for PK does not threaten masculinity as such. Color animates its emptiness and enables the melancholic recoveries of heterosexual manhood that PK has placed in our midst. This crucial distinction intact, the pressing importance of *Racial Castration* is that the book addresses race, sexuality, and class together and creates the premise for more specific analyses of the relational and entirely changeable psychodynamics of material inequality and racial oppression. The short distance between love and hate, the heterosexually proper arrangement between submission and authority, proximity and distance, identification and repulsion, which (white) men are conditioned to affirm, takes on a new and distinctive significance when color is the father.

The unique configuration of difference and desire signaled by that last phrase must be kept in mind as we transition from PK to U.S. neofascism. I do not wish to examine these two phenomena as if they constituted two separate and unrelated systems. In turning to *The Turner Diaries* and its less well-known sequel, *Hunter,* my intention is not just to anatomize the psychic state that the angriest of today's angry white men may mobilize on behalf of a victorious race war. Fascism is evoked, as Theweleit puts it, to recuperate "the multiplicity of living." In this sense, my analysis of the National Alliance attempts to further tease out the "ambivalent emotions," tortured psychologies, and contradictory affections through which the presumed disintegration of white masculinity is lived. Theweleit describes this psychological state as a "vacillat[ion] between interest and cool indifference, aggressiveness and veneration . . . alienation and desire" (*MF,* 24). For him, the "eros of warfare" finds its concrete historical example in the proto-fascist hatred of color exhibited by his German Freikorps. The "multiplicity" that threatens this group, as he puts the matter more succinctly, is "the danger of being-alive itself" (*MF,* 218). One of the tasks that follows is to outline what remains of this legacy today, how racial hatred, specifically given the chimerical presence of a post-white national future, is allied with a certain flustered militancy that I want ultimately to argue is close to PK love. This proximity to PK, and especially to the way this group focuses on father and family, intimates a further-reaching problem for white masculinity than just a comparison between the psychodynamics of 1920s German Freikorps and U.S. neofascism today. Within the shades of difference between PK and U.S. neofascism, my focus remains on what Coach McCartney calls "white masculine difference." I want to suggest, within the uncharted territory of this difference, that aggression and submission are conjoined. To merely draw parallels between historical and contemporary organizations of fascism would be to lighten Adorno's materialist burden of historical specificity, and would limit my analysis to condemning transparently racist and sexist behaviors to an all-encompassing ashcan. That condemnation should be assumed all along. But more difficult work remains. We can best limn the tangled associations between heterosexual "eros" and race "warfare" by asking how the combinations of love and hate cooperate in what have been two differently captivating attempts by white men to think beyond being in the racial majority. PK and U.S. neofascism hold a certain veiled partnership that narrows the psychological distance (never really there) between a torqued-up neoliberal desire to incorporate color into our panoply of national inclusion and the rankest forms of racist violence and aggression yet seen in the homeland. Both PK and U.S. neofascism operate on the brink of what they imagine are the final throes of whiteness. To take that matter seriously is to grapple with a post-white cultural imaginary, which others may mobilize differently one day. For now, the task is to show how these two groups taken together give us a larger, if still foggy, lens through which to glimpse the way white and heterosexual men are psychically invested in race.

As Adorno is Apostolidis's theoretical precursor, and as Butler is Eng's, Deleuze and Guattari's *Anti-Oedipus* provides the critical springboard for Theweleit's analysis of fascism. Of the more applicable contributions this book makes to linking PK and U.S. neofascism is the rejection, common to Foucault, of Freud's repressive hypothesis. For decades theoretical debate between Marxists, psychoanalytic critics, post-structuralists, and queer theorists has circled around this issue. Without detouring too far from the reading of U.S. neofascism that follows, I need to sparingly outline the stakes of that debate. In what has become a canonical postmodern formulation, Deleuze and Guattari set out to revise the idea that desire is a unidirectional programmatic effect of psychological repression. This notion was the one formerly mapped by Freud. They wish to resist an account of the unconscious as given by the traditional Oedipal model on the grounds that it forbids cultural and historical variation. The bionormative tendencies within Freud, such as those David Eng aptly critiques, we have also seen in the homophobic lesser moments of Adorno's authoritarian personality thesis. Male heterosexuality, for example, was once thought a fixed and natural manifestation of working through a course of repression that followed a common archetypal Oedipal complex. By behaving according to the strict requirements of identifying against, and finally with, the father, every man everywhere might achieve the normal forms of heterosexual desire. The rigidity of this system is seen by Deleuze and Guattari as a form of "fascism . . . against the multiplicity of the living." The socially normative process, for example, of Hegelian intersubjectivity becomes, in the Oedipal case they want to demolish, psychologically analogous to the objectification of sexual difference. As Deleuze and Guattari have it, identity formation may remain a linear libidinal transaction, but the line between male child and father is pluralized and leads in every direction.

Again, we have gone at least part way down this road with Adorno. What Deleuze and Guattari want from multiplicity is the same incalculable abundance of object identification that Adorno signals as cultural unreadability. Because of the many ways objects can be named (and indeed, can name back), and because of subjective partiality, the presumption to speak about power relations without being within them is the grand illusion of all social science. Thus, the nagging post-Marxist analogue to the anti-Oedipal critique of repression works in the same way. It critically disrupts the presumed alignment between the relations of production, or economic "base," and the ideological or "superstructural" realm of so-called repressed subjectivity. For Deleuze and Guattari, there can be no representation of the psyche where psychoanalysis is not also confounded by affective excess. Likewise, there can be no explanation of culture as the mere reflection of capitalist modes of production without also producing something else that may contradict your task. The "something else" (termed "whatever") is for Deleuze and Guattari the nongeneralizable singularity at work in Adorno's analysis, and this is what constitutes the aleatory object relations in *Anti-Oedipus*. Deleuze and Guattari define multiplicity in a characteristically ambivalent way in the book's one key term: "desiring-production."[1] "Desiring-production" is the "more or less hodge-podge" reassembly of an object as "*bricolage*": "the pure this-ness of an object produced [and] carried off into a new act of producing" (*AO*, 7). Thus identity cannot be represented by the universal archetypes that entrap us within the worn-out terms of repression. Identity is not a product for Deleuze and Guattari, but "a *producing*/product" (*AD*, 97; emphasis mine). It is, therefore, subject to no totalizing force, while it may resist no force totally. In the sense Adorno would have had it, identity is "an affirmation that is irreducible to any sort of unity" (*AD*, 42). Objects can be identified and/or repudiated any which way in this elaborate and optimistic scheme. Subjectivity can be wrestled from the norm by the libidization of everything; and in this dizzying anti-Oedipal arrangement, who knows who might be your father?

It is easy to get carried away by the freedom promised here. And no doubt one effect of this influential text has been to encourage a kind of anything-goes theoretical rush to trangressive individuality. In the book's preface, Foucault calls *Anti-Oedipus* an "'art,' in the sense that is conveyed by the term 'erotic art'" (*AD*, xii). The comment is meant sympathetically, but also perhaps as a warning: do not expect political assistance by the reading of this text. For that matter, do not expect freedom, Foucault seems to warn. When such expectations occur, as they have, whatever potential the book might have offered as "a strategic adversary of fascism" is lost (xiii). The book's critics proclaim that *Anti-Oedipus* presents us with no oppositional tools for responding to capitalist (or racist, sexist) hegemony. And this is an unimpeachable objection, even if it misses the book's rather different goals. If something provocative might be gleaned from *Anti-Oedipus*, it is the book's attempt to reformulate the agency of multitudes along antifascistic lines. From this angle, to say that its "desiring-production" thesis loses oppositional force is rather a less enabling critique than to say that it too easily infuses the proliferation of difference with radical democratic outcomes. In this schema, desire can infuse all objects with equal political value. This is because "desiring-production" presumes that everything is always available to the "*bricoleur*" inside us all (or where our insides used to be).

My wanting to give some historical specificity to the anti-Oedipal urge returns us to the central issue of fascism as it relates to "the multiplicity of living." According to Foucault, the anti-Oedipal displacement of normative individuality with a multitude of difference "crush[es] the petty varieties of [fascism] that constitute the tyrannical bitterness of our everyday life" (Foucault, xiv). But this formulation is insufficient to the task of coming to terms with either PK or U.S. neofascism. It is insufficient for the same reason Foucauldian notions of

THE EROS OF WARFARE

discipline do not fully account for the multiracial debates of the 2000 U.S. census. (Recall, it was precisely the proliferation of identity's difference that served to undo civil rights.) This is not to dismiss the productive capacities of radically individual object choices, as insisted upon by Deleuze and Guattari. But to recall Rey Chow in another context, "the most important sentiment involved in fascism is not a negative [read repressive] but a positive [read productive] one: rather than hatefulness and destructiveness, fascism is about love and idealism."[2] This statement is consistent with certain aspects of *Anti-Oedipus*. And yet "multiplicity" is at work today in ways that do not altogether productively square off against the disciplined body that Foucault critiques in pointing out the fascism of ordinary life. Reparations and productivity work at the same time and in various combinations in what we have seen of white masculinity so far. And while this dynamic is subject to change, it does not appear to do so randomly or without measurable effect. The multitude has not yet productively antagonized the Oedipal psyche toward any sustainable end. It has not made clear the relational freedoms that Deleuze and Guattari claim to offer. (Granted, the performance of their own critical failure could itself be seen as the stylistic *coup de théâtre* of postmodern theoretical expression.) In the context of white masculinity as it currently *appears to disappear*, the presence of anti-Oedipal multitudes is *illusive* at best, even if they are also, as one can still hope, *allusive* toward more democratically suitable forms of de-individuation.[3] An appropriate description of the agency of multitudes must therefore account, one instance at a time, for how the liberation of "eros" celebrated by Deleuze and Guattari too easily congeals into the concrete bunkers that keep racialized and gendered identities at work against themselves—even, and especially, through what look on the surface like radical forms of racial change. We have encountered one of the ways this sleight of hand is at work in PK's twisted logic of patriarchal post-whiteness. We turn now to what I want to argue is this group's unlikely mirror image, the neofascist group from West Virginia, the National Alliance. Together these organizations live out a certain "eros of warfare" that narrows the distance between the love and hate of color. An account of this narrowing may serve to specify how emergent popular concerns about race in the United States lean ambivalently (as multitudes necessarily do) toward a future without whiteness. If one may say, in the Deleuzian vein, that the multitudes have whispered the announcement of this future, it must also be said that they have so far been unable to claim it.

It would be misleading to suggest that outwardly racialized neofascism is ubiquitous in 2003. By contrast to the mid-1920s, when Theweleit's Freikorps emerged and the Ku Klux Klan claimed 5 million members, it is reported that in 1990 less than 1 percent of U.S. citizens belonged to white supremacist orga-

THE EROS OF WARFARE

nizations.[4] Since the mid-1990s, however, when PK rallies reached their apogee of more than 1.1 million participants in a single year, organized hate has also been on the rise. The number of neofascist groups has nearly doubled in the United States since 1990, from 362 to more than 600 in 48 states.[5] And the number of neofascist groups in the United States jumped by almost 12 percent in 2001.[6] Their financial coffers are minuscule compared to the money that flows unobstructed to those agencies whose more lucrative business it is to ferret hate groups out. But that disparity may change in the future.[7] Neofascist groups once limited themselves to crime for financing their mission, robbing armored cars, banks, and porno stores. Robert Matthews, for example, modeled his fund-raising skills for the Order on *The Turner Diaries* (made famous a second time by Timothy McVeigh), and netted more than $4 million from various heists in 1984. This money found its way to hate groups in seven states. Some of it went to *The Turner Diaries* author, former physics professor—and the Anti-Defamation League's "most important Nazi"—the late Dr. William Pierce.[8] Rather than armed robbery, the current trend in U.S. neofascism is to cultivate legal avenues of support. In 1999, for example, Pierce received $25,000 from a racist millionaire named Richard J. Cotter to fund the National Alliance. Cotter dispersed nearly three-quarters of a million dollars to similar groups nationwide. A more reliable source of money for the National Alliance (hereafter NA) is Resistance Records, a skinhead recording and distribution company that Pierce acquired in 1998. Just a year before that, the company sold 50,000 racist CDs and grossed $250,000. It reportedly generated $1 million in annual revenue in 2001.[9] And a new headquarters for Resistance Records, replete with a video production unit, a performance space that can hold an audience of four hundred, and office space for twelve staff, was completed in 2003. In Europe, where the skinhead recording industry takes in $3.4 million a year, there are 1,500 members of NA. That number is approximately the same tally of NA members in the United States, where there are fifty-one chapters of the group in twenty-five states (though NA claims members in all fifty states).[10] As NA goes pan-European, an international white "nationalism" has become its millennial objective.[11]

"America becomes darker—racially darker—every year," Pierce proclaims in one of his characteristically hateful missives, "and that is the direct result of our government's immigration policy. . . . We white people, we descendants of the European immigrants who built America, will be a minority in our own country. . . ." The impending condition of a post-white "America," he writes, "will spread spiritual poison among our people, so that our spirits become corrupted and our minds become confused." And with "a recession next year [i.e., in 2001–02]," Pierce goes on, "the rise in membership continues [and] should . . .

rise even more rapidly."[12] I introduced this passage by remarking that it was a characteristically hateful missive, and it is. But the hate that this statement reveals shows an uncanny closeness to what we have examined in its inverse, the Christ-like "mestizo" embrace of multiplicity that inspires PK's love of racial difference. The essential point I want to make by joining the two groups is this: the ideological cornerstone for both PK and NA is the unmaking of an American racial majority, a multiracial nation to come. Both groups associate that event with downward class mobility, and both address the diminished condition of whiteness as a "spiritual" (NA's word) problem, one that is predicated on a fevered affective investment in race. The link I want to make between these two groups lies where PK and NA seem to be most divergent in their attitudes about whiteness. As mentioned, both groups encounter the unmaking of whiteness in a "spiritual" way that is entertained by highly masculinized affective extremes. In the passage just quoted from Pierce, "spirit" coordinates uncontrollable forms of defense and aggression, a call to racial warfare that cannot be restrained ("our minds became confused"; but "our membership . . . should rise"). For PK at the opposite extreme, white racial submission is in order. PK beckons a Christ-like surrender to the "mestizo" condition, which its men are no less unable to control (McCartney "on his knees" to blackness; white men "loving" Cooper's multiracial condition, the tears, the hugging, the shouting, and so on). Love and hate fill the same affective function for the men of PK and NA, as together they signal white masculinity's libidinal investment in race. By placing both groups side by side, one sees how affective extremes can commingle, switch back, and create new solidarities of desire from what is also repulsion and fear. As we shall see below, in Pierce's two neofascist novels, color is also addressed to fill the "father-shaped void" exactly as PK would have it. The shadow of difference between these two groups, which is to say their "spiritual" commonality, may thus be addressed as a racialized Oedipal struggle. Three interests converge in PK and NA: the class anxiety of white men, an imagined "postwhite" national future, and the love and hate of color. To further detail this complex psychic arrangement, I will discuss examples from Pierce's two novels.

The Turner Diaries (hereafter *TD*) lay dormant when it was first published in 1978 under the pseudonym Andrew Macdonald.[13] Since Pierce claimed authorship of the book in 1995 and tied it to NA's white minority rhetoric, more than 300,000 copies have been sold though the NA Web site alone. In 1996 New York's Barricade Books purchased the publishing rights to *TD* and planned a first printing of 60,000 trade paperback copies.[14] As the title indicates, *TD* is composed of the personal diaries of Los Angelean Earl Turner, who becomes a "rank-and-file" member of the Organization during the time California becomes a white-minority state. This takes place in the early 1990s, the decade that marks the last years of the "Old Era" of white marginalization in the United States at large. Not only does the "Old Era" refer to a period of multiracial "cosmopolitan chaos," it also refers to a time when the federal government entices whites to intermarry by providing low-interest loans. In the late "1990s OE," black members of the Human Relations board are deputized to search for and confiscate guns, and the Supreme Court rules rape laws unconstitutional because they imply a difference between the sexes that presumes superior masculine strength. In addition to the infamous ammonium nitrate attack on the FBI (enter Timothy McVeigh), Turner responds to these conditions through a long and consistent series of violent racist and sexist acts. Turner murders numerous Jewish merchants and bankers, launches a mortar assault on Capitol Hill, grenades the *Washington Post,* and wages constant guerrilla warfare on pornographic bookstores, especially gay social hangouts. In the ultimate act of commitment to the cause of the race war, Turner commits suicide while unleashing a hand-carried nuclear bomb on the Pentagon. This brings him immortality in the mind of the victorious Organization in the "New Era," as evidenced by the publication of the *Diaries* themselves.

Spun into Turner's overtly racist motivations for joining the Organization, and following its mandates, is a careful attention to class. Moreover, Turner's class concerns are extended to sexuality in ways that mimic the more benevolent psychodynamics of white masculinity that we have seen in PK.[15] Turner is lonely and "depressed" (*TD,* 8)—as he often reminds us—"very, very depressed" (53). This depression is linked in his own mind to class anxiety that mounts without resolution. Turner suffers throughout the novel from the effects of "crime" and "political corruption" (106), "continuing inflation, . . . the gradually declining standard of living" (6), "high unemployment" (33), and "the brainwash[ing] of the proletariat" (101), all of which he believes are effects of "unrestricted capitalism" (106). Turner craves a "band[ing] together . . . of working-class whites" (152), a "new solidarity among workers" who will eventually, like him, form "a kinship of unselfish cooperation to complete a common task" (171). But the "demographic war" he unleashes in order to initiate this fleeting desire for "commonality" is for Turner always also connected to the heterosexual tasks of marriage and fatherhood. This task is what Turner longs for, but never lives to complete. He was, the preface tells us, "35 years old [when he died] and had no mate" (*TD,* iii). At each increasingly colossal scene of antifederalist, racist, or homophobic brutality, he pines "to [hold his] beloved Katherine in his arms" (96). And it is only through their mutual membership in the Organization, for which each of them (first Katherine, then Turner) is ironically also condemned to die, that a "more natural [heterosexual] relationship between the sexes can exist" (57). At least one-third of *TD* is infused with Turner's lamentations over not being able to marry and "have children by Katherine" (204). With his own impending suicide in mind, he attempts to memorialize the "great emptiness" he feels at Katherine's accidental death by writing about their unfulfilled matrimonial love and the spoiled plans for fatherhood. In his diary entries Turner mourns his lost heterosexual career as often as he celebrates the compensatory acts of his continued racist violence (185).

In the hagiography of Turner that furnishes the novel's epilogue, we are reminded that he has chronicled a program for the "war of racial extermination, [where] millions of soft, city-bred, brainwashed whites gradually began regaining their manhood." "The rest," the epilogue states flatly, "died" (207). This conclusion signals a problem with achieving "manhood" through racial purity that goes to the heart of *The Turner Diaries*. If the diaries can be said to have chronicled how a future without whiteness was heroically averted, then it must also be said that the alternative future of white superiority that Turner ushers in is a future its author can document by self-annihilation alone. By destroying himself Turner initiates a program of "racial extermination" that ironically marks his only victory. Turner initiates a "New Era" of whiteness without the burden of any racial difference whatsoever, let alone the burden of a multiracial future he reviles. Indeed, the corresponding promise of the "regaining of manhood" without racial difference never really happens for the novel's leading man. The diaries do not complete the transaction between sexuality and race that Turner, like the book's implied reader, so desperately desires to secure. In his separation from Katherine, Turner denies himself the achievement of marriage and heterosexual fatherhood. And this problem haunts him like PK's "father-shaped void" at each and every turn. Turner finally realizes that the only fitting alternative to reproductive immortality is an "immortality of another sort," "the everlasting life" (204) that he achieves, ironically, by making himself viscerally absent.

Butler's description of heterosexual melancholia in *Bodies That Matter,* a discussion we began with PK, is of interest here as well. She suggests that when "objects fail to qualify as objects of love . . . they assume the mark of destruction. Indeed, they may threaten one's own destruction as well" (*BM,* 27). "But no rage," she continues later in the book, "can sever the attachment to alterity, except perhaps a suicidal rage that usually still leaves behind a suicide note" (*BM,* 195). *The Turner Diaries,* I want to suggest, is precisely that note. Recall, however, that in the application of Butler's thesis to PK, we had to be careful not to collapse the terms "failed objects of love" and racial "alterity," as if they were one and the same. This was so because for PK, unlike what we see in *TD,* the combination of distance and desire that the group's white men seek to reclaim in the "father-shaped void" *does not* equate with an appeal to universal whiteness. To the contrary, an "attachment to alterity" was pursued, not "severed," by PK's treatment of race. White men in this group used color to placate the absence of fatherhood, to grieve, as Butler might put it, the unclaimed object of homosexual love as the "revolutionary" (PK's term) "love" of racial difference. In *TD* this arrangement is adjusted, so that what formerly appeared as PK's racial affections turn—by the slightest psychic variation—into rage.

Midway through *TD*, Turner is captured and anally raped by two black government agents. In the process he discloses the secrets of the Organization, prohibiting him from ever experiencing the racist "solidarities," the "natural" forms of heterosexual love and fatherhood, which Turner dies longing to have. The threats of interracial sexuality that frame the novel are brought to a breaking point in this scene. Not only are Turner's plans for marriage and children foiled by Katherine's death, but the anal rape forces him to carry out an act of racial hatred so sweeping it annihilates the person who hates, and keeps him from loving again. In the case of PK, a racialization of the "father-shaped void" gives men a second, fleeting chance at heterosexual normality, even though whiteness is more or less willingly lost. As we saw in the case of "Grandpa Clyde," the repudiation of homosexuality allows a way for PK men to renew the patriarchal family. And yet this occurs only through the form of racial mixing that in turn provides the basic patriarchal element of PK's spiritual glue. In this case, race mixing seems to ensure—if in an incomplete and melancholic way—the renewed composure of an otherwise antagonized sense of heterosexual self-understanding. But when the imagination of a post-white national future becomes ripped from its heteromasculine moorings, as occurs in the rape scene in *TD*, the attachment to alterity turns love into violence. From there whiteness lives without itself, necessarily, on a suicidal mission for social reconstruction.

If *TD* is a suicide note for whiteness in the way I am suggesting, then it is also perhaps a kind of futuristic ghost story. Better put, *TD* is a story that attempts to address the imagined demise of white masculinity in an expressly "spiritual" way. This is so because the implied suicidal author of *TD* becomes a kind of "immortal" ghostly hero, who tells the story of a victory that leaves Turner's body behind and literally in pieces. The term "spiritual" is also applicable to *TD* because Turner describes his gradual awakening to "racial extermination" (and his own) as an expressly religious conversion from beginning to end. With language that could be lifted directly from PK's mission statement, Turner seeks to join a group of "men of wisdom, integrity, and courage, [over] willful ignorance, laziness, greed, irresponsibility, and moral timidity." These virtues, he continues, "are the way things are reckoned . . . in the Creator's account book" (*TD*, 196). Indeed, Turner begins his diaries by writing, "Only by making our beliefs into a living faith, which guides us from day to day, can we maintain the moral strength to overcome the obstacles and hardships that lie ahead" (9). There are countless examples in *TD* where Turner cites his struggle as the struggle to become a "spiritual man" (42, 52, 71, 74 184, 211). He wants to become, as he remarks, "born again" (74), so as to understand his own life as "an instrument of God" (71), which is created, not incidentally, to remedy the presumed demise of whiteness.

Hunter, the less well-known sequel to *TD,* evokes the ideological lineaments of religion still more directly.[16] In this book, also written by Pierce, Oscar Yeager suffers the same anxieties of class, the same racial hatreds, and the same sexual frustrations as does his fictional forebear, Earl Turner. In a more explicit way than *TD, Hunter* highlights white working-class anxiety, using constantly rising unemployment figures to frame the novel's plot. And as class anxiety is given more prominence in *Hunter,* heterosexual frustration also becomes more pronounced. Above all, besides white supremacy, Yeager craves "becoming a husband and a father" (49, 53, 55, 65, 95, 154, 215 249). He wants a "normal life with Adelaide" (27), his fellow white-racist love interest. Indeed, Yeager's own thoughts of a future with Adelaide are commingled throughout *Hunter* with murdering "queer" and "mixed race couples" (the book begins by mentioning that he has "murdered 22 such couples" already [3]). These acts help Yeager avoid, as he puts it, "the gang rape . . . of my world, my race's world" (57). The aggression Yeager enacts upon a world without whiteness is even more directly linked to class angst. This linkage, too, occurs via racialized homosexual "rape." And as it was for Turner, this class-inflected racism is lived through the desire to recover the heterosexual project of fatherhood, which for most of the novel is remarkable for existing in a "void." Unlike Turner, however, Yeager is able to avoid the bedrock violation of a racial "rape," and he therefore gets the girl and whiteness both. He brings about this victory by "purging himself of spiritual malaise" (9), which foreshadows the pivotal turn in the novel's plot: the turn to evangelical Christianity as a propaganda tool for surreptitiously promoting racial hatred and mobilizing the multitude on behalf of racist violence.

What is uncanny about *Hunter,* published in 1989, some years before PK achieved national prominence, is that the message Yeager and his comrades preach is an ironic inversion of his real racist mandate. And this inversion mirrors the spiritual platform of PK. Yeager's fake promotion of racial promiscuity will, he hopes, stoke the fires of racism that secretly prevails in the sleeping souls of the nation's libertarian masses. In order to stoke this racism, Yeager creates a faux evangelical church and preaches "a religious conviction that a racially mixed America [is] *better* than a white America, that a mulatto child was *better* than a white child, that a white woman who chose a black mate was *better* than one who chose a white" (24; emphasis in the original). Indeed, love and hate operate in *Hunter* in such proximity that the coming race war is the manifest result of post-white racial benevolence. As *Hunter* progresses, this message, which evokes PK's appeal to a Christ-like "mestizo" condition, successfully foments a growing U.S. racist front. And the mobilization of this front allows Yeager to achieve the same heteromasculine objectives as PK, if by an inverted path. The chance at fatherhood that Turner has lost and that Yeager agonizingly pursues throughout *Hunter* hinges upon a sexual violation that is commonly construed as racial "rape." To simply say that there are parallels between PK and U.S. neofascism as exhibited in *TD* and *Hunter* would be to miss the point of their utter inseparability. The relation between the Promise Keepers and the National Alliance is based on a certain evocation of "spirituality," which for both groups focuses masculine "malaise" on an "America" without a white majority. Both PK and NA work through the disintegration of a majority race as, on the one hand, the melancholic love of color, and on the other hand, an equally fixated insistence on programmatic racist aggression. Hate functions in the National Alliance no differently than love does in the Promise Keepers. Love and hate fill the haunted space of white masculinity's "father-shaped void" with equal and indistinguishable aplomb. In addition to exhibiting the same evocation of spirit that motors their racial compulsions, the relation each group has to the other is itself, I would suggest, nothing other than spectral. PK and NA are one another's ideological shadow and, as manifestations of contemporary white masculinity, are finally no more separate than that. Taken together the two groups signal how white masculinity proceeds to live out its own imagined demise. Such a process mobilizes the wildest of affective extremes, where the love and hate of color retain just the shade of difference. It is from the position of this difference (and from within this shade) that the imaginary future of a multiracial nation takes its thoroughly libidinal form.

RACE AMONG RUINS

WHITENESS, WORK, AND WRITING IN THE
NEW UNIVERSITY

BETWEEN JOBS AND WORK

The disaster ruins everything, all the while leaving everything intact.
—Maurice Blanchot

W riting in the university is work. To those fortunate enough to be employed securely in that way, this fact is something we may register or not. But to the multitude of unemployed Ph.D.'s, to disgruntled part-timers, to graduate students whose prospects for tenure-track jobs are increasingly unwinnable, academic life now shares a discomfiting closeness with the harsh travails of labor. On the university's margins, which is to say, within an institutional order where marginality is itself increasingly the norm, any ivory tower distinction between the thinking that goes on in here and the economic frictions we might once have found out there is next to nil. Labor is upon the university. And its unsettling proximity means nothing short of a disaster, not too pessimistic a term, if by signaling our damaged state we might also come clean about the material life of the mind. When the 2002 *Association of Departments of English Bulletin* proclaims "the corporatization of the university," it recites both a dirge and an anthem.[1] In the eyes of those once graced by the university's edifying cultural benefits—called by some our "student-clients"—and for those who seek to join its disappearing tenured ranks, professing English comes close to pushing product in the more strictly commodified sense.[2] The large, nonelite public university feels the push-and-pull of finance more than most.[3]

But to describe the public university's ruin, as Bill Readings has done in his influential book *The University in Ruins,* is to make a more difficult admission than simply reiterating its corporatization.[4] There is an irony—not altogether damning—that the most influential accounts of the university's ruin exist within borders now alleged to be gone. This, too, ends up being a whiteness problem. We have witnessed in Part One of my general argument how the un-making of whiteness portends the general disintegration of racial jurisprudence. This trend is inspired, I wanted to suggest, by a paradox surrounding multira-cial self-recognition, which in turn is supercharged by persistent nationalist fantasies about a post-white America to come. Congressmen, civil rights activists, and anti-essentialist race theorists form an unwitting alliance, I argued, that functions to undo identity politics as usual in the name of getting identity aright. In Part Two, I wanted to detail how deeply sexualized interests in "gaps" and "voids" are at work in more intimate domains, alluding to the ways a post-white imaginary sustains (and bothers) the delicate maintenance of heterosexual masculinity. Somewhere between hyperbolic white racial benevolence and a sui-cidal preoccupation with people of color (particularly black folk), American white men are playing out a drama of racial dissolution and recovery all at once. As we move into Part Three of the book, the focus is still on what I called in my general introduction an economy of absence. From matters of the liberal state, to the nuclear family, I want now to turn a critical eye toward issues of knowl-edge production in the public research university. As the numerous mono-graphs, collections, special issues, official reports, and articles I refer to below will attest, modern institutions of higher learning are increasingly preoccupied with their own dearth, if not death.[5] Rather like the condition of whiteness it-self, one of the most distinguishing features of the university is the academic rush to declare that its better days are past. It would not be a stretch, I think, to suggest that a good part of the work that professors now do is profess the im-possibility of professing in those better days.

This point is not meant to be niggling. In the humanities, to be sure, the task at hand has become less about maintaining a past mirage of autonomous truth seeking and more about wrestling with how the mission of the profes-sional intellectual has lost not just its claim on public financial support, but, equally, its sense of a coherent ideological purpose. Like whiteness, it might be said, in the public university, humanities scholars are trying to learn how to occupy our own absence, as such. The not altogether damning irony I wanted to signal above in reference to Readings's eye-opening book is that the university, now storied to be ruined, has never been more engrossed with itself being here. This ironic preoccupation with what we might call the university's remainders need not signal the end of academic work, however. This cautionary point was, after all, the ambivalent crux of so influential a book as *The University in Ruins*. To the contrary, as Readings might say, this irony may serve to rekindle whatever relevance academe may continue to have. The pushing together of mental and material labor that the university now witnesses produces a unique set of conditions. And under these conditions, the utter rapaciousness of academic entrepreneurialism, its saturation into every scholarly utterance and gesture, can be addressed and encountered head-on. The more difficult admission, it turns out, is that making sense of this head-on encounter may, alas, only occur through the nonobjectifiable kinds of knowledge that the university demands. (Recall Adorno's insistence, in Part Two, that the cultural critic produce nongeneralizable singularities over false universals.) My introductory point here, with Parts One and Two of *After Whiteness* firmly in mind, is that the demand the public university now makes is that we take seriously what we might continue to call an economy of absence. There is a discomfiting overlap between the ideology of writing, in its usual mode as exterior to material influences, and an unusual glimpse, again evoking Readings, into what he calls the de-referentialized way writing functions when materiality breaches the supposed insularity of intellectual life (*UR*, 17 ff.). If Readings is right about de-referentialized knowledge, as I shall insist shortly he is, then accounts of the university from within it are necessarily enmeshed in the ruins they also seek to describe. This difficulty is not insurmountable, though, if to be so enmeshed is also to be able to decipher what was formerly absent from thought: the corporatization of the university in its extant and most predacious of modes.

To seek the decipherability of absence may be the general rule of practice within the ruined university. And symptomatic of it are related shifts in epistemology that converge, more curiously still, with academe's more easily limned conditions of corporatization. These related developments are curious because they are by and large less objectionable than the university's bleak financial state. Alongside shallowing public coffers and in the looming shadow of academic entrepreneurialism are promising transformations in the kinds of work the humanities does and may, with any luck, go on doing. No matter your stake in the smoldering *Kulturkampf* of the 1990s, the financial woes besetting the university are synchronized, counterintuitively, with happier innovations in how knowledge is ordered and made. Boundary crossing of every variety, race and gender matters, canon augmentation, the dis- and re-integration of literature are the expected and proper concerns of humanities scholars today. Fundamental revisions in disciplinarity proceed amidst the state's illiberal demand for market-driven accountability. A desire called diversity reforms the content of curricula, while administrators recalibrate how departments and programs are staffed. Naming new objects, founding new subjects, recombining old procedures, and redividing the divisions, all the while restricting our professional ranks: how to discern this kind of contradiction, this curious moment of disintegration and renewal that exists among the ruins that remain?

In his landmark study of how university intellectuals in the humanities might reliably "distinguish between our 'jobs' and our 'work,'" Richard Ohmann ponders the "freedom of the more privileged academic group to pursue theories and approaches" not directly related to middle- and working-class students.[6] That freedom, for the majority of humanities knowledge-workers, is now remote, if it ever existed. "A new common form of academic institution is emerging," Henry Etzkowitz proclaims with the zeal of an inspired CEO. That "new common form," he continues, is "the contemporary entrepreneurial university."[7] *Business Week*'s call to arms puts the point with sufficient alacrity: "Higher education is changing profoundly, retreating from the ideals of liberal arts and leading-edge research it always has cherished. . . . It is behaving more like the $250 billion business it has become."[8] Forthright comments like these raise questions that sum up the general concerns of what follows: what were those ideals of the liberal arts, and what life remains of them, once said to be past? How do professors occupy the university when the conditions of labor prefigure the academy's demise?

I want to approach these questions in the next four sections of Part Three. First, I want to limn the rise of the corporate university in a more concrete and detailed fashion, giving time to the institutional stories by which humanities scholars and administrators put the question of ruin so dramatically on the board. Of concern here, of course, are the undeniable downturns in financial support for the public university, the replacement of that revenue with ways of funding that orient the university in a market direction, and the university's arrival into a new epoch of private sector managerial order. But as I have also alluded, the convergence between mental and manual labor that occurs in the new university must be explained in lieu of concurrent revisions in knowledge production that portend its changed sociocultural role. Nowhere are the vexed effects of corporatization more violent (nor, I think, more productively discussed) than in English. The ennobling capacity of letters and the ideal of writing as the arbiter of national consensus are historical notions whose prospects are thoroughly transformed by the adjoining of our jobs and our work. The role of the intellectual to mediate between competing economic classes by providing for them an inclusive feel of sociocultural belonging is untenable in the ruined university. This is so, in part, because the academic worker is herself part of a knowledge-economy system that is no longer analyzable—as so much *noblesse de robe*—from a neutral position outside it. Clark Kerr's administrative classic, *The Uses of the University* (and related subsequent books), and Bill Readings's landmark study, *The University in Ruins,* are key texts for addressing a marked shift in the public university's founding democratic sense of purpose. From different quarters, and indeed with diverging agendas, these two authors commonly surmise a problem Readings calls "dissensus" and Kerr lets stand by a simpler name, the "mob." Indeed, the crisis of the liberal state I detailed in Part One on the census is key here. The apparent shift in governmentality from consensual self-disciplinary order to dissensual nationalistic rule finds its cultural analogue, I would argue, in the work of new humanities writing. Both Readings and Kerr allege that an earlier social contract between humanistic knowledge production and the public has completely come apart. And while they may use different language to say so, both authors allude to how such a moment of coming apart is discernable in the form of an unavoidable, almost simultaneous collision. This collision, exemplified by the ruined university, is best understood as a crisis of labor, a forced if also accidental partnership between the once divergent realms of materiality and thought.

The solicitations, enthusiasms, and denouncements surrounding multiculturalism provide further signs of this double event—this collision and this coming apart—that evinces Readings's dissensual agency. It might be said, with rampant claims about the university's dissolution in mind, that diversity claims in higher education present no surer sign that academe has never been more white. In addition to the unprecedented fiscal pressures outlined initially, then, I want to describe how the university adjusts itself toward racial multiplicity through its attention to ethnicity and race (recall the census here, too). In academic multiculturalism, I will suggest, the democratic promise of diversity is more or less reversed. This reversal is related to *Fortune* magazine's declaration that multiculturalism was "one of the most exciting ideas of the 1990s" as the nation moved ever closer to corporatization.[9] There will be important patterns to point out here that connect multicultural fluidity to the university's new corporate order. The university as a consensus-making and integrationist apparatus becomes, in Readings's terms, a de-referential forum appropriate to the new conditions, in particular, of academic labor. As in the census debates, identity studies tends paradoxically toward disintegration, multiplicity, and the pronunciation of post-white singularities that do not cohere to a majoritarian national ideal. I want to argue that, within the corporate entrepreneurial scheme, the transition to post-whiteness remains at least partly a managerial transaction. Academic multiculturalism administers new and more fluid orders of work, even while (more optimistically) that fluidity may give way to forms of democratic collaboration that are misnamed or underexplored. The heightened academic interest in race must be measured against such things as diminished public funding and the demise of universal access to higher education. As it stands, identity studies in the humanities walks a thin line between the democratic promises of civil rights that preceded it and the professionalization of racial identity as an official form of cultural brokering. In the flexible entrepreneurial arrangement that is the new university, each identity holds forth by laying equal claim to whatever distinction. The larger question that remains is how race studies might live up to the democratic potential that may exist in the afterlife of public higher education.

The phenomenon of academic multiculturalism is nowhere more transparently vexed, nor for some more outrageous, than in the rise of so-called whiteness studies. Following the discussion of corporatization and multiculturalism, a subsequent section of what follows explores the ambivalent institutional locale of this relatively new-sprung branch of critical ethnography. The argument here is that the recent attention paid to whiteness, as well-intended as its practitioners (myself included) will plead that it was and is, is best considered within the conditions of ruin that such work both reveals and performs.[10] It is of course remarkable that whiteness, once a wholly unremarkable historical fiction, has in less than a decade been identified as so much cutting-edge (if also highly commodifiable) academic work. And given the so-called rise of whiteness studies, it is becoming standard fare for labor historians and some cultural critics to denounce this relatively new work as an invidious and self-indulgent ruse.

Whiteness studies, the challenge goes, has exacerbated the problem of white hegemony while falsely pretending to unmask it. Whiteness studies is a backhanded gimmick designed to gain professional ground in the leaner, meaner times of academic identity studies. Whiteness studies usurps the margins as so much multicultural capital. Whiteness studies too voluntarily proclaims its own objective self-effacement, and does so—white-negro-like—just to get a bit of the Other (think here of the men in PK). And whiteness studies is often difficult to read, besides. Responses such as these rightly focus our attention on the material realities (and surrealities) of the amassing academic work on whiteness. And I have made analogous critiques of the preoccupation with whiteness earlier in this book regarding the state and family. Even if nobody actually uses the term "whiteness studies" (or worse, "white studies"!) unless they do so tongue-in-journalistic-cheek, writing on whiteness in academe, like all writing situated there, is lucky work if you can get it. Critical responses to the study of whiteness are of great importance, since they are attuned to the ways this work may wrongly play out in spite of its best hopes.

But there is a creeping redundancy in the soon-to-be hoary debate about the political efficacy of whiteness studies. The sometimes hostile rejoinders to the spate of work on whiteness (usually from the left) are not a fatal assault. Rather, such responses continue to generate interest in whiteness studies in ways that seem oddly aligned with its original purview. How to dismiss something already alleged to be gone, without also keeping that thing still in play? Ambivalence and contradiction such as this are common both to the rampant work on whiteness and to the rampant dismissals of it. I want to suggest that such ambivalence remains one of the phenomenon's most salient features. My saying so is not to offer facile postmodern formulations in the place of materialist rigor, nor is it to bow to the pomophobic backlash that characterized the "post-theoretical" later 1990s. What one makes of the rise and fall of whiteness studies (which, because it never existed, did neither, of course) depends, I will argue, on the larger issues of academic labor already at hand. These issues have to do with how work and writing come together (I called it before a collision) in a corporatized institutional environment that jettisons the representational capacities of thought. Coming to terms with such an environment would seem a prerequisite for any effective approach to whiteness in the ruined university. As with the academy itself, whiteness is only interesting once somebody says that it is, ought to be, or is about to be past. In this naggingly postmodern sense, so-called whiteness studies was never—and with hard enough work will never be—unproblematically present as an institutional force. This is so, not because whiteness studies scholars have arranged for color to absolve the contradictions that ail our political souls, but because a lack of institutional force is the *only* force that registers in an intensely exploitative economic arrangement that is itself predicated on absence. The relation between identity and its multitudes is dissensual, nonrepresentable in higher education's de-referentialized operational mode. To say so is to say nothing more than to go on insisting that whiteness studies ought to be regarded as a symptom of labor struggle in the ruined university. Whiteness studies designates just one characteristically bizarre material encounter—tempestuous but, with any luck, soon to be minor—in an array of material encounters that trouble the humanities at large.

The next section of my argument will move from the mixed evaluation of whiteness studies to address just that array of material encounters. Here I have in mind the 1990s U.S. knowledge boom called Cultural Studies, which as the story goes, originated in the heady days of Birmingham some thirty or forty years before. Bill Readings's notion of de-referential knowledge and the forms of experiential dissensus pursuant to it—Kerr's "mob"—are points here brought to bear on the legacy of the British New Left. Through a reexamination of the New Left in its U.S. incarnation, my argument is that the presumed political objectives of U.S. Cultural Studies (hereafter CS) are, and largely remain, confounded by the problem besetting the ruined university. This problem, now crudely in our face as academic corporatization, is the historical problem of how writing and economy relate. Here, as in Parts One and Two of *After Whiteness,* I need to trace the problem of academic writing where it leads, that is, to the question of identity, collectivity, and the demise of consensual representation. Thus, the appropriate term for examining the origins of CS and its legacy is one I have kept in play throughout this book. That term is "multitude," "masses," or "mob." In its appeal to what we might just agree to call the popular, CS has given sufficient challenge to the nationally dictated appeals of high culture. But in doing so, CS has been troubled (fatally, I think) by the tendency to homogenize the ambivalence and excess that are implicit in the mass expressions it wants to name, but does not want to become. That the working class, as the saying goes, must be represented still tends to keep mass culture at a steady and properly objectifiable distance from humanistic writing and thought. Such distancing occurs for the good reason that we may uphold the holy grail of popular opposition we imagine existed over there and in the past, that is, before the welcomed British invasion of Birmingham CS in the 1980s. On the heels of that invasion, popular opposition was itself mourned as being more or less absent, though later, it appears, that opposition has come home *in actu* through graduate student unionization and increased campus activism at the end of the 1990s. The point here is that the written work by which mass culture might be represented out there as radical and transgressive (or not) dissolves in the ruined university. The presumed distance between materiality and thought is, as Readings surmises, propped up on ideological quicksand. In the appropriately dissensual figure of Kerr's "mob," the university's gates are thrown open, and the previous knowledge-economy relation that underwrote our Cold War faith in social coherence all but disappears. As corporatization turns the academic workforce itself into a laboring mass, no position on mass culture escapes the contradictions through which the multitude must live. That an overdue engagement with labor in the ruined university (alas, the real knowledge invasion) occurs simultaneous to the collapse of writing's representational function is the key point to be made about U.S. CS. For it recalls the collision between writing and work, and with that, the economy of absence that is endemic to academic life.

In my attempt to further address these concerns, the renowned cultural historian E. P. Thompson will become an essential figure. In rounding out the CS discussion, I turn here to his work on the eighteenth-century British working class, in particular, his writing on the crowd. Thompson, one of the key New Left originators of British CS in the 1960s, is celebrated to this day as the adopted founding father (and sometimes guiding conscience) of CS in North America. Thompson's work on the historical connection between writing, the multitude, and economy is seminal, I will argue, to the way U.S. CS approaches mass culture and, by implication, attempts to refortify its own troubled representational status in the ruined university. Thus in closing the section on CS, I provide a reevaluation of the famed structure-over-experience debate within CS as traceable to Thompson's magisterial distinction between writing and working-class struggle. Thompson's *Making of the English Working Class* and related essays on the multitude are key texts here. I contend that Thompson's account of the radical press in the late eighteenth century holds writing too distant from popular struggle. Here writing is the means by which representative democratic morality becomes possible. Seen most dramatically in Thompson's philippic against Louis Althusser, this separation is no longer feasible, if it ever was, given writing's currently de-referentialized status in the ruined university. Thompson's difficulties with French post-structuralism belie an underhistoricized notion of political economy as it relates to both identity and knowledge production. Thompson glosses the historicity of this tripartite arrangement and allows, apropos Adam Smith, a false moral continuity between identity and object, and again, between writing and work. What Smith calls the moral sympathy implicit to civil society, Thompson will insist upon as the moral economy of the eighteenth-century crowd. For both, the multitude is an essential factor in establishing, by way of contrast, the fleeting consensus that writing is supposed to maintain. While differing on the promises of the market to foster that consensus, Smith and Thompson both insist that identity proceeds through writing, against the multitude, toward the categorical closure of what Smith calls "gaps." Academics in the humanities, like it or not, are situated hand in hand with the men of PK, who as we have seen also "stand in the gap[s]." Here, though, we may recast the multitude as a democratic force more appropriately situated than identity politics to the challenges writing construes among ruin.

The final section of Part Three turns to the question of ontological "gaps" that motivated Parts One and Two of the book from the angle of contemporary literary studies. After the consensual function of writing has disappeared into the aporatic afterlife of the ruined university, whither the literary text? All that will have been discussed up until this concluding question attempts to address the general challenge marked by Readings in *The University in Ruins*: how to promote the democratic potential of public higher education under conditions of labor that signal the university's demise? The desire behind such a question, which is a desire for and against whiteness itself, is the desire to know something gone. Is literature knowable gone? Better yet, is it knowable only that way? Such authoritative figures as Alvin Kernan, Harold Bloom, and too many others to cite bemoan the Western canon as something irretrievably lost. Literature, as is commonly said, has been—or is about to be—ruined by new knowledge, particularly by the cobelligerent upstarts of multiculturalism and Cultural Studies. Bloom and company may be factually mistaken on literature's real disappearance. The majority of teaching done in English is still recognizably literary, and by most indications will remain so. But it is interesting for the sake of argument to assume what those who are calling for the resuscitation of literature seem to want to be true, that is, that literature is best regarded once dead. It is interesting, for my purposes, because the so-called death-of-literature connects the discipline of English to a kind of performance, for example, that we noted with PK, one that finds purpose in public mourning. Literature, in this scheme, is dressed in its appropriate Bloomian funeral guise of black shrouds. Indeed, the storied demise of literary studies in the university remains the better part of its attraction. True, this kind of mourning beckons certain romantic, almost self-parodic, forms of public longing. But given the collision between economy and writing, it may also portend a barely worked-out kind of hope. For despite what its quixotic self-proclaimed defenders say, literary work as public mourning is consistent with the university in ruin. Moreover, it relates directly to the labor conflicts that we find in the form of the discipline's self-proclaimed demise. Mourning, like academic writing, forgoes the twin ideals of consensus and representation, and insists that there be something more to absence than *just* the condition of not being here. We may well imagine that popular culture and multiculturalism have displaced the study of literature, as some say. But by pursuing literature's alleged disappearance as the best and latest form of literary work, the multitude may yet have its say.

One figure who is sufficiently appealing to mass culture, is multicultural, *and* is literary—and who I want to suggest is up to something like finding labor conflict in the odd remarkability of absence—is Toni Morrison. The text I have in mind is her award-winning nonfiction book, *Playing in the Dark: Whiteness and the Literary Imagination*. This book is commonly taught in university courses dealing with nineteenth-century American literature, but it also works in freestanding seminars on representation, writing, and race. In this text, Morrison's account of American Africanism as an absent cause of canonical literary writing provides effective grounds for thinking critically through whiteness. But her deft attention to causality as that which is generatively gone (I will be calling this labor) has even farther-reaching implications than this. *Playing in the Dark* makes use of writing's necessarily dissensual ends. By attending to absence with such diligence and aplomb, Morrison provides an entirely new paradigm for configuring the value of literary studies. She shows how historically unclaimed affective arrangements can become the basis for more democratic reconfigurations of the work of writing in the future. In such a way, Morrison's own work gestures beyond the ruined university. And she finds in its irrefutable disasters the hope for a democracy whose time is not yet known.

THE MULTIVERSITY'S DIVERSITY

It is a sign of the new masculinity of our age, of the Million Man Marcher or the Ironman or the Promise Keeper, that a man can weep in public. I weep for the future of the humanities for, like the beaten horse, it seems too trivial a thing to acknowledge, and yet its public debasement is a sign and a portent.

—Sander Gilman

In the humanities, why worry? Or, a more apposite question, why is worry such a widespread part of the "beaten," the "trivial," and the "publicly de-based" humanities? There is surely more going on in the epigraph from Gilman than the standard report on academic debasement as offered by another acad-emo-star.[1] Indeed, it is as if membership among the diminishing ranks of the humanities almost requires the PK-like performances of public "weeping" that Gilman offers, ironically or not. As we write ever more books and articles about our wounded, withered state, the only hope for getting beyond our own "trivi-ality," it seems, is to make public appeals, if not for relevance, then at least for mercy. Perhaps, in that sense, the apparent rift between humanities work and a sense of wider cultural significance has itself become the covert sign for entering

the academic club. In signaling that rift here, Gilman reaches out for a pop cultural frame of reference by calling upon PK, and does so less assuredly, with the
hope for his own fleeting sense of public appeal. Gilman wants to connect with
"ages," and like any good humanities professor, he wants to know "signs." But
he is also saying, between "new-manly" sobs, that this connection and this
knowledge are practically doomed from the start. Moreover, Gilman is saying
that this way of being doomed, as far as he can see, sums up the current work of
the humanities. Why else pick the Promise Keepers as the group that best models the future of the humanities? This group, you will recall from Part Two,
seeks to make its sense of white manhood publicly relevant through the "weepy"
performances for which it is well known. These performances, remember, also
alluded to the likelihood that whiteness, if not masculinity, is a thing of the
past. Gilman proclaims the humanities "beaten" in just the same way. Public
weeping and professing go unimpeachably together in the university he describes, because both seek renewal by not being there. Indeed, in that sense the
public and the university (or at least, the humanities) are *not there* in a sort of
mutually confirming way. This is the ingeniousness of Gilman's faux populist
jest. The double disappearance presented in the epigraph—the humanities professor whose public promises have been anything but kept—underscores a new
and unwelcome proposition. The humanities, like masculinity (and we might as
well add whiteness), is most urgently occupied when alleged to be past.
Gilman's apt presentation of professorial tears is the reassurance the humanities
needs that *reassuring the humanities* is doomed. Evidently the best we can do in
the academy—we "new" men, we "new" white men—is to seek our same
doomed company, play out our tears and fears, and pretend for the moment
that someone else cares.

What really makes Gilman's "new-man" soft bravado so resonant in these
difficult times for humanities professors, I want to suggest, has to do with the
new contingencies of academic labor. Numerous voices within the "debased"
humanities have sounded the clarion call of the public university's economic retrenchment. Cary Neslon and Stephen Watt present a compelling account of
"the changing nature of and climate for higher education in the new millennium" in their "devil's dictionary," *Academic Keywords*.[2] With unimpeachable
frankness, Nelson and Watt "make no apology for and offer no retreat from the
very bleak, even apocalyptic, portrait we paint of higher education's prospects"
(*AK,* ix). "Corporatization," they later write, "is here to stay" (*AK,* 94). The portrait Nelson and Watt paint of higher education is as bleak as it is convincing.
In the entry for "The Corporate University," one of the dictionary's most developed items, Nelson sketches the deleterious effects of the university's merger
with business in relentlessly unforgiving terms. There are ten indictments that

underwrite his general charge. These include the performance of corporate contract services and other forms of for-profit partnership with the private sector; corporate influence over teaching content, programs, and faculty lines; and the common practice of paid corporate consultation that faculty engage in to supplement their salaries (more than half of business professors are now so engaged) (*AK,* 89–90). The growing number of professorships sponsored by business, such as the Coca-Cola Professors of Marketing at the Universities of Arizona and Georgia, the Taco Bell Distinguished Professor of Hotel and Restaurant Administration at Washington State, the Burger King Chair at Miami, and the Coral Petroleum Industries Chair at the University of Hawaii at Manoa, are held up for special ire in Nelson's stinging account of higher education's corporate compromise (*AK,* 94). While the majority of these professorships are not (yet) in the humanities, Nelson shows how their existence is symptomatic (and insofar as they affect its operating budget, more than that) of the university's general movement toward the private sector.

With the University of West Virginia's Kmart Chair in mind, Mary Poovey, too, examines how corporatization signals the advent of what she calls the "kept university." Poovey worries that academe's new collusion with business portends the "sacrificing [of] cherished ideals associated with academic freedom for the market values that come with corporate sponsorship."[3] Of particular concern are the redirection of federal and state discretionary funds for higher education and the move toward competitively viable innovations in, for example, technology development. Poovey recalls the Bayh-Dole Act, passed by Congress in 1980, which gives universities the right to patent the results of federally funded research. She details how patent applications from within the university rose from 250 the year before the 1980 bill to 4,800 at the height of the technology boom in 1998. Giving further detail to Nelson and Watt's definition of academic corporatization, Poovey notes that 364 private companies grew directly out of publicly funded academic research in that watershed year, bringing the total number of such companies to 2,578 as of 2001 ("TC," 5).

Harkening back with dismay to Christopher Jencks and David Riesman's more optimistic 1968 book, *The Academic Revolution,* Paul Lauter illustrates what he calls a second "revolution" in academe.[4] The revolution this time is not the relatively well funded and progressive idea of the public research university as it emerged in the United States after the Second World War, but an equally profound transformation, for the worse, in state and federal funding of the university from the 1970s on. Lauter notes the extraordinary (ongoing) cutbacks in the State University of New York and University of California systems. These cuts are unequaled since the university's expansionary period following World War II, he notes ("PC," 76). Though these cuts came during the economic recession of the early 1990s, since then and on the whole, the university did not recover in the remainder of that decade. By 1995–96, appropriations in most states were 8 percent below that of five years before.[5] Between 1980 and the end of the 1990s, the percentage of tax revenue spent on operating budgets for higher education per $1,000 of personal income declined in every state.[6] Lauter thus cites C. Peter Magrath, president of the National Association of State Universities and Land-Grant Colleges, to help proclaim the unambiguous message: "State support for higher education is deteriorating. . . . In a lot of states, where ten years ago 18 percent of the state budget was going to higher education, now it's down to 14 percent" ("PC," 75). In addition to Lauter's grim numbers, one could add the following longer-term trend: 13 percent of revenue for the public university came from the federal government in 1980–81; from states, 46 percent. By 1994–95, those numbers dropped to 11 percent and 36 percent, respectively. In the California system, significant because particularly large, state funding decreased by 29 percent in the mid-1990s. In keeping with President Magrath's dismal forecast, only seventeen states saw increased state appropriations for that year ("TC," 3). And in 2002 the National Conference of State Legislatures (CSL) reported that forty-three states had shortfalls in revenue and would consider cutting higher education the following year.[7] For the fiscal year 2003, CSL has projected an unprecedented $85 billion budget shortfall, which will be added to the $17.5 billion deficit that states grappled with the year before.[8] The two public services destined to take the biggest hits, it will be of no surprise to point out, are health care and public education.

When trends such as these are charted next to the money corporations have channeled into the university, the significance of Lauter's term "revolution" gains its full force and fury. Corporations gave about $850 million in 1985, when public dollars were just about to run scarce. Ten years later, during the period Lauter examines, corporate money found its way into the university to the tune of $4.25 billion ("TC," 6). To put that in perspective, the Department of Education, which Randy Martin reminds us is the government's smallest cabinet-level bureau, has itself a total budget of less than $30 billion.[9] In 1990, for the first time, Medicaid displaced state spending on higher education as the second largest publicly funded concern.[10] As Gary Rhoades and Sheila Slaughter detail, "the largest (share) increase in research expenditures over the past decade has not been from the federal government . . . [nor] from state and local government . . . but from the universities themselves."[11] Indeed, state appropriations account for less than a third of the budget of most public research universities. In an epoch of what Rhoades and Slaughter term academic capitalism, revenue portfolios are diversified according to economic competitiveness. It is therefore of little surprise that, nationwide, CEOs of corporations are now the largest single group of university trustees.[12] Since the 1980s, academic capitalism has become the prevailing ethos of the public university. As Patricia Gumport describes the situation, "economic retrenchment, the rise of market forces, and increased competition for declining public appropriations have . . . eroded [its] foundation."[13]

The effects of capitalist penetration into the university extend beyond the more easily measurable erosion of state and federal funding. Citing Christopher Newfield's pioneering work on academic labor management, Nelson and Watt chart the rise of the corporate university as having produced a whole new managerial technique. According to Newfield, in the corporate university "budgeting becomes *the* fundamental governing principle of the university as a whole. . . . Finance controls the discussion, decides who is asking for too much, who is unreasonable, and when the discussion is over . . . budget crisis becomes budget governance" (cited in *AK,* 90; emphasis in the original). The form of governance referred to here sees the complete restructuring of academic labor so that, to recall the key words of post-Fordism, a more flexible and fluid workforce is produced. Professors thus become, using Gary Rhoades's term, fully "managed professionals." This severely curtails their involvement in professional (or at least fiduciary) decision making and stratifies the workforce into increasingly class antagonistic—if also more diverse and disciplinarily promiscuous—layers.[14] There will be more discussion of the centrality of academic labor to diversity and disciplinarity at several points below. For now, it is important to recall that the repercussions of governing the university via financially mandated crisis, the new standard managerial practice as Newfield suggests, brings us back to the epigraph cited from Gilman and to the general question of the university in ruin. The modern *public* research university is increasingly a part of *private* enterprise. The point of reciting the grim numbers of academic finance, as I have just done here, is to introduce a more difficult series of problems that follow the concern about money. These problems have to do with what Henry Giroux calls "the withdrawal of the state as a guardian of the public trust, and its growing lack of investment in those sectors of social life that promote public good."[15] The devolution of public financial support for higher education ought thus eventually to direct our attention to the vexed question of civil society, and to the changing role of government as it surrenders oversight of the university to the rough-and-tumble dictates of the market. To understand what Giroux alludes to here as the end of the trustworthy state demands that we pause a little longer on the question of how the university is occupied in the wake of its fiscal apocalypse. The stakes of this apocalypse, to recall Nelson and Watt once more, become clear in their introductory essay to *Academic Keywords,* aptly titled "Between Meltdown and Community." Here they cite the chilling words of

William Pater, a senior administrator at Indiana University/Purdue University in Minneapolis, who proclaims, regarding the university's current composition of labor, that "the faculty no longer exists" (9).[16] With that same rhetorical bluntness, the *Chronicle of Higher Education* poses a familiar question: "Is the public research university dead?"[17]

Remarks like these are meant to reveal the displacement of the liberal state by corporatization, and they certainly do that. But they also gesture toward the more complex conceptual questions I posed by way of introduction. Such questions direct us to the peculiar temporality of academic life, that is, how we encounter ourselves as having passed. The way we wrestle with absence in the new university is determined, in part, by the unwelcome pressures of academic corporatization. This demand is implicit in the collision between economy and knowledge that is hastened by the de-evolution of the liberal state. How, then, do humanities faculty continue to work in spite of the claim that higher education (not to mention the faculty themselves) "no longer exists"? In *The Knowledge Factory,* Stanley Aronowitz indicates how it is that the public university is beginning to struggle with its impending absence.[18] He does this by providing a lucid general history of the public research university in the United States, itself barely sixty years old. This history is important to recall, even if only briefly. For in order to begin to come to terms with the faculty's presumed nonexistence, we should know what we say we once were.

Aronowitz traces the rise of the modern public university in the United States to its standard reference point, a period of academic standardization and expansion that was underwritten by Roosevelt's Servicemen's Readjustment Act of 1944, also known as the GI Bill (*KF,* 27). During this period of what is known by the term "massification"—the first "revolution" implied by Lauter above—the university received 1.1 million new students home from the war in 1944. This compares with only 1.5 million students three years before that. By the time of the Sputnik-inspired National Defense Education Act thirteen years later, the public university had doubled its constituency once more. To flesh out the process of academic "massification" in different terms, 15 percent of traditional-aged youth attended college in 1940, while 45 percent attended thirty years later.[19] The country also doubled the number of its colleges and universities in the economically prosperous postwar period. As Aronowitz mentions, this "made the professoriate a major profession" (*KF,* 28). The National Center for Higher Educational Statistics provides an account of this trend as it accelerated a generation after the war. Between 1960 and 1990, the number of colleges or universities rose from 2,000 to 3,595. Full-time enrollments went from 3.5 million to 15.3 million. The population of faculty grew from 281,000 to an astounding 987,000 in that thirty-year period. And federal support for research and development increased apace, from $2 billion to $12 billion (measured in constant 1960 dollars).[20] Higher education's percentage of federal R&D funds grew from 17 percent to 23 percent between 1975 and 1991, before public funding began its precipitous decline after 1992–93.[21] Little wonder then that Aronowitz, like so many others, can continue to speak of the "desacralization of the profession" (KF, 10), alluding to its former gilded age. To mourn the public university's postwar era of expansion is an understandably standard conceit in what are far leaner times.[22]

Clark Kerr has been one of the most renowned promoters of the public research university during its "golden age," and he has of late become one of its most vocal mourners.[23] A former industrial relations specialist, University of California at Berkeley president from 1958 to 1967, and chairman for thirteen years of the Carnegie Commission on Higher Education, Kerr is most widely acclaimed for his 1963 book, *The Uses of the University.* This book was reissued in its fifth edition with a new (and, as we shall see, suitably "beaten-down") introduction in 2001. In the original 1963 take, Kerr mints a descriptive key word for the gilded age administrative vocabulary: multiversity. By this term he means the modern—state-funded, widely accessible, multipurpose—public institution that was characteristic of higher learning during the period described above as postwar "massification." In *Uses,* Kerr traces the gilded age of the modern university a step further back than Aronowitz's GI Bill origins, to Lincoln's historically portentous Morril Land Grant Act of 1862. Here, Kerr cites the most important effects of the Morril Act, quoting directly from it, as the sale of public lands "to promote the liberal and practical education of the industrial classes in the several pursuits and professions in life."[24] To the university's founding concern with the "industrial classes," Kerr adds the windfall of federal support for research that began during World War II, gained momentum throughout the Cold War, and reached its zenith in the National Defense Education Act (NDEA). In Kerr's account, the generous state apportionment we have seen rise and fall fits neatly alongside the university's previous attention to the (white) "industrial classes" specified by Morril.

Kerr's depiction of the multiversity's gilded age maintains an unconflicted arrangement between economy, knowledge, and a happier time of social coherence that the trustworthy (and white-identified) state used to promise. "The university is being called upon to educate previously unimagined numbers of students," he rightly proclaimed in 1963, and it is "inextricably involved in [promoting] the quality of the nation" (*Uses,* 86). As the university found its way to provide stable professional work, not just for its faculty, but for what might otherwise be the antagonistic (white) "industrial classes" targeted by Morril, the university became "a prime instrument of national purpose" (*Uses,*

86). Indeed, the gilded age of public higher education meant for Kerr a "new centrality" in the maintenance of an American identity (*Uses,* 129). This new sense of purpose is presumed to retain its original Morril Act benevolence toward the (white) "industrial classes," even while it celebrates "world-wide [U.S.] military supremacy"[25] (an association for which Kerr would pay a famously high price during the Berkeley Free Speech Movement in the later 1960s). As a "child of [the] middle class" (*Uses,* 118), higher education in the gilded age meant the establishment of an expansive, two-tiered system: the first and most important tier was research-oriented and graduate-student–minded. Thanks to generous state apportionment, this tier was presumed to be held more or less apart from the realm of ordinary class concerns. The second tier of Kerr's multiversity was reserved for teaching undergraduates. These students, by implication, are traceable to Morril's industrial workers, soon to be made professionals as part of the multiversity's charge. This two-tiered system held research and the working classes functionally separate, though it addressed both, in such a way that the "two great forces" of the multiversity—"science and nationalism" (*Uses,* 11)—struck a mutually beneficial balance.

However, the multiversity's two-tiered system of, on the one hand, research, and on the other, the assimilation of workers into a nation of citizen-professionals, also signifies a kernel of anxiety about the socially normative function of modern higher education. This kernel of anxiety intensifies in Kerr's later work as he details the post–gilded age twin evils of student activism and academic corporatization. Both of these, as we shall see, threaten to spoil the multiversity's national assimilationist charge, and replace it with what Kerr can find no other word for than "mob." But even in *Uses*—his earliest work—a kind of fear of dissensus haunts the claim that knowledge and economy can find equilibrium on behalf of the national cause. The research-versus-worker educational system of the multiversity seemed for one blissful moment to balance the call for new knowledge and capitalist demands. But between the soon to be crushing proximity of an unruly student body and the multiversity's Morril Act economic concerns, the administrator's task becomes clear. Kerr's biggest innovation in *Uses* (even if it did not altogether succeed) is the effective treatment of conflict as a matter of managed dissent. Indeed, the strategy invented by Kerr's multiversity is to treat the problem of the *multi-* itself as central to public higher education's national assimilationist mission. From the onset of his administrative career, Kerr called upon the liberal goal of diversity and inclusion as central to his task. He put this priority in no uncertain terms in 1963, as a firm commitment to "pluralism" (*Uses,* 118). For Kerr, such a commitment promised to promote an order of difference that could be maintained within the limits of the multiversity's generously funded adherence to the cause of national belonging. This is an important point to emphasize, as it will return in Kerr's later work on the corporate university with renewed vigor: the period of "massification" in higher education was for Kerr a state-funded and (he hoped *pace* the FBI's harassment)[26] a nationally dictated "*managerial revolution*" (*Uses,* 28; emphasis mine). Kerr's first signature concept in *Uses* was the two-tiered system, which kept research and working-class interests apart. His second innovation, then, meant a more central role—or rather, a pluralistically decentered but farther-reaching role—in adjoining public higher education to national purpose given public financial support. That mass higher education would continue throughout Kerr's long career to have one wary eye on the potential discord that Morril originally addressed in class terms was for now beside the point. As new multitudes of students (and faculty) were channeled through the multiversity's welcoming gates from World War II forward, they were channeled by a new administrative managerial technique that was pluralistically, rather than centrally, inspired. This technique's innovative means of influence, it turns out, was predicated on the disappearance of overt managerial force.

As those who study (and those students who lived through) the 1960s well know, the first real challenge to Kerr's national and multiversal mission came in the form of 1960s student activism, the Berkeley Free Speech Movement, and particularly those constituents of it connected to protest against the Vietnam War.[27] The student activism of this period had a profound effect on Kerr's later assessments of the university's relatively gloomy future. In this later work, a narrative of public financial collapse connects with Kerr's attention to the masses he wanted to make nationally coherent. Whether Morril's mid-nineteenth-century (white) industrial classes, or mid-twentieth-century student war protester, Kerr is haunted by the figure of what he will refer to later as an inassimilable "mob." With the gauntlet-sounding title, *Higher Education Cannot Escape History,* penned by Kerr thirty years later, the multiversity's future is plagued by a darker economic era. This "sad decade," Kerr declares, has wracked the once well-funded multiversity with irrecoverable financial duress (*HE,* 217). Concomitantly, the 1990s have seen higher education's relation to the trustworthy state become muddled. But most frightening of all, the corporate economy may have, alas, set the multiversity toward a belated and fatal encounter with "massive political unrest" (*GT,* 110). This fatal encounter runs contrary in Kerr's later writing to the former dream of pluralism, the lost age of "disciplin[ed] . . . dissent" (*HE,* 203). In a question from 1991, Kerr anxiously proclaims the possibility of academe's transition from assimilated "massification" to just plain "massive unrest." "Has the campus become the center of the 'adversary culture,'" he rhetorically asks, "and is it on a historical 'collision course' with

American society? A new period of massive political unrest, if it should develop, will give an answer to this question" (*GT,* 111). The move from postwar "massification" and national consensus to political restlessness is what Kerr fears most in the public university's post–gilded age. Insofar as the two tiers separating pure research and the education of workers have collapsed in the corporate 1990s, an inassimilable mass destroys the multiversity's national mission. Morril's "industrial classes" are unleashed upon the university under the conditions of market values that have found their intrusive way in. The title of another 1990s offering, *Troubled Times for American Higher Education,* shows the same shift away from Kerr's preferred genre of administrative user's guide to something akin to a forensic report on academe as dispatched by a shattered survivor.[28] By the corporate 1990s, in the "post-modernized, post-industrial society" (*TT,* 195), he laments, the multiversity is written off as an almost total loss.

The point I want to make regarding Kerr's shift from hopefulness to Gilman-like disconsolation is twofold: first, contrary to the pessimistic demeanor he strikes in later work, proclamations of the multiversity's demise, which are widespread in the academy today, do not break from Kerr's original blueprint for an academic "managerial revolution." Rather, Kerr's declarations of loss, like so many others, serve to extend and intensify the decentered administrative task he helped design. Second, the economic collapse that is signaled by declaring the multiversity's demise signals the critical linkage between mass agency, economy, and absence that I have been tracing in various ways in Parts One and Two of this book. Kerr's prevalent worry over the corporate displacement of the multiversity is manifest as an anxiety regarding the multitudes. His fear of massive unrest occupies the position of Morril's "industrial classes," which administrative pluralism was supposed to assimilate within a consensual national framework that was decidedly white.

Regarding Kerr's stated preference for modern (nationally consensual) over postmodern (adversarially massive) kinds of public university life, compare the optimistic Kerr of 1963 to his later, mournful, more guarded (but also, cannily, more up-to-date) late-twentieth-century administrative persona. Upon the publication of *Uses,* the multiversity was proclaimed the nation's new dominant model. Its administrative genius, for a time at least, was to stave off the later named twin specters of postmodernism—equal parts "corporatization" and "fragmentation" (*TT,* 4)—which the multiversity would be forced to concede. As the 1963 gilded age account of Morril, the GI Bill, and NDEA suggests, the combating of class and other forms of fragmentation in a nationalist way constituted the multiversity's original basis and was to remain its one true cause (*Uses,* 15). The multiversity in its gilded age was both plural and sufficiently consensual. Its differences tallied to form, "as a single community, . . . a whole series of communities . . . held together by a common name, a common governing board, and related purposes" (*Uses,* 1). The multiversity—recalling Lincoln's concerns—was to be "itself a class society . . . [its interests] quite varied, even conflicting" (*Uses,* 19). Indeed, the multiversity was to be "partly at war with itself" (*Uses,* 9), a form of warfare that administrative pluralism was designed to win. "Universities," he writes in 1963, "have a unique capacity for riding off in all directions and remaining in the same place" (*Uses,* 17). In a 1972 rejoinder to the student protesters who rattled him just a few years before, Kerr explains his own tolerance for ("disciplined") dissent with new vigor: "what I meant . . . was that the modern university was a 'pluralistic' institution—pluralistic in several senses: in having purposes, not one; in having centers of power, not one; in serving several clienteles, not one" (*Uses,* 137). The multiversity thus "constituted no single, unified community. It had no discretely defined set of customers. [It was a] . . . conglomerate university" (*Uses,* 137). It might thus be suggested—*contra* Kerr—that the multiversity *began* its life in absence, rather than ending up that way. The multiversity was designed (and funded) so as to maintain a national order by the careful multiplication of its already diverse interests. The strategic dispersal of the modern university's administrative center of power is the most important accomplishment of Kerr's managerial revolution, I would suggest. The "protection of the right to dissent" (*GT,* 194) seemed in 1963 to guarantee the national balance between difference and stability, as long as it stayed "disciplined." But the more ruthless economic conditions that beset public higher education in the 1990s give rise to the specter of mass protest, which Kerr desperately forewarns "is going to occur again" (*GT,* 192). The "massification" of public higher education was based on the good intention of placating Morril's (white) industrial class. That this process was to occur through decentered administrative pluralism means that the multiversity was originally designed to keep mass politics from actually arriving on the national scene, and do so in the name of "dissent." But based on Kerr's renewed fear of mass protest and his related declaration of the multiversity's public financial ruin, the persistence of class conflict in higher education seems all but guaranteed.

So far we have distinguished the two personas of Clark Kerr, a golden age enthusiast for multiversal nationalism and a mournful anatomist of the public university's financial and ideological ruin. But is the optimistic Kerr of 1963, in fact, so different from the later, more pessimistic post–cold warrior? Is the public research university of the twenty-first century significantly different in its decentered managerial pluralism from Kerr's original pitch for a "managerial revolution" back in 1963? Again, the revolution he described was in the effectiveness of administrative influence, not via conflict's repression, but via its encouragement, its proper channeling, the officially sanctioned proliferation of antagonism such that no center of power could be recognized, or for that matter, authoritatively opposed. I would suggest that the fragmented university that Kerr later names his postmodern nemesis is rather more accurately an extension of his original plan. Kerr originally put the challenge of the multiversity administrator in the terms of liberal governmentality that we have already limned in Part One. He refers time and again to "the city state of the multiversity" and to "disciplined" dissent. The multiversity "must be inconsistent," he proffers, "but it must be governed—not as a guild once was, but as a complex entity with greatly fractionalized power" (*Uses*, 20). In 1963, when the word "subculture" signified for Kerr the good liberal charge of manageable difference, the multiversity was to be "a city of infinite variety" (*Uses*, 41). The word "factionalized," in this context, was to underscore the same naïve civic-mindedness. Ten years and a stampede of countercultural proclamations later, Kerr designated, not the old twin pillars of science and nationalism, but "the federal government and the protesting students" as the "two great forces" (*Uses*, 132) circumscribing the multiversity's fate. "To the academician," he would comment in 1963—portentously—"the sound made by a new generation often resembles the sound of a *mob*" (viii; emphasis mine).

Kerr's 1982 postscript to *Uses* would plead with that "mob" that the "thrusts of the 1960s could [have been] accommodated within the existing social structures" (*Uses*, 168). But by the postmodern, postindustrialized 1990s, Kerr himself would question whether or not those structures any longer existed. The multiversity was eventually to give over to a new internal war, which, because of corporatization, was no longer winnable in the way he had hoped. In the happier days of Cold War America, when knowledge, economy, and state seemed for a time to operate in separate, determinable, and mutually enforcing spheres, the pluralist multiversity could presume to take a spoonful of dissent as part of its precautionary good health. But "higher education had entered a depressive state by 1980," writes a morose and uncharacteristically defeated Kerr in the 2001 preface to *Uses*. "And [it has] remained there, [in a] Great Academic Depression" (*Uses* 2001, ix). Throughout his later work, Kerr anatomizes the rise of the corporate university and its displacement of the liberal social contract: academe is now "an arm of industry . . . becoming more and more a market economy" (*TT,* 3); and at "almost 30 percent of the GNP" (*TT,* 73), it is an industry, moreover, whose resources are "in jeopardy" as the state bows out of its former financial commitments (*HE,* 217). In a new chapter in the 2001 edition of *Uses*, Kerr echoes Ernest Boyer and Fred Hechinger, noting that "higher education in the United States is no longer at the vital center of the nation's work"

(*Uses* 2001, 210). He draws similarly from Michael Shattock, likening the current state of academe to the monastery at the time of King Henry VIII: "destroyed, with their Monks driven into the Wilderness" (*Uses* 2001, 209). Class conflict in the bandit economy of the corporate 1990s meets Kerr's activist, new-generational "mob" at precisely this point of destruction.

The prodigious afterlife of *Uses*, its trajectory from the optimistic revolution of decentered management described in 1963, to accommodation in the 1970s and 1980s, and finally to a message of "encircling doom" (ix) in the corporatized era of the 1990s, is more an indication of the book's continued relevance than its final, postmodern end. Indeed, it is the very performance of despair, I would suggest, with Gilman and the Promise Keepers in mind, that makes the many prefaces and chapters later added to *Uses* symptomatically relevant texts. In 1963 Kerr founded an administrative mode that sought to govern mass higher education by removing the center of power so as to manage conflict through plurality instead. The multiversity encouraged all forms of dissent so long as they remained "disciplined" (*HE,* 203) and therefore nationally calculable. The multiversity sought balance and endurance, as Kerr rather dramatically said, by promoting its internal diversity as a form of benevolent warfare. The "student rebellion" that Kerr would come to lament in the late 1960s—the "wild card" (*Uses* 2001, 225) of student activism he continues to fear—manifests itself in the 2001 preface to *Uses* in the form of corporate-style factionalization. Both money and the "mob" signal for Kerr the end of the modern university, and indeed, the end of modernity as such. "The traditional university" is not only a "middle-class child," as he said in 1963, but as he reflects in 2001, it is also a "child of the Enlightenment." "Any effective attack on it by the proponents of the postmodern university," Kerr cautions, "will be enormously important" (*Uses* 2001, 217).

The word "attack" here is telling in that it connects Kerr's later worries about postmodernism with his earlier martial language of 1963. But there is a more muted continuity than the literal one hinted at here by the jumbling together of Enlightenment, warfare, and a fear of the "mob." This continuity links the multiversity's original purchase on managerial pluralism to the modes of corporatization Kerr later claims to deplore. The postmodern attack he cautions against in the latest preface to *Uses* is not simply a war on his beloved Enlightenment. Rather, it is an intensification of the warfare Kerr once located there—a war on an older, more trusted way of warring, such that those "disciplined" conflicts that constituted the multiversity in former times widen and eventually rid well-managed academe of any need for consensus whatsoever. The improper absorption of the public university into market relations—the displacement of Enlightenment with corporate values—is objectionable for Kerr, to be sure. But the intrusion of political economy on knowledge production is objectionable because it intensifies dissent outside nationalism in an unthinkably "mob"-like way. Corporatization further fragments the already multiple identity of the multiversity and re-creates it in a phantasmatic, post-national form. In this sense, the academic administrator's role in fostering a fragmented *socius* appropriate to the new corporate epoch only furthers the decentered managerial charge Kerr endorsed in 1963.

Thus it is that the multitude reclaims (or threatens to reclaim) the multiversity in its corporate, postmodern phase. The problem for Kerr is that beyond the (economically minded) 1990s, as traceable to the (culturally minded) 1960s, mobism overtakes the multiversity by inescapably mixing economy and thought. The effect of corporatization marks the return of labor to the university, the reappearance, less consensually minded this time, of Morril's "industrial classes." "We live in an age of too many discontinuities, too many variables, too many uncertainties" (*Uses* 2001, 201), the onetime champion of pluralism maintains. The university is "surrounded by bandits, leading to no clear ultimate distinction" (*Uses* 2001, vii). This rather more worried understanding of the multiversity's diversity is indicative of Kerr's stated preference for Enlightenment over postmodern forms of academic life. But examined more carefully, the "post-" and "modernity" in Kerr's writing are never all that far apart. The bandit economy that he bemoans as the motor of fragmentation thrives by intensifying the processes of conflict he insisted upon to manage the decentered multiversity. The corporatization of higher learning is not the nemesis of the multiversity, but its logical outcome. To declare the multiversity dead is, in the peculiar sense demanded by decentered managerial power, merely to update its actual existence. From its inception, the multiversity administrator negotiated mass conflict by appearing not to be there. Thus, in outlining administrative pluralism in 1963, Kerr was both making a prophecy and contriving a vigil. His "managerial revolution" begins the one true task of the academic at century's end, to proclaim the multiversity's apocalypse and, harder than that, to find relevance in what remains in its wake.

No writer has been more convincing in showing how the modern public research university has, as he says, "outlived itself" than Bill Readings. Since his watershed 1996 book, *The University in Ruins,* is far better known than Kerr's less studied books, a minimal summary of Readings's key tenets is in order. His concepts of de-referentialization and dissensus lend precision to my interest in Kerr's *Uses of the University* and related texts. In addition to that, Readings allows us to reconnect to Parts One and Two of my own argument about the general unmaking of whiteness. According to the central thesis of *Ruin,* the university has entered an epoch in which its Enlightenment mandate has disappeared in every way. In an apt description by one of the book's critics, "the university is in ruins because its civic purpose and ethical meaning have yielded to a variety of local, sometimes contradictory, often competing and overlapping systems of thinking and power that value utility . . . more than truth and more than judgement."[29] In Readings's account, the university has moved from an age of culture to one of excellence; from upholding nationally calculated standards of content to the performance of more fluid, nongeneralizable forms of interdisciplinary, pop- or multicultural knowledge production. As Readings describes it, the global orientation of American interest and influence has been subtended by, in fact, a "hollowing-out" (*UR*, 3) of its earlier sense of internal coherence. We traced this same process as it relates to the 2000 census debates in Part One. The proliferation of complexity, difference, and fluidity according to the state's (and the university's) increasingly promiscuous interest in identity politics effectively empties out the content of culture, or in the case of the census, of race. Insofar as this process also mingles with the university's relegation of knowledge production to the dictates of the market, the discourse of excellence takes its place within the empty location of the representative state. Aligned with its new corporate cause, then, the ruined university denotes a general social condition, which is "less a process of national imperialism, than the generalized imposition of the rule of the cash-nexus in the place of national identity as determinant of all aspects of investment in social life" (*UR*, 3). In many ways Readings's work meshes well with Kerr's. The two key words in *Ruins* already mentioned—derefentialization and dissensus—have to do with describing a relation between economy and knowledge that portends the end of the liberal state and, metonymically, the representative subject. Again, this idea was detailed at length in Part One. "The emergence of the unipolar or managerial state . . . marks a terminal point for political thought. . . . The positioning of the state as the unifying horizon for all political representations indicates that the social meaning lies elsewhere, in an economic sphere outside the political competence of the state" (*UR*, 49).

This is not to say that the collision between economy and knowledge—mourned by Kerr and so many others—rules out the popular awakening of new (and nastier) forms of U.S. nationalism. Recall, for example, how the National Alliance's neofascist musings meshed so easily with the Promise Keepers' conciliatory interest in race. Nor is Readings suggesting that the disintegration of civil society under corporatism means that the state simply vanishes, as it may be tempting to charge. "The idea of national culture," Readings summarily remarks, "as an external referent toward which all the efforts of research and teaching in higher education are directed" (*UR*, 13) is replaced by a relation between society and higher education that, by moving economy closer to thought, sees the latter as "another consumer durable" (27). "The liberal *individual*," by which Readings means identity as representative of a general social consensus, "is no longer capable of metonymically embodying the *institution*" (9; emphasis in the original). And insofar as there is "no longer a subject that might incarnate [this Enlightenment] principle . . . the autonomy of knowledge as an end in itself is threatened" (7). Thus, rather than diminishing the role of the state altogether, Readings more modestly questions its historical longevity as the referent for grounding the relation between identity and thought. From this point the core challenge of Readings's hypotheses emerges. The book itself represents an attempt to imagine the production of new knowledge in the university under the condition of identity's representative absence. Readings attempts to do so, moreover, in ways that exceed the managed nonconformity that underwrites the university's predominantly market-driven goals. With the dissolution of the liberal state, national identity could very well be poised to double back into new and more radical forms of pseudo-nationalist violence. But as might be witnessed by the U.S.A. Patriot Act, the dissolution of civil rights such as those pertaining to privacy and the press is apt to happen in the participatory guise of democracy's own alleged preservation.[30] That possible rise of a participatory fascism in the United States aside, Readings's point is that the public research university is no longer able—nor is it by and large any longer requested—to promote and guarantee the ethical fusion of identity's multitude to the usual (i.e., white, Protestant, male, and heterosexual) American ideal (*UR*, 123).[31] Appropriate to Readings's argument, Georgio Agamben refers to the "planetary bourgeoisie, [which has] freed itself from [the] dreams [of the representative subject] and has taken over the aptitude of the proletariat to refuse any recognizable social identity."[32] This quote, recall, was essential to my closing statements in Part One on the 2000 census. As multiracial self-recognition refuses categorical certainty, the multiversity in its fully developed dissensual mode turns against its assimilative Cold War origins. In so turning, higher education becomes more completely adjoined to the corporate economic agenda that post-national America is now fully committed to serve.[33] The condition of ruin is complex. Originating in a narrowing proximity between capital extraction in a boundaryless bandit economy and the logic of managed difference, the death of modern public higher education that Kerr and others surmise becomes its most socially relevant feature.

To develop Readings's notion of excellence, simply recall the idea attached to the census debates concerning dissensual governmentality. This technique, as we have seen, is predicated on a certain intensity of attention—a kind of hyperattention—to racial identity and difference that results in the paradoxical decomposition of the representative subject itself. Kerr's factious new-generational "mob" is another way of linking Readings's point about social dissensus not just to the "multi-" in the multiversity, but to Readings's sidebar concern with multiculturalism. The new form of governmentality he describes operates through an intensification of Enlightenment concerns to the point of their eventual collapse. Benevolent state interest in, for example, political redress through civil rights is referentially eviscerated. But civil rights are eviscerated by the overproduction of difference and a fetishization of racial multiplicity that higher education is pleased to encourage. Ruin in this sense portends the rise of a new apolitical politics just as the mounting attention to identity portends the evacuation of its content. As regards the relation between multiculturalism and the discourse of excellence in the academy, Readings writes, "excellence is . . . the integrating principle that allows 'diversity' (the other watchword of the university prospectus) to be tolerated without threatening the unity of the system" (*UR*, 32). I want to return to the relation between multiculturalism and institutional unity in a moment. Suffice it to say, for now, that Readings's shrewd account of excellence makes an important caveat regarding the professional rewards attached to a certain kind of academic leftism. The point Readings wants to advance about diversity, to begin with, is that the pursuit of identity politics (which is not to rule out other forms of resistance) is on the whole tragically misdirected. Diversity too often signals a form of academic managerial order that operates in a way appropriate to the cash nexus and that carefully channels the act of racial self-recognition. Rather like Kerr's pitch for "disciplined dissent," the university seeks value and relevance through the proliferation of conflict, not its repression, as in former times. The channeling of diverse cultural interests beyond content toward excellence, that is, beyond referential stability to whatever value the academic market will bear, is another signal of Kerr's decentered administrative mode. This should underscore, as Readings's commentators rarely do, the importance he gives to the imposition of economy on academic life.

Thus, before considering the multiversity's diversity at greater length, I want to underscore Readings's attention to the vicissitudes of academic labor. It ought to be emphasized that the common deconstructive impulses behind his argument about de-referentialization and dissensus are rather uncommonly linked to this issue.[34] Indeed, as if to turn Kerr's Cold War dream of nationalism into the nightmare that, for those who decidedly stayed working-class, it always was, the latest wave of professionals to occupy the university are "proletarianized" (*UR*, 2), Readings contends. In this sense, the beleaguered academic generations of the 1980s and 1990s effectively constitute the fractious presence Kerr bemoaned as the reappearance of a politicized new-generational "mob." Readings reminds us that "short term and part-time contracts . . . (and the concomitant precipitation of a handful of highly paid stars)" (*UR*, 2) are the im-

THE MULTIVERSITY'S DIVERSITY

placable order of the ruined university. "The university is not like a corporation," he says, "it is a corporation" (*UR*, 22). This replacement of the word "like" with the word "is" in this felicitous phrase means that the university's economic ruin sees the demise of its referential capacity and consensual function even as that ruin is articulated by academics lamenting the loss. In contrast to the university's Morril Act/GI Bill pursuit of (white) working-class assimilation, representational justice is complicated in the dissensual university for student and faculty alike. Thus, the trick here is to maintain a critical interest in academic proletarianization without assuming that such an interest escapes the conditions of ruin. The anxious "political piety" that certain left-wing academics are enthusiastic to proclaim reflects "an anxiety of orientation," as Readings keenly puts it (*UR*, 102). This can double back against the best of intentions, as we will see with whiteness studies, and play the very game of dissensus that "political pieties" are supposed to forbid. This is notably true, Readings remarks, in the case of Cultural Studies, about which I will eventually have a good deal more to say. The left academic, he writes, "attacks the cultural hegemony of the nation state" and then worries—or worse, fails to worry—when "global capital engages in the same attack" (*UR*, 102).

This important caveat against the more sanctimonious examples of academic political posturing—both left and right—does not mean to rid the question of power, nor evacuate labor, from the concerns of the ruined university. To the contrary, the idea of ruin is an intensification of politics given a new and unprecedented proximity between academic research and political economy—a proximity that is manifest in Readings's own book insofar as it, too, marks out a wholly dissensual and de-referentialized analytical zone. That such a process of intensification should demand of the university worker a way of demonstrating the scandals of corporate imposition in the ruined, or dissensual, mode is Readings's final challenge. The proletarianization of the professoriate in his careful analysis intimates a form of agency that moves beyond a horizon of disciplined consensus. And as we shall see, in that sense, the conditions of academic work move the professoriate resolutely toward an encounter with inassimilable multitudes that remains to be politically construed. The condition of work Readings describes (and performs) no longer permits the production of "self-identical subjects" as the effect of university knowledge (*UR*, 117). Instead, the ruined university retains something of the agency Kerr signaled by the term "mob." Whether the issue is the rush to diversity or the concurrent turn to mass cultural study, the dissensual persistence of labor within academe remains the primary challenge of occupying the university in ruins.

One able commentator who begins to develop the possibilities of "resistance in ruin" is Robert P. Marzec. His development of dissensus vis-à-vis Readings is useful for transitioning to a consideration of multiculturalism and, later, for assessing the peculiar rise of so-called whiteness studies.[35] Marzec understands dissensus as it relates to a general investment in diversity and cultural heterogeneity within international capitalism. Readings only hints at the connection between multiplicity and race—which Marzec does not explicitly mention either—with his prophetic critique of communicational transparency as the end of "a total world of whiteness" (*UR,* 33). The significance of Marzec's intervention regarding the loss of this same communicational transparency—the content-less advance of academic excellence as an ostensibly post-white development—is to link it more concretely than Readings does to the "isomorphic structure of expanding capitalism" ("SR," 8). Indeed, the publication of scholarly research, Readings's own enterprise, and every other academic book, no matter how radically intended, become in Marzec's rather strict rendition of dissensus the unwitting "creation of an economic product for the advancement of capital" ("SR," 2). Vis-à-vis Deleuze and Guattari, Marzec maintains that isomorphic capitalism features loss itself—or the more psychoanalytically inflected term "constitutive lack"—as its most prominent and exploitative feature. In this sense, drawing on Deleuze and Guattari, "capital does not proceed [in the postmodern epoch] by progressive homogenization, or by totalization, but by taking on the consistency or consolation of the diverse as such."[36] In Marzec's summary of international capital's isomorphic axiomatic, "heterogeneity—more significantly the struggle for different voices to be heard—is being turned against itself. [Capital] is no longer simply a matter of a center, a *polis* enforcing its identity and standards on everything within its grasp" ("SR," 5). Indeed, the market itself "requires a certain peripheral polymorphy" ("SR," 3). In that last pithy phrase, the indictment by implication against academic multiculturalism as a shill for corporate interest is clear enough. The polymorphic capacities of identity studies are renowned. And rote attachment to the margins can make a certain economic sense in a university setting that has its own marginal location within the larger isomorphic capitalist social order.

But the question that remains in this borderline economistic development of dissensus is whether or not subjective polymorphy in the academy is only and absolutely a corporate capitalist ruse. If the significance of the academic turn to marked identity is to simply guarantee the properly capitalistic functioning of constitutive lack, can anything else occur in the nonexistent place of the public research university? This question is meant to follow up on Readings's claim regarding post-white heterogeneity and academic labor, and extend it in a way slightly more forgiving than Marzec would. It is meant as a refusal to square off materiality and writing as falsely dichotomous relations. After the ruined university adjoins them within the cash nexus, economy and writing cannot be reduced so that the former takes explanatory power over the latter. Academic work is not reducible to an anemic state of seamless (or only capitalistically *seamed*) conspiratorial corporate absorption. As I have alluded, the multiversity's afterlife is anatomized by Readings in ways that signal a domestication of Kerr's "mob." This forced connection with the masses is intensified given the university's ruin, but this intensification is by no means a perfect extension of capitalism. This is where I differ, then, with Marzec. In the space between knowledge and political economy—attractive for no longer existing—there remains some political wiggle room, some way for imagining new forms of collective resistance. In this sense, the line of inquiry figured by the university's ruin compares supportively with Nancy Fraser's neofeminist critique of the "practical decoupling of the politics of recognition and the politics of retribution."[37] The question of diversity to which we now turn seeks to take the discontinuities that define identity studies and return them to class in a way that is critical, but decidedly nonabsolute. Multiculturalism, I will suggest, ought to be read with far less certainty than it is in the two prevailing tendencies I have described. Neither the left's iron-fisted reduction of racial marginality to corporate conformism nor the right's mirror charge that race studies is not conformist enough is sufficient to the task of demonstrating a persistent class interest in the ruined university, one that we may detect by evoking none other than Kerr's inassimilable "mob."

What follows, then, locates the communicative imperfections attendant to this form of agency as a matter related not only to corporate interest, but also to unclaimed democratic potential. This discussion is meant to join the wrongly divided concerns of cultural theorizing and political economy under precisely the conditions of generative absence (or constitutive lack) that Readings signals by the term "ruin." Corporate opposition, in this account, also takes its cue from the question of mobilizing what is not supposed to be there. In the multiversity's unprecedented, if incomplete, gesture toward the deconstruction of whiteness, academic work under current conditions seems both to encourage *and* to restrain the articulation of Kerr's activist, new-generational "mob." The modern research university is dissolved under the rapacious conditions of boundaryless corporate capital. That much is more or less granted by the left. But under these same conditions, multiculturalism remains to be heard in the class antagonistic ways in which—to echo Gayatri Spivak—identity both continues to speak in the name of collective better interests and cannot.[38]

To catch multiculturalism behaving badly is an activity whose gotcha-satisfaction is not lost on the culturally conservative wing of the old and slightly newer lefts. Arthur Schlesinger, Jr., Michael Lind, Norman Podhoretz, and Daniel Bell denounce multiculturalism for its widely alleged "disuniting of

America."[39] Newer leftists Todd Gitlin, Michael Tomasky, Christopher Lasch, and Russell Jacoby, those whom Eric Lott refers to as boomer liberals, impugn the so-called rise of identity politics with the same facile reductions.[40] Multiculturalism is simply mass culture's having diminished the one and only politically useful concept called the Enlightenment (Gitlin's favored label), and fractured the potential emancipation of a self-evident universal working class. That this universal working class has had the historically bad manners in the United States to fail to come into its own is a complication that is not registered by the illusive intellectual defense of its allegedly transparent best interests.[41] Multiculturalism is for the cultural-conservative wing of the left "an index of the exhaustion of political thinking."[42] Robert Bork, Peter Brimlow, Gertrude Himmelfarb, Dinesh D'Souza, and others—the looking-glass counterparts to anti-culturalist old New Left commentators—offer the same message from the reactionary right.[43] These more venomous authors have received due comment elsewhere and need not be further addressed here.[44] Suffice it to say that the pitch for cultural homogeneity from both left and right as politically suitable— much less possible—in the current epoch of international capitalism is a question rather more open to debate than either party would like. That this debate must occur under the conditions of intellectual work that has *itself* effectively moved thought and economy ever closer together ought, at the very least, to complicate the form of Enlightenment agency that takes its cue from maintaining just that separation. Class struggle is not only increasingly represented by university writing, it is rather dramatically performed there.

The more trenchant critiques of academic multiculturalism—from within it—focus our attention on both the imposition of political economy on writing and the metonymically related question of Gitlin's nonexistent ideal of Enlightenment consensus. These critiques have struggled to forge a nonreductive and rather more historically specific connection between diversity and labor than the old New Left. They have sought to address how such a connection functions in the university and beyond the busted walls of academe. Arjun Appadurai and Christopher Newfield advance two such critiques. Like Marzec, though well before him, Appadurai rightly comments on multiculturalism's unfolding contradiction: "in the academy the central problem is the reluctance to recognize that the economy of diversity is also the managed economy."[45] Similarly, in Christopher Newfield's resourceful account of "managerial democracy," academic labor and diversity are inseparably linked. His critique of "anti-egalitarian integrationalism" accomplished through decentralized or flexible management is, as already mentioned, essential to any appropriately wary post-Fordist assessment of pluralism's lost democratic charge.[46] Clark Kerr's latest hopes for renewing "disciplined dissent" in the well-managed multiversity should be of little wonder with Newfield's apposite formulations in mind. The "demographic revolution [faced by the multiversity] as historical minorities expand in size and political power" (*Uses* 2001, 218), for example, does not portend for Kerr an example of mob-like postindustrial fragmentation. Or if it does, it is a process of fragmentation that the multiversity can finally live with. For Kerr, the "internecine conflicts . . . [of] the unhappy humanities" may well prove a "wild card" that leads to "postmodern . . . unrest" (*Uses* 2001, 227). But more likely, as he suggests with the expected inflections of combat, the "penultimate ideological battle on campus . . . [of] equality of representation" can be effectively managed by "more cultural forms of consumption" and "more cultural programs [in the multiversity] for the surrounding populations" (*HE*, 181).

Examples of the multiversity's diversity are prevalent enough in corporate academe. Along the ever thinning line between the revolutionary and the retrograde, multiculturalism is positioned by and large in sympathetic relation to the multiversity's new mission, and has therefore become of primary interest in student services and curriculum reform. These are not the clearer-sighted days of civil rights that inspired the first African American studies program at San Francisco State University in 1968 and at Berkeley one year later.[47] In the more than ever multiply cultural university, occupying the president's office on behalf of ethnic studies—as twenty-eight California State University–Northridge students did about that same time—might be administratively welcomed, rather than resulting in the charges of kidnapping and false imprisonment that those students suffered.[48] In less than a college generation, by the 1970s, there existed an estimated eight hundred black studies departments and programs nationwide.[49] It did take twenty additional years for the University of Oregon to establish the first university-wide multicultural requirement. But the Association of American Colleges and Universities reported in 2000 that 62 percent of colleges and universities either have implemented or are in the process of implementing diversity requirements (68 percent supported such a requirement). A larger majority, 94 percent, agreed that "America's growing diversity makes it more important than ever for all of us to understand people who are different than ourselves."[50]

This is by no means to concur with the untenable and viciously motivated claim that multiculturalism is replacing traditional studies in Western history, literature, and civilization. Alarmist overstatement by the National Association of Scholars and other right-wing–funded groups may declare the fall of traditional Anglo-European studies.[51] But, as John K. Wilson reminds us, college and university students read Shakespeare more than Alice Walker by a ratio of about a hundred to one.[52] And as Ramon A. Gutierrez astutely points out, "the multidepartmental [ethnic studies] programs that [rose] in the early 1970s . . .

THE MULTIVERSITY'S DIVERSITY

relied almost exclusively on the resources of established departments for their courses and personnel."[53] The connection between academic multiculturalism and labor management was therefore present from the former's inception, even if in terms other than its constituency would like. This same caveat must be made regarding overexcited predictions of a post-white student body, as if that anxious day were to be coaxed along by the convenient programmatic readiness that administrators are working to provide.[54] It is commonly proclaimed that "minority enrollments at the undergraduate level have increased at all types of institutions in the past 20 years" to about 22 percent, with approximately 19 percent of all degrees awarded each year going to students of color on average.[55] And it is administrative boilerplate that while 94 percent of all students were nominally white in the 1950s, four decades later more than one in six were recorded as being of color. (This of course does not account for the question of regional specificity.) However, proportionate to their national populations, black and Hispanic students trail whites by a substantial margin in enrolling in college after high school, and continue to suffer far higher dropout rates.[56]

The point in rehearsing these statistics, well circulated in academe's managerial circles, should on the one hand be to record the measured success of civil rights upon a previously mostly male and white world of higher education. On the other hand, these statistics signal the somewhat contradictory point that the storied displacement of unmarked subjectivity is a significant part of administrative vocabulary in higher education, not simply the uncomplicated legacy of the culturalist 1960s left. Consider, by way of brief allusion, one particularly graphic example of multiculturalism on deliberate administrative demand.[57] As is suggested in a recent guidebook, one way to "ensure optimal [academic] performance" is by way of "cultural brokering."[58] In this new formulation, "educational and administrative practice" jettisons the old idea of "hierarchy" and replaces it with the university policy of monocultural dissolution that by now we have come to expect: "decentering the dominant Eurocentric perspective and re-centering the view with multiple cultures (including the Eurocentric) as the reference points" (*EM*, 23). There is no need to belabor the point that this thoroughly postmodern rendering of management emanates within a post-Fordist, corporate university order. To the already cited remarks by Marzec, Appadurai, and Newfield, we could add others who indict academic multiculturalism for what Avery Gordon and Newfield call its occulted (but not by much) "multicapitalist" underpinnings.[59] Jon Cruz, like Readings, rightly despairs over diversity's symptomatic complicity with the "fiscal domestic crisis of the state."[60] No less an influential scholar of race than David Theo Goldberg traces the "corporate multiculturalist" ruse back to the Chicago Cultural Studies Group of the early 1990s, who similarly remarked upon "managed multicultural containment" as an instrumental administrative mantra.[61] Peter L. McLaren and Christine Sleeter limn "global capitalist hegemony" as an "eclipse of the original referent system of revolutionary struggle."[62] Cary Nelson's "happy family multiculturalism" and Aronowitz and Giroux's suspicions about diversity's assimilationist tendencies sketch the trouble with the academic fetishization of margins in the same familiar terms.[63] The message behind this litany of return-to-class critique is convincing and clear: corporatization has found its way into the very fabric of the civil rights legacy as it has played ambivalently into the ruined university and all that leftist academics may be expected to accomplish there.

This message is well taken, indeed, to the point of being axiomatic. But does it escape the ambivalent institutional conditions it wrestles to critique? The proximity of corporatization to knowledge in the ruined academy is as severe as it is factually undisputed; what now can be expected of academic work? Each of these critics has picked up on the challenge (I called it above a *feminist* challenge) to remove the historically false separation between political economy and personal experience. Multiculturalism is rightly chided for "putting culture at the center of [class] politics" (Newfield and Gordon), or worse, for "letting culture take charge . . . [so that] political economy . . . disappears almost altogether from contemporary cultural studies" (Goldberg).[64] Without lapsing into the reduction of economy as a strictly instrumental force, as none of these critics want do to, the critique of multiculturalism as a mere corporatist ruse must reinscribe a distance between economy and expression so that a critically satisfying opposition between the two may be reclaimed there. But regarding the class and identity arrangement, how close is too close? What does the joining together of materiality and theoretical expression mean in terms of having to reformulate a theory of knowledge production—call it a post-white analytic—under the conditions of academic ruin? In seeking to describe multiculturalism's relation to corporatization in a university whose own logic is the same, can we assume that the class-based critique of multiculturalism will itself not be held to an encounter with a decidedly class-related if no less dissensual multitude? Putting political economy together with culture, as everyone agrees is the multiversity's next move, means coming to terms with two overlapping sets of nonhierarchically specifiable relations. And if one includes academic writing within this overlap, then the comparison between economy and culture cannot be made in a way that itself escapes the condition of that newly compressed relationship. So what we are beset with in the class and culture combination is a struggle between which state of relationality might be more worth having than the other, as one tries to wiggle toward whatever alternative academics can manage to find. The question is not whether multiculturalism is corporate. Again, that much is axiomatic. Rather, the issue is whether or not academics can designate a way under corporatization to make multiplicity speak such that this agency is reduced to neither of the two existing insufficient alternatives. As it stands, either an Enlightenment return to consensus is called for, or various kinds of post-Enlightenment dissensual mourning are performed. Given the new multicultural mission of the university, to suggest that dissensus is a corporate ruse is a wholly welcome critique. But unless it presumes to transcend the history it is helping to create, that critique will end up dissensual as well.

Wahneema Lubiano joins the "double-edged response to multiculturalism" with the idea that "universities are corporate in their very structures; [they] are workplaces."[65] To repeat Readings's phrase from before, academe is not *like* a corporation, it *is* one. The referential collapse implicit in these two statements signals the peculiar temporality of the university with which we began. The modern public research university is an entity whose unifying mission is past. And its renewed objectives must be sought under the heavy burden of their own unforgiving opacity. For all of that, the ruined university may yet reveal a connection with the multitude, which—as Kerr designated in his vexed relation to the "mob"—remains at its historical core. As stated throughout my argument here, the new conditions of academic labor are demonstrated in the breaching of a wall that historically held political economy and knowledge production apart. Once that separation is said to no longer exist—Readings's farther-reaching point—then neither do the assumptions that upheld the modern public research university. The fact that economy and culture, though belatedly joined, come together in a symptomatically ambivalent and de-referentializing way is entirely consistent with the university's current preoccupation with identity as a dissensual matter. To make the conjunction between dissensus and labor demonstrable in academic writing is a task as difficult as it is perhaps unavoidable, in the race-conscious and corporatized ruins of academe. It is the exigencies of this double dynamic that we examine in the following section on so-called whiteness studies.

AFTER WHITENESS STUDIES

The only responsible course is to deny oneself the ideological misuse of one's own existence, and for the rest to conduct oneself in private as modestly, unobtrusively and unpretentiously as possible, no longer by good upbringing, but by the shame of still having air to breathe, in hell.

—Theodor Adorno

After a smattering of years in the fickle academic spotlight, increasing numbers of scholars are claiming that the laudable goals once promised by the critical study of whiteness have become all but completely perverted. Its egalitarian intentions, which gained their highest regard in American labor history, are being reread by some in a new and ungenerous way. The sheer volume of writing on whiteness seems to have inadvertently released a certain hell-sprung immodesty. Whiteness is perhaps taking on (once again) that unique combination of invisibility and ubiquity that condemned the troubled souls of white folk from the start.[1] Call the contradictions besetting the sensational rise of whiteness studies a dialectics of embarrassment. The desire to critique whiteness, its attraction as an object of serious inquiry, and, paradoxically, its presumed disintegration have entered race studies vis-à-vis a complicated epistemological quandary that remains to be fully sussed out.

As widely reported, in the early to mid-1990s a so-called first wave of whiteness studies was predicated on arguing against its historically unmarked, unified, or presumptively normative condition.[2] Whiteness secretly (if not also, at times, overtly) congealed workers against their own better interests of class solidarity, as ran this worthwhile Du Boisian claim. The new histories of white American labor written at this formative moment in whiteness studies thus sought to divide the race/class axis differently than in the past.[3] Put in the theoretically inflected language that this work tended to eschew, the goal of making whiteness *visible* was partly to promote new and more egalitarian possibilities for making whiteness *divisible*. This writing worked to reconfigure white identity as other than its formerly unremarkable self.[4] That the new divisions assigned to whiteness might eventually reinscribe the same conditional presumptions about agency (as undivided) that the new labor history was supposed to complicate was deemed a theoretical quibble best left to the side. The general hope was that if the ruse of the normative subject were uncovered, modernity's hypocritical appeal to race could also be effectively dismantled.[5] But the fact that academics in the age of managed diversity—and a lot of academics— would seek the undoing of whiteness with such willing abandon has made the agency problem more thorny. Nascent whiteness studies was happy enough to take a theoretical bypass regarding the conditions of its own happening. But debilitating questions are emerging nonetheless, as that work proceeds to amass.

Vron Ware and Les Black express a reasonable and characteristic suspicion about the windfall of writing on whiteness in the later part of the 1990s. They suspect that the disciplinary promiscuity of this scholarship and its general increase may really be a last-ditch majoritarian ruse. Whiteness has become "something of a bandwagon" affair, as Ware and Black put the matter.[6] The rush to remark upon what was heretofore an unremarkable historical category has been "jumped on by a host of writers anxious to explore their particular disciplinary take on the idea of whiteness" (*OW,* 21).[7] A group of earlier whiteness anthologists are more graphically distressed about whiteness studies' perverse multiplication (but not enough to resist it, evidently): "we worry that we will follow a spate of books on whiteness when, in part, we (arrogantly? narcissistically? greedily? responsibly?) believe that maybe this should be the last book on whiteness."[8] The dawn of that self-serving *and* oddly self-effacing day seems unlikely. The spate of books, articles, and conference panels on whiteness that marked the mid-1990s has only gained momentum in more recent years. And this is so despite a certain weary anxiousness that almost always seems to accompany whatever new work appears on this—supposedly disintegrated, disarticulated, or deconstructed—object of study. Perhaps this much might be said about the ambivalent fate of what, all the hand-wringing aside, is nonetheless commonly referred to as an academic subfield: whatever whiteness is at the moment appears inextricably connected to what knowledge in the academy now does. And right now, whiteness is "hell."

The attempt to deny oneself the misuse of one's existence hardly guarantees the "unobtrusiveness" Adorno recommends. And this is so, evidently, with a kind of in-your-face disregard for the widespread political pieties with which this denial is sought. White professors jockey for continued relevance in multi-cultural academe, and do so on administrative decree. But the difficulties implicit to the task of making whiteness visible are difficulties one cannot simply shake on demand.[9] Indeed, the heightened self-consciousness, if not utter discomfort, surrounding whiteness in the form of its study is relevant to surmising how knowledge functions under the current conditions of academic work. Whiteness studies presents a labor problem that cannot be abridged by appealing to the unity of class as if it exists by default at the horizon of whiteness's own dissolution, since that dissolution is also itself going on under the disintegration of academic labor conditions.

In a particularly telling example of how whiteness studies may be linked to what Readings called decentered academic excellence, one public university chair writes, "white studies [sic] . . . sets [the white-majority English department] off from other . . . departments . . . [where the] Anglo-centric perspective of our department's curriculum remains, understandably and justifiably, at the center of what we do" (18). The importance of class to whiteness is manifest in the internal decomposition of the latter's unity as an object of inquiry. But the real difficulties begin when the student of whiteness presumes to escape that unruly fate, locating the same coherency of human (as class) agency on the other side of the post-white future that in some degree the humanities imagines it may (or may not) access. Whiteness studies should not be read as a unique sign of epistemological failure, something to be corrected later by the final, full development of critical, class-based self-consciousness. Rather, whiteness studies is simply one in a series of examples of how epistemological failure becomes the new rule by which the demands of academic labor are sustained.

In her essay "Whiteness Studies and the Paradox of Particularity," Robyn Wiegman offers the first developed critical assessment of what she calls "the academy's latest and—in nearly everyone's opinion—rather confounding antiracist venture, 'whiteness studies.'"[10] Her charges are worth considering at some length because, taken to their end, they go beyond the merely local problem of academic work on whiteness. Bracketing second-wave feminist work on whiteness from the late 1970s—a crucial move—Wiegman recounts the "very recent scholarly archive" ("WS," 123) of work on whiteness since the watershed years of the mid-1990s. This work is arranged into three schools, which serve as a general template for the later critique of whiteness studies: "the race traitor school (which advocates the abolition of whiteness through white disaffiliation from race privilege), the 'white trash' school (which analyzes the 'racialization' of the permanent poor in order to demonstrate the otherness of whiteness within), and the class solidarity school (which rethinks the history of working-class struggle as the preamble to forging new cross-racial alliances)" ("WS," 123). Wiegman suggests that each of these schools particularizes whiteness in such a way that commonly reveals a tacit liberalism. This is manifest, especially in the class solidarity school, as the unchecked appeal to a unified and transparent (also, in the end, white and masculine) subject. This subject moves from the margins of history into the contemporary university without proper attention to the specificities attendant on how whiteness functions at each locality and moment. Thus Marxist-humanist labor history, which is the most highly visible of the three schools, evokes "a universalist narcissistic white logic" ("WS," 149) within the economy of the university, even as it tries to redivide whiteness historically along Du Boisian workerist lines. The inverse narcissism Wiegman identifies within whiteness studies as it stands is predicated on an unscrutinized quest for academic visibility ("WS," 123). White labor history turns against itself as a half-conscious crusade for continued white male dominance in the "downsiz[ed]" and "proletarian[ized] . . . intellectual work force" ("WS," 148) that constitutes the ruined university. With this charge Wiegman disallows class consciousness the objective historical reality that she is right in calling a humanist ruse. By doing so, she treats labor history to a dose of deconstructive feminism that is itself no less attached to the importance of (academic) labor. Whiteness studies is an almost fatal reminder that class struggle is an immovable feast. Using Howard Winant's concept of racial dualism, Wiegman locates a contradiction between the overt antiracist intentions of the most influential historical approaches to whiteness, such as David Roediger's, and the hyped meta-presence of so much white writing within corporate academe. "The texts heralded in the academic press as a 'new humanities sub-field' coalesce as a kind of ethnic studies formulation, but one profoundly divided by the need to destroy its object of study—whiteness—as well" ("WS," 123). Unable to explain whiteness studies as *both* an epistemologically divided practice *and* a phenomenon with a discrete relation to academic political economy, white labor historians are given over to the importation of the historically marginalized white worker as an undertheorized version of themselves.

Wiegman's charges here are unimpeachable, and labor history has yet to respond. The failure within this work to align seamlessly with its proposed object of study—the white male worker—is an index of an unwitting proximity to labor that labor history ironically resists. Thus labor history, poised as it is to pursue this alignment, misses the rather differently situated politics of class that structure the current (re)institutionalization of whiteness as academic work. In Wiegman's argument, the status of the white worker studied by labor historians is moved into an unsettling closeness with the intellectual labor historian himself. But that closeness finally produces an epistemological rupture from which white labor history may never recover. Indeed, Wiegman denies labor history the very certainty upon which the discipline of writing history (in its humanist guise) depends. Labor history wants an economic outside to which it may refer without its own conditions of production being part of the expanded economic equation. However, rather than simply proffering by way of discourse analysis the simpler formulation that there is no outside to knowledge, Wiegman's critique leads to something that is more positive and precise, and certainly more materialist in its theoretical tendencies than discourse analysis is inclined to be. The charge, if we may develop it a little further than Wiegman does, goes beyond the more flatfooted one that insists there is no exterior to knowledge. Rather, Wiegman wants to focus on academic labor as a particular system of work. The importance of this adjustment in focus is that, as the relation between knowledge and economy is moved ever closer in the ruined university, knowledge is also rendered different both in form and function than it was in its humanist trance. Indeed, in the instance of whiteness studies, knowledge is shown as not only different from its object—here the historically marginalized white worker—but, indeed, in conflict with it as the historian loses control of his work. Object and identity misfire in this situation, and the humanist equation between agency and writing is dispelled. The whiteness studies scholar is not the same as the historical worker, as Wiegman insists. Both are immersed in class relations, but insofar as those relations are specific to each, the encounter between writing and the working class (as itself a class relation) is realized in the form of a reversal. This epistemological disruption places the academic unwittingly back into the very political tumults he would more easily prefer to describe. The unmet task for labor history, given this kind of feminist-deconstructive adjustment, is to make political sense of the aporia that Wiegman locates within historical knowledge, without simply smoothing it over.

Given the status of the troubled academic subject of whiteness, Wiegman's solicitation of George Lipsitz makes good sense. Here she posits "the impossibility of the anti-racist white subject" ("WS," 123). But this impossibility may be read (vis-à-vis feminism) in precisely class terms. The charge that whiteness studies is internally divided, that it walks an ambivalent line between destroying and recognizing white identity, is a significant moment of internal division for

AFTER WHITENESS STUDIES

reasons that materialist academic writing should be able to account for. To be sure, the class-based approaches to whiteness that Wiegman repudiates do not grasp the theoretical consequences of a fully materialist understanding of knowledge production. And this lack of theoretical rigor is objectionable, especially under the dubious circumstances of managed diversity. Such work might well be charged with inverse narcissism. Its perceived nostalgia for class unity is admittedly writ too conveniently by white male critics as an unexamined desire for a marginal *and* utterly recentered academic status. Both assuredly radical and highly renowned, the white male academic worker proceeds to fail *upward*. That much conceded, however, Wiegman's argument alludes to a more productive point than just this negative one. This point is important because, in drawing upon a feminist understanding of political economy, it presents a more rigorously materialist adjoining of knowledge, identity, and work than the humanist ones she so effectively critiques. By insisting upon whiteness studies as a particular site of academic labor struggle, Wiegman's is an argument for more, not less, focus on class. But because she herself hardly wants class struggle in the form of naive volunteerism or subjective transparency, contradiction replaces the mythically marginalized white worker to the degree that a prefeminist separation between identity and economy is overcome. The word "impossibility" in the Lipsitz citation might thus be taken in a stronger and more enabling sense than it at first appears in Wiegman's apt repudiation of the sexist and humanist underpinnings of white labor history in the 1990s. She rightly points out that bringing whiteness to the fore in order to interrogate its normative grip runs afoul of the desire to displace it. This conflict raises a more fundamental question about the lack of objectifiable distance between identity and economy, what we called before (vis-à-vis Readings) the absence of representative subjectivity. More than this, she gestures toward a more effective interrogation of academic work than labor historians of whiteness have been able to allow.

Indeed, to supercharge the relation between economy and knowledge is finally the reason she limits whiteness studies to its moment of high visibility in the mid-1990s. "Earl[ier] feminist work," she writes, "is . . . jettisoned from the new multidisciplinary scheme [of whiteness studies]."[11] For the race traitor school, in particular, Wiegman offers special opprobrium. The "race traitor" project, she argues, deals in "overly drawn masculine models of armed retaliation, . . . evacuat[ing] altogether the feminist trajectory of 19th-c. abolitionism. . . . It oscillates between [a form of] universal privilege and minoritized particularity that characterizes not only the history of white subject formation . . . but the critical apparatus of whiteness studies itself" ("WS," 141). Examples of what she is after in this indictment have been enumerated elsewhere at length.[12] The point worth emphasizing here is that her critique of labor history's blindness to the vicissitudes of academic labor relies on its ignorance of feminist-based political economy. "The production of a particularized and minoritized white subject as a vehicle for contemporary critical acts of transference and transcendence," Wiegman writes, "often produces a white masculine position as discursively minor" ("WS," 137). Thus "the unconscious trace of . . . liberal whiteness [is the] reclamation of history [it] so strenuously seeks to disavow" ("WS," 137). For Wiegman, to assume the choice of being other than white in the name of class or some other solidarity is to run the risk of fetishizing the not-white by white default, a simple inversion of a white-inspired binary that twenty years or more of post-structuralist thought forbids with rote suspicion. More offending than to follow the race traitor's line of volunteerism, the most influential labor histories of whiteness betray a class politics set against recognizing the full (i.e., feminist-inspired) implications of class: the antiracist white male academic's need for relevance within an excruciatingly competitive, and even ruthless, professional environment is what Wiegman brings to the fore. She reads white-on-white academic writing through an economic index that figures labor into identity in a more prominent way than the celebrated historians of white workers would choose.

For all of that, it is important to emphasize that the culprit in Wiegman's critique of whiteness studies is less the anti racist intentions of white labor history than the residue of liberal humanism in what pretends to be radically materialist orders of thought. The problem is not that whiteness studies is divided, but that the politics of its divisions are both insufficiently pronounced and incompletely developed as a symptom of labor inside academe. With whiteness studies effectively anesthetized by the paradox of particularity, Wiegman ends her essay by insisting that future work on whiteness should be halted until the "silence about the materiality of its own production in the academy" is remedied and its "institutional form and force" are more critically assessed ("WC," 148). This expansion of labor practice to include knowledge production is crucial to surmising the full force of her argument. The relation between knowledge and economy as portrayed in extant class-based whiteness studies falsely presumes that they will line up in a way commensurate with a unified, or what Readings called "consensual," notion of identity that is pronounced as the lost obligation of nominally designated white men. Wiegman's analysis of whiteness studies as the *recentered* decentering of white masculinity is consistent with her wish, like Fraser's, both to overcome a too-easy split between political economy and knowledge production, and to specify that relation in the post-humanist way it now actually exists. The paradoxical combination of self-description and decomposition that whiteness studies makes available marks the necessity for calling white critique back to a feminist point of origin. By wanting to move whiteness studies into the theoretically more turbulent 1980s, Wiegman's essay posits a formative challenge for further work on the relation between identity, culture, and class. That challenge is to explore feminist forms of (dissensual) agency that take political economy as an essential feature of knowledge production in ruined academe. The performance of paradox surrounding the status of whiteness is politically offensive only if knowledge is presumed to be produced, as humanists presume, in a purely unparadoxical zone. In the university, and as likely in hell, knowledge is hardly produced in that way.

Wiegman's way of bringing writing and political economy together should be kept in mind as political activism is sought to redeem the troubled soul of whiteness studies. The anthology compiled under the name of the landmark 1997 University of California–Berkeley conference, *The Making and Unmaking of Whiteness,* exemplifies this tendency, as well-intended as it is problematic.[13] This volume marks itself immediately by being anxious about its own status, emerging as it does amidst "an increasingly crowded field of edited collections on whiteness" (*MUW,* 17). Of the several additional entries, two provide a personal, activist bent and work to highlight similar selections from the conference that appear interspersed with the rare theoretical chapters. In attempting to hasten the closure of a perceived academic/activist gap, this collection seeks to step through the minefield of reduplication that increasingly characterizes whiteness studies as it stumbles belatedly, often confusedly, toward institutional self-criticism. Heightened awareness of the "proliferation of thinking and writing about whiteness" (*MUW,* 1) is thus duly remarked upon in the book's introduction. Indeed, the amassing attention to whiteness itself receives further mention by (nearly) every other essay in the book. The meta-critical turn of whiteness studies comes because "the status and project of 'whiteness studies' needs consideration" (*MUW,* 1). From there the volume embarks upon a critical assessment of this now sufficiently scare-quoted field, and does so with the studied intention to move whiteness studies outside academic ranks. Just as no one working seriously on the topic uses the term "whiteness studies" unless they are being deliberately—as this volume does variously and at length—"uncomfortable" (14), "ironic" (77, 82), "uncertain" (97), "anxious" (138), "uneasy" (295), or wanting to express plain "outrage" (297) about its own status, while anxiety is held forth as the book's most oft-repeated feature. Whiteness studies as it is written here seeks to fold back into a properly external political good cause whatever other academic "disturb[ances]" (267) it has unwittingly created along the way. Thus, to say again, one of *Making*'s most appealing qualities is the explicitly exhibited desire to forge a cooperative, if not indeed a seamless, link between the ambivalence attendant to the amassing whiteness studies and the adamantine political activist ground it seeks outside academe.

Remarking on the collection's cautionary tone is not to suggest that the book has swapped the less self-reflexively critical goals of the media-hyped Berkeley conference for the meta-critical *study* of the study of whiteness, at least not root-and-branch. The editors want nothing so little as to see the book lapse into an academic tailspin. The final trio of essays are selected so as to remedy the fact that "there were few activists and independent scholars" (*MUW*, 14) at Berkeley in 1997.[14] William Aal's parting shot, "Moving from Guilt to Action: Antiracist Organizing and the Concept of 'Whiteness' for Activism and the Academy," presents an especially strong (but not unique) repudiation of hubristic academic isolationism. "Uneasy with this trend [as] just another career path," Aal suggests that "the process of professionalization takes [academics] away from the community" (*MUW*, 295). The complaint here is understandable enough, but insofar as it leaves unspecified just what assumptions lie behind the term "community," it is wholly misdirected.[15] Indeed, there is a disturbing resonance here between Aal's need for a seamless correspondence between the academic and the citizen, and Clark Kerr's empty Cold War dream of a Berkeley sutured once and for all to national consensus. If the Free Speech Movement gave belated rise to Kerr's new-generational dissensual "mob," perhaps it did so, as Michael Bérubé puts it, "such that the *literal boundary* between inside and outside [academe] became a cite of ideological contestation."[16] On the one hand, editors of the Berkeley whiteness conference want that, too. But that desire, oddly and inexplicably, is presented in Aal's anti-intellectual riposte to the imagined theoretical excesses of whiteness studies in a way that looks a lot like Kerr's fear of the "mob."

In the multiversity as Kerr would have it, word and deed, knowledge and action, inside and out, economy and knowledge are strictly aligned in such a way that the university becomes both the producer and the keeper of the consensual national soul. The relation between the academic and the citizen (never mind the internal relation of the academy to itself) is in this vision based as much upon communicative transparency—unencumbered by the generous domestic hand of the state—as it is the easy cooperation between knowledge production and the self-evident needs of the public. For Kerr, recall, the desire to see the university as the ballast for national consensus means that knowledge is not cluttered by the messier concerns of what he identified as the twin beasts of postmodern factionalism and the university's immersion in economy. The dissensual academic subject and the merging of class politics within the university thus spelled for Kerr the end of an easy adequation between knowledge and the public. For him this meant the end of civil society as such. But recall, too, that Kerr's narrative of ruin, which sounds a good deal like what one reads in Aal's essay in the Berkeley whiteness volume, originates from an unprecedented *consolidation*—and not a *separation*—of what used to be the relatively autonomous realms of academic work and the real (read economically motivated) world. Thus Kerr's desire for the university's tidier Cold War mission tends to mirror Aal's superficially opposing insistence, which expressed the same contradictory lament for our national-consensual past. Aal's essay too conveniently chastises academics for "compet[ing] for control over the territory [of whiteness] by writing in a manner that uses abstract prose" (*MUW,* 309). The appeal here is once again for the academic as good citizen. And it is made as if both positions should not only be brought to exactly correspond, but should remain functionally unchanged in a Kerr-like Enlightenment historical vacuum. As if taking a staple from the larder of the cultural right, Aal casts theory as "career[ist]" and overly "professional[ized]" (*MUW,* 295), impractical for public use, and therefore to be damned. But this charge places the relation of knowledge to wider social forces as a one-way street, moving outward from the university to the public, without any exterior pressure being exercised on knowledge as such. The theorist is criticized for being both too close to unsavory demands labor places on people in their real working lives, and not close enough. Against the "ambivalence" of "the academic book" (*MUW,* 297), Aal suggests that "academics [should] engage fully in a practical effort to make society a just and open space" (*MUW,* 309). Again, these are admirable wishes, and the frustrations they have generated are well-founded. But those frustrations arise in an academic situation in which the old ivory tower boundaries have never been more permeable and the interests of higher education have never been more materially promiscuous. Charging academe with detachment seems a rather facile and self-defeating move. Aal's remarks betray a rather closed understanding of the proximity between knowing and doing as it actually exists in the ruined university. The fact that academic writing can no longer presume to occupy the open space that Aal and the editors of *Making* want to believe still exists, let alone represent popular consciousness at a proper objective remove, is because practical politics are upon academe and condition the work going on there. The ambivalence implicit within whiteness studies—call it, after Readings, its dissensual status—is the result of having engaged with the pressures of material injustice that by no means remain at some erstwhile critical distance. For having the godlike power to keep politics at bay, the "outrage" (*MUW,* 297) expressed by Aal grants academic work too much credit. And for having to work under the conditions of the ruined university that the public shares, he grants academics too little.

Ruth Frankenberg's contribution to the Berkeley volume takes a different tack and joins Wiegman's far-reaching insistence that economy and knowledge not be held separate. Here Frankenberg reexamines the mainstay assumption of her widely acclaimed book, *The Social Construction of Whiteness: White Women, Race Matters,* that whiteness achieves racial hegemony due to its unmarked or invisible status. Frankenberg's critique of David Roediger's introduction to the edited volume *Black on White* indicts him on grounds similar to Wiegman's critique of white labor history. She suggests that his evidently more inclusive approach of locating whiteness studies in black writers remains—by unwitting inversion—a presumptively binaristic countermove that is based on labor's previously noted blindness to gender. Roediger, she writes, "comes ironically close to replaying the very erasure that his collection seeks to confront and challenge" (*MUW,* 77). Like Wiegman, Frankenberg reveals how the most influential work on whiteness continues to retain the universalist shill that was white folks' original sin. The liberatory promises of whiteness studies, once again, are compromised as white men reanimate their formerly normative status by developing a penchant for the margins (*MUW,* 82). Frankenberg notes "an ambivalence about the goals of work on whiteness [which has] a hunger to redeem whiteness and to parallel it to other racial and ethnic locations" (*MUW,* 84). Yet she is not dismissive of the critical study of whiteness on the whole. Its "ambivalence" is salvageable, she seems to suggest, insofar as this work repudiates what she refers to in that last sentence as the dubious attempts of white men to "parallel" some ideal other. Of the 2000 American Studies Association conference, at which there were whiteness studies panels every day, she writes, "on no occasion did I encounter the kind of 'paralleling' of the study of whiteness with that of other ethnic groups that some scholars have dreaded and that much media coverage focused on in the mid-1990s" (*MUW,* 87). It is not just an account of the mid-1990s academic great white hype that links her critique of Roediger to Wiegman's repudiation of class-based humanism, but the term "parallel" that signals the full impact of her respective assessment. On this point, Frankenberg's essay fits with Howard Winant's tentative evocation of the term "deconstruction"; that is, as the necessarily "ambivalent" (because internally divided) description of whiteness as something other than itself (*MUW,* 108). This multiplicity runs counter to Aal's plea for practical politics, and does so precisely because those practical politics are not ducked, but fully and inescapably at work in academe. Class conflict in the corporate university is unremittingly close. Labor struggles within whiteness studies are properly redirected by the feminist move that adjoins economy and thought. Thus Frankenberg's suspicion of "parallelism" in the new visibility of whiteness cautions against the wrongheaded idea that whiteness studies should presume a socially consensual function in the name of academic writing. Its inability to do so is a sign precisely of academe's full immersion in a dissensual *socius* that is the new practical order of work.

To concur with Wiegman and Frankenberg then, whiteness, or whiteness studies, is both gone and still very much among us. In that whiteness remains on the scene by remarking the demise of its formerly normative status, what is being called whiteness studies is really *after*-whiteness studies. To the extent that whiteness is knowable in a university setting that shares the peculiar condition of ruin, it too is knowable only by its being gone. The Berkeley volume seeks a connection between academic work and political commitment, in which the ambivalence assigned to the former is reined in and referentially secured by the latter. On the surface, this is of course hardly a condemnable goal. But under the practical conditions of the university, that goal not only is implausible, but tends to miss the farther-reaching point about academic labor: referential insecurity is itself a manifestation of the very joining of political struggle and writing that the appeal to extracurricular activism is supposed to secure. Those practical conditions of labor that beset the corporate university are what undertheorized appeals to activism as the external referent of knowledge production can allow one to miss. For it is precisely the invasion of materiality on thought—the academy's immanent economic crisis and the proletarianization of its occupants—that subverts the distinction between the object of knowledge and action. By wanting external politics to serve as a template for ensuring a representative function for academic writing, the appeal to activism in *The Making and Unmaking of Whiteness* risks obscuring just how unremittingly close class politics and the university have become. No one should resist linking academic writing to the wider scope of democratic practices (nor can they, really). But neither should this linkage rest on false assumptions about the distance between politically ambivalent academic culture and some politically purer populist exterior. To the contrary, whiteness studies should be taken in the rather more politically exacting light produced by a proximity between writing and political economy. This is a proximity that, by and large, whiteness studies has not figured into its work.

MULTITUDE OR CULTURALISM?

Masses are other people.

—Raymond Williams

At the apogee of the U.S. Cultural Studies boom in the mid-1990s, some ten thousand researched articles, collections, and books could be found on Madonna (and these just in English).[1] Such numbers beckon various conclusions about how to conceive of the legacy of Cultural Studies, its interest in popular, mass, and/or commercial culture, its ability to find political nuance in unlikely places, its hipness, and perhaps its inherent banality. But whatever conclusions one wants to draw on the spate of work inspired by the material girl, it is more or less agreed upon that Cultural Studies was the predominate—certainly, the most celebrated—mode of scholarly inquiry throughout the 1990s. And this was true, oddly, at exactly the time the epitaph of Cultural Studies in the United Kingdom was being written. Its dates have been marked, more or less firmly, from the beginnings of the famed Birmingham Centre for Cultural Studies (BCCS) in 1964, to the downsizing, if not outright abolition, of research-based education at the British polytechnics in 2002. BCCS is gone. But even in its wake, Paul Gilroy is no doubt correct: "Cultural Studies, for good or ill, is everywhere. . . . The mythic well-spring amid Birmingham's red brick is no longer needed."[2] So, on one hand, the dissemination of Cultural Studies (hereafter CS) within the humanities in the United States (and "everywhere" else, for that matter) is of little dispute. But, on the other hand, its original orientations, let alone its continued relevance, are left somewhat more obscure. Now that CS is both gone and "everywhere" at the same time, the task of defining it remains one of the more nettlesome aspects of its legacy. Ross Chambers suggests that CS is a way of seeking the "occulted context[s]" within which otherwise mystifying processes (the determination of cultural value, the formation of human relationships, the distribution of wealth) operate.[3] But if CS is about finding these occulted contexts, then the serious difficulty in contextualizing CS itself should be no small wonder. CS marks one of those peculiar moments in the history of knowledge, more widespread than the one already named regarding whiteness studies, wherein the vast contextual determinations placed upon knowledge production extend to a degree that the knower—now subject to the same intense relationality—cannot be certain of the status of his work.

This difficulty, I want now to argue, appears in CS as an unfinished encounter with what Williams refers to above as the "masses." "The masses," for good historical reason, are always "other people," he suggests. And if U.S. CS has prospects other than (or rather, in addition to) the domesticated one some say it now enjoys, the second part of Williams's maxim should be kept in mind as well. "Other people," he seems to suggest, should not be reduced to the ideal inversion of us. With regard to so-called whiteness studies, this problem plays out in the guise of margin-sensitive white (male) academics as they wrongly assume the easy progress of their work. Though my insistence on an analytical function for the "masses" will leave the explicit question of race to the side for a while, the critiques of white labor history offered by Wiegman and Frankenberg remain essential to the discussion of CS that follows. In placing white critique within the context of academic labor (and indeed, in forbidding white men the ruse of context-less-ness), their charges beckon a more general discussion of how interdisciplinary, and pop-cultural humanities work manifested itself during its headiest days. Toward fostering that discussion, I want to continue to develop the feminist adjoining of knowledge and economy that now exists under the conditions of a proletarianized and thoroughly de-referentialized corporate university. Rey Chow's rejection of "those supporters of CS who think that the study of 'culture' means that there is no longer a need to engage with theory" targets a form of culturalist escapism that is too often featured in the standard multicultural-CS partnership.[4] Chow's caveat is kept firmly in mind in what follows. Within the current culture of, shall we say, studying culture, the presumed fiction of an intellectual/mass cultural divide is vulnerable to those earlier feminist critiques of whiteness that we have already traced. The subsequent envelopment of academe within farther-reaching social processes takes to task the same anti-theoretical clamor Chow sees attendant to race. The struggle in CS to distinguish between culture and economy, and to secure in the latter an ideologically exterior referential anchor, has provided CS with a theoretical riddle that marks the same state of impasse we have tagged to whiteness studies. In an attempt to move beyond such an impasse, I want to offer an account of CS that traces the shibboleth of BCCS activism—Fredric Jameson called it "the desire called the organic intellectual"[5]—to one of CS's unsuspecting founders, the renowned scholar of the British eighteenth century, E. P. Thompson. By this historical move, I mean to reframe the question of CS's relation to the "masses" and make clear the way CSers make "other people" occupy that form of collective agency that is, in fact, no "form" of agency at all. Within whiteness studies, this meant examining white masculinity on the academic margins (think, too, of the Promise Keepers). Here, feminist scholars of whiteness charged, the critique of whiteness produced (by performing) the very racial power play it wanted to get away from by simply objectifying it as an apt historical target. Jameson remarks of CS's similarly lost political soul that "the status of the intellectual as observer intervenes between the object of knowledge and the act of knowing" ("CS," 39). This intervention is for him significant because, by it, CSers inadvertently come up against an impossible moment of truth when the entirely historicizable question of "the social role and status [of] intellectuals returns [to our attention] with a vengeance" ("CS," 50). The ambivalent status of whiteness and the work of white academics are oddly intertwined, it could be said. What I want to suggest regarding CS at large is something similar. I want to suggest that the historically important question of intellectual status portends nothing short of the return of Williams's "masses as other people." With Kerr, we referred to this problem in similar terms as the occasional encounter with antiformalist brands of collective agency. This was writ, recall, as the multiversity's fear of and preoccupation with a new-generational "mob." Thompson's thesis regarding the moral economy of the eighteenth-century crowd, together with his explicitly antitheoretical investment in keeping the production of knowledge outside economic relations, connects this same thread to the formation of CS's ambivalent legacy. Wiegman's and Frankenberg's insistence, it must be kept in mind, is that the relation between writing and economy should not be construed so as to allow for the false creation of parallel identities where multiplicity actually resides. Writing and economy should not, in other words, keep academics outside the politics of work. This problem can be opened up with a vocabulary that has been well developed in the debate over the worth of CS. To cite Ellen Messer-Davidow in *Disciplining Feminism,* it is none other than the problem of an actor/structure dualism—a theoretical analogue to the personal/political divide—that kept labor studies of whiteness blind to the pressures of labor exacted on that work itself, again, throughout the ruin of the 1990s.[6] So too, I want to argue, does labor place upon CS the same disorientation. In Simon Wortham's deconstructive register, "a mixture of constatives and performatives, [of] statements and acts" constitutes CS's legacy.[7] To say again, we have already seen this in whiteness studies. My suggestion here is that such a "mixture" imparts a new proximity between work and writing that CS's historicist originators, like E. P. Thompson, never surmised.

Everyone knows the story of CS's origins, how it began in Britain, unnamed, sometime around the late 1950s; and everyone grants that it was a practice closely connected with political activism and the teaching of (nonacademic) workers. Even though British CS is associated with important books by the likes of Richard Hoggart, Raymond Williams, and E. P. Thompson,[8] its roots are in broader, extracurricular social movements. Sometimes with excitement, and sometimes as a stern reminder of the apparent political detachment of U.S. academic life, we hear tell, for example, of the thriving numbers of New Left Clubs and Centers that existed across Great Britain by 1961.[9] For U.S. leftist intellectuals eager to embrace CS's immigration some twenty years and more later, such organizational centers, combined with the short-lived proliferation and conversion of the British polytechs, intimate a rare and enviable vision in the more professionalized scene of U.S. academe. In the lore of CS's lost but well-recited history, one reads of its grassroots mission, its democratically inspired, anti-elitist, interdisciplinary commitment to adult education. From there one can easily extrapolate CS's original concern with British workers, cooperating toward the better future made available, in part, through the stewardship of a brave and lonely intellectual vanguard. Indeed, a dozen issues before the journal's editorial reorientation in the 1960s under Perry Anderson, the first issue of the *New Left Review* declared with a sense of optimism barely possible today that "we are in our missionary phase."[10] It is tempting to cite British CS as an example of golden age solidarity between academics and the masses. By referring to a location outside those fallen "brick walls" to which Gilroy refers, work in CS can become a way of walling off the mass-cultural complexities, contradictions, and ambivalences that haunt U.S. CS from within ruined academe. In the usual telling of its history British CS is made to function as an index of stony activism, of philosophical certainty and political purity, a kind of "Wonder Years" version of the radical life of the mind.[11] This scenario subtends today's conscience-sensitive hunt for the ways and places in which U.S. CS works and does not.

Of course, the memory of Birmingham CS is at best a troubled fit within the different conditional mandates of U.S. academe. To begin with, the institutional marginality and the decidedly low professional profile of scholarship and teaching within CS were a good deal more pronounced in Great Britain in the 1960s than they could be in the United States in the academostar–crazed 1980s and 1990s. Until it was established as an independent unit in 1974, the only full-time faculty members at the Centre were Hoggart and Hall. There were two half-timers, Richard Johnson in history (who eventually succeeded Hall as the BCCS director), and Michael Green in English. Most folks who were associated with the Centre could hardly have hoped for (nor indeed, may have wanted) academic careers. Originally, British CS was hardly a fast track toward professional security, nor was it a tollbooth or gatekeeping device channeling legions of graduate students to the jobs they might be lucky enough to secure. But neither should the institutional marginality of British CS be too hastily elided with a romantic polarization between, on the one hand, an impoverished but engaged life of activism and teaching, and on the other, a stoic denial of scholarly writing and research (think here of the ambivalent Berkeley volume on whiteness discussed in the preceding section) in which one is sufficiently distant from labor exploitation. Though he started in adult education and was active in the Campaign for Nuclear Disarmament, by 1965 E. P. Thompson had published two major books, edited three collections, written a number of pamphlets, and authored seventeen articles, all from a farmhouse retreat or bishop's palace in Halifax, Leamington Spa, or Warwick.[12]

Indeed, Thompson is exactly the right player to recall for complicating the myth that makes British CS the redeemer of U.S. academe's lost political soul. In particular, around the issue of working-class authenticity that he and other members of the BCCS front line attempted to find and preserve, there rumbles an impending imbroglio that underwrites the ongoing debate over agency, economy, and the production of knowledge. We have seen this debate ensue regarding the exigencies of so-called whiteness studies. And I will eventually argue that it originates within the historical emergence of political economy itself in the eighteenth century. But before getting to that broader historical point, consider the anguish implicit in Raymond Williams's remarks over his split allegiances to the by no means pure phenomenon of working-class culture. Consider, too, what he wants to hold forth in his own writing as a commitment to working-class opposition:

MULTITUDE OR CULTURALISM?

when you recognize in yourself the ties that still bind, you cannot be satisfied with the old formula: Enlightened minority, degraded mass. You know how bad most "popular culture" is, but you also know that the irruption of the "swinish multitude" . . . is the coming to relative power of your own people.[13]

The "old formula" is measured for Williams as much by cultural elitists like Edmund Burke, Matthew Arnold, and F. R. Leavis as it is by the British Communist Party.[14] This original instance of a de facto intellectual elitism colliding with radical politics in theory is, in fact, the best place to seek the legacy of British CS. At the height of U.S. CS in the mid-1990s, the most distinctive feature of this discipline-which-is-not-one is the very ambivalence over the political status of mass culture. Williams attends to this problem by citing the "multitude . . . [as] your [his] own people." This ambivalence is manifest, originally, through the "old formula" of cultural elitism that makes Edmund Burke the unlikely bedfellow of the British Communist Party; and it is manifest in another way, in the voluminous examples of academically decoded popular resistance served up in the CS section of a Barnes and Noble superstore near you. The problem Williams is alluding to here in the evocation of multitudes is one that is developed in his classic essay "Base and Superstructure in Marxist Cultural Theory," which appeared in the *New Left Review* in 1973.[15] For radical writing to work as reliably as sober political commitment demands it should, the dynamics of conflict identified by Williams with the term "multitude" always have to be kept at some academically objectifiable remove.

Under the conditions of academic labor as they existed during CS's ubiquitous U.S. rise in the 1980s and 1990s, CS, like whiteness studies, has seen the distance between economy and writing narrow to the point of nonexistence. Williams's famed expansion of culture as "a whole way of life" comes to mean, in the current context as in the original, that political economy must be reconfigured in this more inclusive way.[16] CS is made barely distinct, on this order, from what it singles out as the object of its work. And in that sense, CS struggles to negotiate the same perplexing combination of academic visibility and political banality that whiteness studies negotiates in America's imagined postwhite phase. The moment CS came to the United States, it did so on the precondition that the disciplinary identity of academic work was gone. Beyond that, as Meaghan Morris suggests, through its unchecked proliferation CS comes to look banal, disposable, ineffective. In other words, CS becomes inadvertently complicitous with the power plays of commerce and coercion it wants to locate in the ambivalent world of mass culture that academics are trained to keep outside.[17] CS, as Bill Readings rightly surmises, is the university's most prominent symptom of ruin, even while CS represents its last best hope. CS shares an arrangement with the humanities generally, and U.S. society at large, that must draw a certain sort of strength from the forced encounter with absence (the absence of the university itself, of cultural content, and, as we have been detailing, of whiteness).[18] What such an impasse seems to signify, in fact, is an overavailability of resistance within popular culture as the culture and economy opposition is rendered ever less operative in the wake of the liberal state. As we stumble along the dotted line between Madonna studies and missionary work, the difference between CS's tendency to "sleuth for subversiveness" and the opposite desire to rage against the popular culture machine is a difference that has never been *less* distinct. The collision between culture and economy that takes place in U.S. academe has seen CS's ambivalence come home.

Of course, the layered misadventures that have befallen job seekers in literary studies are plain on this score. Disastrous market conditions await the recent English Ph.D., as everyone knows. No graduate student escapes the stultifying phrase "academic Great Depression," which designates the referential absence of English while implying an economic upturn that never actually arrives.[19] How do we figure CS's unfinished political business into a professional environment that eats its own young? If scholarly research in the United States has seen a relative boom in CS over the last ten years, it seems likely that this is due at some level to an institutional demand for it. An English professor at a major U.S. research university writes in 1992 of the reconfiguration of his department: "our revisions [to a CS graduate curriculum] seemed attractive: in 1991 applications . . . increased by 288 percent over the previous five years, while the increase in applications to the Ph.D. was 547 percent. . . . Our department," he continues, "has received some recognition in news stories, journal articles, and institutional histories as one of several pioneering the development of CS curricula and programs."[20] That the rise in graduate applications bears a causal correlation to making CS an official part of graduate training is, of course, questionable.[21] But these remarks are telling in other ways. CS in America, with ironies and contradictions, I think, very close to its and the country's anguished hearts, has taken on a certain entrepreneurial bent. The development of CS, having occurred primarily at research institutions as part of the latest turn in professional training, has conceivably produced a cohort of theoretically minded new Ph.D.'s who are destined for rather different kinds of jobs, if they get jobs at all. Michael Bérubé has it right, no doubt: "the discipline [of English] thinks it's going from literature to culture, and the market tells us we're going from literature to technical writing."[22] One might add that in going from "literature" to "technical writing"—and in going to a less insulated, less secure, less privileged work-a-day existence (for us and for increasing numbers of our students)—CS is coming, alas, to a kind of materialist engagement *in spite of* its overt materialist pretensions. This engagement is dictated according to the appropriately vulgar realities of labor exploitation, un- and underemployment.

The *ADE Bulletin,* the *MLA Newsletter,* the *Chronicle of Higher Education,* and other official publications bring the message of a disintegrating profession with sadistic regularity. During the years of CS's most rigorous importation, from 1976–77 through 1991–92, not once did more than half of the new Ph.D.'s in English and foreign languages receive tenure-track jobs.[23] These numbers were, of course, compounded by an increase in the numbers of new Ph.D.'s on the market during those years, in English, from a low in 1987 of about 650 to 850 in 1991.[24] Similarly, between CS's watershed years of 1990 and 1994, when "missionary" work gave over to Madonna studies, the number of full-time faculty decreased at 28 percent of the English departments at research institutions. Two-thirds of them increased the number of TAs, and 25 percent increased the number of part-timers.[25] Reliance on adjuncts and part-time faculty increased from 22 percent in 1970 to more than 40 percent at the time CS achieved its high profile in 1993.[26] And accordingly, between 1975 and 1993 the number of non–tenure-track faculty appointments in higher education increased 88 percent, with 65 percent of the overall population of faculty and graduate assistants in the university designated as having "temporary" status.[27] "Will Marry for Health Insurance," "Full-Time Justice for Part-Time Faculty," and "We Don't Have Part-Time Rents" are the catchphrases that capture the mood of the new transitory workforce in higher education.

What kinds of conclusions might be drawn from these numbers, especially insofar as they reach into the tough issues of political struggle and, implicitly, CS's alleged abandonment of teaching and political activism? One way to recover from CS's backdoor politicization is to try and connect with its lost purity, making sure to seal one's scholarly pursuits ever more deliberately and securely against what Nelson calls "the daily messages of consumer capitalism . . . [that] encourages the sort of anxious cynicism about how one markets oneself" in pursuit of an academic job.[28] For Nelson, as for the editors of the Berkeley whiteness volume, this is best done via a certain suspicion about theory, which effectively assures that the refusal to "separate academic and political life, a separation that CS has sought to overcome" (*MTR,* 58), will be met. But again, once this separation is overcome, will political good conscience be restored, career advancement taught to heel, or the angst-ridden connection between career and labor dismissed? The adoption of CS within the downsized humanities suggests that the adjoining of knowledge and politics lands the unsuspecting scholar—in spite of better intentions—in another starting place than purity. Consider Nelson elsewhere. "Haunted by the knowledge that all I can do at the moment to help [graduate students] is write one more book," he writes, "adding, at ironic minimum, yet one more line to my own vita" (*MTR*, 156). Elsewhere, Nelson and Michael Bérubé lament graduate training and under-paid labor as a "cruel joke the academic economy has played on . . . students."[29] In these frank admissions, the difficulty of keeping the antagonistic interests of good politics correctly divided from career advancement is apparent. The tendency on behalf of easing one's conscience to distinguish between action and object turns in on itself in the form of CS's own begrudged institutionalization. Evident in Nelson and Bérubé's candid remarks is the nervous desire to end the imposition of economy upon the academy, or short of that, to keep economy at a more manageable distance from knowledge than the terms "joke" and "irony" imply. As CS attempts to sift the transgressive parts of popular culture from its more retrograde elements, Madonna studies may have done very well for those making ends meet in academe's remaining (but shrinking) professional-managerial class. The professional lot for most other academics will be working, not at some preferred representative distance from the messiness of mass culture, but rather starkly within it, as part of the disempowered workforce for whom it is much easier to speak. Academic labor in the corporate university means that humanities Ph.D.'s are being rather differently popularized than tenured radicals may be able to know. The work of academic writing, especially as one may pursue the ambivalent practice of CS, means being pushed up against a material problem that, for all that materialist training or lack of it, cannot be kept outside the fabric of one's work. In this sense, political struggle within ruined academe becomes less something found by dividing mass culture from the ability to represent it in the books one writes (or might have written), and more a point at which one finds oneself beginning to think and to write. The redefinition of professor as worker is being made a symptom of "the down-sizing of America."[30] And this comes to the majority of service sector academics in an experientially (and epistemologically) dissensual way, cluttering the presumed agreement between economy and thought, and erasing the distinction between action and object.

The desire to do more than simply describe labor is referred to by Nelson as a kind of "haunting." In that sense, one is heartened by the adjoining of labor consciousness in academe to the psychic discomfort of its highest achievers. In another sense, though, PK's melancholic "new" white men come to mind in the ghostly figure of the humanities' lost claim on the social significance it once presumed to have. Sander Gilman's faux populist grief stands in for the reluctant acknowledgment that appeals to labor outside academe are muddled by the

MULTITUDE OR CULTURALISM?

class conflict going on there. The task of maintaining political good conscience while doing CS in the academy is made dubious by the market conditions that make one desire it. Economy is fully upon the writing that academics produce, and no amount of rewriting will keep materiality at its former more comfortable distance. The term "activism," when it appears in writing, too conveniently redivides knowledge from the encounter with labor that CS says it wants, since that writing is always also being acted upon. This process of being acted upon is why the phrase "minimally ironic" remains attached to CS work. To redeem the task of activism as external reference, that is, where the academic actor is presumed to escape labor's paradoxical reversals, is the stated goal of a certain backlash that follows CS's theoretical excess. But this backlash, I would suggest, is something CS has been courting all along. It is traceable to a well-cultivated ambivalence that CS both hates and wants, a suspicion that agency is absent in the humanities, and that it went the way precisely of the academic's fleeting moral claim on society as fake consensus.[31] This is, of course, to reiterate an earlier point we have traced in Bill Readings. Recall, he too claims that agency is all about absence in the humanities. The cultural content of its disciplines has been evacuated. Its disciples have been replaced with more fluid cadres of transdisciplinary workers who have little attachment to maintaining cultural fixity, and who are themselves, by cruel extension, unlikely to find stable work. This situation, recall, designates what Readings famously calls academic "excellence." And, as I have been arguing, it is a sign (one that is ironically predicated on the impossibility of fully reading it) that performing labor struggle is the unclaimable basis of humanities writing itself. Along those lines, I have suggested that CS's own troubled emergence in the United States among the university's ruins is none other than a manifestation of labor's ambivalent sign. That the backlash against the emptying of humanities as political economy's late arrival to it is advanced by academics who claim to give labor its most credible due, thus signals a second level of irony. And it is that backlash against CS, and more generally, against theory, to which I now want to turn. What I want to show is how this backlash is traceable to a long-standing and under-interrogated preoccupation with mass culture as part of CS's 1960s origins in eighteenth-century British studies. This is why E. P. Thompson, long regarded as one of CS's unwitting founders, will be a key figure in what is offered below. Moreover, I want to suggest, we must start any assessment of CS's troubled future in U.S. academe by jettisoning the assumption, recalling Williams, that the "masses" are other than us.

To get a sense of the backlash I have in mind, consider a promotional blurb from a recent book catalogue, which provides the following reassurance: "this book is a breath of fresh air in the increasingly dusty room of texts without human agents behind them. It is an important book," the pitch continues, "[in] its restatement of 'hard' history against cultural studies. . . . Historians have gone too far down the road with cultural theory and are in danger of negating their own vocation."[32] After years of disruption, "theory" is, alas, firmly bracketed by the return of a prodigal discipline, "hard history," which promises to endow "human agency" with an erstwhile pretheoretical vigor. In the presumed wake of CS, which it ought be said ranges from the "dustiest" of textual preoccupation to the "freshest" examples of transgressive ingenuity, a book that promises to amend current scholarly practice, while at the same time secure "the popular" in history, makes it a doubly urgent read. But at closer look this double urgency bespeaks a curious slippage of terms. "The popular" as "human agency" is quietly succeeded by a wary, but effectively recuperative, sideward glance at the apparent overpopularity of "theory." What makes this pitch successful is how it conjoins the "vocation" of writing in a preferred adamantine, "hard histor[ical]" form—certified by the recital of an object's pure evidentiary status—with "popular contention," now freed from the immoderate influence of wayward "theoretical" prose. Again, it is an irresistible sell. But insofar as "the popular" and writing are mutually implicated historical problems—as indeed, we shall see that they are—writing is even "harder" work than the market allows.

It is important to point out that the atoning book referred to by the blurb cited above is Charles Tilly's *Popular Contention in Great Britain, 1758–1834*. Indeed, Tilly is one of our most eminent and prolific writers on eighteenth-century popular dissent. By necessity his name evokes E. P. Thompson's, whose rehabilitation of popular culture from its long-standing Burkean dismissals is ubiquitously cited as a *locus classicus* of British CS.[33] But what of this debt to Thompson? Specifically, what of his thesis on the "moral economy" of the eighteenth-century English crowd, and his parallel indictment of Louis Althusser—the two most distinguished contributions Thompson made to the legacy of CS in America?

In the crowd's capacity to resist the encroaching advance of the new political economy, Thompson suggests that the eighteenth-century bread riot harkens back to an earlier Tudor notion of traditional rights concerning the price of grain. In opposition to middlemen, samplers, and forestallers, "grievances operated within popular consensus as to what were legitimate and illegitimate practices in marketing, milling, and baking. . . . This constitutes the moral economy of the poor."[34] Thompson's numerous examples of consensual price setting by direct crowd action throughout the first decades of the eighteenth century would seem unimpeachable on this count. In the 1740s, and in riots ensuing from the grain dearths of 1756 and 1766, the crowd is seen to select deliberate targets, bypassing bakers and pursuing millers and merchants as more appropriate objects of redress. Moreover, the "moral economy" of the crowd "derived its sense of legitimation from the paternalist model" ("ME," 208) and the "compassionate traditionalism" of the seated country gentleman ("ME," 211). Riot is situated by an under-interrogated client/gentry "reciprocity" that works at artificial distance from market imperatives so that experience, "compassion," "mutuality," and "sympathy" (Thompson's terms) underwrite "moral" transgressions of the market.[35] In question here is by no means the antagonistic presence of riot outside capitalist sociability. Rather, with the troubled desire for "human agency" that hovers around U.S. CS in mind, we need to clarify in ways Thompson did not how the "moral economy" thesis bleeds into capitalism's own foundational terms. For Thompson, "in the eighteenth-century the market remained a social as well as an economic nexus" ("ME," 256). And similarly, from a later essay, "Patricians and Plebes": "they [the pre-industrial workers] favored paternal social controls because they appeared simultaneously as economic and social relations, as relations between persons, not as payments for services."[36] At stake in this momentary historical alignment, that is, before "relations between persons" were displaced by "economic rationalization" ("PP," 39), is the inclination in the "moral economy" argument to grant subjectivity allowances that appear to slip too easily beyond its relationship to market forces. The assessment of paternalist good conscience and the client/gentry bond as a fleeting alliance against classical political economy begins to weaken here.

What are the tenets of "morality" as Thompson presents them? We know that there is more at stake in this term than the raw data of the riots themselves. Rather, "moral economy impinged very generally upon eighteenth-century government and thought, and did not only intrude at times of disturbance" ("ME," 189). Indeed, riot itself is eventually sublimated in the "moral economy" argument to "thought," that is, to the consensual dimensions of the plebe/patrician social contract.[37] Already Clark Kerr's nervousness about the new-generational "mob," together with its postmodern analogue, the proximity in the ruined university between thinking and work, is traceable to this preferred Enlightenment insistence on communicative reason and the knowledge/economy dyad. The ambivalent charges of whiteness studies and the nervous "minimal irony" Nelson evokes when class consciousness serves to lengthen the academostar's curriculum vitae stem from Thompson's diminished precapitalist separation between the crowd and its paternalist benefactor. The "moral economy" gained its benefits in the early part of the eighteenth century, Thompson writes, "less in riot [than] by threat," "the anxiety of the authorities," "the anticipation of riot" ("ME," 242). "There is a sense in which rulers and the crowd needed each other, watched each other, performed theater and counter theater to each other's auditoriums. . . . This is a more active and reciprocal relationship than the one normally brought to mind under the formula 'paternalism and deference'" ("PP," 57). The efficacy of riot appears here as an intersubjective (precapitalist) experiential imperative, a "consenting alliance" between gentry and client whose "moral" capacity precedes the forces of the market so as to transgress them: the plebe/paternalist relationship, Thompson suggests, "appeals to a moral norm—what ought to be men's reciprocal duties" ("PP," 203). But "morality" as such, as Thompson later begrudgingly conceded, is a good deal closer to the mandates of political economy than his contextualization of food riots as a matter of social conscience and mutual "watching" would allow. To say so is not to begin an "academic language game" ("MER," 349), a charge Thompson would make of his critics (though this oversight returns in the ruined university precisely as a question of knowledge). Rather, a closer look at morality in its proximate historical relation to early modern capitalism reveals an unacknowledged debt to the liberal moral philosophy of the eighteenth-century Scottish Enlightenment.[38] This legacy will foster Thompson's eventual philippic against Althusser. From there, as we shall see in a moment, it will beset CS with an inability to come fully to terms with the historical collapse between knowledge and economy—the same collapse Clark Kerr bemoaned, and the same one feminists point out in the troubled rise of whiteness studies.

For Thompson, Adam Smith's "victory" in the corn trade debates between 1767 and 1772, the years that saw the capitalist repeal of anti-forestalling legislation, is presented in "the moral economy" argument as "a direct negative to the disintegrating Tudor policies" ("ME," 203). Reminded by his Cambridge antagonists of the market's explicit moral imperatives insofar as Smith—a "civic moralist"[39]—would have them, Thompson offered that "the 'morality' of Adam Smith was never the matter at issue" ("MER," 270). He describes his own comments on Smith as in fact "deferential, mild, and agnostic" ("MER," 277). This is an unsatisfactory response given the "general rules of morality" and "sympathetic" observation that Smith saw as central to civil society in its commercial form. The nature of reciprocity within Smith's capitalist *socius,* it must be said, begins to blur the "moral" versus "market" antinomy that is foundational to Thompson's early formulations of early modern popular culture. Taking from Hutcheson and Hume and foreshadowing Bentham, Smith's ideal of moral "sympathy" as described in *The Theory of Moral Sentiments,* and nearly twenty years later in *The Wealth of Nations,* is important here. For Smith too, a dynamic of mutual watching produces an intersubjective zone of reciprocity. The inequities experienced by the sufferer strike an experiential, or what Smith calls an "imagined," chord of mutuality in the sufferer's sympathetic witness. "For every rich man, there must be at least five hundred poor, and the affluence of the few supposes the indigence of the many," Smith would write in *The Wealth of Nations*.[40] But the inherent inequities of wealth were for Smith already resolved socially, in the arena of civil society where—according to Smith's Lockean rule—one also finds "the security of property . . . [and] the defense of the rich against the poor" (*WN*, 181). The boundaries of morality for Smith are thus contained within a capitalist form of government produced within civil society. As is evident in Book Two, Chapter Three of *The Wealth of Nations*, which echoes his blueprint of "moral sentiment" in the earlier treatise of 1759, "partial" behavior on either side of class division is reduced to the supra-materialist realm of character, conduct, and mutual respect.[41]

Thus, conflict writ as "moral" restraint is a historically necessary condition for the advance of markets, not inimical to them. For Smith, economic contradictions, rather than potentially confronted by a pre- or anticapitalist moral exchange "between persons" as in Thompson's paternalism, are resolved in precisely that (subjective) arena in the guise of "moral sympathy."[42] In a society necessarily unequal, the capitalist spectator finds experiential "correspondence" within civil society as "fellow feeling" (*TMS*, 10). And this is insufficiently distinguishable from Thompson's allegedly precapitalist gentleman/client relation. Far from standing outside, and thereby in opposition to, the market, sympathetic experience and (unequal) moral reciprocity are seen as effects surreptitiously congenial to the market in its earliest historical forms. Thus, to find within popular agency the rational correspondence of individual feeling is to move inadvertently within the very market relations that collective action is alleged to be opposing.

We have not in this overview of sympathetic morality traveled far from a concern over the loss of "human agency" attached to CS—that notion of stony activism that keeps knowing and doing at some economically unsullied mutual distance. Indeed, underneath current debates over the textual proclivities of CS and the hard questions theory asks of history is the tacit endorsement of Enlightenment intersubjectivity that attends Thompson's crowd. This same misdirected melding together of self-interest with collective response is what Wiegman and Frankenberg want rightly to pin to the overly volunteerist desires for post-whiteness that inform much of white labor history. When a cultural zone of mutual reciprocity is posited outside economy, the shadowy presence of consensus as moral experience becomes the preferred way of envisioning popular struggle. This account of the popular, which underwrites CS's interest in the masses, is traceable to Thompson, but finds its origins with Enlightenment rationalizations of affect that need to be redressed.

Adam Smith's theory of moral sympathy develops the individuation of the masses further along the lines Thompson has drawn. "We suppose ourselves the spectators of our own behavior," he writes, "and endeavor to imagine what effect it would, in this light, produce upon us. This is the only looking-glass by which we can, in some measure, with the eyes of other people, scrutinize the propriety of our own conduct" (*TMS*, 16). The primary feature of the moral "looking glass" is that it is circular: "the creation of an imaginative self-projection into an outsider whose standards and responses we reconstruct by sympathy."[43] In Smith's formula, the expression of outward sympathetic feeling is only the initial step in an infinite spectatorial chain. The sympathizing subject not only corresponds with his own experience of pleasure or suffering with the object of his gaze, but internalizes this correspondence such that the first subject/object relation is reproduced as the secondary "propriety" of voluntary self-restraint.[44] "A prison is certainly more useful to society than a palace" (*TMS*, 30), Smith would remark in anticipation of Bentham's panopticon. But the disciplinary procedures spelled out by Foucault are in Smith's much earlier example rather more efficient, softer in appearance but no less material in effect, than the bricks and mortar of education or early modern punishment.[45] For Smith, the "propriety" implicit in his circular moral gaze is at work by epistemological necessity, and indeed, at the level of language itself. Unlike the spectator of Hutcheson and Hume, both of whom gave prominence in their ethical theories to spectatorial experience, Smith's morality is found in the voluntary (read "social" or "cultural") domain of "impartial" communicative exchange. "Society and conversation . . . are the most powerful remedies for restoring the mind to . . . that equal and happy temper, which is so necessary to self-satisfaction" (*TMS*, 23).

A communicative ethic such as the one Smith prescribes, presumed concurrent to the market at its normative core, operates somewhat differently than Habermas's otherwise similar formulation of the Enlightenment public sphere.[46] In accordance with Habermas, Smith's spectator may be traced to the polite conversation of imaginatively presumed equals characteristic of the early-eighteenth-century coffeehouse. Indeed, Smith's moral "spectator" can be traced directly to Joseph Addison's journal by that very name.[47] But in the place of Habermas's disinterested rational critical debate, Smith offers room for the more affective and potentially conflict-ridden dimensions of feeling summed up in the term "rational admiration" (*LRBL*, 61). This term allows for the redoubled correspondence, as we have seen in moral sympathy, first between the spectator and his object, and then in the objectification of the looking-subject as, in turn, appropriate in the eyes of an "impartial" (if absent) third-party witness. But the term "rational admiration" also, perhaps in a more perfidious fashion, embraces—indeed, would seem to require—the occasional violence of "unnatural objects" so as to extend its seamless observational advance. In his 1746 essay "Principles Which Lead and Direct Philosophical Inquiries," Smith sums up "the advance of knowledge" as follows: "Wonder, Surprise, and Admiration, are words which, though often confounded, denote in our language, sentiments that are indeed allied. . . . What is new and singular, excites that sentiment which in strict propriety, is called Wonder; what is unexpected, Surprise; and what is great or beautiful, Admiration."[48] The singular object "stands alone in [the spectator's] imagination as if it were detached from all the other species of that genus to which it belongs" (*EPS,* 40). To "get rid of that Wonder," Smith continues, requires the "connecting principles" of philosophy as an "art which addresses itself to the imagination" (*EPS,* 46).

Smith's definition of philosophy, which is coterminous with the "imitative arts" associated with belles lettres (and later "literature"), is essentially a narratological—or one is tempted in the 1740s to say "novelistic"—foray into the self-evident sequencing of phenomena within their proper "species and genera" (*EPS,* 40).[49] In moving from "surprise" to "admiration," the goal of knowledge is to seek in "the class[ification] of things" (*EPS,* 39) the same continuity of objects that is fundamental to moral sympathy. From the "momentary loss of reason" experienced when an object is "dissimilar," "unexpected," "strange," "disjointed," or for that matter, "new," agitation is anesthetized within a "natural order of succession." "Philosophy," as Smith defines it, "by representing the invisible chains which bind together all these disjointed objects, endeavors to introduce order" (*EPS,* 37). This order takes place by "the endeavor to arrange and methodize all [the mind's] ideas" (*EPS,* 37). By thus putting "extraordinary and uncommon objects" into "proper classes and assortments," philosophy redresses the imagination such that it "may fill up the *gap,* [and] like a bridge, may . . . unite those seemingly distant objects, [so] as to render the passage of thought betwixt them smooth" (*EPS,* 42; emphasis added). For Smith, the "mind takes pleasure," and is therefore "relaxed," "in observing the resemblances that are discoverable between different objects" (*EPS,* 36).

As it functions to designate the classificatory mistakes that knowledge is prone to produce outside the temporality of novelistic sequence, Smith's key term "gap" is important to emphasize. It designates the agency of "multitudes" as the unrepresentable—but nonetheless *generative*—basis for knowledge production. In this sense, class struggle finds an epistemological analogue in classification struggle, or what we might better call the persistent dotting in CS of the lines that separate disciplinary difference within the history of writing. In another early essay, "The First Formations of Language," Smith refers to the mind's innate generic sensibility as a process of assorting "the great multitudes of objects," a process central to language itself (*LRBL*, 205). For Smith it is the presence of "multitudes" within the association of words that hurries the mind toward object correspondence at the experiential level. The "fellow feeling" between sufferers (below) and witnesses (above) an antagonistic class divide is thus previously played out in a prepolitical, horizontal continuity between objects and language in thought. Multiplicity ("surprise" and "wonder") is immanent to meaningful discourse under capitalism, and always threatens to upset its otherwise natural experiential harmonies ("rational admiration"). But again, interruption within Smith's commercial *socius* is effectively recuperated—before it ever fully speaks—in the production of knowledge itself and at the semiological level in the correspondence of words to things.[50] Indeed, the more potentially violent the "uncommon object," the more satisfying its eventual adequation in "metaphysical" exchange (*EPS*, 35).

Thus, for Smith, morality is method, subjectivity a careful social grammar. Both work together to keep the production of knowledge in a cooperatively detached relation to economy. Thought, by the necessity of category, keeps the "multitude" at bay, and this is so even though thought demands the occasional interruption of the "new." Recalling the new-generational "mob" that, on the order of Nelson's "minimal irony," "haunts" ruined academe, Smith becomes Clark Kerr's ideal multiversity occupant. And depending on what version of collective agency CS wants to have, depending, that is, on what proximity the multitude is presumed to have to academic writing, Adam Smith may be the real ghost dogging CS's troubled soul. The definition of sympathetic moral spectatorship as "emotions . . . just and proper, and suitable to their objects" (*TMS*, 16) finds its premise according to Smith in the very habits of thought. The modern social arrangement of the market, one might say, is granted through a philosophico-hermeneutic technique that is itself a matter of associational mandate: "smoothing out" otherwise "unexpected," "violent," or "convulsive" objects by the "habit of the imagination" to arrange each disruption according to its moral "propriety" (*EPS*, 41). It is falsely assumed by the terms "natural," "impartial," "experiential," or "moral" that Enlightenment "habits of imagination" can be cordoned off from, so as to "smooth out," the more pressing contradictions that constitute the Enlightenment project as a whole. Those contradictions continue on the order of postmodern academe's intensified encounters with absence. In the way the humanities mourns its transdisciplinary ruin and the academy's absorption by the market, and in the way we witness the fast rise and fortunate fall of so-called whiteness studies, Smith's dreaded "gaps" could not be more evidently in play. In my account of Thompson and Smith, to seek from those contradictions a moral foundation for knowledge would be a task, wittingly or not, that is circumscribed within the field each attempts to describe. The "moral economy" of the English crowd is manifest, not opposed to the accumulation of wealth as Thompson would have it, but when he reads back upon mass action an exterior rationale that reproduces a philosophical legacy formed at the moment of mass domestication. The conflict within CS stated before as the "text" versus "agency" (or "academic" versus "activist") debate thus rears its troubled head again. But in discussion of Thompson and Smith, this takes place less as a matter of theoretical excess against Enlightenment objectivity, and more as an antitheoretical confusion about the Enlightenment's ongoing effect. The securing of objects of knowledge in experience, and the freedom "hard history" promises to give "agency" at some post-theoretical (or appropriately post-"popular") date, is by now familiar terrain. But perhaps this terrain is even more familiar than that. Perhaps the relationship between theory—as a practice of multitudes—and its current discontents is best understood as the latest example of thought in a centuries-old series of "smooth" repetitions.

How else to describe Thompson's second most important contribution to CS's U.S. legacy, his infamous imbroglio with Louis Althusser's alleged theoretism, which played out during CS's nascent stages of the 1960s? Motivating Althusser's call thirty-odd years ago for the delimiting features of materialist practices of writing is the notion, put simply, that objective facts emerge and circulate as social and historical forces that move in many directions. In relation to these forces, consciousness and experience play a secondary role. This is by now a boilerplate Marxist proposition.[51] Here Althusser takes up the more difficult issue posed by Sartre of "a plurality of epicenters of action."[52] History through a Sartrean template contains no unidirectional force conversing with human consciousness—especially consciousness writ as "moral experience"—which somehow remains anterior to the historical forces that consciousness may seek to describe. For Althusser, in contradistinction to Smith and, as we shall see, Thompson, a convenient shorthand would be to say that the objects of materialist history retain the status of a multitude. And they maintain this status precisely on account of a materialist conjoining between knowledge and economy that the ruined public research university now witnesses at large. In the Althusserian sense, objects of knowledge are, to repeat a well-known term, overdetermined by a mass of incommensurable—but nonetheless real—influences and meanings. The totality of this complex arrangement is unavailable for pure description because there is *no place* for writing that is anterior to the material forces that knowledge seeks to measure (and that "no place," it should be said again, is exactly what is crucial to our work). Thus, Althusser's enigmatic phrase: "while the economy is determinate in the last instance, that instance never comes."[53] The status of this generative absence, which has achieved a new urgency given, for example, the aporic functions of whiteness studies in the ruined university, marks essential locations for establishing not the dismissal but the adjoining of labor to thought. The ongoing debates around CS and academic agency thus ought to be located here, in the attempt to disrupt the circularity between identity and object, and relocate within Smith's dreaded "gaps" the agency of multitudes that CS encountered (unwittingly) by the academic labor market's default. The right coordinates of the CS debate might be redrawn according to these lines then, with Nelson's "minimal irony" in unabashed full view. That debate has signaled, it would seem, not the recent excesses of cultural theory that empirical dialogue will eventually contain, but a cultural turn *from* theory, played out in the 1960s by the rise of the British New Left, and indeed, played out two centuries before that by the likes of Adam Smith.

In an account of knowledge production as a "moral" imperative where experience is determinate, collective agency is reduced to the unfettered collation of objects in the inquirer's mind. Between the Marxist terms "social being" and "social consciousness," Thompson inserts an "experiential" or "cultural" zone to which the archivist retains an unmediated pass. But a closer look at this arrangement—*pace* the charge against Althusser—reveals how the troubled term "culture" prohibits an account of the relation between experience and an openness to knowledge as itself a historically specific relation. What the term "culture" ensures in this guise is an act not of dialogue, however one may configure it, but again of a quiet circularity. "Empirical dialogue" in the "cultural" zone functions the same for effective historical agents as it does the right-thinking historian: the "rational evidence . . . adduced by men and women" in history mimics the historian's "dialogue . . . between thought and its objective materials."[54] Indeed, Thompson presents a historical method that betrays a kind of mirroring of mirroring. The historian's mandate to maintain "the openness with which one must approach all knowledge" (*PT,* 168)—an initial mirroring—is mirrored in a second sense by the way "the people" are themselves supposed to have risen to self-consciousness in their own historical circumstance. The apparent slippage with which we began, between historical method and historical object, remains one of the most troubling features of *The Poverty of Theory.* Bearing in mind Smith's "moral looking glass," the spontaneous and circular nature of Thompson's historical object ("the people") is a reduplication not only of his own historical method, but in the end, of the limits of eighteenth-century philosophy in its ability to reduplicate the mirroring process itself.

To interrupt this process of reproduction is the point of Althusser's first essay in *Reading Capital*—an invitation precisely to challenge the bait-and-switch between individuated sympathetic experience and the generative absence, or "gaps," that Smith assigned to "multitudes." In "From 'Capital' to

MULTITUDE OR CULTURALISM?

Marx's Philosophy," Marx's own reading of Smith (as Althusser's rereading of Marx) is presented as an interrogation of "the mirror myth of immediate vision and reading."[55] In defiance of Smith's various subjective correspondences, Althusser recalls Spinoza to posit "a theory of the opacity of the immediate" (*RC*, 16). This evocation of theory seeks a "protocol of reading [for] what classical economy does not see," namely, the generative absence in Smith's *Wealth of Nations*—Marx called it "labor power" (*RC*, 23)—which is visible only in multiple forms. Once again, the ideological lineaments of the ruined university as an institution predicated on its own absence (and that of the humanities, of whiteness, and so on) are traceable to this rift within the Thompson and Althusser debate.[56] On the basis of seeing absence as the location of labor power, as Althusser insists, the first of Smith's philosophical goals is diminished and the stakes of contemporary CS are more fully revealed: capitalist contradiction is no longer resolved in the "social" or "cultural" field of "imagined" reciprocity, but is brought to bear within knowledge in its materialist potential for subjective and social interruption (e.g., "multitudes"). Althusser, thus, defines a "fact" as "a mutation in the existing structural relations" (*RC*, 102). That he refuses to seat knowledge too far outside these "existing structural relations," as we have seen with Thompson's evocation of the term "culture," marks the challenge to Smith's second philosophical accomplishment: to move knowledge from the realm of consensual rational experience by locating it within "the conditions of its production" (25). In this alternative to Enlightenment epistemological reflex, the identification of objects that experience forbids come to hinder the silent guarantees of capital. This, of course, is precisely the challenge Readings identifies as the work of writing in the ruined university—a matter equally of cognitive and material struggle. And to ignore it, recalling a handy example, is to miss the significance of whiteness studies as an academic labor conflict born (necessarily) from a dialectic of embarrassment.

HOW COLOR SAVED THE CANON

> The Canon, far from being the servant of the dominant social class, is a minister of death.
>
> —Harold Bloom

Class, death, and the canon—could there be a more apposite combination of items with which to conclude this long argument about the importance of generative absence to the work of writing in the ruined university? Give Harold Bloom this much, at least: literary studies has become the official phantasmatic discipline of the humanities. CSers and anti-CSers, theorists and traditional literary types would seem to hold this notion in common. And the battered discipline's large itinerant workforce, its part-timers, frustrated job seekers, and disgruntled TAs, are burdened with having to live within those same shadowy institutional conditions. English is a ghostly enterprise, perhaps like no other humanities discipline, in that it is everywhere and nowhere at once. So Bloom may have something with regard to canonicity and death, though this "something" is perhaps not as far as he would like from the political concerns the epigraph eschews. Consider, if the best literature is also grieved as that writing that most purposefully administers absence, then the canon, as yet another chimerical force, cannot *simply* be an instrument of power. That instrumentality depends, to stay within Bloom's entrenched Romantic-Oedipal lexicon, on what profundity literature's own death might deliver once its epitaph is written by the next author in line. To the extent that representation and labor are intertwined in English, literature is, as Bloom indicates without making the crucial labor connection, an important example of the kind of knowledge-activity we have been tracing all along. It is yet one more material encounter with the newly disappeared.

Think here of PK weeping, whiteness studies, or Althusser's focus on the opacity of the immediate, and the notion of generative absence that I am reading in Bloom will make sense. Against the morbid refusal of politics in his detached Byronic register, a more earthbound set of questions about the significance of literature remains intact beyond its celebrated wake: how is literature beholden to dominance in the ruined university, not just among and between classes, but inseparable from that, when such writing is associated with the question of race? And yet how, given its widely proclaimed and fairly recent dissolution, is literature not simply reducible to class or racial dominance as such? The epigraph from Bloom, wittingly or not, begs the same questions regarding epistemological "gaps," mass agency, and labor power that we have put to the men of PK, multiculturalism, whiteness studies, and CS already. And it invites us to put these questions to the lately very salable proclamations of literary demise (or we should more precisely say, its double demise, since literature's death for Bloom occurs both categorically as a discipline, and rhetorically as an aesthetic practice). Specifically, we might ask, what relevance remains of English, once gone, for rekindling those lost democratic futures that founded the modern public research university and superficially sustained it while higher education found its wary way through the challenges of "massification" after World War II? The epigraph from Bloom, I am suggesting, provokes an interest, appropriate to the dissensual order we have been limning for some time, in what can only be described as an interest in afterlives. In a sense he may miss altogether, the death reference insists upon the democratic purposes of literary work. These purposes, I want to argue beyond Bloom, are worth holding on to precisely for not being there. In this sense, as all along in *After Whiteness,* we are still wrestling with an economy of absence.

Before getting to how that matters for literary studies, I will provide a short summary of what has been offered so far. I have maintained, close to Readings, that the peculiar temporality active in the key term in that last group of sentences—afterlife—is the predominate mode of working in the humanities as the university articulates its own fiscal and epistemological disasters. My shorthand for giving academic writing its contemporary materialist bearing beyond Readings has been to place collective over individual agency at each and every turn. There was Clark Kerr's career-spanning fear of the new-generational "mob." This linked his investment in maintaining national consensus to the forms of corporatist postmodern fragmentation that was (and remains) the multiversity's logical extension. The multiversity's appeal to cultural brokering in the wake of the 1960s helped soften the collision between economy and knowledge that came later. And this multicultural appeal occurred, recall, while racial multiplicity negotiated the unsuspecting return of class politics to the university in the muted and dissensual form that Kerr finally despised. Then there was the question of CS's ambivalent investment in mass culture, which I argued was an earlier example of what whiteness studies suffers, only on a grander and more career-rewarding scale. CS's association with the masses, recall again Kerr's new generational "mob," doubled back as irony, once it rendered popular struggle a point of reference external to the labor conflicts that the university was living when CS arrived stripped of class. In this sense, the CS academostar became a double agent as the humanities pruned its ranks, intensified its productivity, and annihilated its own middle class. The ironic reemergence of class, I wanted to show, comes by way of that peculiar temporality that the ruined university demands. Class came to CS in a belated way, like death itself, after CS was a tenured and salaried part of the university. Class came to CS by default, in other words. My account of CS's eighteenth-century origins argued, next, that the historical appeal to popular culture in the likes of E. P. Thompson cordons itself off from the agency of multitudes in the same way. In his unacknowledged philosophical debt to Adam Smith, which maintained the same fear of what Smith called "gaps," Thompson's moral economy argument keeps writing and political economy at bay so as to maintain the twin Enlightenment ideals that falsely hold the politically committed scholar of popular culture apart from the popular itself. Those ideals were traceable to Smith as corresponding sympathetic spectatorship, and correlatively, the desire to reduce mass action to the kind of rational macro-subjectivity that the early capitalist *socius* required. Thus, referring both to the role of writing in cultivating humanist agency and its function in the hoped-for maintenance of knowledge without categorical "gaps," I described Smith's moral spectatorship as the "novelization" of multitudes. Regarding David Roediger's attempts to originate the critical study of whiteness in black authors, Frankenberg rejected the same eighteenth-century philosophical hangover as the antimaterialist ruse behind what she called subjective "paralleling." (Wiegman made the same feminist case against humanist white labor history.) By contrast, Althusser's locating labor power within epistemological absence helped set the stage for linking writing back to political economy within the ruined university. My focus on generative absence, a materialist rehabilitation of Smith's dreaded "gaps," was meant to shed new light on academe. Public higher education, I wanted finally to show, is beset with the ambivalence of masses that can no longer be held separate from the knowledge that is supposed to represent them.

Thus has the argument proceeded so far. In what remains, I want to focus on one more moment of institutional finitude in the array of others detailed so far. By this I mean that peculiar form of representation we still call literature, and its bearing on the kind of questions we still have to ask about whiteness in its own supposed wake. Specifically, I want to address how imaginative writing, when encountering race or pretending to avoid it, attends to labor as generative absence. What follows, then, is admittedly something on the order of a Bloomian deathwatch, but with a decidedly materialist twist. I want to counter his tears and fears by making the *unsympathetic* suggestion that (white) literature's so-called death is just what (white) literature needs, if its imagined absent place within the ruined university is to function usefully, or function at all. The turn to imaginative writing in this sense is meant to reclaim Smith's dreaded categorical aporia—writ here within both a disciplinarity and racial register—and to do so, risking my own form of hyperbole, with an interest in labor I still intend to say is massive. I want to take seriously the continued claims of popular culture upon literary writing in its supposed afterlife, instead of adhering to those pernicious forms of subjective correspondence that are built into the Enlightenment's nagging universalistic claims. Thus below I turn to Toni Morrison's formulation of American Africanist reading as an alternative to the antitheoretical dismissal of absence (literary and otherwise), showing how her work offers an understanding of literature where the connection between writing and economy comes, via race critique, fully and uniquely to the fore. My elaboration of what Morrison calls "whiteness and the literary imagination" is not concerned with the so-called death of literature as a missed opportunity for the Enlightened evolution of the masses. And neither does it conceive of post-whiteness as a revolutionary spark portending some foreseeable moment of unified collective agency that white male academics can unproblematically assign. The attempt here is to make sense of the displacement of literary studies and to offer a nondismissive account of the work produced by those left writing within it. This account of literary whiteness is not offered to prescribe democracy's future by the preservation of certain canonical authors or literary texts. Rather, following Morrison's cue, I hope to clarify how literature may yet signal one or two of democracy's still occulted historical burdens.

That literary studies has been killed in a war on Western culture, done in by the profligate triumvirate of CS, multiculturalism, and/or theory, is a hackneyed but utterly widespread charge. The staleness, if not the downright meanness, of this allegation is easy enough to expose. John K. Wilson's point about the predominance of Shakespeare over Alice Walker in undergraduate English courses (he cites a ratio of about a hundred to one, you may recall) has already been noted. Wilson has similar revelations about the multicultural undergraduate requirement, which we can now add to this earlier remark. Consider, for example, that while in 1990, 46 percent of colleges required a multicultural course, requirements in Western civilization also rose at that time, from 43.1 percent on the heels of the civil rights movement in 1970 to 53 percent in 1990.[1] Skirmishes in 2002 over the core curriculum at the University of Chicago, and at Stanford University in 1988, join a myriad of exaggerated declarations characterizing the Western literary canon's demise.[2] But a 1995 MLA report shows that traditional authors in undergraduate introductory English courses, far from having been disregarded, retain their expected pride of place. For the American survey, the top five authors likely to appear in such courses are Hawthorne (66 percent), followed by Whitman, Dickinson, Twain, and Emerson. For the British survey, such radical upstarts as Chaucer (89 percent), then Shakespeare, Milton, Wordsworth, Pope, and Donne top the roster. By notable contrast, James Baldwin, Langston Hughes, and, of course, Alice Walker, are cited with frequencies of less than 1 percent. Toni Morrison, who comes in at a hardly threatening 1.8 percent of frequency, trails the American Puritan Cotton Mather, who comes in at 2.1 percent.[3] Trends in job availability only confirm this scene. The English Ph.D. seeking academic work in 2001 in one of the offending disciplines, for example, gay and lesbian studies, would be about ten times *less* likely to find a job than the new classics doctorate; one hundred times less likely, when compared to jobs offered in British literature, which is still the dominant force of its namesake, English. Far from displacing the Western canon in terms of job demand, multiethnic literatures made up only half the numbers of British jobs during the 2001 hiring season.[4]

Contrary indications regarding both curricula and the job market notwithstanding, the National Association of Scholars and its ilk have declared literature's expiration with risibly embellished regularity.[5] Since the mid-1980s, when interdisciplinary studies rolled into departments of English in the hollow horse of Birmingham CS, literary critics have been poised to defend themselves against a shibboleth horde of imperious multicultural theorists. (Stopping to examine university budgets or considering the domestic crisis of the state would be for such critics politically distasteful.) Even among more moderate voices, literature's funeral bell is sounded and heard. Alvin Kernan's suitably titled book

The Death of Literature registers a more historically inflected (and more justifiable) concern that "book culture, of which literature is a central part, is disappearing."[6] Kernan's subsequent edited volume, *What's Happened to the Humanities?* also hunts for a logic by which to explain "the humanities' . . . lost ground," a loss that is more or less conceded.[7] Robert Scholes, in *The Rise and Fall of English*, is "interested in returning to the roots of English studies," having also identified the discipline in a diminished, postlapsarian state.[8] Harold Bloom, not to be outdone, is caught somewhere between an elitist insistence on high aesthetic purity and righteous punk-rock self-effacement. In no less mandarin a venue than *Newsweek*, Bloom echoes Hamlet or Sid Vicious, it is not clear: literary studies has "no future," he remarks.[9] (It might also be worth noting that for all his right-wing supporters, Bloom himself is a culturally conservative socialist.) The death-of-literature refrain is not purchased exclusively by those who argue on behalf of preserving the sanctity of traditional literary texts, however. Its epitaph is as likely to be written by the cultural right as by the left. In a 1990 book describing the rise of CS, Anthony Easthope gives a marginally Bloom-like intimation that literature's so-called death is a feature built into its very capacity for living. Easthope declares, with exactly the right amount of qualification to make the statement just, that "'pure' literary studies, though dying, remains institutionally dominant in Britain and North America."[10] Ten years later, one of the first and most influential chroniclers of CS's U.S. incarnation, Patrick Bratlinger, seals off the bardicidal scene and asks the nervy question, *Who Killed Shakespeare?*[11]

How to make sense of literary studies insofar as it has conceded its own categorical vacuity—pitched its own absence—with such ubiquitous fervor and force? The disciplinary lacuna attendant to the phantasmatic displacement of traditional critical habit is worth taking seriously here. Death has a kind of prescience in contemporary literary practice. And along the shifting borders of humanities knowledge, there is some clarity on how the sticky tenacity of imaginative writing gets another chance at connecting with the democratic potential it only ever pretended to have. There is some clarity, too, in recollecting the short history of literature as publicly relevant discourse, regarding identity's own disintegration as an academic labor concern.[12] Think here of multicultural displacement as a politics of category writ back into economy via literature's imagined demise, and call this, broadly, a class-as-classification struggle. Recall, once more, the persistence of Adam Smith's multitude (as well as Kerr's "mob"). The multitude was regarded by Smith first and foremost as a generic mutation, which the Enlightenment division between materiality and thought, as much as the disciplinary divisions between knowledges themselves, was designed to make rationally calculable. If new objects were left unrecuperated by consensus-producing sympathetic reflection, "gaps" occurred and gave rise to the categorical misfires that threatened the system with incalculable difference. Again, this was Smith's "novelization" of multitudes. It was accordingly within Smith's epistemological "gaps" where Althusser located the relational opacity of labor and, in *Reading Capital* (the full weight of those two words becoming clear), attempted to reconnect political economy and writing. In considering disciplines along eighteenth-century lines, then, the categorization of knowledge was itself a way of adequating subjects to objects on profit's behalf. Under these historical circumstances, the imagination becomes the quintessential tool for assuring that identities are individuated, while their differences are too conveniently pacified and allied. Imagination deployed affect as detached moral sympathy in the separation between materiality and knowledge. In this way, the encounter with aporia, today everywhere the rule, was considered fatal to the disciplinary arrangements secured by the Enlightenment. It should hardly be surprising, then, that absence comes once again to mark the limit of literature's historical advance.

But it is also according to this historical trajectory that literature finds renewed relevance, and does necessarily, I am suggesting, within its own wake, as much as within the wake of whiteness. Thus, in spite of two hundred years and more of anxious prohibition, the so-called death of literature forces the Enlightenment's final and most penetrating question: what sense can the displaced discipline make of displacement *itself* as a way of making writing relevant to the democratic potential of masses? To ask this question is to look for what Pierre Machery calls the "determinate insufficiency" of a literary text. And this insufficiency is made more pressing now that the unified (and unifying) qualities of imaginative writing, though by some still desired, are universally declared to be gone. Machery goes on to ask the literary critic to demonstrate "the unconsciousness of *the* work" (emphasis mine), which insofar as literature is a materially situated enterprise means also making clear the unconsciousness of academic labor.[13] Literature, in this context, elicits the generative force of absence that attends to disciplinary "gaps" instead of smoothing them over. To say the word in the contemporary *post*-literary sense reconnects imagination and labor, even though that connection occurs in formerly (and formally) unidentifiable ways. The place of whiteness in the ruined university might be approached again from this angle. The academic turn to whiteness, I have been trying to suggest, is not a supplement to the CS *versus* literature, theory *versus* activism, or structure *versus* experience debates that marked the last two decades of humanities scholarship. Neither is whiteness studies bereft of the contradictions implicit within the more recent business of managed multiculturalism, as we have already seen. Rather, the stresses and strains regarding

HOW COLOR SAVED THE CANON

nonnormative subjectivity are the symptoms of having to work in the ruined university, where absence is the name of the game. Moreover, in spite, or indeed, as a direct result, of the ambivalence attendant to so much work on the unremarkable race, attention to whiteness can occasion a more nuanced understanding of the vicissitudes of academic labor. Not only that, but I want also to suggest that whiteness can provide the opening for collective practice that does not reduce to self-evident forms of individual agency, nor to its various facile inversions.

Catherine Belsey makes sense of the death-of-literature mantra in ways that are helpful for further assessing the prevailing sense of absence in the ruined university. Belsey takes the reactionary backlash that constitutes literature's imagined demise seriously, and in this she provides a workable transition to Toni Morrison's critique of literary whiteness in *Playing in the Dark*. Belsey begins by noting the "cry of anguish from white heterosexual men," whose voices, as we have recorded, fill the formerly hallowed halls of "English studies in the postmodern condition."[14] In the avowal of literature's forced dissolution, she detects the "ghosts and revenants" of white masculine self-marginalization, a haunting whose consequences by this time are more than familiar. In the enactment of public lament, Belsey unpacks the anxious logic behind the way white male academics are now reaching for their "uncanny double" ("ES," 135). Think here not only of Sander Gilman's appeal to the Promise Keepers and of Bloom's gloom beamed across C-SPAN, but also of the psychic recipe of white labor history that has been the object of feminist critique. White literary mourning is, in this sense, characteristic of a greater great-white-hype than just whiteness studies. It is the bait-and-switch that is the rush to marginality within the humanities, and indeed within an ambivalent nation at large. By appealing to an absent canon, Belsey writes, the white male literary scholar "brings the subject to the edge of a confrontation with its own relativity, [and] paradoxically, also permits it to back away again, reaffirm[ing] the distance between the subject and the unthinkable condition of existence" ("ES," 136). Recalling Wiegman on the new psychology of dominance through difference, one recalls the humanistic drive she located in white labor history—a kind of recoil against, and recovery from, the dreaded "gaps" between knowledge and the best of political intention. In Belsey's version of Bloom, as in Wiegman's take on David Roediger, the "unthinkable condition" of white male identity is *both* properly fixed in a specific context *and* "paradoxically" dissociated from its own presumptive transparency and self-understanding. For feminist critics of white masculinity as it plays out in the academic arena, the least and most self-serving work is shot through with the same damning contradiction. In Wiegman's case against humanist labor history, the historian keeps labor at an unwitting distance, and thereby avoids the materialist feminist demand for a nonobjective, post-white analytic. In Belsey's argument, the same trick allows Bloom a parting Romantic shot at the coveted marginal center.

Literature's swan song thus mimics the complaints, Belsey indicates, of "white heterosexual men who have reached the point of salary and scale when they ought, in the normal course of things, to have expected a certain deferential attention, only to find that they have been upstaged by lesbian critics half their age" ("ES," 126). Such candid, exacting, and appropriately unsympathetic criticism of those who used to (and do still) make up the professional elite of English certainly levels the academic playing field (at least at the top). But there is a more productive point to Belsey's depiction of "the end of literary criticism" ("ES," 123) than just a parallel jostling between divergent sexualities or different generations as they compete for academic stardom. Although Belsey does not stress the matter here, this more productive point has to do with how the white literary subject's death—how its "determined insufficiencies," recalling Machery—may go on to animate the material significance that imaginative writing has tried for too long to resist. Belsey's remark about "salary" in that scathing quote above casually gestures toward the larger task at hand. To delineate this task requires one more move in this discussion of literary absence. We still need to situate the rhapsody of dissonance surrounding canonical literature within the context of labor and pay. Toni Morrison's work on whiteness, I want now to propose, enables one to conceive of canonical literary writing in exactly those terms.

My interest in Morrison, for these limited purposes, is focused primarily on her nonfiction best-seller, *Playing in the Dark: Whiteness and the Literary Imagination*.[15] The first significant item one notices upon opening this influential book is—to evoke the term precisely—its remarkably *massive* appeal. The book, like Morrison herself, is a media triumph. The radical socialist news journal *In These Times* remarks upon the "hard racial truths that [*Playing in the Dark*] contains." Calling the argument "daring, profound, and painful," the *Voice Literary Supplement* similarly draws attention to how Morrison shows that "the temptation to enslave others . . . has shaded our national literature." Yet *Newsweek,* the venue in which Bloom gave literature "no future," calls Morrison a "classic American writer squarely within the tradition of Poe, Melville, Twain, and Faulkner." I evoke these publicity blurbs, first, to establish that imaginative writing ("classic" and "national literature") and labor (the "racial truths" of "slavery") exist inseparably, if utterly antagonistically, in Morrison's public reception; and, second, to suggest that this inseparability extends to her own embattled place within a canon alleged to be gone. Regarding the "shady" prospects of the canon wars, identity *is* what writing *does*, in Morrison's work.

Writing, she remarks, "needs another for completion." But Morrison offers a decisive caveat regarding literature's continuation, insofar as that continuation is the canon's effective demise: "as far as the future is concerned," she notes, "all necks are on the line."[16]

The first task of *Playing in the Dark* is to debunk the hypocrisy of Enlightenment universality, and with it the "sycophancy of white identity" when it appears as an unmarked and normative ideal (a more common event in the 1980s and early 1990s than it is in the aftermath of whiteness studies). More important than simply debunking Eurocentrism, however, Morrison offers a further-reaching hypothesis regarding the syncretic and relational nature of race and of whiteness as such. By the term "American Africanism," she means to signal the implicit location of Africa within American whiteness, so near to the false idea of ontological purity because it is so desperately feared (*PD,* 7). Thus "from the overwhelming presence of black people in the United States," Morrison seeks to revive "one of the most furtively radical impinging forces on the country's literature" (*PD,* 5), which heretofore has been its absent cause. In this sense, Morrison suggests in her Nobel Prize lecture, "word-work . . . is generative."[17] Its "*absences* are so stressed, so ornate, so planned, they call attention to themselves" ("UT," 11; emphasis mine). Literature is for her, quite clearly, an encounter with "a presence-that-is-assumed-not-to-exist" ("UT," 19); an active engagement *with,* but as importantly *by,* the "*absences* of vital presences" ("UT," 15; emphasis mine). The affective arrangements she attaches to literary practice are meant to elicit neither the "summoning [of] false memories of stability, [nor] harmony among the public" (*NL,* 14). While "narrative," working in a lexicon that takes her close to Adam Smith, is "one of the principal ways in which we absorb knowledge" (*NL,* 7), Morrison writes, literary absence resists articulation by the "infantile heads of state" (*NL,* 15). The democratic ideals of literature are for Morrison conceptually incalculable, to use a term from my account of the census, since "the future of freedom" one might find there is predicated on the "fear and longing" of and for another who is everywhere and nowhere at once. Morrison calls this a "haunting . . . from which our early literature seemed unable to extricate itself" (*PD,* 33).

But before white academics might celebrate the belated visibility of difference as something whiteness may now welcome as its own, a certain materialist-inspired self-critical pause regarding "colored whiteness" is in order.[18] The temptation upon reading certain passages of *PD* is to seek a false continuity of oppression between nominally black and white American dreamers. But its materialist challenge is to come to terms with the unevenness of how racial categories position us in different ways, in different times and places, and with local, and inconsistent, effects. Frankenberg called this the need to resist false parallels between blackness and whiteness. She, like Morrison, forgoes the attempt to read history or literature for mixed-racial consensus, wanting to avoid an Enlightenment return to formalist agency that jettisons the term "radical" (Morrison's term) from the absent presence of American Africanism. The necessary caveat, then, is to tread carefully around what Doris Sommers calls "the ravages of facile intimacies" that white folk bring to "minority writing." The misguided tendency here is to substitute "self-authorizing method" for the "discontinuities" that were implicit in the desire to debunk white normativity in the first place.[19] As white male academics may be tempted to celebrate their own belated marginal status, we have seen from Belsey, Wiegman, and others how whiteness studies may turn back against its better self. Within the mandates of multicultural fluidity that the ruined university demands, and under the conditions of managed multiculturalism, who knows what effects white writing in the margins may prove to have in times to come? This question calls for one last move regarding Morrison, which is to transition from the concern with afterlives to concerns pertaining more directly to future challenges to capital. We may now address absent causality as a matter of labor power, which, in Morrison's account of race and writing, is hiding in only obvious locales.

Given what we have covered so far, there are at least three forms of absence in Morrison's texts. The first two are manifest in the theory of ontological syncretism implicit in American Africanism: blackness and whiteness are inseparable, she suggests. Therefore, the distance implicit in presumptive white purity is false, and covers an occulted racial proximity. The absence attendant to formerly unmarked white purity and the absence that is the unrecognized generative force of Africa are both alluded to here. But they are alluded to in their own, by no means commensurably quantifiable, ways. The way to tell the difference between what are no longer the identities of blackness and whiteness at all, but are relations, depends on the third absence Morrison engages: the very absence at work in the so-called death-of-literature phenomenon as it plays out in the ruined university as labor struggle. Peggy Kamuf calls literature, in this sense, "a division in fiction . . . a division which continues to divide."[20] Recalling the canon debate, she asks, "What do we teach *as* literature?" And she replies, in a lexicon reminiscent of Readings, "the question seems to go to the very border along which . . . the university . . . sets itself off from the outside" (*DL,* 4). Literature redivides and collapses the inside/outside division in the process of its own failed institutionalization. Think here not just of the American canon and the white identity attached to it, but the interrupting aporetic functions of writing that even the most critically minded whiteness studies scholars can hardly pretend to escape. Within her own deconstructive reserve, Kamuf would seem to be taking seriously Morrison's call for an encounter with absence as writing's generative force. As literary studies remarks upon its own divided state, race calls on labor in the ruined university, and thereby unleashes materiality on thought.

Morrison, I want to emphasize, is clear in her writing about the exploitative nature of capitalism. And this concern is explicitly related to her own interest in what Adam Smith resisted as categorical "gaps." As Sommers cautions, the "murderous mutuality" (*PC*, 31) that can result when white folk presume to "know the Other well enough to speak for him or her" (*PC*, x) is a result of a particularly academic disrespect for the opacity of academe's own conditions of labor. That those conditions, for white men who work in whiteness studies in particular, are for others to speak of ought to be made clear in Morrison's insistence both on the critical capacity of "holes and spaces" in language, and the identification of African presence as the absent cause of the American literary canon. But again, in addition to her primary concerns of imaginative writing, or one should say, inseparable from writing itself, generative absence is for Morrison both a racial operation and an explicit class concern: "black people," she writes, "have always been used as a buffer in this country between powers to prevent class war."[21] Whiteness is both an ego-reinforcing device and a way of distributing wealth and managing poverty. That point holds economically, politically, as well as in literary-aesthetic terms. But the force of Morrison's take on American Africanism is still further reaching than that. The two relations we call culture and economy can themselves no longer be held as separate in the ruined university. Representation is a political matter by its very historical nature. And thus, Morrison insists that those "holes and spaces" in her work be left open for an unnamed future point of democratic potential that requires as much textual as material redistribution. Her appeal to generative absence mimics the death-of-literature crowd in the same way it draws attention to whiteness. But that appeal works to register the race *and* class inequities that are symptomatically available in both.

Morrison writes in another context of "the deepest and earliest secret of all: that *just as we watch other life, other life watches us*" (emphasis in the original).[22] Scholars of whiteness and white scholars of literature, whether they are optimistically self-critical or pessimistically mournful, will do better than they have, if that line is kept close at hand. Whether the controversy now surrounding whiteness will end usefully or not, is something others will no doubt reveal.

NOTES

NOTES TO INTRODUCTION

1. This figure is cited in Barbara Kantrowitz and Pat Wingert, "What's at Stake," *Newsweek,* January 27, 2003, 35.

2. For accounts of American Renaissance conferences in 1998 and 2000, see respectively, "A Convocation of Bigots: The 1998 *American Renaissance* conference," *Journal of Blacks in Higher Education [JBHE]*, autumn 1998, 120–24; and Peter Novobatzy, "Bigots in Jackets and Ties: The 2000 *American Renaissance* Conference," *JBHE,* summer 2000, 117–24.

3. This quote, from *Time* magazine's "New Face of America" special issue (discussed below) is cited in Lauren Berlant, *The Queen of America Goes to Washington City* (Durham: Duke University Press, 1997), 200.

4. Mike Hill, "America's Biennial Gathering of Academic Racists," *JBHE,* spring 2002, 118–27.

5. Mike Hill, "Vipers in Shangri-la: Whiteness, Writing, and Other Ordinary Terrors," in *Whiteness: A Critical Reader,* ed. Mike Hill (New York: New York University Press, 1997), 1–18.

6. See, for example, Ross Chambers, "The Unexamined," in *the minnesota review*'s special issue "The White Issue" (fall 1996): 141–56.

7. The main event that marked the arrival of whiteness studies was the conference at the University of California–Berkeley in 1997, "The Making and Unmaking of Whiteness."

8. Fred Pfeil, *White Guys: Studies in Postmodern Domination and Difference* (London: Verso, 1995), 7.

9. "Hispanic and especially black households saw faster income growth during the boom [of the 1990s] than non-Hispanic whites, and have taken smaller hits in the bust. . . . Since 1999, men's incomes have fallen . . . while women's have continued to rise" (4). See Doug Henwood, "Not Such a Good Year, 2001," *Left Business Observer* 103 (December 18, 2002): 4–5. More recently, see *Newsweek*'s special issue, "She Works, He Doesn't: The

Latest Twist in Jobs and Family, Why 30 Percent of Working Women Earn More Than Their Husbands," May 12, 2003.

10. Levin's "research" has been bankrolled by the Pioneer Fund, a New York City–based foundation headed by a Harvard Law School graduate and tax attorney, Harry F. Weyher. Through his white-collar contacts in New York and elsewhere, Weyher has funneled more than $3.5 million into research supporting eugenics.

11. Hence the subtitle of this book uses the word "an" instead of "the" American majority. See, for example, Michael Zweig, *The Working Class Majority: America's Best Kept Secret* (Ithaca: Cornell University Press, 2000).

12. This fact was widely discussed as proof at AR that Buchanan's selection of Ezola Foster as a running mate was a PC compromise, and that his racial sentiments were sufficiently to the right. The proposed title of Buchanan's book is confirmed in an editorial piece, "Citing Neo-Nazi and Racist Sources, Buchanan Sounds the Alarm," *Intelligence Report,* summer 2002, 3.

13. It might also be noted here that for the richest 1 percent of the country the federal tax rate fell from 69 percent in 1970 to 40 percent in 1993, while for the median family it rose from 16 to 25 percent. On the precipitous bloating of CEO wages, see Kevin Phillips, *Wealth and Democracy: A Political History of the American Rich* (New York: Broadway, 2002).

14. Hill, "Vipers in Shangri-la," 2.

15. Of particular importance to this discussion are the following: bell hooks, *Ain't I a Woman* (Boston: South End Press, 1981); Cherríe Moraga and Gloria Anzaldúa, eds. *This Bridge Called My Back: Writings of Radical Women of Color* (Watertown, MA: Persephone Press, 1981); and Marilyn Frey, "On Being White: Thinking toward a Feminist Understanding of Race and Race Supremacy," in *The Politics of Reality: Essays in Feminist Theory* (Trumansburg, NY: Crossing Press, 1983), 110–27. See also Debra A. Castillo and María-Socorro Tabuenca, *Border Women: Writing from La Frontera* (Minneapolis: University of Minnesota Press, 2003).

16. As a point of pride at AR conferences, the vast majority of speakers boast postgraduate degrees. Many hold M.A.'s or Ph.D.'s from leading research institutions. Yale University, Cambridge University, the University of North Carolina, California State University at Northridge, and the University of London were just some of the alma maters claimed at the 2002 event.

17. Berlant, *Queen of America,* 175. Hereafter cited in text as *QW.*

18. Michael Warner, *Publics and Counterpublics* (New York: Zone Books, 2002), 188. Hereafter cited in text as *PCP.*

19. Susan Gubar, *Racechanges: White Skin, Black Face in American Culture* (New York: Oxford University Press, 1997), 34; Gubar cites Haraway's response to Eve on p. 46.

20. David Roediger, *Colored White: Transcending the Racial Past* (Berkeley: University of California Press, 2002), 7. Hereafter cited in text as *CW.*

1. The reference is typically cited in W. E. B. Du Bois, *The Souls of Black Folk* (New York: Penguin, 1996 [1903]), 1, 13, 35. He originally used the phrase in his address to the American Negro Academy in 1900. For this reference, see "The Present Outlook for the Dark Races of Mankind," in *The Oxford W. E. B. Du Bois Reader,* ed. Eric Sundquist (New York: Oxford University Press, 1996), 47–48. For a striking account of Du Bois's use of the phrase "the color line" throughout his long career, see Ira Katznelson, "Du Bois's Century," *Social Science History* 23, no. 4 (winter 1999): 459–74.

2. The standard references to critical white labor history are Theodore W. Allen, *The Invention of the White Race,* vols. 1 and 2 (London: Verso, 1994, 1997); David Roediger, *The Wages of Whiteness: Race and the Making of the American Working Class* (London: Verso, 1991); and Noel Ignatiev, *How the Irish Became White* (New York: Routledge, 1995). More recently, see Matthew Frye Jacobson, *Whiteness of a Different Color: European Immigrants and the Alchemy of Race* (Cambridge: Cambridge University Press, 1998); and John Hartigan, Jr., *Racial Situations: Class Predicaments of Whiteness in Detroit* (Princeton: Princeton University Press, 1999). For an overview of what she rightly calls "the class solidarity school," see Robyn Wiegman, "Whiteness Studies and the Paradox of Particularity," *boundary 2,* 26, no. 3 (fall 1999): 115–50. I address Wiegman's essay and the objections it raises regarding Roediger's work in Part Three of this book on "the rise and fall of whiteness studies."

3. W. E. B. Du Bois, *Black Reconstruction: An Essay toward a History of the Part Which Black Folk Played in the Attempt to Reconstruct Democracy in America, 1860–1900* (Philadelphia: Albert Saifer, 1935), 680. Hereafter cited in text as *BR*.

4. Karl Marx, cited in John Bellamy Foster, "Marx and Internationalism," *Monthly Review* 52, no. 3 (July–August 2000): 15.

5. Karl Marx, *The Critique of the Gotha Programme* (1875), also cited in Foster, "Marx and Internationalism," 17.

6. William Julius Wilson, *The Declining Significance of Race: Blacks and Changing American Institutions,* 2d ed. (Chicago: University of Chicago Press, 1980), 5–7.

7. Anthony Appiah critiques Du Bois's suturing of race to a perfect class dialectic in "The Uncompleted Argument: Du Bois and the Illusion of Race," in *"Race," Writing, and Difference,* ed. Henry Louis Gates, Jr. (Chicago: University of Chicago Press, 1985), 21–37.

8. See Nancy Fraser, "From Redistribution to Recognition? Dilemmas of Justice in a 'Postsocialist' Age," in *Justice Interruptus* (New York: Routledge, 1997), 11–40. I discuss Fraser more directly in Part Three of this book.

9. Michael Warner, "The Mass Public and the Mass Subject," in *The Phantom*

Public Sphere, ed. Bruce Robbins (Minneapolis: University of Minnesota Press, 1993), 243.

10. G. W. F. Hegel, *The Philosophy of Right,* in *Hegel: The Essential Writings,* ed. Frederick G. Weiss (New York: Harper, 1974 [1820]), 284.

NOTES TO SECTION 1.2

1. Langston Hughes, "Census," in *Simple's Uncle Sam* (New York: Hill and Wang, 1965), 1. Hereafter cited in text.

2. Ian Hacking, "Biopower and the Avalanche of Printed Numbers," *Humanities in Society* 5, nos. 3–4 (summer–fall 1982): 281. Also of interest here is Tukufu Zuberi, *Thicker Than Blood: How Statistics Lie* (Minneapolis: University of Minnesota Press, 2001).

3. Andrew Ross suggests, by way of contrast to Hacking, that "struggles for cultural equity . . . cannot afford to ignore numerical assessments of recognition and redistribution—not in a nation-state so devoted to statistical forms of expression in government and in economic life." But as will become clearer below, that the struggle for equity has proceeded so diligently through "numerical assessment" is precisely what enabled the nation-state's detachment from previous interests in "cultural equity." See Andrew Ross, "Claims for Cultural Justice," chap. 9 in *Real Love: In Pursuit of Cultural Justice* (New York: New York University Press, 1998).

4. Diane McWhorter, *Carry Me Home: Birmingham, Alabama, the Climactic Battle of the Civil Rights Revolution* (New York: Simon and Schuster, 2001), 43. Hereafter cited in text.

5. On the original complexities and political shortfalls of the U.S. civil rights movement of the 1960s, see George Lipsitz, *The Possessive Investment in Whiteness: How White People Gain from Identity Politics* (Philadelphia: Temple University Press, 1998), which contains a particularly good critique of the Federal Housing Administration. See also Thomas Sowell, *Civil Rights: Rhetoric or Reality?* (New York: William Morrow, 1984); Howard Zinn, *SNCC: The New Abolitionists* (Boston: Beacon Press, 1964); Herb Haines, *Black Radicals and the Civil Rights Mainstream, 1954–1970* (Knoxville: University of Tennessee Press, 1980); and Jack Bloom, *Class, Race, and the Civil Rights Movement* (Bloomington: Indiana University Press, 1987).

6. For the unacknowledged debt civil rights owes militant black radicalism, see Haines, *Black Radicals.*

7. Not that this would by any means guarantee the equal treatment of black voters, as the Bush election made painfully clear. See John Lantigua, "How the GOP Gamed the System in Florida," *Nation,* April 30, 2001, 11–16.

8. Margo Anderson, *The American Census: A Social History* (New Haven: Yale University Press, 1988), 210. Her book with Stephen E. Fienberg, *Who*

Counts? The Politics of Census-Taking in Contemporary America (New York: Russell Sage, 1999), provides a more contemporary account of the census, with an emphasis on the debilitating effects of undercounting. For a contrasting opinion, see Peter Skerry, *Counting on the Census? Race, Group Identity, and the Evasion of Politics* (Washington, D.C.: Brookings Institution Press, 1999). The activist group "race traitor" suggests that whites should "ignore the Census," in hopes that "for once the white folks will be undercounted" (*New Abolitionist,* May–June 2000, 5). On undercounting generally, see also Harvey M. Choldin, *Looking for the Last Percent: The Controversy over Census Undercounts* (New Brunswick: Rutgers University Press, 1994). For a more critical history of the census, see Melissa Nobles, *Shades of Citizenship: Race and the Census in Modern Politics* (Stanford: Stanford University Press, 2000); and Richard Polenberg, *One Nation Divisible: Class, Race, and Ethnicity in the United States since 1938* (New York: Viking, 1980). More generally, see Bryant Robey, *The American People* (New York: Dutton, 1985); a former census director, A. Ross Eckler, provides a more celebratory and technical account in *The Bureau of the Census* (New York: Praeger, 1972). Also see Herbert Scott, *Census USA: Fact-Finding for the American People, 1790–1970* (New York: Seabury Press, 1968).

9. Office of Management and Budget (OMB), "Statistical Policy Directive no. 15" (1977), available at http://www.fedworld.gov/ftp.htm#omb.

10. In the *Monthly Labor Review,* a standard source of debate on federal statistical policies, Ruth B. Mckay and Manuel de la Puente report an increased public sense of "confusion" and "suspicion" regarding the U.S. census. See their article, "Cognitive Testing of Racial and Ethnic Questions," *MLR,* September 1996, 8–12. On the general fragility of current race categories, see Lawrence Wright, "One Drop of Blood," *New Yorker,* July 25, 1994, 46–55; and Dennis Barron, "How to Be a Person, Not a Number," *Chronicle of Higher Education,* April 3, 1998, B8. F. James Davis, *Who Is Black? One Nation's Definition* (University Park: Pennsylvania State University Press, 1991) remains one of the most trenchant critiques of the ironic twists and turns of the enforcement of the "one-drop rule" of black hypo-descent. See also Michael Omi, "Racial Identity and the State: The Dilemmas of Classification," *Law and Inequality* 15, no. 7 (1997): 14–28.

11. Clavert Dedrick, head of the federal Statistical Research Division, was sent to California in 1942 to supervise the statistical work necessary for the internment of innocent Japanese. See Anderson, *The American Census,* 194.

12. This point is well made by Mike Davis in *Magical Urbanism: Latinos Reinvent the U.S. City* (London: Verso, 2000). Hereafter cited in text as *MU.* On U.S. Latino agency and its relation to a white U.S. majority, see Neil Foley, "Becoming Hispanic: Mexican Americans and the Faustian Pact with Whiteness," in *Reflexiones 1997: New Directions in Mexican American Studies,* ed. Neil Foley (Austin: University of Texas Press, 1997), 53. For a general account

of the demographics of U.S. Latinos/Hispanics, see Frank Bean and Marta Tienda, *The Hispanic Population of the United States* (New York: Russell Sage, 1987). Theodore Allen focuses on the formal category of "Hispanic" and its relation to OMB Directive 15 in "The Category 'Hispanic' and the U.S. Census" (unpublished manuscript).

13. See Barbara Vobejda, "How Kansas Is Central to Americans," *Washington Post,* April 29, 1991, A9.

14. Roman de la Campa, "Latinos and the Crossover Aesthetic," in Davis, *Magical Urbanism.* The exploration of "mixed" Latino agency has its origins in important feminist texts of the 1980s. Most notably, see Gloria Anzaldúa, *Borderlands/La Frontera: The New Mestiza* (San Francisco: Spinsters/Aunt Lute, 1987). On feminist contributions to mixed-identity debates more generally, see Mike Hill, "Vipers in Shangri-la: Whiteness, Writing, and Other Ordinary Terrors," particularly the section "The Feminist Origins of White Critique," in *Whiteness: A Critical Reader,* ed. Mike Hill (New York: New York University Press, 1997), 1–20. On Latin American approaches to U.S. multiculturalism, also see John Francis Burke, *Mestizo Democracy: The Politics of Crossing Borders* (College Station: Texas A&M University Press, 2003).

15. In addition to previous references, on the "Latino-ization of the U.S. city," see Peter McLaren, "Fashioning *Los Olvidados* in the Age of Cynical Reason," in *Revolutionary Multiculturalism* (Boulder: Westview, 1997), 1–15.

16. See Dale Maharidge, *The Coming White Minority: California's Eruptions and America's Future* (New York: Random House, 1996).

17. U.S. census 1964, cited in Maria Root, ed., *The Multiracial Experience: Racial Borders as the New Frontier* (London: Sage, 1996), 56. For an updated account of multiracialism, see Yvette M. Alex-Assensoh and Lawrence J. Hanks, eds., *Black and Multiracial Politics in America* (New York: New York University Press, 2000); and Jill Olumide, *Raiding the Gene Pool: The Social Construction of Mixed Race* (London: Pluto Press, 2001).

18. Statistics cited in Davis, *Magical Urbanism,* 6–7. According to a 1997 U.S. census report, nearly half of the United States' 25.8 million foreign-born residents came from Latin America, with Mexico accounting for 28 percent of that number. By 1999, the number of foreign-born residents living in the United States had increased to 26.4 million, 50.7 percent of which came from Latin America.

19. The 2000 census estimates America's foreign-born population at more than 28.3 million, with the majority from Latin America and Asia. This number is up from 26.4 million in 1999. For various episodes of the popular declaration of a "post-white America," see Tom Morganthau, "The Face of the Future," *Newsweek,* January 27, 1997, 58–60. The coming "white minority" draws especially excitable attention when new divisions of wealth accompany it. On the minority-majority status of Silicon Valley, which is 49 percent

white in 2000, see Karen Breslau, "Tomorrowland, Today," *Newsweek,* September 18, 2000, 51–53.

20. Cited in Alfredo G. A. Valladão, *The Twenty-first Century Will Be American* (London: Verso, 1996), 44. The Census Bureau reports that Mexican-born immigrant men have a median annual income of $16,800; women, $13,700.

21. Andrew Hacker, *Two Nations: Black and White, Separate, Hostile, Unequal* (New York: Scribner, 1992).

22. Walter Benn Michaels, *Our America: Nativism, Modernism, and Pluralism* (Durham: Duke University Press, 1995).

23. See Walter Benn Micheals, "The No Drop Rule," *Critical Inquiry* 20, no. 4 (summer 1994): 758–69.

24. Henry Louis Gates, "Statistical Stigmata," in *Deconstruction and the Possibility of Justice,* ed. Drucilla Cornell et al. (New York: Routledge, 1992), 340.

25. For a list of dates on the progress of U.S. and colonial antimiscegenation laws from 1514 through 1987, see Werner Sollors, "Appendix B: Prohibitions of Interracial Marriage and Cohabitation," in *Neither Black nor White, Yet Both* (Oxford: Oxford University Press, 1997), 395–410.

26. Given how recent the history of prohibitions surrounding multiracialism are in the United States, proclamations on behalf of "the multiracial generation" and "the new face of race" come from the popular press with astonishing regularity. For an example of glossy-magazine ebullience, see Tom Morganthau, "What Color Is Black?" in *Newsweek,* February 13, 1995, 63–65. Lisa Jones Townsel provides a more evenhanded account in "Neither Black nor White," *Ebony,* November 1996, 45–56. For more characteristic examples of the standard positive version of the story, see John Leland and Gregory Beals, "In Living Color," *Newsweek,* May 5, 1997, 58–60; Jon Meacham, "The New Face of Race," *Newsweek,* September 18, 2000, 38–41; and, on Tiger Woods as the new American racial template, Jack E. White, "I Am Just Who I Am," *Time,* May 5, 1997, 30–35. My statistics on "the multiracial baby boom" are taken from Root, *The Multiracial Experience,* xiv–xv. Hereafter cited in text.

27. See Eric Schmitt, "Experts Clash over Need for Changing the Census," *New York Times,* April 24, 1997, A17.

28. See *Time* magazine's special issue, "The New Face of America" (fall 1993). This image has generated at least two critical scholarly responses to multiracialism. Focusing predominately on changes in the black/white color axis, Susan Gubar traces general trends in multiracial imagery in *Racechanges: White Skin, Black Face in American Culture* (New York: Oxford University Press, 1997). Closer to my own argument, Lauren Berlant sees the image as symptomatic of an emergent post-white U.S. nationalism. See *The Queen of America Goes to Washington City* (Durham: Duke University Press, 1997), 200–208. I will complicate the "new nationalism" hypothesis below.

29. While the Census Bureau has kept no official data on U.S. multiracialism, a Princeton University study in 2000 estimates that as many as 16.5 million people, or 6 percent of the country, so identify. See Association of MultiEthnic Americans, Inc. at http://ameasite.org/. For a list and summary descriptions of U.S. multiracial activist groups, see Nancy G. Brown and Ramona E. Douglas, "Making the Invisible Visible: The Growth of Community Network Organizations," in Root, *The Multiracial Experience,* 323–40. For an account specifically of the most influential group, Susan Graham's Project RACE, see Hannah Beech, "Don't You Dare List Them as 'Other,'" *U.S. News and World Report,* April 8, 1996, 56.

30. H.R. 830, 105th Congress, 1st session, "To amend chapter 35 of title 44, United States Code" (February 25, 1997). This bill proposes "to require that collections of information that ask a respondent to specify a racial classification or ethnic classification from among a list of classifications shall provide an opportunity for the respondent to specify, respectively, 'multiracial' or 'multi ethnic.'"

31. On the World Health Organization, see Hacking, "Biopower and the Avalanche of Printed Numbers," 280. In what he identifies as the logical extension of the 1960s civil rights movement, Charles Byrd, an activist and the editor of the *Interracial Voice,* suggests that proper state recognition of multiracialism equates with "an individual identifying with the totality of his or her being." See Bryd's editorial, "Has *The New York Times* Pronounced the Multiracial Initiative Dead?" *Interracial Voice,* January–February, 1997, http://www.webcom/~intvoice/arhives.html.

32. U.S. Department of Education, *Racial and Ethnic Classifications Used by Public Schools* (Washington, D.C.: NCES, 1996), iii.

33. In the 1850 census the term "mulatto" was used; and in 1890 populations could be identified as "quadroon" and "octoroon." The new decision is not substantially different from the interagency recommendations issued in the 1977 mandates of OMB Directive 15. For the 2000 census standards, see *Federal Register* 62, no. 131 (July 9, 1997).

34. See William O'Hare, "Managing Multiple-Race Data," *American Demographics,* April 1998, 44.

35. On dealing with the likely confusion over selecting numerous racial categories for the 2000 census, see Joel Perlman and Mary C. Waters, *The New Race Question: How the Census Counts Multiracial Individuals* (New York: Russell Sage, 2002).

36. Genaro Armas, "Black, Hispanic Totals Nearly Equal," *Associated Press,* March 8, 2001, electronic press release.

37. *Federal Register* 62, no. 131 (July 9, 1997): 36906.

38. G. Reginald Daniel, *More Than Black? Multiracial Identity and the New Racial Order* (Philadelphia: Temple University Press, 2002), 3. Hereafter cited in text. It should also be noted than Daniel, as he states in the book, is

a former advisory board member of Project RACE, which is endorsed by Newt Gingrich and other conservative politicos who run ideologically contrary to Daniel's own stated goals.

39. *Hearings before the Subcommittee on Census, Statistics, and Postal Personnel,* April 14, June 30, July 29, November 3, Serial no. 103-07 (Washington, D.C.: U.S. Government Printing Office, 1993). Hereafter cited in texts.

40. David Theo Goldberg, *Racial Subjects: Writings on Race in America* (New York: Routledge, 1997), 33. Hereafter cited in text as *RS.*

41. David Theo Goldberg, *The Racial State* (London: Blackwell, 2002), 9. Hereafter cited in text as *TRS.*

42. See Michel Foucault, *Discipline and Punish: The Birth of the Prison* (New York: Vintage, 1979).

43. The reference here is to Michel Foucault's work on "individuation," which he articulated, famously, in *Discipline and Punish,* 33 ff.

44. Given the hollowing out of its former liberal content and commitments, the state is clearly poised to become more intrusive. As the Patriot Act reveals, and as I have been arguing from another angle, the state's interest in identity can appear to dissipate at the same time the relation between citizenship and state interest becomes more absolute.

45. Christina Ling, "Census: Black-White Integration Remains Elusive," *Reuters,* September 13, 2001, electronic press release.

46. This statistic is found in Root, *The Multiracial Experience,* 55. On the ironic connection between the self-imposed rule of hypo-descent (or "one-drop rule") and the rearguard postures of the civil rights legacy, see Davis, *Who Is Black? One Nation's Definition.* Davis cites the same statistics on black "multiracialism" as Root, and is widely cited. See references to Davis, for example, in Lise Funderburg, *Black, White, Other: Biracial Americans Talk about Race and Identity* (New York: William Morrow, 1994), 16. Citations on multiracialism as a national phenomenon have become too numerous to list. However, see variously Werner Sollors, ed., *Interracialism: Black-White Intermarriage in American History, Literature, and Law* (Oxford: Oxford University Press, 2000); Heather M. Dalmage, *Tripping on the Color Line: Black-White Multiracial Families in a Racially Divided World* (New Brunswick: Rutgers University Press, 2000); Alex-Assensoh and Hanks, *Black and Multiracial Politics in America*; Martha Hodes, ed., *Sex, Love, Race: Crossing Boundaries in North American History* (New York: New York University Press, 1999); and Naomi Zak, ed., *American Mixed Race: The Culture of Microdiversity* (Lanham: Rowman and Littlefield, 1995).

47. In a letter presented at the congressional hearings in 1993, the nation's top civil rights leaders expressed "extreme concern that [the] new [multiracial] category will inadvertently cause confusion and inconsistent reporting." See *Hearings,* 224. An editorial by Charles Byrd in the *Interracial Voice* (September

5, 2000) "The Political Realignment: A Jihad against 'Race' Consciousness," blames the NAACP directly for maintaining the "one-drop rule" and discouraging multiracial census reclassification. *Interracial Voice* is found online.

48. See, again, Dalmage, *Tripping on the Color Line*, who is mindful of the possibility that the multiracial movement will "undermine the already shrinking protections in place for African Americans" (151).

NOTES TO SECTION 1.3

1. This now common thesis is typically attributed to Michael Omi and Howard Winant's influential *Racial Formation in the United States: From the 1960s to the 1980s* (New York: Routledge, 1986). This work and "racial formation" theory more generally are cited throughout the 1993 congressional hearings. The National Research Council's report, *Spotlight on Heterogeneity: The Federal Standards for Racial and Ethnic Classifications* (Washington, D.C.: National Academy of Sciences, 1996), contains pivotal subsections on "identity as a social construct," 18. The notion has been popularized in the national dailies. See Ethan Bronner, "Inventing the Notion of Race," *New York Times,* January 10, 1998, B7.

2. See Eva Knodt, "Toward a Non-Foundationalist Epistemology: The Habermas/Luhmann Controversy Revisited," *New German Critique* 61 (winter 1994): 77–100.

3. These estimates are taken, respectively, from Will Kymicka, *Multicultural Citizenship: A Liberal Theory of Minority Rights* (Oxford: Clarendon, 1995), 1; and James Tully, *Strange Multiplicity: Constitutionalism in an Age of Diversity* (Cambridge: Cambridge University Press, 1995), 3.

4. For a lucid overview of the CRT/CLS split, see Gary Minda, *Postmodern Legal Movements* (New York: New York University Press, 1995), 106–27, 167–88; and Larissa MacFarquhar, "The Color of the Law," *Lingua Franca,* August 1996, 40–47.

5. Richard Delgado, *Critical Race Theory: An Introduction* (New York: New York Universtity Press, 2001), 7. Hereafter cited in text as *CRTI.*

6. Introduction to *Critical Race Theory,* ed. Kimberlé Crenshaw et al. (New York: New Press, 1995), xxiii. Cited hereafter in text as *CRT.*

7. Cited by Kimberlé Crenshaw, "Race, Reform, and Retrenchment: Transformation and Legitimation in Antidiscrimination Law," in Crenshaw et al., *Critical Race Theory,* 108.

8. See Derrick Bell, "*Brown v. Board of Education* and the Interest-Convergence Dilemma," *Harvard Law Review* 93, no. 518 (1980); cited in Delgado, *CRTI,* 34.

9. Juan F. Perea, "The Black/White Binary Paradigm of Race," in *Critical Race*

Theory: The Cutting Edge, 2d ed., ed. Richard Delgado and Jean Stefancic (Philadelphia: Temple University Press, 2000).

10. Leslie Espinoza and Angela P. Harris, "Embracing the Tar-Baby: LatCrit Theory and the Sticky Mess of Race," in Delgado and Stefancic, *Critical Race Theory,* 440.

11. Karl Marx, "Contribution to the Critique of Hegel's *Philosophy of Right,*" in *The Marx-Engels Reader,* 2d ed., ed. Robert C. Tucker (New York: Norton, 1979), 17. Hereafter cited in text as "CCH."

12. G. W. F. Hegel, *The Philosophy of Right,* in *Hegel: The Essential Writings,* ed. Frederick G. Weiss (Harper, 1974 [1820]), 284.

13. Michel Foucault, "Governmentality," in *The Foucault Effect: Studies in Governmentality,* ed. Graham Burchell et al. (Chicago: University of Chicago Press, 1991), 103.

14. Louis Althusser, "Marx's Relation to Hegel," in *Montesquieu, Rousseau, Politics and History,* trans. Ben Brewster (London: Verso, 1971), 163–86. Hereafter cited in text as "MRH."

15. Clearly there are different "Hegels" in play on the issue of the other's constitutive role in identity formation. Althusser's Hegel is not, for example, Judith Butler's. To the contrary, Butler wants to emphasize, vis-à-vis Kojève, the role of negation on consciousness, which is closer to Althusser's suspicion about liberal humanism than the Hegel he wants to critique. I will address the issue of identity and negation more completely in Part Two of *After Whiteness* on race and male sexuality with regard to the Promise Keepers. Meanwhile, see Judith Butler, *Subjects of Desire: Hegelian Reflections in Twentieth-Century France* (New York: Columbia University Press, 1987), esp. vii–ix.

16. *Non-response Follow-up Enumerator Manual: U.S. Census 2000* (Washington, D.C.: U.S. Bureau of the Census, 1999), D-547, 6.4. Hereafter cited as *NF.* When the enumerator visited me during the composition of this book, I asked half in jest to be recognized as "proletariat." She was initially amused, as any state official would be. But when I expressed reluctance at the race question, experimentally, she left, as the manual says, "remember[ing] to smile" (*NF,* 4). I later discovered that she confirmed my racial identity, appropriately enough, by contacting my landlord.

17. Ibid., 4–5.

18. *Findings on Questions on Race and Hispanic Origin Tested in the 1996 National Content Survey: Population Division, Working Paper no. 6* (Washington, D.C., 1996).

19. See statements on behalf of the state's recognition of the multiracial category by the following conservative politicians and pundits: Newt Gingrich, cited in Steven A. Holmes, "Gingrich Outlines Program on Nation's Race Relations," *New York Times,* June 19, 1997, A12. Susan Graham's Project RACE

touts Gingrich as one of the group's staunchest supporters. See also Dinesh D'Souza, "The One Drop of Blood Rule," *Forbes Magazine,* December 2, 1996, at http://www.forbes.com/forbes/; and George Will's *Washington Post* editorial (October 5, 1997) cited in *Project RACE Newsletter,* at http://www.projectrace.com.

20. D'Souza, "The One Drop of Blood Rule."

21. On this topic, see Angela D. Dillard, *Guess Who's Coming to Dinner Now? Multicultural Conservatism in America* (New York: New York University Press, 2002). President Bush's veiled pronouncements against the University of Michigan's affirmative action policies only confirm the right-wing backslide on civil rights.

22. See Ward Connerly, *Creating Equal: My Fight against Racial Preferences* (New York: Encounter Books, 2000). That Senator Hubert Humphrey, a Democrat from Minnesota, was one of the CCRI's principal supporters in Congress is evidence of the bipartisan support for the multiracial movement.

23. Ward Connerly, "Loving America," *Project RACE Newsletter,* September 28, 2000, online.

24. Ed Fletcher, "Racial Data Ban Won't Make Fall Ballot," *Sacramento Bee,* June 27, 2002, A3.

25. The one difference here is that Zak begins from the premise that all race, including multiracialism, is bunk. The others embrace multiracialism as an autonomous racial category to end up at the same eventual dismissal of race.

26. David A. Hollinger writes prodigiously on race as a simple matter of choice. See his *Post-Ethnic America* (New York: Basic Books, 1995), particularly pp. 3–4, 19, 21, 40, 118. For an argument that attempts to extend civil rights to "miscegenated subjectivity" in a similarly facile way, see Ross Posnock, "Before and After Identity Politics," *Raritan,* fall 1995, 95–115.

27. Werner Sollors, *Beyond Ethnicity* (Oxford: Oxford University Press, 1996), 151. See also Sollors, *Neither Black nor White, Yet Both* (Oxford: Oxford University Press, 1997). My misgivings about Sollors on this issue are similar to those of Michael Awkward, who writes that Sollors's work "serves to disguise [a] desire to dominate regions and discourses of blackness." Such would seem to be the case with the census debates over multiracialism as well. See Michael Awkward, *Negotiating Difference: Race, Gender and the Politics of Positionality* (Chicago: University of Chicago Press, 1995), 84 ff.

28. Naomi Zak, *Race and Mixed Race* (Philadelphia: Temple University Press, 1993), 165.

29. See Eric Lott, who writes of "cultural miscegenation" that this work "reinstalls a consensus nationalism redolent of exeptionalist and cold-war nationalist approaches to ethnicity." For Lott, the argument for a multiracial right of recognition would produce, at best, what he cleverly calls "mixed" results for conceiving of greater material equality in the United States and beyond. Against Hollinger and company, Lott argues instead for a socialist-inspired,

black-led mass political movement. See "Boomer Liberalism," *Transition,* no. 78 (1998): 26.

30. Ibid., 26.

NOTES TO SECTION 1.4

1. Nathan Glazer, multicultural adversary lately turned advocate, could surely be added to the mix. Glazer contends that racial categories have become so unwieldy during the 2000 census that black people are the only group worth counting, since they "have a clear sense of their identity." See "Parsing Race in the Census," *Chronicle of Higher Education,* October 4, 2002, B4.

2. See special issues, "After Seattle: A New International-ism?" *Monthly Review* 52, no. 3 (July–August 2000); and "Free Trade/Fair Trade: Special WTO Issue," *Nation,* December 6, 1999. For a sober assessment of worker benefits on all sides of the international divide, see David Bacon, "Globalization: Two Faces, Both Ugly," *Dollars and Sense,* March–April 2000, 18–23, 40–41. For a critical assessment of NAFTA's effect on U.S. labor, see John R. MacArthur, *The Selling of "Free Trade": NAFTA, Washington, and the Subversion of American Democracy* (New York: Hill and Wang, 2000).

3. Harold W. Stanley et al., eds., *Vital Statistics on American Politics,* 2d ed. (Washington, DC: Congressional Quarterly, Inc., 1990), 320.

4. See Stephen F. Cohen, *The Failed Crusade: America and the Tragedy of Post-Communist Russia* (New York: Norton, 2000); and David Hoffman, *The Oligarchs: Wealth and Power in the New Russia* (New York: Public Affairs, 2002).

5. For essays on the myths of "globalization," see Leo Panitch, "The New Imperial State," *New Left Review* 2 (March–April 2000): 2–20; and Fredric Jameson, "Globalization and Strategy," *New Left Review* 4 (July–August 2000): 69–74. My thoughts on planetary capitalism have been aided by Michael Hardt and Antonio Negri, *Empire* (Cambridge: Harvard University Press, 2000).

6. Alfredo G. A. Valladão, *The Twenty-first Century Will Be American* (London: Verso, 1996). Hereafter cited in text as *TC.*

7. Nicos Poulantzas, *Classes in Contemporary Capitalism* (London: New Left Books, 1975). This argument should be contrasted with the influential writing of Eric Hobsbawm, who in *The Age of Extremes* makes the counterargument that the multinational corporate order portends a time of "dwarf states or no states at all" (New York: Random House, 1996), 281. For an extension of Poulantzas's view, which corresponds to the careful disintegration of the bourgeois state in the rise of a new world order, see Richard A. Falk, *Human Rights Horizons: The Pursuit of Justice in a Globalizing World* (New York: Routledge, 2000).

8. This is a concise summary of Poulantzas's thesis by Panitch, "The New Imperial State," 13.

9. Kenichi Ohmae, *The End of the Nation State: The Rise of Regional Economies* (New York: Free Press, 1995), 4. Hereafter cited in text as *EN*.

10. Panitch, "The New Imperial State," 5.

11. Masao Miyoshi, "Sites of Resistance in the Global Economy," *boundary 2*, spring 1995, 63. The idea that flexible national borders are embedded in the acceleration and expansion of capital causes Timothy Brennan to distinguish between "cosmopolitanism" ("the comfortable culture of middle-class travelers") and "internationalism" (which seeks the material conditions for abolishing difference) (77). See Brennan, "Cosmopolitanism and Internationalism," *New Left Review* 7 (January–February 2001): 75–84.

12. Again, see Hardt and Negri, *Empire*.

13. David Armstrong, "Dick Cheney's Song of America: Drafting a Plan for Global Dominance," *Harper's Magazine*, October 2002, 76.

14. Thus my account of flexible citizenship contrasts with that of Slavoj Zizek, who writes of multiculturalism that "it is as if the positive charge of pathetic patriotic identification . . . has been seriously eroded" (42). Nothing could be farther from the truth. The key point here is that patriotic fervor—the Bush Doctrine's notice that "you are either with us or against us"—spreads best once internal national difference is evacuated. This is my point in joining the implications of the 2000 census to the idea of a "World-America." See Slavoj Zizek, "Multi-Culturalism; or, The Cultural Logic of Multinational Capitalism," *New Left Review* 225 (September–October 1997): 28–51.

15. Sandra Day O'Connor, as quoted in *Left Business Observer* 98 (October 18, 2001): 3.

16. Valladão, *The Twenty-first Century*, 190.

17. Jürgen Habermas, *The Structural Transformation of the Public Sphere* (Cambridge: MIT Press, 1989). Hereafter cited in text as *STPS*.

18. John Keane, *Civil Society: Old Images, New Visions* (Stanford: Stanford University Press, 1998), 23.

19. Robert K. Fullinwider, ed., *Civil Society, Democracy, and Civic Renewal* (Lanham: Rowman and Littlefield, 1999), 2.

20. Benjamin Barber, "Clansmen, Consumers, and Citizens: Three Takes on Civil Society," in Fullinwider, *Civil Society*, 20.

21. See Daniele Archibugi et al., eds., *Re-imagining Community: Studies in Cosmopolitan Democracy* (Stanford: Stanford University Press, 1998); Judith Shklar, *American Citizenship: The Quest for Inclusion* (Cambridge: Harvard University Press, 1991); Will Kymicka, *Multicultural Citizenship: A Liberal Theory of Minority Rights* (Oxford: Clarendon, 1995); Anne Philips, *The Politics of Presence* (Oxford: Clarendon, 1995). Defenses of the public sphere are by no means limited to the liberal left. For a feminist take, see, most no-

tably, Seyla Benhabib, *Situating the Self: Gender, Community and Postmodernism in Contemporary Ethics* (New York: Routledge, 1992); and Nancy Fraser's well-known essay, "Rethinking the Public Sphere: A Critique of Actually Existing Democracy," in *Habermas and the Public Sphere,* ed. Craig Calhoun (Cambridge: MIT Press, 1992), 109–41. For an anticapitalist endorsement of Habermasian "civic morality," see Carl Boggs, *The End of Politics: Corporate Power and the Decline of the Public Sphere* (New York: Guilford, 2000).

22. For a now standard criticism of Habermas on this score, see Fraser, "Rethinking the Public Sphere." See also Johanna Meehan, ed., *Feminists Read Habermas: Gendering the Subject of Discourse* (New York: Routledge, 1995).

23. See Calhoun, *Habermas,* 425–30; and Jürgen Habermas, *Between Facts and Norms* (Cambridge: MIT Press, 1996), 329–87. Hereafter cited in text as *BFN.*

24. See Jürgen Habermas, *The Inclusion of the Other: Studies in Political Theory* (Cambridge: MIT Press, 1998), i. Hereafter cited in text as *IO.*

25. Jürgen Habermas, *The Philosophical Discourse of Modernity* (Cambridge: MIT Press, 1990), i. Hereafter cited in text as *PDM.*

26. Robert Williams calls Hegel "the first thinker of difference." See his appropriately titled book, *Recognition: Fichte and Hegel on the Other* (Albany: SUNY Press, 1992), xiv. For an able if overenthusiastic account of Hegel's politics of recognition as the basis for an ethical community overseen by the state, see Shlomo Avineri, *Hegel's Theory of the Modern State* (Cambridge: Cambridge University Press, 1972).

27. Axel Honneth, "Integrity and Disrespect: Principles of a Conception of Morality Based on the Theory of Recognition," *Political Theory* 20, no. 2 (May 1992): 5. This emphasis on Hegel's "intersubjectivist innovation" is elaborated in his book, *The Struggle for Recognition: The Moral Grammar of Social Conflicts* (Cambridge: MIT Press, 1996). A similar argument for the "politics of cultural recognition," indistinguishable from the later Habermas, is found in James Tully, *Strange Multiplicity: Constitutionalism in an Age of Diversity* (Cambridge: Cambridge University Press, 1995).

28. Charles Taylor, *Hegel* (Cambridge: Cambridge University Press, 1975), 153. Taylor later minimizes his interest in Spirit and replaces it with culture, as in "multicultural diversity." On this see Taylor, *The Ethics of Authenticity* (Cambridge: Harvard University Press, 1992), 37.

29. Jürgen Habermas, "Struggles for Recognition in the Democratic Constitutional State," in *Multiculturalism: Examining the Politics of Recognition,* ed. Amy Gutmann (Princeton: Princeton University Press, 1994), 126. The volume's contents are in direct response to Charles Taylor, as the volume's subtitle suggests.

30. For a very different account of the politics of recognition and a critique of Habermas's "uni-multiculturalism," see Alexander Garcia Duttman, *Between*

Cultures: Tensions in the Struggle for Recognition (London: Verso, 2000); and William E. Connolly, *The Ethos of Pluralization* (Minneapolis: University of Minnesota Press, 1995).

31. Charles Taylor, "The Politics of Recognition," in Gutmann, *Multiculturalism,* 61. Hereafter cited as "PR" in text.

32. Habermas, *Inclusion of the Other,* 107.

33. Jürgen Habermas, "Remarks on Legitimation through Human Rights," *Modern Schoolman* 75, no. 2 (January 1998): 87–100.

34. Hegel's rather nefarious writings on Africa are found in *Race and the Enlightenment: A Reader,* ed. Emmanuel Chukwuddi Eze (London: Blackwell, 1997), 109–53. This reference, which is taken from Hegel's later writings of 1822–28, is found on page 127. Henry Louis Gates's objections to Hegel's Africa are well known. See his *Figures in Black: Words, Signs, and the "Racial" Self* (Oxford: Oxford University Press, 1987), 19–25.

35. On what they call the "withering of civil society," see Michael Hardt and Antonio Negri, *The Labor of Dionysus: A Critique of State-Form* (Minneapolis: University of Minnesota Press, 1994). This book has been influential in my thoughts on the U.S. census, as has Michael Hardt's companion essay, "Affective Labor," *boundary 2,* 26, no. 2 (1999): 89–100. However, I first encountered the notion of the withering of civil society in Etienne Balibar, *Masses, Classes, Ideas* (New York: Routledge, 1994).

NOTES TO SECTION 1.5

1. Giorgio Agamben, *Means without End: Notes on Politics* (Minneapolis: University of Minnesota Press, 2000), 16. Hereafter cited in text as *MWE.*

2. Jacques Derrida, "Force of Law: 'The Mystical Forces of Authority,'" in *Deconstruction and the Possibility of Justice,* ed. Drucilla Cornell et al. (New York: Routledge, 1992), 16.

3. Jacques Rancier, "Politics, Identification, and Subjectivization," in *The Identity Question,* ed. John Rajchman (New York: Routledge, 1995), 67.

4. J. K. Gibson-Graham, Stephen Resnick, and Richard Wolff, "Class in a Poststructuralist Frame," in *Class and Its Others,* ed. J. K. Gibson-Graham et al. (Minneapolis: University of Minnesota Press, 2000), 8.

5. See Brian Massumi, "The Autonomy of Affect," in *Deleuze: A Critical Reader* (London: Blackwell, 1996), 217–40.

NOTES TO SECTION 2.1

1. See, for example, the scholarly journal *Masculinities.*

2. Barbara Ehrenreich, foreword to *Male Fantasies: Women, Floods, Bodies, His-*

tory, by Klaus Theweleit, trans. Stephen Conway, vol. 1 (Minneapolis: University of Minnesota Press, 1987), ix. Hereafter cited in text.

3. Hannah Arendt, *The Origins of Totalitarianism* (New York: Meridian Books, 1958), 156. Hereafter cited as *OT* in text. Ernesto Laclau maintains that, according to Arendt, "fascism rises from the suppression of the nation-state and the emergence of imperialism, the crisis of the class system and its values, and the autonomization of the individual in modern mass society" (86). This last element is objectionable to Laclau, as it underestimates the complexity of fascism, particularly, the "relative autonomy of the fascist state and the mass mobilization which preceded its coming to power" (88). Laclau's support for the "autonomy of popular democratic interpellations" aside (125, 142), he likewise signals Arendt's fear of what she calls "mass man." See Ernesto Laclau, *Politics and Ideology in Marxist Theory* (London: New Left Books, 1997).

4. Feminist historical critiques of the "conjugal patriarchal family" and its connection to the liberal public sphere are well known. See, for example, Joan Landes, *Women and the Public Sphere in the Age of the French Revolution* (Ithaca: Cornell University Press, 1988); see also two volumes that contain critiques of Habermas from feminist and materialist perspectives: Johanna Meehan, ed., *Feminists Read Habermas* (New York: Routledge, 1995); and Mike Hill and Warren Montag, eds., *Masses, Classes, and the Public Sphere* (London: Verso, 2000). On the tensions between nationalism and the public sphere, see Jürgen Habermas, "Remarks on Legitimation through Human Rights," in the *Modern Schoolman* special issue "Globalization," 75, no. 2 (January 1988): 87–99; and Lisa Lowe, *Immigrant Acts: On Asian American Cultural Politics* (Durham: Duke University Press, 1996).

5. Max Horkheimer and Theodor Adorno, "Authoritarianism and the Family Today," in *The Family: Its Function and Destiny,* ed. Max Horkheimer and Theodor Adorno (New York: Harper, 1949), 362. Friedrich Engels defines modern society as comprised of "the system of the family . . . dominated by a system of property." Here he adds an economic dimension to the understanding, postulated by the anthropologist Lewis Henry Morgan in 1877, of the developmental stages of human history from a "primitive" system of rank and familial descent to a society based on commodity production, private property, and the modern state, with the unique arrangement of monogamous marriage and gendered divisions of labor based on a new conception of home. See Engels, *The Origins of the Family, Private Property and the State* (New York: International Publishers, 1972 [1884]), 72.

6. Slavoj Zizek, *Did Somebody Say Totalitarianism? Five Interventions in the (Mis)Use of a Notion* (London: Verso, 2001), 3. Hereafter cited as *DS* in text.

NOTES TO SECTION 2.2

1. See Promise Keepers' official homepage: http://www.promisekeepers.org/.
2. Letter from Bill McCartney, January 3, 2002. And see PK's newsletter, *The Promise Keeper* 5, no. 1 (January–February 2002): 4.
3. Beginning in 1997, the Center for Democracy Studies (CDS) at the Nation Institute began publishing *PK Watch,* in order to "educat[e] local activists, clergy," and local politicians on PK's "attack . . . at the positions of women in society." CDS is an organization that "monitor[s] and report[s] on organized efforts to undermine the rights of women, people of color, labor." See "Not the Rose Bowl, You Don't," *PK Watch* 1, no. 1 (March 1997): 2. Similarly, Political Research Associates has assembled an "Organizer's Information Packet" called *Challenging the Promise Keepers* (1997).
4. Statistics cited in John M. Higgins, "A Humanist among the Faithful," *Humanist,* September–October 1997, 23.
5. See Laurie Goodstein, "A Marriage Gone Bad: Struggles for Redemption," *New York Times,* October 29, 1997, A17.
6. On the colossal growth of PK through the mid-1990s, see Rupert Cornwell, "Tough Guys for God? It's a Miracle—This Year a Million Men Will Attend Rallies Organized by the Promise Keepers, America's Fastest Growing Religious Group," *Independent* (UK), June 5, 1996, 2; and Ron Stodghill, "God of Our Fathers," *Time,* October 6, 1997, 32–40. For a detailed explanation of PK's "mobilizing paradigm," see Center for Democracy Studies, *Promise Keepers: The Third Wave of the American Religious Right* (November 1996).
7. Dane Claussen, introduction to *Standing on the Promises: The Promise Keepers and the Revival of Manhood,* ed. Dane Claussen (Cleveland: Pilgrim Press, 1999), 2.
8. By the end of 1997, PK receipts were down 27 percent, having fallen from a projected $117 million to $85 million. In 2001, PK's revenue dropped further, to $51 million. In 1997 PK congregated 1.1 million souls, compared with 200,000 men attending conferences in eighteen cities in 2000. In 2002 the number of stadium events went down to sixteen. For an analysis of variations in PK membership and financial solvency, see Frederick Clarkson, "The Culture Wars Are Not Over: The Institutionalization of the Christian Right," *Public Eye* 7, no. 1 (spring 2001): 1–18.
9. Since 1996 McCartney has dedicated PK's conferences to addressing what he calls the "giant of race"—"the subtle spirit of white superiority [that] has alienated and wounded our brothers and sisters in the Church." See his autobiography, *Sold Out: Becoming Man Enough to Make a Difference* (Nashville: Word Publishing, 1997), 175. Here McCartney describes the nearly 40 percent negative reaction to his 1996 "reconciliation" theme, and speculates that the turn to race has been responsible for the decline in membership after 1997.

10. This statement headlines the PK official homepage.
11. McCartney also had early ties in Boulder to the Vineyard Christian Fellow-ship, whose interests in "signs and wonders," faith healing, and other cultish miracles has drawn criticism from other evangelical movements. Among the more obvious connections between PK and Vineyard is their use of "disciple-ship" or "shepherding" to control church members. See Joe Conason et al., "The Promise Keepers Are Coming: The Third Wave of the Religious Right," *Nation,* October 7, 1996, 11–19.
12. Quoted in Political Research Associates, *Challenging the Promise Keepers,* 5. Amendment 2 sought to amend the Colorado state constitution to forbid state and municipal agencies from guaranteeing nondiscriminatory practices toward those with "homosexual, lesbian, or bisexual orientation." Amend-ment 2 passed in 1992, but was eventually overturned by the U.S. Supreme Court. For analysis of Colorado's Amendment 2, see Laurie Schulze and Frances Guilfoye, "Facts Don't Hate, They Just Are," in *Media Culture and the Religious Right,* ed. Linda Kintz and Julia Lesage (Minneapolis: Univer-sity of Minnesota Press, 1998), 327–44. See also Amy Gluckman and Betsy Reed, "The Hoax of 'Special Rights': The Right Wing's Attack on Gay Men and Lesbians," in *Homoeconomics: Capitalism, Community, and Les-bian and Gay Life,* ed. Amy Gluckman and Betsy Reed (New York: Rout-ledge, 1997), 209–22. Reaction on the right against gay civil rights oc-curred simultaneously with widely publicized exaggerations concerning gay men's wealth. On the mobilization of heterosexual class anxiety by the right, see Amy Gluckman and Betsy Reed, introduction to *Homoeconomics,* xi–xxxi.
13. Quoted in *Calculated Compassion: How the Ex-Gay Movement Serves the Right's Attack on Democracy* (Somerville, MA: PRA, 1998), 20. McCartney stumped for Colorado Amendment 2 and spoke at an Operation Rescue rally. On PK's predictable stance on reproductive rights, see Donna Minkowitz, "In the Name of the Father," *Ms.,* November–December 1995, 64–71.
14. Quoted in Political Research Associates, *Challenging the Promise Keepers,* 5.
15. Ibid., 1.
16. See Linda Kintz, *Between Jesus and the Market: The Emotions That Matter in Right-Wing America* (Durham: Duke University Press, 1997). Kintz also writes critically of PK's "symmetrical structure of homologies" (10), its "logic of purity" (121), and its investment in "rigid binaries" (263). As we shall see below, this take on PK's obviously rightward gender politics de-emphasizes the group's rather more complex treatment of race, which includes the pitch for a "mestizo" Jesus. On the politics of family and the Christian right more generally, see Kintz's essay, "Charity, Mothers, and the Mass-Mediated Na-tional Soul: A Defense of Ambiguity," in Kintz and Lesage, *Media Culture and the Religious Right,* 115–39.

17. Ann Burlien, *Lift High the Cross* (Durham: Duke University Press, 2002), xv. Hereafter cited in text as *LH*.

18. On the turn to family as a nationalist concern, see Michael Warner and Lauren Berlant, "Sex in Public," in Michael Warner, *Publics and Counterpublics* (New York: Zone Books, 2002), 187–208.

19. Lauren Berlant sees the rightward politicization of the family as part of a more general rise of "infantile citizenship," in which women and reproductive rights are reduced to objects of hypermasculine protection. See *The Queen of America Goes to Washington City* (Durham: Duke University Press, 1997).

20. See Rob Boston, "Bush League," *Church and State,* November 2000, http://www.au.org/cs01.htm. The Christian Coalition's annual convention drew just a thousand attendees in 2000. See Clarkson, "The Culture Wars Are Not Over."

21. Citations for Gallagher found in Bill Berkowitz, "The Marriage Movement," *Z Magazine,* July–August 2002, 12–16. Also see James Q. Wilson, *The Marriage Problem: How Our Culture Has Weakened Families* (New York: Harper-Collins, 2002). Wilson proclaims marriage the social corrective for everything from drunkenness to poverty.

22. Quoted by Bob Saunders, "Bush's Christian Guru Aims to Reshape America," *Toronto Globe and Mail,* January 13, 2001; rpt. in *Public Eye* 15, no. 1 (spring 2001): 12.

23. See Bill Berkowitz, "Tilting at Faith-Based Windmills: Over a Year in the Life of President Bush's Faith-Based Initiative," *Public Eye* 16, no. 2 (summer 2002): 22–26.

24. Nancy Guerin, "Marital Dis," *Metroland,* August 9–15, 2001, 11.

25. Quoted in Judith Stacy, *In the Name of the Family: Rethinking Family Values* (Boston: Beacon Press, 1996), 120.

26. Judith Stacy, "Family Values Forever," *Nation,* July 9, 2001, 26–28.

27. Juliet Mitchell, *Women's Estate* (New York: Random House, 1973), 154.

28. Eve Kosofsky Sedgwick, *Between Men: English Literature and Male Homosocial Desire* (New York: Columbia University Press, 1985), 14.

29. Michèle Barrett and Mary McIntosh, *The Anti-Social Family* (London: Verso, 1982), 48.

30. Edward Shorter, *The Making of the Modern Family* (New York: Basic Books, 1975).

31. Stacy, *In the Name of the Family,* 45.

32. Stephanie Coontz, introduction to *American Families: A Multicultural Reader,* ed. Stephanie Coontz (New York: Routledge, 1999), xii.

33. Statistics cited in Barbara Kantrowitz and Pat Wingert, "Unmarried, with Children," *Newsweek,* "The New Single Mom" special issue, May 28, 2001, 46–55.

34. See the Family Work Institute's ten-year study released in 1997, *National Study of the Changing Workforce,* available at http://www.familiesandwork.org.

35. See Doug Henwood, "Trash-O-nomics," in *White Trash: Race and Class in America,* ed. Matt Wray and Annalee Newitz (New York: Routledge, 1997), 177–92. Henwood writes, "While it's well known that hourly wages have been falling for twenty years, it's less well known that women's earnings have risen while men's have fallen" (193). His point is not to lessen the continued disparity between men's and women's wages, but to specify certain new vulnerabilities entertained by white men during decreasingly secure times for all workers. On this point, see too Fred Pfeil, *White Guys: Studies in Postmodern Domination and Difference* (London: Verso, 1995).

36. For an early critique of this tendency, see Barrett and McIntosh, *The Anti-Social Family.*

37. Stacy, *In the Name of the Family,* 7. Hereafter cited in text.

38. John M. Swomley, "Storm Troopers in the Culture War," *Humanist,* September–October 1997, 12.

39. Higgins, "A Humanist among the Faithful," 25.

40. Evans, quoted by Frederick Clarkson, "Righteous Brothers," *In These Times,* August 5, 1996, 15.

41. Russ Bellant, "Mania in the Stadia: The Origins and Goals of the Promise Keepers," *Front Lines Research,* May 1995, 7.

42. Nancy Novasad, "God Squad: The Promise Keepers Fight for a Man's World," *Progressive,* August 1996, 27. This focus on Evans is the view commonly held in more progressive Christian media. See, for example, Jon D. Spalding, "Bonding in the Bleachers: A Visit to the Promise Keepers," *Christian Century,* March 6, 1996, 260–61. Spalding's treatment of Evans is indistinguishable from that of the more radical secular coverage presented in *In These Times.*

43. In fairness to Clarkson's article in *In These Times,* PK's rather more "inclusive" treatment of race is mentioned, though its relation to gender is left unexplored.

44. McCartney "on his knees" to black men in the PK foot washing ritual is discussed in more detail below. The theme of "submission" to God, and between men of different races, is constant in McCartney's PK writing. Jesus, his autobiography maintains, was heard by the Father "because of his submission" (284). See McCartney, *Sold Out,* 79, 181, 185.

45. Tony Evans, *Let's Get to Know Each Other* (Nashville: Thomas Nelson Publishers, 1995), 20. Hereafter cited in text as *LG.*

46. Gloria Anzaldúa, *Borderlands/La frontera* (San Francisco: Spinsters/Aunt Lute, 1987), 78.

NOTES TO SECTION 2.3

1. Frantz Fanon, *Black Skin, White Masks,* trans. Charles Markmann (New York: Grove, 1962 [1952]), 12. Hereafter cited in text as *BS.*

2. Useful feminist critiques of Fanon include Diana Fuss, *Identification Papers* (New York: Routledge, 1995); and Gwen Bergner, "Who Is That Masked Woman? or The Role of Gender in Fanon's *Black Skin, White Masks,*" *PMLA* 110, no. 1 (January 1995): 75–88. Lee Edelman, *Homographesis: Essays in Gay Literary and Cultural Theory* (New York: Routledge, 1994), 42–75, provides a queer critique of Fanon's reliance on a normative sexual paradigm.

3. McCartney, foreword to *Let the Walls Fall Down,* by Bishop Phillip Porter (Orlando: Strang, 1996), 7.

4. Porter, *Let the Walls Fall Down,* 93. Hereafter cited in text.

5. Wellington Boone, *Breaking Through: Taking the Kingdom into the Culture by Outserving Others* (Nashville: Broadman and Holman, 1996), 7. Hereafter cited in text.

6. References to Martin Luther King are a predominate feature of PK literature, including McCartney's autobiography. References to the 1950s civil rights movement were abundant at PK's Washington, D.C., demonstration "Stand in the Gap" in 1997.

7. Joseph Garlington, *Right or Reconciled?* (Shippensburg, PA: Destiny Image, 1998), 78.

8. Patrick Means, *Men's Secret Wars* (Grand Rapids: Fleming H. Revell, 2000), 54. Hereafter cited in text as *MS.*

9. Bill McCartney, *Sold Out: Becoming Man Enough to Make a Difference* (Nashville: Word Publishing, 1997), xxvii.

10. Rod Cooper, *We Stand Together: Reconciling Men of Different Color* (Chicago: Moody Press, 1995), 16. Hereafter cited in text as *WS.*

11. Ken Abraham, *Who Are the Promise Keepers? Understanding the Christian Men's Movement* (New York: Doubleday, 1997). Hereafter cited in text as *WA.*

12. See Ken Abraham, "God Loves Losers, Too," in *What Makes a Man?* ed. Bill McCartney (Colorado Springs: NavPress, 1992), 56–58.

13. George Lundskow, "Are Promises Enough? Promise Keepers Attitudes and Character in Intensive Interviews," in *The Promise Keepers: Essays on Masculinity and Christianity,* ed. Dane S. Claussen (Jefferson, NC: McFarland, 2000), 56–75. Cited hereafter in text.

14. Sylvia Ann Hewlett and Cornel West, *The War against Parents: What We Can Do for America's Beleaguered Moms and Dads* (New York: Houghton Mifflin, 1998). Hereafter cited in text as *WP.*

15. Susan Faludi, *Stiffed: The Betrayal of the American Man* (New York: William Morrow, 1999), 227. Cited hereafter in text as *SB.*

16. For example, Hewlett and West, *The War against Parents,* 196, 210.

17. Gregg Lewis, ed., *The Power of a Promise Kept: Life Stories by Gregg Lewis* (Colorado Springs: Focus on the Family Publishing, 1995), 1. Hereafter cited in text as *PP.*

18. McCartney, *What Makes a Man?* 157.

19. Because of its allegedly progressive treatment of race, PK has been endorsed for renewing "civil society" within an increasingly fragmented sense of national identity, making the United States "an ever widening and inclusive community of . . . reciprocating others." For this term "community," read "dissensual nationalism," as I described in Part One regarding the census. See Bryan W. Brickner, *The Promise Keepers: Politics and Promises* (New York: Lexington Books, 1999), 70, 73. The appropriateness of such an endorsement aside for the moment, it must be said PK does not follow the dictates of "purity and control" that are historically associated with masculinity. PK's insistence on "racial reconciliation" does not follow the program of the "imagined fraternity of white men" outlined, for example, by Dana D. Nelson in *National Manhood* (Durham: Duke University Press, 1998). Neither, as we shall see further below, does PK exactly adhere to the argument presented by Sally Robinson that white masculinity reasserts itself through a new identity politics of increased white masculine visibility and victimhood. If PK is guilty of exhibiting white masculinity on those terms, it does so with a relation to color not accounted for in Robinson's reading of wounded white men. See her book, *Marked Men: White Masculinity in Crisis* (New York: Columbia University Press, 2000).

20. See Martin Duberman's critique of the materialist left's "politics of exclusion" in *Left Out: The Politics of Exclusion* (New York: Basic Books, 1999).

21. Marjorie Garber, "Two Point Conversion," in *One Nation under God? Religion and American Culture,* ed. Marjorie Garber and Rebecca L. Walkowitz (New York: Routledge, 1999), 295, 300. Cited hereafter in text as *ON.*

22. Jean Hardistry, *Mobilizing Resentment: Conservative Resurgence from the John Birch Society to the Promise Keepers* (Boston: Beacon Press, 1999), 8.

23. See Michael Messner, *The Politics of Masculinity: Men in Movements* (Thousand Oaks, CA: Sage, 1997), hereafter cited in text as *PM*; and Michael Kimmel, "Patriarchy's Second Coming as Masculine Renewal," in *Standing on the Promises: The Promise Keepers and the Revival of Manhood,* ed. Dane Claussen (Cleveland: Pilgrim Press, 1999), 115–25, hereafter cited in text as "PS." The tendency in "masculinity studies" developed, in part, by Messner and Kimmel, is generally to study men's sexuality through a feminist lens and to marginalize the relationship between men's gender difference and race. For early examples of this problem, see Antony Easthope, *What a Man's Gotta Do: The Masculine Myth in Popular Culture* (London: Paladin, 1996), in which race is not mentioned at all in the critique of male "universality," 1. Joseph Boone begins an attempt to think out of the paradox of "men in feminism" by "exposing the latent multiplicity and difference in the word

me(n)." This is exactly PK's charge regarding race, although with decidedly less than feminist results. See Boone, "Of Me(n) and Feminism: Who(se) Is the Sex That Writes," in *Between Men and Feminism*, ed. David Porter (New York: Routledge, 1992). This volume, like Boone's essay, is in part a response to the strained attempts to find common ground between feminist-inspired male scholarship on men and previous feminist work by and on women, without appearing to appropriate academic and political turf. The "triggering event" for this discussion remains Alice Jardine and Paul Smith's edited volume, *Men in Feminism* (New York: Methuen, 1987). A more recent meditation on the turn to masculinity in gender studies is provided by George Yúdice, "What's a Straight White Man to Do?" in *Constructing Masculinity*, ed. Maurice Berger et al. (New York: Routledge, 1995), 267–83. On this note, see also Tom Digby, ed., *Men Doing Feminism* (New York: Routledge, 1998). The first sustained volume on the interrelation between race and masculinity is Harry Stecopoulos and Michael Uebel, eds., *Race and the Subject of Masculinities* (Durham: Duke University Press, 1997).

24. Judith Newton, "A Reaction to Declining Market and Religious Influence," in Claussen, *Standing on the Promises*, 37. Hereafter cited in text as "RD."

NOTES TO SECTION 2.4

1. Paul Apostolidis, *Stations of the Cross: Adorno and Christian Right Radio* (Durham: Duke University Press, 2000). Hereafter cited in text as *SC*.
2. Theodor Adorno, *Prisms*, trans. Samuel Weber and Sherry Weber (Cambridge: MIT Press, 1981), 19, 23.
3. On conservative public policy groups more generally, see Ellen Messer-Davidow, *Disciplining Feminism: From Social Activism to Academic Discourse* (Durham: Duke University Press, 2002).
4. This would include the writing on "mass deception," published with Max Horkheimer, in *The Dialectics of Enlightenment*, trans. John Cumming (New York: Continuum, 1998).
5. G. W. F. Hegel, *The Philosophy of Right*, in *Hegel: The Essential Writings*, ed. Frederick G. Weiss (New York: Harper, 1974 [1820]), 284.
6. Adorno, *Prisms*, 9.
7. Theodor Adorno, *Minima Moralia: Reflections from Damaged Life*, trans. E. F. N. Jephcott (London: Verso, 1974), 16. Hereafter cited in text as *MM*.
8. "Authoritarianism and the Family Today," in *The Family: Its Function and Destiny*, ed. Max Horkheimer and Theodor Adorno (New York: Harper, 1949). Hereafter cited in text as "AF."
9. Sigmund Freud, *Civilization and Its Discontents*, trans. J. Strachey (New York: Norton, 1962), 74.

10. Antony Easthope, *What a Man's Gotta Do: The Masculine Myth in Popular Culture* (London: Paladin, 1996), 195. Hereafter cited in text as *WM*.

11. Theodor Adorno et al., *The Authoritarian Personality* (New York: Norton, 1982 [1950]), 361. Hereafter cited in text as *AP*.

12. Adorno's notion of the "big little man," who is attracted to both submission and dominance in a mutually extreme way, is treated by Wilhem Reich in similar terms. See Reich, *The Mass Psychology of Fascism*, trans. Vincent R. Carfagno (New York: Farrar, Straus and Giroux, 1970). For an apt critique of Reich that extends to his theory of the orgasm and the development of his infamous "Orgon Energy Field Meter," see Jeffrey Weeks, *Sexuality and Its Discontents: Meanings, Myths, and Modern Sexualities* (New York: Routledge, 1985), 141–69. Susan Sontag offers a variation on the theme of egomania and servitude in her analysis of fascist film aesthetics. See Sontag, "Fascinating Fascism," in *Movies and Methods,* ed. Bill Nichols, vol. 1 (Berkeley: University of California Press, 1976), 38–43.

    The performances of male suffering exhibited by PK are markedly different from the more typical pictures, stemming from nineteenth-century popular and literary culture, of the black man suffering at the hand of whites, and the white women subject to black sexual threat. This is not to say that this fantasy is absent from current media melodrama. See, for example, Linda Williams, *Playing the Race Card: Melodramas of Black and White from Uncle Tom to O. J. Simpson* (Princeton: Princeton University Press, 2001). For an analysis of male suffering and hegemony in nineteenth-century historical context, see Christopher Newfield, "The Politics of Male Suffering: Masochism and Hegemony in the American Renaissance," *differences* 1, no. 3 (1989): 55–87. Robyn Wiegman makes the trenchant suggestion that a politics of male suffering that underwrites a form of heterosexual male bonding can be found in the field of American studies. See her essay, "Fiedler and Sons," in *Race and the Subject of Masculinity,* ed. Harry Stecopoulos and Michael Uebel (Durham: Duke University Press, 1997), 45–70.

13. Theodor Adorno, *The Stars Down to Earth and Other Essays on the Irrational in Culture* (New York: Routledge, 1994), 64.

14. For a critique of Adorno's ahistorical treatment of the heterosexual family, see Mark Poster, *Critical Theory of the Family* (New York: Seabury, 1978). Michèle Barrett and Mary McIntosh offer a critique of Christopher Lasch's *Haven in a Heartless World: The Family Besieged* (New York: Basic Books, 1977) that runs along the same lines. Like Adorno at his lesser moments, Lasch sees the family as the last stronghold of the realm of the private, now invaded by public policy and increasing "state manipulation," where "the Oedipal crisis is his foundation for the development of responsible adulthood." See Barrett and McIntosh, *The Anti-Social Family* (London: Verso, 1982), 111–12.

15. Again, these faults are common to Wilhelm Reich in *The Mass Psychology of Fascism*.

16. On melancholy's relation to politics more generally, see Colin Campbell's assertion that "every revolt against social power eventually passes into a state of melancholia." Campbell, "Socialism: Utopian and Melancholy," *JPS: The Journal for the Psychoanalysis of Culture and Society*, spring 2002, 123.

17. It is again perhaps better to say here a certain Hegel. The Hegel critiqued by Althusser is moderately consistent with Butler's reworking of his notion of ideology in *The Psychic Life of Power* (Stanford: Stanford University Press, 1997), 110–13. I realize that in her earlier work Butler attempted a rereading of Hegel through Kojève in order to retain the same agency of "negation" I am suggesting is ruled out by Hegelian object "adequation." See Butler, *Subjects of Desire: Hegelian Reflections in Twentieth-Century France* (New York: Columbia University Press, 1987), 63 ff. Hereafter cited in text as *SD*.

18. David Savran, *Taking It Like a Man: White Masculinity, Masochism, and Contemporary American Culture* (Princeton: Princeton University Press, 1998), 33.

19. David Eng, *Racial Castration: Managing Masculinity in Asian America* (Durham: Duke University Press, 2001), 2. Hereafter cited in text as *RC*. Eng does not want to "emphasize sexual difference over and above every other type of social difference"; he declares that "it is indispensable to incorporate socially and historically variable factors into what hitherto has been rather ahistorical and essentializing psychoanalytic formulations of the construction of subjectivity" (5). Eng's revision of psychoanalysis is oriented by important work in feminism and queer studies. This work opened up the possibility for anti-essentialist work on identity, which nevertheless takes the matter of sexuality and desire as an important structuring principle for the arrangement of other forms of social difference. In addition to the citations to Butler already mentioned, see Elizabeth Abel et al., eds., *Female Subjects in Black and White: Race, Psychoanalysis, and Feminism* (Berkeley: University of California Press, 1991); and Ann Pellegrini, *Performance Anxieties: Staging Psychoanalysis, Staging Race* (New York: Routledge, 1997).

   By working against the foreclosure of cultural and historical variations within the psychodynamics of race, *Racial Castration* differs significantly from more orthodox analyses of masculinity and whiteness, for example, that of Kalpana Seshadri-Crooks in *Desiring Whiteness: A Lacanian Analysis of Race* (New York: Routledge, 2000). Hereafter cited as *DW*. In this book, Whiteness (always with a capital *W*) is a "master signifier" that operates so as "to fill the constitutive lack of the sexed subject" (*DW*, 7). While Seshadri-Crooks grants that "the values attached to male and female are historically contingent," she insists that a "historicist genealogy of the discursive construction of race" must be avoided in favor of a psychoanalytical mode of analysis that locates sexual pleasure at the core of race (Lacan over Foucault)

(*DW*, 7). That the "prophylactic" function of Whiteness as it "dissimulates the object of desire" should be any less subject to historical explanation for being sexually motivated is an unconvincing hypothesis. For Seshadri-Crooks, Whiteness "subtends the binary opposition between 'people of color' and 'white,'" while "this hierarchical opposition remains unacknowledged due to the effect of difference engendered by this master signifier" (*DW*, 20). There are two problems with this formulation in the context of PK and the imagined demise of whiteness that I have been describing. First, it provides no basis on which to describe the interactions, "subtended by whiteness," between differently colored or multiracial groups; and second, it tends toward reducing racial object "adequation" (the "binary opposition" she critiques as an effect of Whiteness) into a sexual logic of "unconscious anxiety" that escapes class and historical variation. Her evocation of the Lacanian unconscious is limited to a set of Saussurian linguistic dynamics that do not appear to change over time. Indeed, Whiteness as a "master signifier" needs nominally "white" people to operate as such. But what happens when white men are willing to give way to others?

20. Elsewhere, the insistence that whiteness exists as a fictionally normative, universal, "unmarked" or invisible racial category has been referred to as a premise of "first-wave" white critique. This work was initiated by, among others, Kobena Mercer, Fanon, bell hooks, Toni Morrison, and others. See Mike Hill, "Vipers in Shangri-la: Whiteness, Writing, and Other Ordinary Terrors," in *Whiteness: A Critical Reader,* ed. Mike Hill (New York: New York University Press, 1997), 1–18. I am suggesting here, by contrast, that whiteness is fast becoming a *marked* category in both the popular and academic registers.

21. Raleigh Washington and Glen Kehrin, *Breaking Down Walls: A Model for Reconciliation in an Age of Racial Strife* (Chicago: Moody Press, 1993), 85. Hereafter cited in text as *BD*.

22. See Rodney Cooper, *We Stand Together: Reconciling Men of Different Color* (Chicago: Moody Press, 1995). The following citations are from *Breaking Down Walls,* coauthored by Washington and Kehrin.

23. These references are from Rodney Cooper, *Double-Bind: Escaping the Contradictory Demands of Manhood* (Grand Rapids: Zondervan, 1996), 82.

NOTES TO SECTION 2.5

1. Gilles Deleuze and Felix Guattari, *Anti-Oedipus: Capitalism and Schizophrenia* (Minneapolis: University of Minnesota Press, 1983), 7, 42, 44. Hereafter cited in text. Georges Bataille describes "the psychology of fascism" in similar terms, as a Hegelian problem of "the recuperation of negativity" that protects "homogeneity [in order to] obliterat[e] various unruly forces." See Georges

Bataille, *Visions of Excess: Selected Writings, 1927–39*, ed. and trans. Allan Stoekl (Minneapolis: University of Minnesota Press, 1985), 139.

2. Rey Chow, *Ethics after Idealism: Theory, Culture, Ethnicity, Reading* (Bloomington: Indiana University Press, 1998), 16.

3. The notion *ideology = illusion/allusion* is an Althusserian formulation. See "Ideology and Ideological State Apparatuses (Notes towards an Investigation)," in *Lenin and Philosophy*, trans. Ben Brewster (New York: Monthly Review Press, 1971).

4. By 1927 membership in the Klan fell to 350,000, and to 1,500 by 1974. In 2001 its numbers were in the mere hundreds. See Jessie Daniels, *White Lies: Race, Class, Gender, and Sexuality in White Supremacist Discourse* (New York: Routledge, 1997), 3–15. On the general role of religion in the racist right, see Michael Barkun, *Religion and the Racist Right: The Origins of the Christian Identity Movement* (Chapel Hill: University of North Carolina Press, 1994); Richard Abanes, *American Militias: Rebellion, Racism, and Religion* (Denver: Intervarsity Press, 1996); and Morris Dees, *The Gathering Storm: America's Militia Threat* (New York: HarperCollins, 1996); more generally, see Michael Novick, *White Lies, White Power: The Fight against White Supremacy and Reactionary Violence* (Monroe, ME: Common Courage Press, 1995).

5. *Intelligence Report* 101 (spring 2001): 14, composed by Morris Dees of the Southern Poverty Law Center, reports white racist homepages at four hundred.

6. *Intelligence Report* 105 (spring 2002): 6.

7. As *Harper's* reports, the Southern Poverty Law Center is one of the most profitable charities in the country, earning $27 million in 1999, and spending only $13 million on civil rights programs.

8. William Pierce used this money for the reprinting costs of *The Turner Diaries*, as well as to fund the National Alliance. NA was formed in 1974 as a splinter group of the 1960s neo-Nazi National Youth Alliance. For details on the origins of NA, see Barkun, *Religion and the Racist Right*.

9. This figure is cited in *Nation*, July 22–29, 2002, 22.

10. See "Facing the Future: The Neo-Nazi National Alliance Struggles to Survive under a New Chairman," *Intelligence Report* 107 (fall 2002): 31–37.

11. On the skinhead recording industry and Pierce, see "Money, Music, and the Doctor," *Intelligence Report* 96 (fall 1999): 10.

12. Quoted in *Intelligence Report* 101 (spring 2001): 15.

13. Andrew Macdonald, *The Turner Diaries: A Novel* (Hillsboro, WV: National Vanguard Books, 1980 [1978]). Hereafter cited in text as *TD*.

14. Walden Books and others have decided not to carry *TD* after an outcry from the Southern Poverty Law Center and other civil rights groups.

15. Abby L. Ferber writes that "in white supremacist discourse, the regulation of sexuality is governed not only by a compulsory heterosexuality, but by a

compulsory interracial sexuality, which desires to maintain the illusion of racial purity." See Ferber, *White Man Falling: Race, Gender, and White Supremacy* (Lanham: Rowman and Littlefield, 1998), 22. This is entirely applicable to *The Turner Diaries*. But the more interesting significance of this dynamic is how heterosexuality is maintained within the kind of white masculinity touted by PK through exactly the opposite treatment of race. Thus Ferber's point that "interracial sexuality . . . comes to signify the erasure of all difference . . . and threat[ens] the boundaries of whiteness" (24) does not hold true for PK if the group is part of "the reactionary men's movement" she describes elsewhere (149).

16. Andrew Macdonald, *Hunter* (Hillsboro, WV: National Vanguard Books, 1994). Hereafter cited in text.

NOTES TO SECTION 3.1

1. Reed Way Dasenbrock, "One and a Half Cheers for the Corporate University," *ADE Bulletin* 130 (winter 2002): 42. That privatization and market values generally are gaining momentum in American colleges and universities is ubiquitously reported. For an overview of this trend, see James J. Van Patten, *Higher Education Culture: Case Studies for a New Century* (New York: University Press of America, 2000). See also "Unionists Delve into University Corporatization," *Voice,* December 2002, 10.

2. Luce E. Weber uses the words "students" and "clients" interchangeably and without irony in her essay, "Survey of the Main Challenges Facing Higher Education," in *Challenges Facing Higher Education at the Millennium,* ed. Warner Z. Hirsch and Luce E. Weber, (Phoenix: American Council on Higher Education, 1999), 5.

3. On the devolution of state and federal budgets for higher education funding, see Sheila Slaughter and Larry L. Leslie, *Academic Capitalism: Politics, Policies, and the Entrepreneurial University* (Baltimore: Johns Hopkins University Press, 1997); David Breneman, *Higher Education: On a Collision Course with New Realities* (Washington, DC: Association of Governing Boards of Universities and Colleges, 1993); and Andrew Delano Abbott, *The System of Professions: An Essay on the Divisions of Expert Labor* (Chicago: University of Chicago Press, 1988).

4. Bill Readings, *The University in Ruins* (Cambridge: Harvard University Press, 1996). Hereafter cited in text as *UR.*

5. Among many other journals that have done special issues on the changing state of the university, consider the *minnesota review*'s multivolume focus on institutional politics and material life, which has addressed everything from cultural studies (nos. 43 and 44) to activism in the academy (nos. 50 and 51).

6. Richard Ohmann, *Politics of Letters* (Middletown: Wesleyan University Press, 1987), 22, 12.
7. Introduction to *Capitalizing Knowledge: New Intersections of Industry and Academia,* ed. Henry Etzkowitz et al. (Albany: SUNY Press, 1998), 1.
8. Cited in Henry Steck and Michael Zweig, "Take Back the University: Only Unions Can Save Academic Life" in *Campus, Inc.: Corporate Power in the Ivory Tower,* ed. Geoffry D. White with Flannery C. Hauck (Amherst: Prometheus Books, 2000), 297. According to Zelda F. Gamson, "the property owned by colleges and universities has been estimated to be worth over $200 billion, total expenditures to be $175 billion, and annual research and development expenditures to be about $20 billion." See Gamson, "Stratification in the Academy," in *Chalk Lines: The Politics of Work in the Managed University,* ed. Randy Martin (Durham: Duke University Press, 1998), 103.
9. Cited by Ishmael Reed in *Multi-America: Essays on Cultural Wars and Cultural Peace,* ed. Ishmael Reed (New York: Penguin, 1997), xxvii.
10. My 1996 introduction to the *minnesota review*'s "White Issue" attempts, incompletely, to signal that irony and inversion were implicit in the task of criticizing whiteness. It was already in the air at the time that whiteness rearticulated itself as "bad faith Mc-Multicultural niche-marketing." See Mike Hill, "Introduction: Through the Ethnographic Looking Glass," *minnesota review* 47 (winter 1996): 6 ff.

NOTES TO SECTION 3.2

1. The term belongs to Jeffrey Williams. See "Academostars," special issue of *minnesota review* 52–53 (2000).
2. Cary Nelson and Stephen Watt, *Academic Keywords: A Devil's Dictionary* (New York: Routledge, 1999), ix. Hereafter cited as *AK* in text.
3. Mary Poovey, "The Twenty-first Century University and the Market: What Price Economic Viability?" *differences* 12, no. 1 (2001): 1. Hereafter cited in text as "TC."
4. Paul Lauter, "'Political Correctness' and the Attack on American Colleges," in *Higher Education under Fire: Politics, Economics, and the Crisis of the Humanities,* ed. Michael Bérubé and Cary Nelson (New York: Routledge, 1995), 73–90. Hereafter cited in text as "PC." The first academic revolution, which was in the era of post–World War II expansionism, is described in Christopher Jencks and David Riesman, *The Academic Revolution* (Garden City: Doubleday, 1968).
5. Ami Zusman, "Issues Facing Higher Education in the Twenty-first Century," in *American Higher Education in the Twenty-first Century: Social, Political, and Economic Challenges,* ed. Philip G. Altbach et al. (Baltimore: Johns Hopkins University Press, 1999), 111.

6. Carol Frances, "Higher Education: Enrollment Trends and Staffing Needs," *TIAA-CREF Research Dialogues* 35 (1998): 1–23.

7. See Mark G. Yudof, "Is the Public University Dead?" *Chronicle of Higher Education,* January 11, 2002, B24; and Ben Gose, "The Fall of the Flagships: Do the Best State Universities Need to Privatize to Thrive?" *Chronicle of Higher Education,* July 5, 2002, A19.

8. See Barbara McKenna, "In the Eye of the Storm: Unions Chart a Course through a Second Year of Turbulent Budget Deficits," *On Campus,* February 2003, 4–7.

9. Randy Martin, introduction to *Chalk Lines: The Politics of Work in the Managed University,* ed. Randy Martin (Durham: Duke University Press, 1998), 3.

10. Patricia Gumport et al., eds., *Trends in United States Higher Education* (Stanford: National Center for Postsecondary Improvement, 1997), 24.

11. Gary Rhoades and Sheila Slaughter, "Academic Capitalism, Managed Professionals, and Supply-Side Higher Education," in Martin, *Chalk Lines,* 59.

12. Ronnie Dugger, "Introduction: The Struggle That Matters Most," in *Campus, Inc.: Corporate Power in the Ivory Tower,* ed. Geoffry D. White with Flannery C. Hauck (Amherst: Prometheus, 2000), 23; Wesley Shumar, *College for Sale: A Critique of the Commodification of Higher Education* (London: Falmer Press, 1997), 65.

13. Gumport et al., *Trends in United States Higher Education,* 23.

14. Gary Rhoades, *Managed Professionals: Unionized Faculty and Restructuring of Labor* (Albany: SUNY Press, 1998), 8.

15. Henry Giroux, "Critical Education or Training: Beyond the Commodification of Higher Education," in *Beyond the Corporate University: Culture and Pedagogy in the New Millennium,* ed. Henry Giroux and Kostas Mysiades, (Lanham: Rowman and Littlefield, 2001), 8.

16. This statement is literally true in the sense that of the 2.6 million knowledge workers in the academy, only 43 percent are faculty or TAs. See Martin, introduction to *Chalk Lines,* 13.

17. Yudof, "Is the Public University Dead?" B24.

18. Aronowitz is focused, as am I, on the short sixty-year history of the modern public university post–World War II. See his book, *The Knowledge Factory: Dismantling the Corporate University and Creating True Higher Learning* (Boston: Beacon Press, 2000), 10. Hereafter cited in text as *KF.*

19. See Robert Geiger, "Ten Generations of Higher Education," in Altbach et al., *American Higher Education in the Twenty-first Century,* 61.

20. Alvin Kernan, "Introduction: Change in the Humanities and Higher Education," in *What's Happened to the Humanities?* ed. Alvin Kernan (Princeton: Princeton University Press, 1997), 4.

21. See Gumport et al., *Trends in United States Higher Education,* 20. Regarding

the decline in public funding, see Zusman, "Issues Facing Higher Education," 110.

22. Radically rising tuition and fees and a marked increase in student loans have provided the harsh backdrop for the move from public to private funding in higher education. For example, tuition and fees nearly tripled at four-year colleges and universities between 1976 and 1989. And as Randy Martin notes, the percentage of students borrowing to attend college increased 22 percent between 1990 and 1994. On tuition, see Zelda F. Gamson, "Stratification in the Academy," in Martin, *Chalk Lines,* 107; and on student loans, see Martin's introduction to the volume, 9.

23. Kerr uses the term "golden age" to distinguish between the great postwar period of public university expansion and "a descent into a time of troubles." See Clark Kerr, *The Great Transformation in Higher Education, 1960–1980* (Albany: SUNY Press, 1997), 109. Hereafter cited in text as *GT.*

24. Clark Kerr, *The Uses of the University* (Cambridge: Harvard University Press, 1982 [1963]), 52. Hereafter cited in text as *Uses.* See also references to the postwar university in Kerr, *Higher Education Cannot Escape History: Issues for the Twenty-first Century* (Albany: SUNY Press, 1994), 163. Hereafter cited in text as *HE.*

25. Clark Kerr, *The Uses of the University,* 5th ed. (Cambridge: Harvard University Press, 2001), 199. This updated edition of Kerr's 1963 manifesto is hereafter cited in text as *Uses 2001.*

26. Consider the odd campaign of disinformation and harassment set upon Kerr by Hoover's FBI during UC Berkeley's Free Speech Movement. This harassment of the Free Speech Movement student protesters at UC Berkeley is reported in the *Nation,* July 8, 2002, 7.

27. Kerr's nervousness about the Free Speech Movement is more evidence for his interest in what he called "disciplined" over other, less clearly patriotic, forms of collective dissent. Recall, the act that helped spawn the movement at Berkeley was the barring of nonacademic political groups from the campus, a point that further shows how the multiversity was dependent on the Cold War separation between knowledge and political matters, at least at that level of the university's occupants. On the Free Speech Movement, see Stanley Aronowitz, *The Death and Rebirth of American Radicalism* (New York: Routledge, 1996), 66–67; and more directly, David Lance Gaines, *The Free Speech Movement* (Berkeley: Ten Speed Press, 1993).

28. Clark Kerr, *Troubled Times for American Higher Education: The 1990s and Beyond* (Albany: SUNY Press, 1994). Cited hereafter in text as *TT.*

29. Harold Hellenbrand, "The University of Excellence," *ADE Bulletin* 130 (winter 2002): 25.

30. Consider, once again, the myriad new forms of FBI surveillance in our midst given the U.S.A. Patriot Act, not least disturbing of which is the unprecedented monitoring of library use.

31. This does not rule out the possibility that white masculinity may be poised to make a certain comeback vis-à-vis performances of majoritarian abjection. The preceding part of this book on the Promise Keepers and the National Alliance should have made that cautionary point abundantly clear. A correlate suggestion was that mainstream claims to patriarchy are increasingly adopting the discourse of marginality instead of insisting on the strictly normative maintenance of white supremacy as in former times. A pertinent example of this Anglo bait-and-switch is, of course, the current assault on affirmative action, which began in the leaner and meaner time of higher education's era of post-massification, with *Regents of University of California v. Bakke* (1978). In this case, a white plaintiff, Alan Bakke, challenged the admissions standards of UC Davis's medical school, using Title VI of the 1964 Civil Rights Act and the Constitution's Equal Protection Clause. With the help of right-wing–funded legal groups, such as the Center for Individual Rights, other such examples of co-opting civil rights have occurred in Texas (1996), Washington (2000), and Michigan (2001). See Margaret A. Burnham, "Affirmative Action Cases in Higher Education," *Public Eye* 16, no. 2 (summer 2002): 4–5. For a full analysis of the assault on affirmative action, and in particular, its connection to right-wing–funded think tanks and policy groups, see Ellen Messer-Davidow, *Disciplining Feminism: From Social Activism to Academic Discourse* (Durham: Duke University Press, 2002), 270–74.

32. Giorgio Agamben, *The Coming Community,* trans. Michael Hardt (Minneapolis: University of Minnesota Press, 1993), 62. Cited by Readings in *Ruins* on page 49. Hereafter cited in my own text as *CC.*

33. I have in mind here, of course, the avalanche of corporate scandals that reached top branches of the federal government in the summer of 2002. These episodes include President George W. Bush's questionable (i.e., unreported) sale of stock at Harken Energy upon the company's collapse, and Vice President Dick Cheney's stewardship of the scandal-ridden Halliburton Corporation. It ought also be noted in considering the profile of the Bush cabinet that the secretary of the treasury, secretary of labor, and chief of staff were all former CEOs.

34. Paul Delany concedes Readings's "competitive postmodern university" hypothesis, but construes this as a facile causal effect of theory's academic market value. See his essay, "The University in Ruins: Bill Readings and the Fate of the Humanities," *Profession,* 2000, 94.

35. Robert P. Marzec, "The Scene of Research and the Crisis-Event: Resistance in Ruins," in "Universities II," special issue of *Crossings* 3 (1999): 1–17. Hereafter cited in text as "SR."

36. Gilles Deleuze and Felix Guattari, *A Thousand Plateaus,* trans. Brian Massumi (Minneapolis: University of Minnesota Press, 1987), 436–37. Cited by Marzec in "SR," 3.

37. Nancy Fraser, *Justice Interruptus: Critical Reflections on the "Postsocialist" Condition* (New York: Routledge, 1997), 5.

38. The reference is to Spivak's well-known essay, "Can the Subaltern Speak?" anthologized, among other places, in *Marxism and the Interpretation of Culture*, ed. Cary Nelson and Lawrence Grossberg (Chicago: University of Chicago Press, 1988), 271–316.

39. These writers are named by Stanley Aronowitz in *The Death and Rebirth of American Radicalism* as embodying the "attack on multiculturalism as a subversion of American, Enlightenment values," 188. The quote, of course, is taken from Arthur Schlesinger, Jr., *The Disuniting of America* (New York: Random House, 1991).

40. See Eric Lott, "The New Liberalism in America: Identity Politics in the 'Vital Center,'" in *The Making and Unmaking of Whiteness*, ed. Birgit Brander Rasmussen et al. (Durham: Duke University Press, 2001), 214–34.

41. An oft-cited example of an Enlightenment-based critique of the U.S. left as being overly concerned with identity politics can be found in Todd Gitlin, "The Rise of 'Identity Politics': An Examination Critique," in Bérubé and Nelson, *Higher Education under Fire*, 308–19; and at further length in Gitlin, *The Twilight of Common Dreams: Why America Is Wracked by Culture Wars* (New York: Henry Holt, 1995).

42. Russell Jacoby, *The End of Utopia* (New York: Basic Books, 1999), 33.

43. See Robert H. Bork, *Slouching towards Gomorrah: Modern Liberalism and American Decline* (New York: Regan Books, 1996); Peter Brimlow, *Alien Nation: Common Sense about America's Immigration Disaster* (New York: HarperCollins, 1996), both of which were *New York Times* best-sellers. See also Gertrude Himmelfarb, *One Nation, Two Cultures* (New York: Knopf, 1999).

44. See, in particular, Aronowitz, *The Death and Rebirth of American Radicalism*, 188–89; and Jeffrey Williams, ed., *PC Wars: Politics and Theory in the Academy* (New York: Routledge, 1995).

45. Arjun Appadurai, "Diversity and Disciplinarity as Cultural Artifacts," in *Disciplinarity and Dissent*, ed. Cary Nelson and Dilip Parameshwar Gaonkar (New York: Routledge, 1996), 24.

46. Christopher Newfield, "What Was 'Political Correctness'? Race, the Right, and Managerial Democracy in the Humanities," in Williams, *PC Wars*, 128.

47. See Libby V. Morris and Sammy Parker, *Multiculturalism: A Source Book* (New York: Garland, 1996), 3. For additional information on the relation between diversity and demographic trends, see Timothy K. Conley, ed., *Race, Ethnicity, and an American Campus: A Report and Recommendations* (Peoria: Office for Teaching Excellence and Faculty Development, 1996); for the connections between the civil rights movement, its legacy, and the institutionalization of multiculturalism, see Christine Sleeter and Peter McLaren, eds., *Multicultural Education, Critical Pedagogy, and the Politics of Difference*

(Albany: SUNY Press, 1995); and J. A. Banks, ed., *Multicultural Education: Issues and Perspectives* (Boston: Allyn and Bacon, 1989).

48. See Thomas J. la Belle and Christopher Ward, *Ethnic Studies and Multiculturalism* (Albany: SUNY Press, 1996), 73.

49. Morris and Parker, *Multiculturalism*, 4.

50. Quoted in fall 2000 from the National Survey on Diversity Requirements Web site: http://www.aacu-edu.org. For more detailed calculations regarding domestic versus international diversity on US campuses, see la Belle and Ward, *Ethnic Studies and Multiculturalism*, 117–18.

51. National Association of Scholars, *Losing the Big Picture: The Fragmentation of the English Major since 1964* (Princeton: NAS, 2000).

52. John K. Wilson, "The Canon and the Curriculum: Multicultural Revolution and Traditionalist Revolt," in Altbach et al., *American Higher Education in the Twenty-first Century*, 429. On the fact that the still traditional nature of the undergraduate curriculum is still intact, see Francis Oakley, "Ignorant Armies and Nighttime Clashes," in Kernan, *What's Happened to the Humanities?* 71; and Rhoades and Slaughter, "Academic Capitalism," 55.

53. Ramon A. Gutierrez, "Ethnic Studies: Its Evolution in American Colleges and Universities," in *Multiculturalism: A Critical Reader*, ed. David Theo Goldberg (Oxford: Blackwell, 1994), 160; see also Carrie Tirado Bramen, "Minority Hiring in the Age of Downsizing," in *Power, Race, and Gender in Academe: Strangers in the Ivory Tower?* ed. Shirley Geok-Lin and Maria Herrera-Sobek (New York: MLA Press, 2000), 112–31.

54. See, representatively, not only Kerr as mentioned, but also Conley in *Race, Ethnicity, and an American Campus*, who sympathetically links "geography and demographics" with "the changing American/international marketplace" (11). These twin phenomena are what "key campus officials" must finally seek to control (13).

55. These numbers are taken from the U.S. Department of Education National Center for Educational Statistics Web site in the fall of 2001: http://nces.ed.gov/programs/coe/2001. See also Lynn Hunt, "Democratization and Decline? The Consequences of Demographic Change in the Humanities," in Kernan, *What's Happened to the Humanities?* 17–31.

56. Myrtis H. Powell, "Campus Climate and Students of Color," in *The Multicultural Campus: Strategies for Transforming Higher Education*, ed. Leonard A. Valverde and Louis A. Castenell (Walnut Creek: Altamira Press, 1998), 96, 99. For relative enrollments for students of color, see also la Belle and Ward, *Ethnic Studies and Multiculturalism*, 69.

57. Managed multiculturalism can also lead to scandal, as witnessed by the digital imposition of black and Asian faces among groups of white students on the cover of university publicity brochures. See Lila Gutterman, "Doctoring Diversity II," *Chronicle of Higher Education*, October 13, 2000, A12.

58. Frances K. Stage and Kathleen Manning, *Enhancing the Multicultural*

NOTES TO SECTION 3.2

Campus: A Cultural Brokering Approach (San Francisco: Jossey-Bass, 1992), 2. Hereafter cited in text as *EM*.

59. Avery Gordon and Christopher Newfield, introduction to *Mapping Multiculturalism*, ed. Avery Gordon and Christopher Newfield (Minneapolis: University of Minnesota Press, 1996), 13.

60. Jon Cruz, "From Farce to Tragedy: Reflections of Race at Century's End," in Gordon and Newfield, *Mapping Multiculturalism*, 19.

61. David Theo Goldberg, introduction to *Multiculturalism: A Critical Reader*, 8.

62. McLaren and Sleeter, *Multicultural Education*, 9–10.

63. See Cary Nelson, *Manifesto of a Tenured Radical* (New York: New York University Press, 1997), 35; and Stanley Aronowitz and Henry Giroux, *Education Still under Siege* (Westport: Bergin and Garvey, 1993), 161.

64. Gordon and Newfield, introduction to *Mapping Multiculturalism*, 2. They expand on the unresolved theoretical antagonisms between class and culture in their later essay in the volume, "Multiculturalism's Unfinished Business," 78 ff. Goldberg is quoted in *Multiculturalism*, 14.

65. Wahneema Lubiano, "Like Being Mugged by a Metaphor," in Gordon and Newfield, *Mapping Multiculturalism*, 70.

NOTES TO SECTION 3.3

1. There are at present too many anthologies on whiteness to cite. But, in addition to the Berkeley conference volume discussed below, a representative list might include Richard Delgado and Jean Stefancic, eds., *Critical White Studies: Looking behind the Mirror* (Philadelphia: Temple University Press, 1997); Michele Fine et al., eds., *Off White: Readings on Race, Power, and Society* (New York: Routledge, 1997); Ruth Frankenberg, ed., *Displacing Whiteness: Essays in Social and Cultural Criticism* (Durham: Duke University Press, 1997); Mike Hill, ed., *Whiteness: A Critical Reader* (New York: New York University Press, 1997); Joel L. Kinchloe et al., eds., *White Reign: Deploying Whiteness in America* (New York: St. Martin's, 1998). See more recently Chris Cuomo and Kim Hall, eds., *Whiteness: Feminist Philosophical Reflections* (Lanham: Rowman and Littlfield, 1999); and Cynthia Levine-Rasky, ed., *Working through Whiteness: International Perspectives* (Albany: SUNY Press, 2002).

2. Speaking perhaps too hastily, I called the desire to talk about whiteness as an unmarked normative racial category a "first wave" of white critique. See Mike Hill, "Vipers in Shangri-la: Whiteness, Writing, and Other Ordinary Terrors," in Hill, *Whiteness: A Critical Reader*, 2.

3. The most widely recognized of the white labor historians are Theodore W. Allen, *The Invention of the White Race*, vols. 1 and 2, (New York: Verso, 1994–1997); Noel Ignatiev, *How the Irish Became White* (New York: Rout-

ledge, 1995); and David Roediger, *The Wages of Whiteness: Race and the Making of the American Working Class* (London: Verso, 1991).

4. On whiteness and the visibility/divisibility relation, see Ross Chambers, "The Unexamined," in Hill, *Whiteness: A Critical Reader,* 187–203.

5. David Palumbo-Liu has argued, convincingly, that the historical patholo-gization of color contaminates whiteness with the fear of its own lack of pu-rity and the loss of its presumed national integrity under the ideological pressures of globalization. See chapter 9, "Double Trouble: The Pathology of Ethnicity Meets White Schizophrenia," in his book *Asian/American: Histori-cal Crossings of a Racial Frontier* (Stanford: Stanford University Press, 1990), 295 ff.

6. Vron Ware and Les Black, *Out of Whiteness: Color, Politics, and Culture* (Chicago: University of Chicago Press, 2002). Cited hereafter as *OW* in text.

7. Calling whiteness heretofore unremarkable is not to say that it was unre-markable to everyone, only that it was predominately so given the very na-ture of a majoritarian national ideal. This is an exceedingly important point. Clearly, as David Roediger has chronicled in his volume of black-on-white writing, whiteness was hardly regarded as unmarked by its African American others. See Roediger, ed., *Black on White: Black Writers on What It Means to Be White* (New York: Schocken, 1988). More on this volume's alleged gender blindness below.

8. Fine et al., *Off White,* xi–xii. I have written at greater length about the vol-ume's interest in corporate diversity training in "'Souls Unclothed': Race, Writing, and the Fantasy of Knowing," *Review of Education/Pedagogy/Cul-tural Studies* 20, no. 3 (fall 1998): 25–34.

9. Robert Ochsner, "A New Chair's Perspective, White and Black, of English Studies," in "The University of Excellence," special issue of *ADE Bulletin* 130 (winter 2002): 18.

10. Robyn Wiegman, "Whiteness Studies and the Paradox of Particularity," *boundary 2,* 26, no. 3 (fall 1999): 115–50. Hereafter cited in text as "WS." See critiques of white labor history from within its own ranks with a special cluster of essays on the topic in *International Labor and Working-Class History* 60 (fall 2001): 1–202. In particular, see Eric Arnesen's contribution to that issue, "Whiteness and the Historian's Imagination," 3–32; and his review of Roediger's edited volume, *Colored White,* in the *New Republic,* available at http://www.tnr.com/doc.mhtml?I=20020624$s=arenson062402&c=1. For confirmation that the worry over the status of knowledge about whiteness in the academy "has become something of a stock scene in whiteness studies" (186), see Mason Stokes, *The Color of Sex: Whiteness, Heterosexuality, and the Fictions of White Supremacy* (Durham: Duke University Press, 2001). An al-ternative critique of this work advances the contrary thesis that the many cri-tiques of whiteness have lately resulted in too much "fragmentation" (36). This is rather the opposite point than saying that whiteness studies scholars

have come to academic prominence by producing and then manipulating white marginality on normative grounds. See Zeus Leonardo, "The Souls of White Folk: Critical Pedagogy, Whiteness Studies, and Globalization Discourse," *Race, Ethnicity and Education* 5, no. 1 (2002): 29–50.

11. In the 1997 introduction to *Whiteness: A Critical Reader,* I attempted to locate the paradoxes and contradictions surrounding whiteness studies precisely in early 1980s feminism, and then tried to link that, in a cursory way, to "a new international." I had not fully realized at that point that labor was redefining whiteness much closer to my own workplace in academe. See the section of that earlier introduction called "Other People's Modernism: The Feminist Charges of White Critique," 4 ff. In *White Guys: Studies in Postmodern Domination and Difference* (New York: Verso, 1995), Fred Pfeil offers a rare early critique of whiteness via the essential factor of masculinity. I have compared Pfeil and Frankenberg to Ignatiev, critically and at greater length, elsewhere. For this, see "Trading Races: Majorities, Modernities, Critique," in *Education and Cultural Studies: Toward a Performative Practice,* ed. Henry Giroux and Patrick Shannon (New York: Routledge, 1997), 139–52. My own insistence in adjoining gender and whiteness appears in a 1996 essay, "Can Whiteness Speak? Institutional Anomies, Ontological Disasters, and Three Hollywood Films," in *White Trash: Race and Class in America,* ed. Matt Wray and Annalee Newitz (New York: Routledge, 1997), 18–29.

12. See Mike Hill, "What Was (the White) Race? Memory, Categories, Change," *Postmodern Culture* 7, no. 2 (January 1997), www.iath.virginia.edu/pmc.

13. Birgit Brander Rasmussen et al., introduction to *The Making and Unmaking of Whiteness* (Durham: Duke University Press, 2001), 17. Hereafter cited in text as *MUW.*

14. My own recollection as a participant in this event is that community interest found its way into the venue, not ideally, in the conference's large and vocal nonacademic audience. This audience was comprised of a good number of major media representatives, many of whom thought the event was a twisted pitch for academic white pride. It would be sadly interesting if they turned out, after all, to be right.

15. Aal's mistake is simply the ungenerous and unfounded assumption that academics cannot be both theoretical and politically active, a particularly U.S. suspicion. For plenty of arguments to the contrary, see "Activism and the Academy," a special issue of *minnesota review* 50–51 (fall 1998).

16. Michael Bérubé, *The Employment of English: Theory, Jobs, and the Future* (New York: New York University Press, 1998), 189.

NOTES TO SECTION 3.4

1. Cited in Ioan Davies, *Cultural Studies and Beyond: Fragments of Empire* (New York: Routledge, 1995), 138.
2. Paul Gilroy, "Cultural Studies and the Crisis in Britain's Universities," *Chronicle of Higher Education,* July 26, 2002, B20.
3. Ross Chambers, "Reading and Being Read: Irony and Critical Practice in Cultural Studies," *minnesota review* 43–44 (1995): 113–30.
4. Rey Chow, *Ethics after Idealism: Theory, Culture, Ethnicity, Reading* (Bloomington: Indiana University Press, 1998), 7.
5. Fredric Jameson, "On Cultural Studies," *Social Text* 34 (1993): 24. Hereafter cited in text as "CS."
6. Ellen Messer-Davidow, *Disciplining Feminism: From Social Activism to Academic Discourse* (Durham: Duke University Press, 2002), 11.
7. Simon Wortham, *Rethinking the University: Leverage and Deconstruction* (Manchester: Manchester University Press, 1999), 9.
8. These books, of course, are Richard Hoggart, *The Uses of Literacy* (New York: Oxford University Press, 1970 [1958]); Raymond Williams, *Culture and Society* (London: Chatto and Windus, 1958); and E. P. Thompson, *The Making of the English Working Class* (New York: Vintage, 1963).
9. These include organizational centers such as the Campaign for Nuclear Disarmament (CND), the Workers Educational Association (WEA), and the National Council of Labor Colleges (NCLC).
10. Cited in Davies, *Cultural Studies,* 12.
11. This is a point made first by Stuart Hall, reluctant spokesperson for the Birmingham "legacy," and the director of BCCS by 1970. Hall wants to be neither the "tableau vivant," CS's "spirit of the past resurrected," nor "the keeper of the conscience of Cultural Studies." See Hall, "Cultural Studies and Its Theoretical Legacies," in *Cultural Studies,* ed. Lawrence Grossberg et al. (New York: Routledge, 1992), 277.
12. Ioan Davies calls Thompson "the ideal example of the 'free-born Englishman's' (or aristocratic) radicalism." See Davies, *Cultural Studies,* 50.
13. Cited in Patrick Bratlinger, *Crusoe's Footprints: Cultural Studies in Britain and America* (New York: Routledge, 1990), 45.
14. Hall speaks eloquently of coming to CS through the *problem* of Marxism: "backwards: against the Soviet tanks in Budapest." See Hall, "Cultural Studies and Its Theoretical Legacies," 279.
15. A *locus classicus* for CS's subsequent revision of the economistic version of the base/superstructure equation is Raymond Williams's article "Base and Superstructure in Marxist Cultural Theory," which appeared originally in the *New Left Review* in 1973. The reprint is found in Williams, *Problems in Materialism and Culture* (London: Verso, 1980), 31–49.

16. This phrase, which has for some time been a CS slogan, is found in Raymond Williams, *The Long Revolution* (London: Chatto and Windus, 1961).

17. See Meaghan Morris, "Banality in Cultural Studies," in *The Logics of Television,* ed. Patricia Mellencamp (Bloomington: Indiana University Press, 1990), 14–43.

18. Readings elaborates on the paradoxes of cultural absence that surround CS in the U.S. academy in "Culture Wars and Cultural Studies," in *The University in Ruins* (Cambridge: Harvard University Press, 1996), 89–118.

19. Erik D. Curren, "No Openings at This Time: Job Market Collapse and Graduate Education," *Profession,* 1994, 57–61.

20. Philip E. Smith II, "Composing a Cultural Studies Curriculum at Pitt," in *Cultural Studies in the English Classroom,* ed. James Berlin and Michael J. Vivion, (Portsmouth: Boynton/Cook Heinemann, 1992), 47, 63.

21. Not unlike other graduate students of the generation who came on the market in the mid-1990s, I found my initial optimism for gainful employment buoyed by William G. Bowen and Julie Ann Sosa, *Prospects for Faculty in the Arts and Sciences, 1987–2012* (Princeton: Princeton University Press, 1989). This book infamously predicted a 1990s bull market for first-time hires at a time when there would be more jobs in the humanities than there would be new Ph.D.'s to fill them. A survey of doctoral students in English in 2001 shows by contrast how grim the feelings about future employment are among the profession's disheartened new recruits. Polling students in twenty-seven doctoral-granting universities, this survey finds that less than 43 percent believe that a career in academe is a realistic possibility. See Linda Ray Pratt, "In Dark Wood: Finding a New Path to the Future of English," *ADE Bulletin* 131 (spring 2002): 33. And, sadly, the numbers for 2000–01 Ph.D. placement support this pessimism. For graduates in English, a mere 410 of the 976 of those applying for tenure-track jobs (42 percent) actually found them. This compares with 372 of 1,102 (34 percent) in CS's heyday of 1996–97; and 385 of 845 graduates (45.6 percent) in 1983–94. See "Findings from the MLA's 2000–01 Survey of Ph.D. Placement," *MLA Newsletter,* winter 2002, 14.

22. Michael Bérubé, "Peer Pressure: Literary and Cultural Studies in the Bear Market," *minnesota review* 43–44 (1995): 139.

23. Richard Holub, "Professional Responsibility: On Undergraduate Education and Hiring Practices," *Profession* (1994): 81.

24. "Facts and Figures," *ADE Bulletin* 106 (winter 1993): 62.

25. "Highlights of the MLA's Survey of Ph.D. Granting Modern Language Departments: Changes in Faculty Size from 1990–94," *ADE Bulletin* 109 (winter 1994): 47.

26. The date 1993 is significant for being the same year as the weighty volume by Grossberg et al., *Cultural Studies,* cited above, regarding Hall's backpedaling over CS's popularity in the United States. Regarding part-time employ-

ment, see Ana Marie Fox, "Study Shows Colleges' Dependence on Their Part-Time Instructors," *Chronicle of Higher Education,* December 1, 2000, A12.

27. Cited by the AAUP's "Statement from the Conference on the Growing Use of Part-Time and Adjunct Faculty," available via the American Federation of Teacher's Web site: www.aft.org. Also see the MLA's consistently damning tallies in, "MLA Committee on Professional Employment," at http://www.mla.org.

28. Cary Nelson, *Manifesto of a Tenured Radical* (New York: New York University Press, 1997), 55. Hereafter cited in text as *MTR.*

29. Michael Bérubé and Cary Nelson, eds., *Higher Education under Fire: Politics, Economics, and the Crisis of the Humanities* (New York: Routledge, 1995), 19.

30. Sandra M. Gilbert, "President's Column," *MLA Newsletter,* summer 1996, 5.

31. For an apt response to the backlash against "cultural studies" and a recuperative assessment of CS's apparent professional excesses, see Lauren Berlant, "Collegiality, Crisis, and Cultural Studies," *ADE Bulletin* 117 (fall 1997): 4–9.

32. The book is Charles Tilly, *Popular Contention in Great Britain, 1758–1834* (Cambridge: Harvard University Press, 1995). Like E. P. Thompson, Tilly may be placed within a tradition of "Marxist humanism," the same theoretical tendencies Wiegman rightly pins on Roediger. Both Tilly and Thompson evoke the term "moral" to challenge what they perceive are the economistic tendencies of classical Marxism. See Charles Tilly and Louise Tilly, eds., *Class Conflict and Collective Action* (Beverly Hills: Sage, 1981).

33. The CS scholars who cite Thompson as an originator of CS are too numerous to list. But see, representatively, Valda Blundell et al., eds., *Relocating Cultural Studies: Developments in Theory and Research* (New York: Routledge, 1993). In this volume, in particular, see Grossberg's contribution, "The Formations of Cultural Studies: An American in Birmingham," 21–66. This essay names Thompson, rightly, as the critical locus for the nagging debate in later CS between structuralism and culturalism, which I shall trace to Thompson's own unclaimed investment in the Scottish Enlightenment. Two other influential citations of Thompson as a CS originator are Fred Inglis, *Cultural Studies* (London: Blackwell, 1993); and Cary Nelson and Dilip Parameshwar Gaonkar, "Cultural Studies and the Politics of Disciplinarity: An Introduction," in *Disciplinarity and Dissent,* ed. Cary Nelson and Dilip Parameshwar Gaonkar (New York: Routledge, 1996), 1–22.

34. E. P. Thompson, "The Moral Economy of the English Crowd in the Eighteenth Century" (1971), rpt. in *Customs in Common* (New York: New Press, 1991), 188. Hereafter cited in text as "ME."

35. Elizabeth Fox Genovese suggests, though with less specificity than I have here, that "both paternalism and liberalism have a moral base . . . [and] were both part of ruling class ideologies" (166). See Fox Genovese, "The

Many Faces of Moral Economy," *Past and Present* 58 (February 1973): 161–68.

36. E. P. Thompson, "Patricians and Plebes" (1974), rpt. with additions in *Customs in Common*, 38. Hereafter cited in text as "PP."

37. Thirty years later Thompson sought to distance himself from "overly consensual and holistic notions of the term 'cultural,'" and likewise was concerned that "consensus . . . may serve to distract attention from social and cultural contradictions" (6). See introduction to *Customs in Common*. Thompson also sought to distance himself from the term "reciprocity" in revisiting the "moral economy argument," suggesting that this term "does not imply equity of burden or obligation" (343). See "The Moral Economy Reviewed," in *Customs in Common*. These statements do not change the implications of the present argument in relation to Smith and to CS's ambivalent status in U.S. academe. Smith's prescriptions for capitalist morality could contain—indeed, were designed precisely to contain—both conflict and correspondence simultaneously. That these may become unaligned given certain historical conditions intimates the continued presence of what he calls the multitude, equally within the legacies of the Enlightenment and CS. "The Moral Economy Reviewed" is hereafter cited in text as "MER."

38. See A. W. Coats's suggestion to this effect in "Contrary Moralities: Plebes, Paternalists, and Political Economists," *Past and Present* 54 (February 1972): 130–33.

39. See Nicholas Phillipson, "Adam Smith as Civic Moralist," in *Wealth and Virtue: The Shaping of Political Economy in the Scottish Enlightenment*, ed. Istvan Hont and Michael Ignatieff (Cambridge: Cambridge University Press, 1983). The term is J. G. A. Pocock's. See his "Cambridge Paradigms and Scotch Philosophers" in the same volume.

40. Adam Smith, *Wealth of Nations*, ed. Lawrence Dickey (Indianapolis: Hackett, 1993), 177. Hereafter cited in text as *WN*.

41. Indeed, Smith was reprimanded at Oxford for reading John Locke, who was himself banned by the university in favor of Christian rationalism. See Athol Fitzgibbons, *Adam Smith's System of Liberty, Wealth, and Virtue: The Moral and Political Foundations of The Wealth of Nations* (Oxford: Clarendon, 1995).

42. Thus Smith uses the key term "frugality" in hopes of trimming capitalist greed. Recognized by capitalist fellowship as a "moral" necessity, frugality thus checks the unrestrained accumulation of wealth. See *WN*, 67 ff. On "morality," the key text is Adam Smith's neglected earlier treatise, *The Theory of Moral Sentiments* (Indianapolis: Liberty Fund, 1984). Hereafter cited in text as *TMS*.

43. See Lawrence Dickey's essay in *WN*, "Economics and Ethics in Smith's Theory of Capital Accumulation," 213 ff.

44. Adam Smith, *Lectures on Rhetoric and Belles Lettres* (Indianapolis: Liberty

Fund, 1985), 10. Hereafter cited in text as *LRBL*. Getting aright our relation to sympathetic objects in thought, we then "voluntarily submit" and "render ourselves . . . proper objects" (*TMS,* 119).

45. Michel Foucault, *Discipline and Punish: The Birth of the Prison* (New York: Vintage, 1979).

46. Jürgen Habermas, *The Structural Transformation of the Public Sphere* (Cambridge: MIT Press, 1989).

47. After the Act of Union with Scotland in 1707, Edinburgh saw a proliferation of spectatorial clubs and societies. See Pockock, "Cambridge Paradigms," 242. Before assuming his post as professor and chair of moral philosophy in 1752 at Glasgow, Smith was since 1748 a lecturer in rhetoric and belles lettres at Edinburgh. Direct references to Joseph Addison are found in several places in *TMS* as well.

48. Adam Smith, "The Principles Which Lead and Direct Philosophical Inquiries," in *Essays on Philosophical Subjects* (Indianapolis: Liberty Fund, 1982), 33. *The Principles* was published posthumously in 1795. Hereafter cited in text as *EPS.*

49. In his few comments on the history of the novel, Smith cites Romance as an unnatural object in relation to which Richardson's formal realism creates the more stable standard. On the process of excess and recovery in the history of the novel, see Clifford Siskin, *The Work of Writing: Disciplinarity, Professionalism, and the Engendering of Literature in Britain, 1700–1830* (Baltimore: Johns Hopkins University Press, 1997). "The novelization of the multitudes" is a topic I address at greater length in Mike Hill, "Towards a 'Materialist' Rhetoric: Contingency, Constraint, and the Eighteenth-Century Crowd," in *The Role of Rhetoric in an Anti-Foundationalist World: Language, Culture, Pedagogy,* ed. Michael Bernard-Donalds and Richard Glejzer (New Haven: Yale University Press, 1998), 128–46.

50. In this Smith is similar to his mentor, Henry Home, Lord Kames. For British influence on Smith's theory of interpretation, see Joel C. Weinsheimer, *Eighteenth-Century Hermeneutics: Philosophy of Interpretation in England from Locke to Burke* (New Haven: Yale University Press, 1993).

51. See Karl Marx, *A Contribution to the Critique of Political Economy,* in *The Marx-Engels Reader,* ed. Robert C. Tucker, 2d ed. (New York: Norton, 1978), 5.

52. On Sartre and Althusser, see Perry Anderson, *Arguments within Western Marxism* (London: Verso, 1980), 52 ff. This is by no means to match Althusser with Sartre root and branch. The two divert especially on the question of agency. As Gregory Elliot notes citing Jean-Pierre Cotten, ultimately, "*Reading Capital* . . . is an 'anti–*Critique of Dialectical Reason.*'" See Elliot, *Althusser: The Detour of Theory* (London: Verso, 1987), 64.

53. Louis Althusser, *For Marx* (London: Verso, 1990 [1965]), 111. See Michael Sprinker's cogent summation of the concept of "last instance" in "Politics

and Friendship," in *The Althusserian Legacy*, ed. Michael Sprinker and Ann Kaplan (London: Verso, 1993), 206.

54. E. P. Thompson, *The Poverty of Theory* (New York: Monthly Review Press, 1978), 175, 39. Hereafter cited in text as *PT.*

55. Etienne Balibar and Louis Althusser, *Reading Capital* (London: Verso, 1997 [1968]), 10. Hereafter cited as *RC* in text.

56. The proper Marxian coordinates for the notion of what I am calling, *contra* Smith, "generative absence" is Volume One of *Capital*, where Marx most fully theorizes his famous labor theory of value. Peter Hitchcock provides a tidy formulation of Marx's revolutionary opposition between the relations of "use" and "exchange": "Marx wants to convey how an unseen relation nevertheless constructs a social reality, but then he resists a representational imperative by pointing to use value's absent presence in exchange." See Hitchcock, "They Must Be Represented? Problems in Theories of Working-Class Representation," *PMLA* 115, no. 1 (January 2000): 23. The most consistent and articulate theorist of Althusserian materialist aporia is Etienne Balibar. See his *Masses, Classes, Ideas* (New York: Routledge, 1994). Regarding "use value" as a relational alternative to the manner in which commodity fetishism occults labor value by way of "exchange" (i.e., by the false universality of money), see Gayatri Chakravorty Spivak, "Scattered Speculations on the Question of Value," in *In Other Worlds: Essays in Cultural Politics* (New York: Routledge, 1987), 154–75.

NOTES TO SECTION 3.5

1. John K. Wilson, "The Canon and the Curriculum: Multicultural Revolution and Traditionalist Revolt," in *American Higher Education in the Twenty-first Century: Social, Political, and Economic Challenges*, ed. Philip G. Altbach et al. (Baltimore: Johns Hopkins University Press, 1999), 428.

2. Thomas Bartlett, "The Smearing of Chicago," *Chronicle of Higher Education,* June 28, 2002, A10–12.

3. Cited in Francis Oakley, "Ignorant Armies and Nighttime Clashes," in *What's Happened to the Humanities?* ed. Alvin Kernan (Princeton: Princeton University Press, 1997), 74.

4. See "Count of Positions in the October 2001 JIL," *MLA Newsletter,* summer 2002, 10.

5. The NAS report is cited above, as *Losing the Big Picture: The Fragmentation of the English Major since 1964* (Princeton: NAS, 2000).

6. Alvin Kernan, *The Death of Literature* (New Haven: Yale University Press, 1990), 5. Kernan also says that the number of undergraduate English majors is decreasing (6). Michael Bérubé draws different conclusions in terms of

percentage of degrees awarded in the humanities, and enrollments relative to the social sciences. See Bérubé, "Days of Future Past," *ADE Bulletin,* spring 2002, 22. Here the crisis of English is properly placed in graduate education.

7. Alvin Kernan, "Introduction: Change in the Humanities and Higher Education," in Kernan, *What's Happened to the Humanities?* 6.

8. Robert Scholes, *The Rise and Fall of English: Reconstructing English as a Discipline* (New Haven: Yale University Press, 1998), ix–x.

9. Ken Shulman, "Bloom and Doom," *Newsweek,* October 10, 1994, 75.

10. Anthony Easthope, *Literary into Cultural Studies* (New York: Routledge, 1991), 5.

11. Patrick Bratlinger, *Who Killed Shakespeare? What's Happened to English since the Radical 1960s* (New York: Routledge, 2001).

12. One thinks here of Alvin Kernan's highly informative historicization of the literary reader as a member of the general public. This, too, he argues, is an eighteenth-century construct now gone the way of history. See his *Samuel Johnson and the Impact of Print* (Princeton: Princeton University Press, 1987).

13. Pierre Machery, *A Theory of Literary Production* (New York: Routledge, 1978), 79, 92.

14. Catherine Belsey, "English Studies in the Postmodern Condition," in *Post-Theory: New Directions in Criticism,* ed. Martin Mcquillan et al. (Edinburgh: Edinburgh University Press, 1999), 126. Hereafter cited in text as "ES."

15. Toni Morrison, *Playing in the Dark: Whiteness and the Literary Imagination* (New York: Vintage, 1993). Hereafter cited in text as *PD.*

16. Toni Morrison, *The Dancing Mind: Speech upon the Acceptance of the National Book Foundation Medal for the Distinguished Contribution to American Letters* (New York: Knopf, 1997), 14; and "Unthinkable Things Unspoken: The Afro-American Presence in American Literature," *Michigan Quarterly Review* 28, no. 1 (winter 1989): 19. Hereafter cited in text as "UT."

17. Toni Morrison, *The Nobel Lecture in Literature* (New York: Knopf, 1993), 22. Hereafter cited in text as *NL.*

18. The term "colored whiteness" is from David Roediger, *Colored White: Transcending the Racial Past* (Berkeley: University of California Press, 2002).

19. Doris Sommers, *Proceed with Caution, When Engaged with Minority Writing* (Cambridge: Harvard University Press, 1999), xiii, xi, x. Hereafter cited in text as *PC.*

20. Peggy Kamuf, *The Division of Literature; or, The University in Deconstruction* (Chicago: University of Chicago Press, 1997), 6. Hereafter cited in text as *DL.*

21. Danielle Taylor-Guthrie, ed., *Conversations with Toni Morrison* (Jackson: University of Mississippi Press, 1994), 164, 255.

22. Toni Morrison, "Memory, Creation, and Writing," *Thought* 59, no. 235 (December 1984): 390.

INDEX

Abel, Elizabeth, 242
Abraham, Ken, 101
absence, 16, 36, 50, 70, 139, 144, 153, 194, 202, 208, 214; and labor, 146
academics, 164; and diversity, 164; and multiculturalism, 3, 141–142, 166, 168, 170; and professorial labor, 141, 152, 166, 184, 190, 193, 204, 212
Adorno, Theodore, 14, 80, 108–114, 116–117, 120, 122–124, 139, 175; and homophobia, 122; and male heterosexuality, 124; and the modern state, 113
affirmative action, 51–52
Agamben, Georgio, 163
Allen, Theodore W., 23, 252
Althusser, Louis, 17, 49, 110, 195, 197, 202–204, 208, 211; and absence, 202, 208; and labor, 208, 211; and multitudes, 202
ambivalence, 79, 106, 139, 144, 175, 180, 183, 193; and the academic book, 182; and masculinity, 120
American Africanism, 146, 208, 214, 215
American Renaissance, 1–4, 8
American Studies Association, 183
Anderson, Perry, 188
Anzaldúa, Gloria, 92, 218
Apostolidis, Paul, 14, 80, 107–113, 117, 123

Arendt, Hannah, 80
Arnold, Matthew, 190
Aronowitz, Stanley, 153–154, 171
Asian American masculinity, 117
authoritarianism, 114–115

Balibar, Etienne, 83, 232, 260
Bambara, Toni Cade, 8
Barrett, Michèle, 88
Bell, Daniel, 167
Belsey, Catherine, 212–213
Berkeley Free Speech Movement, 155–156
Berlant, Lauren, 9, 86
Bérubé, Michael, 191, 193
Birmingham Centre for Cultural Studies, 186–189
Black, Les, 174
Black Reconstruction, 22
Bloom, Harold, 17, 146, 205–206, 210, 213
Bratlinger, Patrick, 210
British Communist Party, 190
British National Party, 3, 6
British New Left, 16, 144, 203
Bush Doctrine, 58
Butler, Judith, 14, 80, 115–117, 119–120, 123, 130

California Civil Rights Initiative, 52
Campaign for Nuclear Disarmament, 255

Campus Crusade for Christ, 85
census, 40; and check all that apply op-
    tion, 39; and civil rights, 31; congres-
    sional hearings in 1993, 40; history of,
    12, 220; 2000 census, 12, 29, 38–39,
    41, 44, 47–49, 51, 54, 58, 68, 76, 90,
    163; U.S. Census Bureau, 30; U.S.
    census count of 1790, 30, 38
Chambers, Ross, 217, 253, 255
Chow, Rey, 126, 186–187
Christian Coalition, 108
Christian radio, 84
civil rights, 12, 25, 27, 29–31, 34, 39, 69,
    97–98, 142, 163–164; end of, 47, 52
civil society, 13, 49, 58, 60–61, 162, 181
class: anxiety, 13, 132; conflict, 77; ex-
    ploitation, 28; struggle, 168, 216
Claussen, Dane, 102
Cold War, 159, 181–182
colonialism, 94–95
Colorado Amendment Two, 81
Colorado for Family Values, 86
Community Marriage Covenants, 87
Connerly, Ward, 52, 56
contradictions, 173
corporate university, 15, 138, 149, 156,
    183
corporatization, 161, 171
Crenshaw, Kimberlé, 46
Critical Legal Studies, 45–46, 50
Critical Race Theory, 12, 25, 45–46
crowds, 195–196, 198, 202
Cruz, Jon, 170
cultural miscegenation, 53–54, 56
Cultural Studies, 16–17, 143, 165, 185,
    188, 190–191, 193–194, 198, 202,
    206–207; and academic labor, 190,
    193; and ambivalence, 144, 193

Davies, Ioan, 255
Davis, Mike, 33–36
de-disciplinary state, 58, 71
Defense of Marriage Act, 87
de la Campa, Roman, 33–34
Deleuze, Gilles, 123–126, 166
Delgado, Richard, 47

de-referential, 16, 139, 141; and the cen-
    sus, 164
Derrida, Jacques, 70
desiring-production, 125
Dillard, Angela D., 228
discipline, 40, 60, 70; and the state, 41
dissensus, 58, 61, 141, 165, 183; and na-
    tionalism, 54
diversity, 15, 105, 155, 164
D'Souza, Dinesh, 51, 168
DuBois, W. E. B., 21–23, 26, 36, 51, 67,
    69, 176; Black Reconstruction, 22; and
    masses, 23–24, 26, 36, 51
Duberman, Martin, 239

Easthope, Anthony, 113–114, 210
Ehrenreich, Barbara, 78
Eng, David, 14, 80, 115, 117, 119,
    122–124; and the Oedipalization of
    race, 117
Engels, Friedrich, 89–90
Enlightenment, 13, 25, 41, 76, 111,
    160–161, 163–164, 168, 182, 196,
    198, 208, 210–211, 214; and the state,
    29
enumeration, statistical, 30
excellence, 162, 194

Family Research Council, 86, 102
Fanon, Frantz, 7, 94–96, 122
fascism, 77–78, 109, 113–114, 121, 125
fatherhood, 86
feminism, 177
Fine, Michele, 253
Focus on the Family, 85, 87, 102,
    108–109
Foley, Neil, 221
Foucault, 29, 40, 45, 49, 124–125, 199
Frankenberg, Ruth, 182–184, 186–187,
    207, 214
Fraser, Nancy, 25, 167, 179
Freud, Sigmund, 113, 115, 117, 124; nar-
    cissism, 117
Frye, Marilyn, 8
function, 208
Funderburg, Lise, 225

INDEX

and masculinity, 93, 98–99; and the
mestizo condition, 99, 128, 133; multiracial appeals, 106; Oedipal failure,
115; and racial reconciliation, 97, 118;
right-wing political affiliations, 100;
and wages, 103; white masculine difference, 99; white masculine submission,
92; and whiteness, 93, 100; and white
self-abnegation, 100
public sphere, 60–61

Race and Ethnic Target Test, 51
race traitor, 176, 178–179
racial reconciliation, 118
racial self-recognition, 29
Rancier, Jacque, 56, 63
Readings, Bill, 15–16, 138–141,
144–145, 161–167, 175, 178–179,
190, 194, 206–207, 215; and de-referentialization 16, 139, 141, 164; and
dissensus, 141, 164–165, 183; and excellence, 163–162, 194; and ruin,
162–163
Rhodes, Gary, 151–152
Roediger, David, 11–12, 176, 183, 207,
212
Ross, Andrew, 220

Saxton, Alexander, 11
Scholes, Robert, 210
Sedgwick, Eve, 88
self-recognition, 25, 29, 45, 48, 55, 58,
62, 68, 80
Seshadri-Crooks, Kalpana, 242
Slaughter, Sheila, 151
Sleeter, Christine, 171
Smith, Adam, 17, 145, 197–201, 203,
207–208, 210, 216; and gaps, 145,
201, 203, 216; and the multitude, 201,
203, 210; theory of moral sympathy,
197–99, 201; theory of species and
genera, 200
Smith, Paul, 240
Sollors, Werner, 53–54
Sommers, Doris, 215–216
species and genera, 200
Spivak, Gayatri, 167

Stacy, Judith, 89
state, 25–26, 28, 40, 44–46, 52, 68, 214
Stokes, Mason, 253

Taylor, Charles, 13, 25, 59, 61–64, 69,
110; and the politics of recognition,
65, 110
Theweleit, Klaus, 77–78, 123
Thompson, E. P., 17, 24, 144–145,
187–189, 194–199, 201–203, 207;
and Cultural Studies, 198; and the
English crowd, 195–196, 198; the
moral economy, 196, 202; and the
multitude, 207
Tilly, Charles, 195
Tomasky, Michael, 168
totalitarianism, 114
Turner Diaries, The, 15, 80, 122, 127–131;
and heterosexuality, 131; and self-annihilation, 130
2000 Census, 12, 29, 38–39, 41, 44,
47–49, 51, 54, 58, 68, 76, 90, 163

university, 137, 145; and absence, 139;
and academic labor, 141; and civil society, 162; and the Cold War, 159; and
corporatization, 138, 171; and diversity, 155; and labor, 137
U.S.A. Patriot Act, 4, 163
U.S. Census Bureau, 30
U.S. census count of 1790, 30, 38
U.S. Cultural Studies, 90

Valladáo, Alfredo G. A., 57, 69
Voting Rights Act of 1965, 30

wage labor, 103, 110
Ware, Vron, 174
Warner, Michael, 9, 26
Watt, Stephen, 149, 150, 152
West, Cornel, 102, 103, 104
white labor history, 176, 183
white masculinity, 78, 123
white minority, 3, 7, 34, 68, 78, 128,
222
whiteness, 8, 93, 100, 121, 176, 183; and
sexuality, 5; white heterosexual men, 5,

267

ABOUT THE AUTHOR

Mike Hill is Assistant Professor of English at the State University of New York at Albany. He is the editor of *Whiteness: A Critical Reader* (also available from NYU Press), and the coeditor of *Masses, Classes, and the Public Sphere.*